Pillars
of **Faith**

Pillars
of Faith

A Reasonable Approach to the
Foundations of Judaism

PINCHAS TAYLOR

Mosaica Press, Inc.

© 2014 by Mosaica Press

Typeset and designed by Rayzel Broyde

ISBN 13: 978-1-937887-35-3   ISBN-10: 1937887359

Published and distributed by:

Mosaica Press, Inc.

www.mosaicapress.com

info@mosaicapress.com

Contents

כס"ד

Rabbi Zev Leff

Rabbi of Moshav Matityahu
Rosh HaYeshiva—Yeshiva Gedola Matityahu

הרב זאב לף

מרא דאתרא מושב מתתיהו
ראש הישיבה—ישיבה גדולה מתתיהו

D.N. Modiin 71917   Tel: 08—976—1138 טל'   Fax: 08—976—5326 'פקס   ד.נ. מודיעין 71917

Dear Friends,

I have read portions of the manuscript "Pillars of Faith" by Rabbi Pinchas Taylor. The author presents as he says, "The Foundations of Judaism for the Rational Mind". Although no tenet of Judaism can be proved one hundred percent empirically and rationally as belief in the foundations are mitzvos and hence dependent on one being able to exercise free choice in affirming or denying them, however one can prepare the way to make that choice easier by understanding the rational basis for those beliefs and the means to negate the arguments that undermine those beliefs.

The author presents an admirable depth and breadth of knowledge both in the sphere of Torah and the spheres of science and other worldly knowledge to accomplish this purpose. The ideas presented are anchored in true Torah sources.

The work covers a vast array of subjects and is presented in an interesting and comprehensible manner. This work will both be an invaluable aid to introduce one to the foundations of Jewish belief and also to inspire and strengthen the faith of those already on a Torah path.

I commend the author on a job well done and pray that Hashem Yisborach grant him life, health and the wherewithal to provide further works to benefit the community.

Sincerely,

With Torah blessings

Rabbi Zev Leff

בס"ד

RABBI GEDALIA DOV SCHWARTZ
3001 W. Chase
Chicago, IL 60645

"Pillars of Faith, Foundations of Judaism for the Rational Mind" is a valiant effort to understand and explain many of the challenging religious beliefs of Torah Judaism. Although the author Pinchas Taylor is not personally known to me, his research and analysis of many of the major foundations of Torah Faith is most impressive. My perusal of his work, although a rather cursory one, has piqued my interest and curiosity to read and pay attention to his very clear and logical explanations of many difficult and complicated subjects. He has delved into a vast array of the scientific and philosophical writings of many scholars of all backgrounds, and has made many incisive comments from authentic Rabbinic sources.

I believe this book will both stimulate and enlighten any reader seeking clarification and understanding of the essentials of Torah true Judaism.

Gedalia Dov Schwartz

בס"ד

שמואל קמנצקי
Rabbi S. Kamenetsky

2018 Upland Way
Philadelphia, PA 19131

Home: 215-473-2798
Study: 215-473-1212

ה' אדר א תשע"ד

Honorable Rabbi Taylor, שליט"א

 Congratulations on the success of your endeavor to clarify the foundations of Jewish beliefs. Your book, *Pillars of Faith*, will enlighten the understanding of all who follow the laws of the Torah, and serve as a source of knowledge and inspiration for those who are seeking a life of truth.

May you be blessed with continued success in sharing your knowledge with כלל ישראל.

Sincerely Yours,

S. Kamenetsky

Rabbi Yisroel Dov Webster
1840 58th Street
Brooklyn N. Y. 11204
718-236-9244, Fax 259-8941
Email Rabbiyd@aol.com

ישראל דוב וועבסטער
אב"ד שערי משפט
מח"ס יד ליולדת, לב איטא ג"ח

14 Adar I 5774

L'Kovad HaRav Pinchas Taylor

I have read portions of your manuscript "Pillars of Faith" and have found it true to its title. You

have laid down the fundamentals and foundation of Judaism in your sefer. The sefer is written in

a clear and easy to understand format of our Torah and its Mitzvos. It is in my opinion that this

sefer is very useful to everyone to get a better grasp of Judaism. You show that you have a great

depth of knowledge our Torah and science whereby you are able to disseminate its teachings

through this sefer. May Hashem Yisborach grant him much success with this sefer.

Sincerely

Yisroel Dov Webster

American Friends of Kollel Shaarei Horaah
110 N. 11th Avenue
Highland Park, NJ 08904
732.719.4258

Michtav Beracha

I was excited to read significant sections of Rabbi Pinchas Taylor's masterpiece "Pillars of Faith".

It is obvious that the author has invested much time and energy in researching the principles of Emunah and presenting them in a clear and logical manner. He has taken great efforts to clarify the basic principles of our faith, and to elaborate upon their rational foundations in a style that is accessible both to those learned in Jewish tradition as well as to newcomers.

Furthermore, his presentation of classic Jewish sources complemented by contemporary scientific writings, offer a unique perspective on the topic in a style that many different readers will find engaging.

The need for works of this type is self-evident, and it has potential to fill a significant void.

Therefore, I wish the author much success in his continuing efforts to spread a clear understanding of the basic philosophy of Judaism, both through this work and in his other endeavors.

Rabbi Peretz Moncharsh

רב ודיין בירושלים עיה״ק

רחוב עוזיאל 3 ירושלים
בית וגן

בס״ד

מכתב ברכה

אני שמח לשמוע שהחבר שלי מוערך היקר והעמיתה, ר 'פנחס טיילור, הכין לפרסום ספר חדש
על הנושא של אמונה. הרב טיילור הוא חוקר מלומד מאוד וירא שמים, מוכשר כדי להאיר את
עיני דורנו בתובנות שלו על נושא חשוב זה.

מגבלות זמן ושפה שמנעו ממני התחייבות סקירה מעמיקה של כתב היד שלו, עם זאת, אני כבר
יכול לשמוע מאחרים שהעבודה היא גם רומן ואמין. לכן אני מושיט את ברכתי למחבר שהוא
צריך להיות מוצלח בכל העשייה שלו בהוראה ובהפצת תורה השם צריך לברך אותו ואת
משפחתו

לכבוד גדול יותר של תורה

הרב צבי שלום רוזן

Letter of Approbation

I was delighted to hear that my esteemed dear friend and colleague, Rabbi Pinchas
Taylor, has prepared for publication a new *sefer*, entitled Pillars of Faith, on the
subject of *Emunah*. Rabbi Taylor is very learned and a *yiras shomma'im*, highly
qualified to enlighten our generation with his insights on this important topic.

Time and language limitations have prevented me from undertaking a thorough
review of his manuscript; however, I have been able to hear from others that the work
is both novel and reliable. Therefore, I extend my blessing to the author that he should
be successful in all his endeavors in teaching and spreading Torah and Hashem should
bless him and his family.

For the greater honor of Torah,
Rabbi Tzvi Shalom Rosen

ערב יום כיפור, תשע"ד
September 9, 2013

בס"ד

Dear Rabbi Pinchas Taylor,

Thank you for the opportunity to review your *sefer* **Pillars of Faith**. In my opinion you have successfully presented fundamental concepts of Judiasm in a way that speaks to the thinking individual.

The *sefer* is a pleasure to read because your commentary is rooted in today's language which can be easily understood. It is of benefit whether one is new to Judaism or a long-time learner.

The result is that you deliver a unique set of tools to help a person bridge Torah and the scientific community. This *sefer* is a manual for helping one heighten his or her awareness of the Creator, beginning from the moment one wakes, opens his eyes, and begins to observe the world around him. One cannot help but feel invigorated after beginning the day with such a deep understanding. It has a cumulative effect.

This *sefer* is a tremendous aid for *emunah*. It is a reflection of your commitment to Torah and your overwhelming desire to educate others. May you merit to see your *sefer*, **Pillars of Faith**, warmly received and well circulated amongst *Klal Yisrael*.

With Torah blessings and warmest regards,

Rabbi Daniel Channen
Director, Issur V'Heter

יצחק צבי
אושינסקי

דיין בית הדין הרבני חיפה

מחבה"ס אורות המשפט ג'ח, אורחות משפט,
הלכות אבלות ועוד

קרית יערים - טלזסטון
02-6540106

בס"ד

_____

מכתב ברכה

הנני בא לספר בשבחו של הרב פנחס טיילור מארה"ב אשר הנני מכירו זה זמן.

לא יצא לי לקרוא את ספרו, אך הנ"ל מוכר אצלי כחכם בעל מידות מוסריות טובות ובעל יראת שמים.

אברך את המחבר שיזכה לקדש שם שמים ברבים וירבה אהבת ה' ויראתו בקרב כלל ישראל.

מוקירו

יצחק אושינסקי

Letter of Approbation

I would like to take this opportunity to praise my longtime acquaintance Rabbi Pinchas Taylor.

I cannot express an opinion regarding the *sefer* (which I have not read, because my English is limited) but I can say that the author is known to me as being a Torah scholar and a man of fine personality traits, upstanding, and a G-d fearing person.

I extend my blessing that he may have the privilege to sanctify the name of G-d among people and to increase the intensity of the love and fear of G-d among all the house of Israel.

With all my respect,

YITZCHAK
OSHINSKY

JACOB AGID

This page is dedicated to a true hero and an extra special man.

He was the greatest man from "The Greatest Generation."

From humble beginnings in Brownsville, New York, he was always a man of the strongest moral character and sincerity. He always had a simple faith in G-d and lived life with modesty and a humble spirit.

He was a great patriot, a proud American, and dedicated to the American dream. Although he was awarded great honors and medals during his service in the Second World War, he never boasted or bragged—in fact, he never discussed them at all.

He was always a man who loved life, and was always very active. He loved working—no matter what the task; walking—no matter what the distance; and driving—no matter where the destination.

His zest for life and ever-present good nature was always inspiring to his family. He was an outstanding husband, a dedicated father, grandfather, and great-grandfather. He taught everyone to never complain and to never give up.

May his repose be in Paradise, and may the Master of compassion bring him under the cover of G-d's wings and bind his soul in the bond of life.

May we all soon merit seeing him once again, with the coming of Moshiach speedily in our days.

THE AGID FAMILY

לע"נ

פייבע דוד בן לייזער ע"ה

RICHARD DENNIS
RUBIN

Richard, as a son, husband, father, and boss, was an exemplary human being and an exemplary Jew.

He told us to always give with an open heart and to give opportunity to those who may not otherwise have it.

He taught us the principles of honesty, philanthropy and determination, which we continue to practice today.

Richard always stressed the importance of knowing and never forgetting your roots; that we must uphold our Jewish heritage and support the Jewish community.

We will continue to make light and bring light to others as he so graciously did during his life on Earth.

May G-d grant him everlasting peace, and bring our dear father and husband under the cover of His wings for all eternity.

Amen.

THE RUBIN FAMILY

JACOB MARVIN

This dedication is for a remarkable husband and extraordinary father whose depth of wisdom, love for life, and unbridled compassion for family and everyone and everything, is far beyond the scope of expression.

A seeker of knowledge who believed in what this book represents.

Your impact on those who were fortunate enough to have known you will last lifetimes, and your legacy is far greater than you could have imagined.

Our hearts will forever cherish your beautiful spirit and we will never cease to miss our "Hero."

RENA, DALIA, AND STEPHANIE MARVIN

לע"נ
דוד בן אברהם ע"ה

DAVID GREENBAUM

To my Duvid
My dearest, my love I love you so
I just thought I'd write to let you know
How grateful I am to G-d each day
For having let you find your way
Through your winding path of life
To find me and make me your wife
You've given me so much of your love
And things I couldn't even dream of
Our three little daughters—I love them so
You're a wonderful father to them I know.
I pray that my love you'll always be
And that you'll never ever get tired of me
I know I'll never stop loving you
No matter what the years may bring
My life just started, it's very true
The day you gave me my wedding ring.
In loving memory to a wonderful husband and father.

THE GREENBAUM FAMILY

לע"נ

דוד בן יוסף ע"ה

DAVID LEWIS

Dedicated to the memory of our father David ben Yosef Lewis.
A kind, loving soul who sought to do right by his family; his sense of
humor, and his heartfelt warmth. He was a true blessing to all that
he touched. May the thoughts and spirituality of this book give all its
readers a renewed respect for their own family.

THE LEWIS FAMILY

לע"נ

מיכאלה לאה בת יוסף שמעון ע"ה

MIKAELA TICK

Dedicated to the memory of Mikaela Tick, who left this world far too
early.
May the teachings in this book bring her merit on High, may the spiritual principles in this book help all to find comfort, may its teaching
bring her merits, and may we all grow and be blessed from her eternal
memory.

THE LEWIS FAMILY

ACKNOWLEDGMENTS

I first would like to thank G-d Al-mighty for bringing this project to fruition.

I would also like to thank the Lubavitcher Rebbe *zt"l*, whose teachings continue to inspire and galvanize me to grow spiritually and impact my circle of influence in the world.

It is with deep appreciation that I thank my wife Miriam, who is extremely talented and, among other things, a fantastic mother. She took time at the end of her hectic days to review and revise major segments of this work. She offered encouraging and constructive feedback. She is also praiseworthy for all of the toil that she does on a daily basis caring for our children, all of whom are still in diapers.

I would like to thank my parents and my extended family for always being interested and enthusiastic about all the projects that I embark on.

I am indebted and appreciative to our friends and colleagues, the Posner and Pink families, who are a constant source of support, and to the Chabad of Plantation community as a whole.

I would also like to express thanks to the learning institutions that I had the privilege to study under for so many years, and in particular to the Rabbonim at the Rabbinical College of America.

I am grateful to Rabbi Zev Leff *shlita*, Rosh Yeshiva of Yeshiva Gedola Matityahu in Modi'in, Israel, for looking over major segments of this work and offering much encouragement. Likewise, I would like to thank Rabbi Gedalia Dov Schwartz *shlita, av beis din* of both the Beth Din of America and the Chicago Rabbinical Council, Rabbi Shmuel Kamenetsky *shlita,* Rosh Yeshiva of the Talmudical Yeshiva of Philadelphia, Rabbi Yisroel Dov Webster *shlita, av beis din* Sha'arei Mishpat, and Rabbi Peretz Moncharsh *shlita,* Rosh Kollel of Kollel Shaarei Horaah in Beitar, Israel, who looked over significant portions of the manuscript. Also I would like to make a personal thank you to Rabbi Tzvi Rosen, Rabbi Don Channen, and Rabbi Yizchak Oshinsky for their endorsements.

Last, but certainly not least, I want to express tremendous appreciation to the staff at Mosaica Press, who were an absolute pleasure to work with. Rabbi Doron Kornbluth's editing abilities were extremely impressive and thorough. His comments were enlightening and helped open up the writing to a broader audience. Rabbi Yaacov Haber was such a *mentch* who patiently answered questions and provided practical guidance when needed. The love that these two have for spreading Torah is genuine and admirable, and was a major contributing factor in deciding to work together with them.

INTRODUCTION

There once was a Jew named Isaac who lived in Krakow, Poland. He had a recurring dream about a buried treasure at the base of a bridge far away in Prague, near the royal palace. The dream came so often and was so vivid that Isaac finally decided to embark on the arduous journey to Prague in search of this treasure.

When Isaac arrived at the spot that he had seen in his dream, he became very excited, but before he could begin digging he was approached by a guard who, sensing that Isaac was not a local, questioned his presence at the bridge. When Isaac told the guard about his treasure dream, the guard laughed hysterically, because it was quite a distant journey to take for a dream. The guard chuckled that he himself had recurring dreams about a man named Isaac from Krakow who has a huge treasure chest buried under the floorboards of his own house, but, said the guard, he never thought to actually travel there.

When Isaac returned home, he lifted up his floorboards and, beneath his oven, he found a large buried treasure.[1]

---

1   Story told over by Rabbi Moshe Alshich in his commentary to Parshas Ki Savo. See also *Sippurei Tzaddikim*, Nitzavim.

S ome imagine that the only way to find the special treasure of life is to search far away, while in reality that beautiful treasure lies hidden beneath the floorboards in their own home. A Jewish person need look no further than his own faith to guide him in wisdom, meaning, and purpose throughout his life. Judaism is beautiful, logical, and contains a depth of spirituality unparalleled anywhere in the world.

Many Jews do not seem to feel this way. Why not? I can only speak from my own experiences in answering this question. From my vantage point, these perceptions are often rooted in insufficient understanding of Jewish thought. Popular opinions are based upon Hebrew School knowledge learned before the Bar- or Bat-Mitzvah ceremony rather than through assiduous study. All too often, the Bar-Mitzvah ceremony marks an end in Jewish involvement rather than a beginning. The child grows up drinking the waters of secular society, molding his worldview according to its model, and retains an eleven-year-old understanding of his faith. Is there any wonder that the thinking Jewish adult lacks appreciation for Jewish teachings? Can one appreciate *anything* that he only has an eleven-year-old's understanding of?

Given the fact that, through no fault of their own, many adults have a limited understanding of Judaism, combined with a pop culture unimpressed with religious tradition, it is almost inevitable that many Jews are uncomfortable with, and not accepting of, basic Jewish tenets. This is, in fact, an expected outcome. History, too, is replete with examples of experts who steadfastly refused to think outside of their "established" fields. The societies in which they lived limited their perspective as to what could be deemed truth. Despite concrete evidence, they were unable to break out of the cultural paradigms present in their times.

During the Enlightenment period, a cultural movement that began in the late seventeenth century, astronomers decided that meteorites do not exist. This era was known to arbitrarily reject inherited knowledge from previous generations and instead insist that everything be fully rational. Many museums in Europe actually threw out their meteorite specimens, considering them nothing more than humiliating reminders of a superstitious past. Antoine Lavoisier, father of modern chemistry, declared, "Stones don't fall from the sky, because there are no stones in the sky!" It was only at the beginning of the nineteenth century that the academics of the time were forced to concede and make an about-face.

An editorial in the *Boston Post* in 1865 talks about a man named Joshua Coppersmith who was arrested in New York for attempting to extort funds from the "ignorant and superstitious." What was his crime? He was exhibiting a device that he said would convey the human voice at any distance over metallic wires so that it will be heard by the listener at the other end. He called it a telephone. The article continues, saying that "well-informed people know it is impossible to transmit the voice over wires and that were it possible to do so, the thing would be of no practical value." It then congratulates those who incarcerated this "schemer."[2]

In the beginning of the twentieth century, when the Wright brothers claimed to have built a flying machine, it was dismissed as a hoax by the scientific journals, newspapers, the US military, and most American scientists. In fact, just weeks prior to the first flight at Kitty Hawk, Simon Newcomb, professor of mathematics and astronomy at Johns Hopkins University, published an article that powered human flight was "utterly impossible."[3] Experts were so convinced, and on purely scientific grounds, that they rejected it as impossible without troubling themselves to believe the reports and examine the evidence.[4] Likewise, American inventor Lee Deforest said, "To place a man in a multi-stage rocket and project him into the controlling gravitational field of the moon where the passengers can make scientific observations, perhaps land alive, and then return to Earth—all that constitutes a wild dream worthy of Jules Verne. I am bold enough to say that such a man-made voyage will never occur,

---

2   Quoted from Edward Evenson, *The Telephone Patent Conspiracy of 1876* (2000), pg. 118.

3   *The Independent*, October 22, 1903.

4   The examples of meteorites and flight have been paraphrased from Richard Milton, *Alternative Science* (1996).

regardless of all future advances."[5] Also, Britain's Astronomer Royal, Sir Harold Spencer Jones, famously said "space travel is bunk" only two weeks before Sputnik 1 was launched into space by the Russians.[6]

These statements, which are just the tip of the iceberg, were made by the experts of the day, and in many cases reflected a broader mindset of the time in which they were said. The cultural atmosphere of criticism and skepticism became even more pronounced in the Age of Enlightenment. One byproduct of this era was the mentality that naturalism should always trump the supernatural. Better to bend over backwards, sometimes even counterintuitively, to apply naturalistic reasoning rather than to consider a more straightforward approach that may include the supernatural. The ideas of the Enlightenment have had a significant and lasting impact on the culture of the Western world. Remnants of this worldview still rule the day in segments of our society.

With this same mindset, some are quick to reject Jewish fundamentals based upon theoretical deduction and social conditioning rather than from observation or experience. These thoughts may result from cognitive dissonance, conformity, or other biases, and may follow these tenets: *Everything must be explained naturally. We cannot invoke the concept of G-d. Since there is no G-d, then clearly the Torah is just a compilation of ethical stories to help us live better lives, not a Divine manual. It must have been compiled by a group of writers. Traditional Judaism must have different roles for men and women because it is archaic and a product of the chauvinism that existed in the ancient world. The Jewish dietary laws must be an outgrowth of what was perceived as healthy in the ancient society. There simply cannot be a Messiah who will lead the world to perfection, or that the dead will one day live again in physical bodies.* All of these concepts are simply dismissed without further consideration.

Jewish life is meant to be a journey toward freedom and authenticity, becoming free from outside influences in order to become one's true self. This quest began with the instruction that G-d gave to Abraham,

---

5   Lewiston, *Morning Tribune* via Associated Press, February 25, 1957.
6   Milton, *Alternative Science*, pg. 22.

the first Jew, to "go to yourself," empowering him to leave the predominant worldviews of his day and look toward his essential self. The Jewish people after him are likewise vested with the same ability and charged with this same mission.[7]

This book attempts to clearly explain reasonable approaches to some key foundations of the Jewish faith. In this work, I believe that the spiritual seeker will be able to gain a solid understanding of the core of Jewish belief. In addition to being a starting point for those who find themselves at the beginning of their Jewish spiritual journey, this work also offers the seasoned student of Torah learning a tremendous resource to solidifying his own beliefs and outlooks.

My only concern in writing this work was that if the reader should find an answer to be in error, insufficient, or unsatisfactory in his eyes, then let it be seen as a deficiency in the author rather than in the Torah or the works of the sages. I hope that the reader finds the information contained within to be both interesting and enlightening, and that it galvanizes him toward a deeper appreciation of our faith and continued learning and exploration.

Pinchas Taylor
Adar, 5774
Feb. 2014

---

7   Based on *Likkutei Sichos*, vol. 5, pg. 58.

G-D

The first pillar of Judaism is the belief in G-d.

Many philosophical questions are related to this topic: Is there a logical approach to G-d's existence? Are there signs of design in the universe? How is a Jew to view Darwinian evolution? What is the age of the universe, and does it matter? If G-d knows what will be in the future, doesn't that impinge on free choice? If G-d is overseeing the world, why is it that bad things seem to happen to good people?

Let's begin to explore.

REASONABLE APPROACH TO BELIEF IN G-D

Faith In The Divine

The most central idea in Judaism is that the universe was created for a reason, by a Purposeful Being, and that human beings play the key role in achieving that purpose.[8] In fact, since the dawn of time, until the present day, and across all culture lines, the vast majority of human beings have believed in and sought connection with some form of deity.[9] In truth, this fact itself points to the existence of a Creator, as it would be very ironic that a godless and aimless existence spontaneously generated and evolved all of its human specimens with the exact same defect of believing the opposite—that there is a Maker and a purpose.[10]

---

8   *Mesillas Yesharim* 1:1; *Derech Hashem* 1:1, 2:1. See also Rambam, *Yesodei HaTorah* 1:1.

9   This phenomenon has remained more or less stable through the present day. World population statistics regarding belief in a deity are difficult to assess because of different factors, however, there was a poll in 2005 by Cambridge University that showed that 88 percent of the world population considered themselves believers. Using the United States alone, a Gallup Poll taken in 2008 showed that a staggering 94% of Americans believe in some type of Higher Power (gallup.com/video/109111/majority-americans-believe-god.aspx). See also Gallup and Catelli, *The People's Religion: American Faith in the 90s* (1989), pgs. 45, 58. A survey of religious beliefs in the United States, performed by Baylor University in 2007, showed that only 4 percent of Americans explicitly classify themselves as atheists. The other 7 percent of the population who define themselves as having "no religion" seem to be merely disconnected from an official religious institution, as opposed to disconnection from the concept of a deity. See Rodney Stark, *What Americans Believe* (2008).

10   Some have theorized that the human being is weak and seeks comfort in the idea of a G-d

Often, within even the most strident opponent of the Divine is an unperceived sense of faith and belief. In the Jewish community, this phenomenon is obviously manifest. Even those Jews, who typically do not practice Judaism, and even classify themselves as non-believers, seem to have a small flame of essential faith that occasionally shines forth. How many Jews flock to synagogue for the High Holidays, make a Passover Seder, or light Chanukah candles despite their insistence of disconnection?[11] How many self-proclaimed atheists make a point of saying *kaddish* for a loved one, or at least lighting a *yartzeit* candle on the anniversary of their passing? At the core of every Jew is an inextinguishable spark of faith. It is only that sometimes this faith becomes clouded; however, it is never fully forgotten.

---

in order to cope with his struggles. Karl Marx favored this line of thinking, and famously called religion the "opiate of the masses." For this reason he predicted that when socialism integrated itself into society, the need for G-d would go away. This, of course, did not take place. Sigmund Freud was also known to explain that the human mind invented the idea of G-d because of its inability to cope with the uncertainties of life. According to them and others, G-d is merely a comforting delusion. While this topic truly deserves and requires a more lengthy discussion, it is worth noting the fallacy in this line of thinking. This claim only appears valid when one bases himself on the worldview that G-d does not exist. If G-d does exist, then the exact same line of thinking shows that atheism is the comforting delusion, in which one avoids responsibilities for his actions. Czesław Miłosz, a Nobel Prize-winning Polish poet, witnessed Nazism and Stalinism first-hand. He recalls Marx's comment and eloquently points out its flaw and irony, saying, "Religion, opium for the people. To those suffering pain, humiliation, illness, and serfdom, it promised a reward in an afterlife. And now we are witnessing a transformation. A true opium for the people is a belief in nothingness after death—the huge solace of thinking that for our betrayals, greed, cowardice, [and] murders, we are not going to be judged. The true opiate in modern times is the idea that there is no G-d, so that all can do as they please." See *New York Review of Books*, November 19, 1998, pg. 17.

11   In researching their book *American Grace*, authors Robert Putnam and David Campbell found that half of all American Jews doubt G-d's existence. Compare this with a recent study that shows that upwards of 75 percent of Jews in America light Chanukah candles and participate in a Passover Seder (see PowerPoint presentation at bjpa.org/ Publications/ details.cfm? PublicationID=13566). Granted, this is a somewhat limited scope, as it is only Americans. If the rest of the world were factored in, it is likely that the number of participants in these religious practices would be even a greater percentage, even among those who claim to be disconnected.

ARE SCIENCE AND RELIGION REALLY AT ODDS?

THE NEW WIND OF ATHEISM

In the arena of scientific thought, there are several names that have, ironically, turned the idea of *disbelief* in G-d into a religion in and of itself.[12] This recent crusade against the Divine by a handful of outspoken individuals has come to be known as "New Atheism." One such individual is Richard Dawkins, world-renowned evolutionary biologist, who constantly speaks and writes about his abhorrence of the concept of G-d and religion. His position as trusted scientist enables him to quickly and easily disseminate a convincing argument against the existence of G-d. He and his contemporaries reach a broad audience and have the power to influence many opinions.

The line of thinking brought about by New Atheism actually looks down at religious beliefs and considers religion to be something that is *bad* for a person. The scientific assessment of religion as good or bad seems ironic and invalid. Science cannot make moral judgments. The inability to determine ethical value is one of the limitations of science. One must then ask the question: What scientific or empirical proof is the conclusion that "religion is bad" based on? Furthermore, if personal well-being is the scale upon which religion is to be measured, studies show that religion is actually quite positive for a person.[13]

One may also wish to consider how deep the New Atheist writers' understanding of religion goes, and how qualified they are to make such

---

12   Michael Ruse, philosopher of science at Florida State University, is himself a skeptic, yet at the same time is outspoken about the irony of turning atheism into a religion in its own right, and is quoted numerous times as describing Dawkins and his writings as something that makes him "embarrassed to be an atheist."

13   Interestingly enough, recent Gallup polls showed that the very religious in general had higher levels of well-being than their less-religious counterparts. Also, one Gallup study, published by the *New York Times*, actually showed that the most observant Jews in America live the happiest lives out of all. (See economix.blogs.nytimes.com/2011/01/07/american-jews-lead-the-happiest-lives/?_php=true&_type=blogs&_r=1).

staunch conclusions. Hans Jurgen Eysenck, professor of psychology at the University of London, says, "When scientists leave the particular field in which they specialized, they are just as ordinary, pig-headed, and unreasonable as anybody else, and their unusually high intelligence only makes their prejudices all the more dangerous."[14] A medical scientist may do well making the diagnosis, but should call upon the theologian to guide the moral way to proceed. A Nobel Prize-winning physicist may have the expertise of a high-school student in American History. This point is illustrated by Terry Eagleton, professor of cultural theory at the National University of Ireland, in his review of Richard Dawkins's *The G-d Delusion*. There he writes: "Imagine someone holding forth on biology whose only knowledge of the subject is the *Book of British Birds*, and you have a rough idea of what it feels like to read Richard Dawkins on theology."[15]

Parenthetically, it is worth noting that several of the most influential and outspoken representatives of New Atheism are "Anglo-Saxon males of Protestant upbringing from remarkably similar backgrounds of privilege and power."[16] Many of their arguments emphasize that there is no redeeming factor to G-d or religion whatsoever. Logically, this is not the case, since one can easily see the monetary donations, volunteering, acts of Good Samaritans, etc, all done in the name of G-d and religion and all universally acknowledged as "good."[17] One can

---

14   Hans J. Eysenck, *Sense and Nonsense in Psychology* (1968), pg. 108.
15   Terry Eagleton, "Lunging, Flailing, Mispunching: A Review of Richard Dawkins' *The God Delusion*," *London Review of Books*, Oct. 19, 2006. Likewise, philosopher Alvin Plantinga, in an essay entitled "The Dawkins Confusion," said that many of his arguments would "receive a failing grade in a sophomore philosophy class." Even atheist philosopher Thomas Nagel called his arguments in this book "amateur."
16   Besides Dawkins, some of the most outspoken leaders in the New Atheism include Sam Harris, author of *The End of Faith*, Daniel Dennet, author of *Breaking the Spell*, and Christopher Hitchens in his bestseller *God is Not Great*. For a study of their comparative backgrounds, see Balzell, *The Protestant Establishment: Aristocracy and Caste in America* (1987). For the "maleness" of the New Atheist movement, see Beattie, *The New Atheists*, pgs. 126-28. There are also surprisingly few African-American atheists. This information is cited from and expounded upon in Allister McGrath, *Why God Won't Go Away* (2010), pg. 36.
17   Although some religions do have unfortunate histories of bloodshed and hate, contrary to popular belief, only a small minority of recorded wars were primarily motivated by

therefore conclude that perhaps the New Atheists' arguments are not exclusively driven by logic. Someone who vehemently disagrees on a strictly intellectual level is almost always able to find at least some positive aspects in what they oppose, though they disagree with the idea as a whole. Someone who is emotionally driven to oppose an idea can be blinded by their emotions to completely disregard an entire concept without giving it any redeeming value, though logically there is redeeming value there. It would seem that acceptance of science should not play a role in determining one's acceptance of G-d. A statement such as, "I believe in science, [therefore] I don't believe in G-d," is flawed. One does not beget the other as the proponents of New Atheism would lead one to believe.

DO SCIENTISTS BELIEVE IN G-D?

Where do scientists fit in statistically with belief? Are the majority non-believers? As it turns out, scientific discovery or openness to scientific inquiry is not synonymous with godlessness. Referencing a number of scientists with religious faith, Stephen Jay Gould, a prominent evolutionary biologist and Harvard professor, said that science and religion constitute non-overlapping spheres. In his *Rocks of Ages,* he wrote, "Either half of my colleagues are enormously stupid, or else the science of Darwinism is fully compatible with conventional religious beliefs—and equally compatible with atheism."[18] This idea is furthered by renowned evolutionary biologist and former director of the Human Genome Project, Francis Collins. He is outspoken about being a scientist and a believer—and finds no contradiction between

---

religious disputes. See C. Phillips and A. Axelrod, *Encyclopedia of Wars* (2007). The New Atheists will quickly point out how fundamentalism fuels Al Qaeda, but are silent on the role of religion in the civil-rights movement. The New Atheists should at least admit a variety of good things that religion has brought to the world. According to this logic, Dr. Jeremy Ginges, assistant professor of psychology at the New School, writes that it is equivalent to saying, "Science produced a nuclear bomb, therefore, we should throw away science." See Scott Atran and Jeremy Ginges, "Religious and Sacred Imperatives in Human Conflict," *Science*, 336 (2012): pg. 855.

18   Steven Jay Gould, "Impeaching a Self-Appointed Judge," *Scientific American* 267, no. 1 (1992): 118–21.

the two. Additionally, try telling Dr. Owen Gingerich, former Research Professor of Astronomy and Science History at Harvard, and a senior astronomer at the Smithsonian Astrophysical Observatory, that science means rejection of G-d. In his recent work, *G-d's Universe*, he spells out very clearly that the universe hints at design and purpose and that this in no way impinges on the scientific arena.[19] Thomas C. Emmel, professor of zoology at the University of Florida is noted for saying, "To me, the concept of G-d is a logical outcome of the study of the immense universe that lies around us."[20]

SCIENTISTS AND STATISTICS

In 1916, researcher James Leuba conducted a survey by active scientists of the time. The questions presented to them surrounded the idea of belief in a personal G-d; namely, if they believe in a G-d who communicates with humanity and to whom prayer may be directed in expectation of receiving a response. The numbers showed about 40 percent believed in this kind of G-d, 40 percent did not, and 20 percent were unsure. He predicted that the percentage of nonbelievers would greatly spread as education improved.

The same survey, with the same questions, was conducted in 1997. Those who believed remained a steady 40 percent, whereas the number of non-believers in a theistic G-d grew slightly to about 45 percent, and 15 percent unsure. To the extent that both surveys are accurate readings, this means that 55 percent of scientists either believe in G-d or don't know. While the number of non-believers seems to have risen slightly, the difference is hardly significant. It appears that "Western theism has not lost its place among U.S. scientists, despite their intellectual preoccupation with material reality."[21]

Furthermore, because the questions on the survey were so narrowly phrased, the results probably underestimate the extent of religious

---

19   Some facts and ideas gleaned from McGrath, *Why God Won't Go Away.*

20   Henry Margenau and Roy Varghese, *Cosmos, Bios, and Theos* (1992), pg. 166.

21   E.J. Larson and L. Witham, "Scientists Are Still Keeping the Faith," *Nature* 386 (April 3, 1997): pgs. 435–436.

sentiment among scientists.[22] Additionally, one must also take into account how many scientists are atheists on grounds other than science and bring those preconceived sentiments to their science, rather than basing their atheism on their science. Dr. John Lennox, renowned professor of mathematics at Oxford, explains that many atheist scientists are not compelled by science to accept a natural or materialistic explanation of the universe; instead, the commitment to materialism comes first.[23] Simply, for most scientists in the atheist camp, science has not led to their atheistic conclusions, but is instead a tool to express and validate preconceived notions.

ABSOLUTE PROOF?

Judaism believes that the existence of G-d is logical, reasonable, and verifiable. At the same time, there is no such thing as a mathematical-style "absolute proof" for anything in the human experience. Everything must be relied upon by a certain degree of faith. When one enters a building or flies on an airplane, there can never be a full guarantee that the building will not collapse or that the plane will not malfunction. It is assumed that they will function as they are meant to. Although the probability of an accident is slim, there is always a minor risk that is taken.

---

22   Rodney Stark, a professor of sociology and comparative religion at the University of Washington in Seattle, said that because the questions in the Leuba survey are so narrowly phrased, the results probably underestimate the extent of religious sentiment among scientists. Several recent surveys of American college professors, he said, show that professors are almost as likely to express a belief in G-d as are Americans as a whole. See Natalie Angier, "Survey of Scientists Finds A Stability of Faith in God," *New York Times*, April 03, 1997.

23   Lennox says that, "Some atheists are quite explicit that their atheism comes first. Richard Lewontin, an evolutionary biologist, who said it wasn't science that compelled him to accept a materialistic explanation of the universe. It was an *a priori* materialism." The following is one such quote that is very telling: "It is not that the methods and institutions of science somehow compel us to accept a material explanation of the phenomenal world, but, on the contrary, that we are forced by our *a priori* adherence to material causes to create an apparatus of investigation and a set of concepts that produce material explanations, no matter how counter-intuitive, no matter how mystifying to the uninitiated. Moreover, that materialism is an absolute, for we cannot allow a Divine Foot in the door." See Richard Lewontin, "Billions and Billions of Demons," review of *The Demon-Haunted World: Science as a Candle in the Dark*, by Carl Sagan, *The New York Review*, January 9, 1997, pg. 31.

The likelihood for success in these scenarios is brought out through logical sequence, and the small chance of risk is disregarded due to a certain "faith" that everything will be ok. This is a faith that is based on logic. Just as one does not need 100 percent proof before doing most things in life, so too one should not require absolute proof to believe.

While it is true that there are millions of people who are afraid to fly in airplanes, or do other activities that the majority has no issue with, these phobias are *emotionally* bent and not based on reason. All of the evidence in the world could be presented, but such a person would still have an aversion toward these activities. In order to get onto the airplane, it must both make reasonable sense to the person and he must be emotionally open to such an idea.

Likewise, the same is true when it comes to faith. Philosophers have presented many reasonable approaches to belief in G-d. They are not "proofs" per se or guarantees, but are reasonable approaches for belief in the Divine. For one who is open to belief in G-d, they serve as reasonable steps that lead to faith; however, if someone is emotionally closed to the idea, all of the approaches in the world will still not be heard.

Some religions promote a dogmatic, blind, or baseless faith. This is comparable to one who enters an abandoned or rickety building or chooses to fly on an antiquated and rusty airplane and believes everything will be okay. He is not basing his faith on any sound foundations, and therefore the faith is empty and untrue. Judaism encourages a reasonable faith.

In Judaism, faith in the existence of G-d is a conclusion founded upon sound logic. Some of the classical approaches to faith have been demonstrated through philosophical deduction, and as time went by these approaches came to include elements of scientific assertion. Together, they demonstrate the inner consistency and coherence of belief in G-d, not its evidential foundations. The following are some of the classic approaches to the existence of a Creator.

THE FIRST CAUSE OR COSMOLOGICAL APPROACH

The cosmological proof is perhaps the most basic reason why people believe in G-d. It is an approach that has penetrated every human culture; though it takes on different forms, the basic premise is universal.[24] This approach begins to answer the question of anyone who has ever asked, "Where did this all come from?" "Why is there something[25] and not just nothingness?"

There is a beginning.[26] The foundation of all of logic is that *for every cause there is an effect, and every effect has a prior cause.*[27] The physical universe was at one time non-existent and came into being from nothing; therefore, there must have been a First Cause that brought it into existence.[28]

To take this logic further, we must then say that *nothing creates itself.* Everything in the realm of the physical is limited. Causes are limited in number and necessitate a First Cause. This First Cause must be self-existent, having neither beginning nor end, because everything that has an end must have a beginning. Anything physical has a beginning,

---

24 Although the First Cause approach is inherently Jewish, being that its premise is so logically obvious, many other non-Jewish philosophers and theologians have made similar approaches along the same line of thinking. Some examples might be the medieval Arabic approach called the Kalam cosmological argument, named after a specific Islamic philosophy. See also Thomas Aquinas, *Summa Theologica.*

25 I.e., a universe.

26 Rabbi Shlomo Wolbe opens his book *Pathways: A Brief Introduction to the World of Torah* (1983), pg. 15, with some food for thought: "A radioactive atom disintegrates in a specific amount of time. Uranium, after a chain of transitions, emits helium and becomes lead. The conversion process is absolute and irrevocable. If the final transfiguration of every uranium atom is lead, then ipso facto it must have a beginning. Physical substance is not eternal. There is a beginning to everything, but what caused everything to come into existence?"

27 Reliance on cause and effect is so embedded into the psyche that it is accepted even without proof or explanation. Nobody has ever seen or measured a particle or wave of gravity. The only proof we have that it exists is the fact that physical bodies move. The effect—that physical bodies move—must have a cause; this cause has been called "gravity." This is accepted even without tangible evaluation of the force.

28 See R. Saadia Gaon, *Emunos v'Deos*; the Rambam in *Moreh Nevuchim* furthers the idea to include the concept of "motion." Motion is always produced by a previous motion, which necessitates an initial mover.

and all causes must be created. It can be inferred from here that the world has a non-corporeal, self-sustaining First Cause.

In other words, this First Cause must be "uncaused" because there cannot be an infinite regression of causes. It must be timeless, and by definition, changeless, because it was from this First Cause that time was set into motion. Since it created space, it must therefore also transcend space and be immaterial, not physical. This transcendent First Cause of the universe is a disembodied mind that purposely brought the nothingness into a state of somethingness. This First Cause in Judaism is called Hashem, or G-d.[29]

Thousands of years after its formulation, this classic philosophical approach still rings true. Contemporary philosophers have put forth more refined versions of it, but the main point is consistent.[30]

THE UNIVERSE POINTS TO A FIRST CAUSE

Despite the prevalence of this theory among philosophers and theologians, until the twentieth century the scientific community generally believed that the natural world was eternal, without a beginning, and therefore needed no further explanation. Something without a beginning does not require a cause or an explanation because it has always been.

In modern times, however, "…almost everyone now believes that the universe, and time itself, had a beginning at the Big Bang."[31]

When Edwin Hubble first proposed a beginning point in the 1920s based on the expansion rate of the universe, many scientists could not yet accept this theory. Only after several later proofs (including the discovery of the cosmic background radiation in 1964) were scientists ready to accept the idea. With the emergence of the Big Bang theory,

---

29   Based on *Chovos HaLevavos*.

30   Some non-Jewish philosophers downplay or dismiss the logical persuasiveness of this argument. Nonetheless, one can find ample source material that upholds the First Cause approach, beginning with Germaine Grisez, *Beyond the New Theism: A Philosophy of Religion* (1974), along with many others brought down in Mayer Schiller, *The Road Back* (2001), pg. 254, note 7.

31   Steven Hawking and Roger Penrose, *The Nature of Space and Time* (1996), pg. 20.

the universe in every aspect—namely space, time, energy, and matter—came to have a definite beginning.

There is a remarkable point where Big Bang cosmology and traditional theology intersect. An "eternal universe" is no longer considered an option. This begs the question, "What caused this universe to come into existence?" The answer also seems unavoidable.[32] Over the years, cosmologists have suggested other theories in an attempt to avoid this absolute beginning and its implications of a "Beginner," but none of these theories has shown itself to be as plausible to the scientific community as the Big Bang theory.[33] Arthur Eddington, a well-known British astrophysicist (and atheist) divulged his feelings, saying, "Philosophically, the notion of a beginning of the present order of nature is repugnant to me. I should like to find a genuine loophole."[34]

The prevalent belief among scientists today is that there was a beginning, which makes belief in a Creator more tenable. Prominent astrophysicist Robert Jastrow put it this way: "For the scientist who has lived by the faith in the power of reason, the story is like a bad dream. He has scaled the mountains of ignorance; he is about to conquer the highest peak; as he pulls himself over the final rock, he is greeted by a band of theologians who have been sitting there for centuries."[35]

Notable theoretical physicist Christopher Isham writes, "Perhaps the best argument in favor of the thesis that the Big Bang supports theism is the obvious unease with which it is greeted by some atheist physicists. At times this has led to scientific ideas, such as continuous

---

32   Author Simon Singh writes that "an eternal universe seemed to strike a chord with the scientific community, because the theory had a certain elegance, simplicity, and completeness. If the universe has existed for eternity, then there was no reason to explain how it was created, when it was created, why it was created, and Who created it. Scientists were particularly proud that they had developed a theory of the universe that no longer relied on invoking G-d." See Simon Singh, *Big Bang: The Origin of the Universe* (2005), pg. 79.

33   Prominent English astronomer Fred Hoyle, for example, surmised and endorsed theories that defended an eternal universe even long after most of his collegues had accepted the idea. It is clear that he supported infinite time because it was more in sync with his atheistic beliefs. See Ian Barbour, *When Science Meets Religion: Enemies, Strangers, or Partners* (2000), pg. 42.

34   Singh, *Big Bang,* pg. 281.

35   Robert Jastrow, *God and Astronomers* (1978), pg. 254.

creation or an oscillating universe, being advanced with a tenacity which so exceeds their intrinsic worth that one can only suspect the operation of psychological forces lying very much deeper than the usual academic desire of a theorist to support his or her theory."[36]

WORSHIPPING THE FIRST CAUSE

The concept of a First Cause is logical, and described as such in Jewish literature.

In the first of the Ten Commandments, G-d introduces Himself as the One "who brought you up out of the land of Egypt."[37] The sages write that G-d is saying that I, the logical First Cause, am the same Being that took you out of the land of Egypt. In other words, the commandment being instructed here is not necessarily to believe in G-d, the initial causation of the universe, because that is a logical necessity. A commandment is not needed to teach something dictated by innate intellect. Instead, this command is to believe that this First Cause is synonymous with the One who redeemed the Jewish people from slavery and is involved in their lives.[38] By the way in which the commandment is phrased, the Jewish G-d is also not a distant deistic god that abandoned the universe once it was created, but rather that G-d has an active involvement in His Creation.[39]

The non-physical, self-sustaining, uncaused Being, Who transcends time and space, is the nucleus of Judaism. G-d, in essence, is also distinct from Creation, negating the concept of pantheism. As First Cause, G-d does not depend on anything in His Creation. The Jewish G-d has no components.[40] He is described as the ultimate simplicity

---

36 Christopher Isham, "Creation of the Universe as a Quantum Process," in *Physics, Philosophy and Theology: A Common Quest for Understanding* (1988), pg. 378.

37 *Shmos* [Exodus] 20:2.

38 The Rambam (*Yesodei HaTorah* 1:1–6) explains that the command is to know that there is a G-d that is in control of the universe. However, the Ran (*Derashos HaRan* 9) argues and writes that belief in a G-d, a First Cause, is logical. The command is needed to teach that this same Being is the One who took us out of Egypt and is involved in our lives.

39 After all, He took them out of the land of Egypt. See *Kuzari* 1:1:2 that negates deism.

40 G-d does not have components or attributes like strength or kindness, since these components would cause Him to be what He is, and He has no cause. If G-d theoretically did

and His essential Oneness and absolute unity are foundations of the Jewish faith.[41] A Jew must retain a belief in this absolute unity. Clearly, then, adding any element of plurality to G-d's essence or requiring any mediator to G-d is antithetical to Jewish teachings and hence forbidden for a Jew. Thus, the concept of a trinity would be ruled out as an acceptable belief for a Jewish person.[42]

CREATION REFLECTS ONENESS

The cornerstone of Jewish prayer is the *Shema*, which is the verse "Hear O Israel, the L-rd our G-d, the L-rd is One."[43] *Echad*, the term used by the verse to describe G-d's Oneness, can mean *one* in a sense that comprises different elements. The Talmud explains that this term specifically is used in order to highlight that G-d's Oneness permeates every dimension of existence.[44] Even in the framework of existence, where other entities exist, all is encompassed by His Oneness.[45]

Similar to the way in which Judaism portrays one absolutely "simple" Creator as responsible for both the creation and operation of nature, many modern scientists believe there to be a fundamental unity that underlies the physical world. They seek out a grand unified-field theory. They hope to find the simple unifying factor between the natural

---

not have these components, then He would be different; however, G-d is not dependent on His creations. When terms like "strength" and "kindness" or "wisdom" are used to describe G-d, it is through the human vantage point, not something contained in His essence.

41 This is the second of the Rambam's Thirteen Principles of Faith.

42 A non-Jew must recognize G-d as part of his Seven Laws of Noah, the moral code for humanity. He is not held to the same parameters of unity. For a gentile, belief in a mediator or triune godhead may be an acceptable form of worship. The concept is discussed in rabbinic literature as being *shituf*, a partnership, where the individual believes in G-d as the Supreme Being but that there is power allotted to another force or entity as well. The Rambam seems to be strict (*Melachim* 9:3), but other sources imply that non-Jews are allowed to have such a belief. See Rama, *Orach Chaim* 156; Tosofos to *Brachos* 2b, *Sanhedrin* 63b; Ran, end of chapter one in *Avoda Zara*, and Rabbeinu Yerucham, 17:5.

43 *Devarim* [Deuteronomy] 6:4.

44 The Talmud (*Brachos* 13b) says that the letters of *echad*—*alef, ches, dalet*—have the numeric equivalent of 1, 8, 4. This indicates that G-dliness pervades the one earth, seven heavens (and this world), and in all four cardinal directions.

45 See Rabbi Dov Ber Schneuri of Lubavitch, *Imrei Binah* 20a.

forces of gravity, electromagnetism, and the strong and weak atomic forces. Perhaps this essential unity in Creation that is being sought out is a reflection of the inherent unity of the Creator.[46]

This contemporary scientific outlook is related to a philosophical teaching explained by one of the greatest medieval sages, Maimonides (also known as the Rambam). The Rambam views the whole universe as one unified organism. All of the integrated parts of planet Earth and the entire cosmos are to be seen as functioning as one greater whole.[47] The concept of a cosmic unity helps one understand a subject addressed by the Chassidic masters.[48] They write that physical objects are not physical, but rather they are a conglomeration of four essential elements: earth, fire, air, and water. The Divine "word" is the unifying force, the power of amalgamation that perpetually fuses the four elements into a physical entity. The unity of the universe is qualitatively different than that of the Creator, since the universe is a compound unity, while the Creator has a "simple" unity—not consisting of any parts. Notwithstanding, the oneness in the cosmos foreshadows a simple source of all within it.

Aside from the Oneness that is found in the universe, there is also plan and purpose embedded into the Creation by the Purposeful Creator. These signs of purpose or design are the foundations of the teleological approach to G-d's existence.

---

46   There are a minority of physicists that do not seek a unified theory, believing the world to be a conglomeration of multifarious forces. Even this outlook may highlight the unique Oneness of the Creator. R. Saadia Gaon in *Emunos v'Deos* relates that because Divine unity is such an exclusive concept, the universe must be a multiplicity, because nothing else could be considered truly united. Both he and the Rambam (to be mentioned in the main text) both teach that the construct of Creation is indicative of Divine unity; however, they both explain how in opposite ways. For more on this concept, see Norman Lamm, "The Unity of God and the Unity of the World: Saadia and Maimonidies," in *Torah and Wisdom: Studies in Jewish Philosophy, Kabbalah, and Halacha—Essays in Honor of Arthur Hyman*, ed. Ruth Link-Salinger (1992), pgs. 113–118.

47   See Rambam, *Moreh Nevuchim* 1:72.

48   The idea of a perpetual Creation was taught by the Baal Shem Tov, founder of the Chassidic movement. Based on the *Midrash Tehillim* on 119:89, he explains that when G-d originally created the world, those words continue to stand and keep Creation in existence at every moment.

TELEOLOGICAL

The Teleological Approach is also a very common and reasonable approach to the existence of G-d. Based on the demonstrable existence of order, design, and direction of purpose in nature, it is clear that the universe was produced through an intelligent Creator.

This approach is nearly two thousand years old and is not limited to Jewish sources. In the writings of the sages, perhaps the first to make reference to this approach was Rabbi Akiva, who said, "Just as a house indicates a builder, a garment a tailor, and a door a carpenter, so too does this world tell that the Holy One, Blessed be He, created it."[49]

Rabbeinu Bachya, in his magnum opus *Duties of the Heart*, wonders how a rational being can entertain the idea that the world came into existence by chance, without a Creator. He asks:

> If ink were poured out accidentally on a blank sheet of paper, would it be possible that proper writing should result?... Since this appears impossible in the case of characters whose form is conventional, how can one assert that something far finer in its art, and which manifests in its fashioning a subtlety infinitely beyond our comprehension, could have happened without the purpose, power and wisdom of a wise and mighty designer?[50]

In modern times, the same sentiment is expressed in a slightly different way, saying that a room full of monkeys hacking away at a typewriter for infinite time would never produce the work of Shakespeare. A similar line of thinking was taken by one of the greatest scientists of all time: Sir Isaac Newton, a believer in G-d who studied the Bible every day[51] and also extensively studied the Talmud, commentaries of the Rambam, and a Latin translation of the *Zohar*. He wrote that the "beautiful system of the sun, planets, and comets, could only proceed

---

49   Rabbi Akiva: *Midrash Temurah* 3. In truth this approach was also the reasoning of our patriarch Abraham 4,000 years ago, who came to the conclusion of monotheism by seeing a common link and Designer in Creation.

50   *Chovos HaLevavos, Sha'ar HaYichud* 6.

51   See John Tiner, *Isaac Newton: Inventor, Scientist and Teacher* (1975).

from the counsel and dominion of an intelligent Being... This Being governs all things..."[52]

It is reported that an atheist colleague of Newton saw a model solar system on his desk and asked who made it. Newton responded that nobody did. Newton's colleague smiled and repeated the question, insisting that someone must have made it and that he should be told. Newton pointed out to him the absurdity of accepting that the actual solar system was created through luck and chance, and yet the model of it—with all of its craftsmanship and clear intelligence—must have had a maker.

In the early 1800s, the teleological approach was popularized by British theologian William Paley in his work *Natural Theology*, which introduced the famous "watchmaker analogy." He reasons that if one were to find a watch in the forest, with all of its springs and gears fashioned with intricacy and purpose, it would be obvious that it had not formed there by natural processes but instead must have been made by a watchmaker. So too, if one considers the sophistication and sense of purpose, or "intelligence," found in every detail of the natural world, one finds far more complexity than in a watch, and therefore, he concludes, the world requires a Maker.

Rabbi Elchonan Wasserman *zt"l* writes that common sense teaches that it is impossible for Creation to show this design and purpose by itself and it is therefore obvious that the world has a Creator. He questions how a child can be required to believe in G-d when even the greatest philosophers have failed. He also asks how non-Jews can be required to believe in G-d if they have not been taught the Torah. How can they be held accountable? He answers that the belief that G-d created the world is self-understood by any intelligent being.[53] There is no need for any knowledge of philosophy, or the need for proper instruction in order to grasp this idea, rather the person needs to simply open his eyes.[54]

---

52   *Newton's Philosophy of Nature: Selections from his Writings*, p. 42.

53   *Kovetz Mama'arim*, Mama'ar Al HaEmunah 1-5.

54   That is not to say that everything appears to the human onlooker as perfect, just that a purposeful Creation implies a purposeful Creator. Many times there are other factors in

Those who argue that belief in G-d is infantile, irrational, and something that should have been abandoned centuries ago must explain why so many only find G-d while in university or later in life. Antony Flew was the twentieth century's most vociferous atheist. He taught at Oxford, Aberdeen, Keele, Reading, and at York University in Toronto. For fifty years, his articles, books, and debates focused on disproving G-d. His work, *G-d and Philosophy*, is a classic in the atheist study arena. In 2004, at age eighty-one, he finally became a believer and declared all of his previous works invalid and obsolete. It was the scientific aspects connected with the teleological approach that finally convinced him.[55] Flew writes "...the journey of my discovery of the Divine has thus far been a pilgrimage of reason. I have followed the argument where it has led me. And it has led me to accept the existence of a self-existent, immutable, immaterial, omnipotent, and omniscient Being."[56]

MIRACLES ALL AROUND

Only habit and routine prevent us from being astounded by everything that we see at every moment. The Baal Shem Tov, the founder of the Chassidic movement, said the only difference between nature and a miracle is the frequency.[57]

All too often, there is a lack of appreciation for Divine workings that operate before our eyes. The work of the Creator can be very apparent in His creations. There are those who profess that they would believe in G-d if He would just show Himself. This is comparable to one who begs for water to drink while standing waist deep in a crystal-clear

the life of a person, like severe challenges or negative experiences that turn one off from the idea of G-d. For more on this topic, please see the chapter in this work concerning bad things happening to good people.

55 Gary Habermas, "My Pilgrimage from Atheism to Theism: An Exclusive Interview with Former British Atheist Professor Antony Flew," Biola University, December 9, 2004.

56 Antony Flew, *There is a God: How the World's Most Notorious Atheist Changed His Mind* (2007), pg. 155. Professor Flew said that the driving forces behind his epiphany were the information he read in a book written by Roy Varghese, *The Wonder of the World*, and in Gerald Schroeder's *The Hidden Face of God*.

57 *Keser Shem Tov*, ch. 119, 256.

wellspring. Sometimes the mind is closed to the idea of G-d, for various reasons, and even the greatest revelation would be written off with some sort of naturalistic explanation. One must allow himself to see the Divine in the world around.

The study of molecular biology seeks to trace the origin of life. Researchers in this field are beginning to appreciate the extreme improbability of inanimate matter transforming into living cells. Dr. Harold Klein, chairman of the National Academy of Sciences Committee, which reviews origin of life studies, concluded that, based on the complexity of even the simplest bacterium, it is impossible to imagine how life could have ever been created on its own.[58]

In the human body, the profound intricacy of the brain alone speaks volumes about design. The brain has recently been called "the most complex object in the universe."[59] It seems counterintuitive to deem such an entity befitting of this title to be the result of randomness and chance. Furthermore, much like Newton's colleague agreed that his *model* solar system needed a designer but denied that the *actual* solar system needed one, it is likewise ironic that all agree that electrical pumps and dialysis machines require designers, yet at the same time are willing to write off the *actual* heart and kidneys as the results of lucky chances. If one throws into the package the complexity of each cell in the body, the details of the eye, the perfectly coordinated circulatory, muscular, skeletal, digestive, and nervous systems, and the interdependency that they have between one another, it becomes more and more apparent that nature was designed with plan and purpose.

With proper examination, every object in the world speaks volumes to enrich faith, as the Psalmist writes, "Every one of them You have made with wisdom."[60] The reader is encouraged to read the Jewish texts that comprehensively enumerate the unfathomable complexities

---

58   *Scientific American* (Feb. 1991), pg. 104.
59   R. Grant Steen, *The Evolving Brain: The Known and the Unknown* (2007). See also Isaac Asimov, "In the Game of Energy and Thermodynamics You Can't Even Break Even," *Smithsonian* 1 (August), pg. 10.
60   *Tehillim* [Psalms] 104:24.

in the human body, the natural world, and the universe at large.[61] Plan and purpose show themselves all over the natural world.

Consider a seed. It is far from a simple matter. The seed is a programmer, with hundreds of thousands of instructions of how to proceed once put into the ground. These instructions are inscribed on the tiniest of strands on the helix of the DNA molecule. To write the seed's planned instructions on paper would take ten thousand fat library volumes. Besides the instructions, the seed also possesses the apparatus to carry out these plans. Within the seed are a complex of industrial installations and factories.[62]

Consider bananas. Before they are ripe they are green and camouflaged among the leaves, hard to peel, and give stomach aches to those who eat them. When ripe, they turn yellow to become more noticeable and appealing to the eater, easy for the eater to detach from the tree, easy to peel, and easy to digest. In other words, the fruit "knows" of eaters, who have eyes that distinguish color, possess stomachs, have senses of smell and taste, like sweet foods, have hands to pick the fruit, and have complex digestive systems that are compatible with the fruit's makeup.

Consider pollinated plants. Flowers that are pollinated by insects purposely attract the insects by their nectar, their color, and their scent. The plants "know" the necessity of propagating their kind; that pollination is necessary for propagation; that insects exist and participate in this process; that insects seek nectar; and that insects can discern color and smells. The entire existence of the bee depends on the nectar, and the entire existence of 100,000 flowers and fruits depends solely on the bee. They must have developed contemporaneously, for if they were slowly progressing over millions of years, where did the bees feed and how did the flowers produce fruit during this time?[63]

Consider egg shells. They must be a very exact thickness: strong

---

61   The teleological approach can be found in the writings of the Rambam, also the *Chovos HaLevavos*, Sha'ar Habechinah, Chazon Ish in *Emunah u'Bitachon*, the Steipler in *Chaye Olam*, and Rabbi Avigdor Miller in "The Universe Testifies," *Sing You Righteous*, pg. 130.

62   Yaakov Astor, *Rav Avigdor Miller on Emunah and Bitachon* (2012), pg. 204–205.

63   Miller, "The Universe Testifies," #405.

enough to hold the developing creature within, but thin enough that the animal can break out at the right time. Furthermore, the egg of each species has to be a different precise thickness. Were the eggshell not the perfect thickness in the first generation, there could be no second generation. Although thousands of degrees of thickness were possible, the fact that the shell was not too thick or thin is indicative of the work of a Designer.

The examples of purpose and interdependency are virtually endless the deeper one looks everywhere in Creation. Some wish to simply write off these intricacies as part of "Mother Nature." Nature is neither chemical nor energy. Empty slogans like "nature will find a way" or "nature plans ahead" shirk the evidence of premeditated purposefulness. In doing so, any deeper exploration of the question "how things came to be as they are" is evaded. Nature can either be intelligence or accident; there is no third option. One simply cannot say that "Accident will find a way," or that "Accident plans ahead." Substituting the word "nature" for other words like "adaptation" does not fix anything either. The principle remains the same: it is either intelligence or accident.[64]

THE ANTHROPIC PRINCIPLE

The teleological approach stresses that evidence of plan and purpose assumes a Creator. Interestingly, there is a scientific principle called the Anthropic Principle that has been developing since the 1970s. It was during this time that the Big Bang theory became firmly established, and thus physicists began to theorize about alternative scenarios for the development of the universe. The Anthropic Principle, from the Greek word *anthropos* meaning "man," states that the universe seems to have been designed for the existence and sustaining of mankind, as very slight changes in natural law, and the disappearance of many highly improbable past events, would make human life impossible. While different than the teleological argument, it shares some common theological implications.

---

64   Based on ibid., #291, 292.

Professor Steven Weinberg, a very prominent American theoretical physicist, explains that "life as we know it would be impossible if any one of several physical quantities had slightly different values... One constant does seem to require incredible fine tuning. This constant has to do with the energy of the Big Bang. If the energy of the Big Bang were different by one part in 10^{120}, there would be no life anywhere in our universe."[65] Astrophysicist Michael Turner of the University of Chicago puts this probability into perspective, comparing it to "throwing a dart across the entire universe and hitting a bullseye one millimeter in diameter on the other side."[66]

John Wheeler was formerly Professor of Physics at Princeton University and ranks with Einstein as one of the most consequential physicists of the twentieth century. In discussing these observations, he asks: "Is man an unimportant bit of dust on an unimportant planet in an unimportant galaxy somewhere in the vastness of space? No! The necessity to produce life lies at the center of the universe's whole machinery and design." He continues, saying that "slight variations in physical laws such as gravity or electromagnetism would make life impossible."[67] The following are just the tip of the iceberg of examples of fine tuning in the universe:[68]

- Any change in the proportions of the force of gravity and electromagnetism would not allow for midsize stars like the sun, only cooler "red" stars or hotter "blue" ones. Both are incapable of sustaining life.[69]

- If the gravitational force were *increased*, stars would be too hot

<hr />

65   Steven Weinberg, "Life in the Universe," *Scientific American* (Oct. 1994), cited from Gerald Schroeder, *The Science of God* (1997), pg. 5.

66   Quoting Schroeder, ibid.

67   John Wheeler, *Reader's Digest* (September 1986): pg. 107.

68   A very comprehensive list of "coincidences" needed to sustain life on Earth can be found in John Leslie's book *Universes*. See also Guillermo Gonzalez, "Solar System Bounces in the Right Range for Life," *Facts & Faith*, v. 11, no. 1 (1997); Adam Burrows and Jonathan Lumine, "Astronomical Questions of Origin and Survival," *Nature* 378 (1995), pg. 333; and other sources listed by Hugh Ross, "Big Bang Model Redefined by Fire," in Dembsi, *Mere Creation* (1998), pg. 372.

69   Brandon Carter, "Large Number Coincidences and the Anthropic Principle in Cosmology," in *Confrontation of Cosmological Theories with Observational Data* (1974), pgs. 295–298.

and burn up quickly and unevenly. If force were *decreased*, stars would be so cool that nuclear fusion, which burns in the core of stars, would have never ignited.

- If the nuclear strong force were *increased* as little as two percent, protons would be prevented from forming, producing a universe without atoms. *Decreasing* the force by five percent would lead to a universe without stars. No elements heavier than hydrogen would form.

- Think of the mysterious nature of water. Water is a unique substance, lighter as a solid than it is as a liquid (i.e., ice floats). If ice did not float, the oceans would freeze from the bottom up, and the Earth would now be covered in ice. Life would not be able to form in these conditions.[70]

Similar "lucky coincidences" that the universe has the perfect format for life on Earth can be found in electromagnetic force, ratio of number of protons to number of electrons, ratio of electron to proton mass, mass density of the universe, entropy level of the universe, expansion rate of the universe, average distance between galaxies, density of galaxy cluster, decay rate of protons, average distance between stars, and a plethora of additional precise factors. Once again, they cannot simply be dismissed as natural laws of physics; they are rooted in either accident or plan.

Prominent physicist Paul Davies observed that "scientists are slowly waking up to an inconvenient truth—the universe looks suspiciously like a fix. The issue concerns the very laws of nature themselves. For forty years, physicists and cosmologists have been quietly collecting examples of all too convenient 'coincidences' and special features in the underlying laws of the universe that seem to be necessary in order for life, and hence conscious beings, to exist. Change any one of them and the consequences would be lethal. Fred Hoyle, the distinguished cosmologist, once said it was as if a super-intellect has monkeyed with physics."

70　See John Barrow and Frank Tipler, *The Anthropic Cosmological Principle* (1987), pgs. 143–144, 524–541. Life would not be possible because many scientists say that life evolved from primitive sea life.

ALTERNATE UNIVERSES AS AN ALTERNATIVE TO DESIGN

A fine-tuned universe, where everything is precisely how it needs to be for life to be sustainable, hints at a plan, a purpose, and implying perhaps even a Purposeful Designer. In order to prevent the possibility of such a thought (that the universe was intentionally created for life), some scientists have come to rely on the "multiverse" model of existence. This essentially means that there are many other "parallel universes" very similar to ours that have different rules and natural laws that they follow. *This* universe happens to be the one that has the proper configurations necessary for life to exist, but there are other universes where this is not the case.

Dr. Alan Lightman, professor of physics at MIT, writes that the multiverse approach undermines the very premise of science as a description of reality. Instead, scientists claim that in the "cosmic lottery hat" of infinite universes, *this* happens to be the one that allows for life. Also, by definition, these "other universes" cannot be traced, measured, or have any conceivable means of proving their existence. Their entire existence is limited to faith. This is quite ironic, since faith in the existence of infinite, untraceable, accidental universes is perfectly acceptable to them, yet the premise of a single and purposeful universe, created by a traceable (yet not openly evident) Creator is laughable.

A FURTHER GLIMPSE OF PRECISION

The solar system is a fascinating spectacle to consider. The radius of the nucleus of an atom is 10,000 times smaller than the radius of the full atom itself. Interestingly, the radius of the sun is smaller than the radius of the solar system by approximately the same amount. In other words, an atom is like a miniature solar system. "This kind of similarity demonstrates that the gigantic solar system and the tiny atom, which is invisible to the naked eye, are different details of the same creative design or different products of the creativity of one and the same intelligent Creator."[71]

---

71   Joseph Davydov, *God Exists: New Light On Science and Creation* (2000), pg. 30.

A. C. Morrison, former president of the New York Academy of Science, writes that the perfect order in the solar system is one of the reasons that he believes in G-d. The rotational pattern of the planet Mercury always keeps the same half turned toward the sun. The planet is desolate on one side because of the intense heat, and on the other because of the bitter cold. The Earth, on the other hand, rotates on its axis at a little over one thousand miles per hour. Were it slower, the prolonged heat of day, or cold of night, would not allow vegetation to grow. If its rotations were faster, vegetation would not receive enough sunlight each day to grow. If the Earth were slightly closer or further from the sun, it would be scorched or frozen over.[72]

The moon, on average, is about 240,000 miles away from the Earth. The sun is about 400 times more distant than the moon, and the sun is also about 400 times larger than the moon. It is intriguing, to say the least, that from the Earth, the sun and moon are at just the right distances to have the same apparent size, hence the possibility of the perfect fit during a full solar eclipse.

Furthermore, the size and distance of the moon are just right to stabilize the Earth's perfect tilt and keeps it from wandering between the gravitational pulls of the sun and Jupiter.[73] Even if the Earth, sun, and moon were in their perfect spot, but Jupiter were a little bit farther or smaller, Earth would be blasted by asteroids and comets. If Jupiter were closer or larger, its gravity would pull Earth outside of the zone where life is sustainable.

If the solar system was arranged as perfectly as it is, but it was in a different part of the Milky Way, life would also be prevented. Were it *closer* to the center of the galaxy, Earth would likely collide with many comets and asteroids. Additionally, the tightly packed area of stars would pull its orbit out of the life zone. If it were located *farther* from the center of the galaxy, the solar system would not contain enough heavy elements for a life-supporting planet.

---

72   Morrison, "Seven Reasons Why a Scientist Believes in G-d," *Reader's Digest* (Oct. 1960), pgs. 72–74. See also Michael Denton, *Nature's Destiny* (1998). See also Barrow and Tipler, *The Anthropic Cosmological Principle*, pgs. 567-569.

73   Brownlee and Ward, *Rare Earth* (2000), pgs. 36-40.

If the Earth was in the same location in the galaxy, but factors in the galaxy's rotation were different, or the positioning of other galaxies was altered, then life on Earth would also not work. The Milky Way is in a rather unpopulated area of the universe, so there is little if any gravitational pull from other galaxies. This stabilizes the galaxy and the orbit of the sun.

It is simply amazing how so many celestial entities in both the local and distant universe had to be perfectly aligned in order to facilitate life on this planet.

These, along with innumerable other factors, make life anywhere else in the universe practically impossible, says Donald Brownlee, professor of astronomy at the University of Washington. "Almost all environments in the universe are terrible for life. It's only Garden-of-Eden places like Earth where it can exist."[74] The precision that goes into making our planet habitable shows a "Higher Intelligence" that did it purposefully. In the words of astronomer Allan Sandage, "I find it quite improbable that such order came out of chaos. There has to be some organizing principle. G-d to me is a mystery but is the explanation for the miracle of existence, why there is something instead of nothing."[75]

Volumes could be written on the depths of this subject, but for the purposes here it will have to suffice concluding with the words of American astronomer George Greenstein: "As we survey all the evidence, the thought insistently arises that some supernatural agency—or, rather, Agency—must be involved. Is it possible that suddenly, without intending to, we have stumbled upon scientific proof of the existence of a Supreme Being? Was it G-d who stepped in and so providentially crafted the cosmos for our benefit?"[76]

---

74   William Broad, "Maybe We Are Alone in the Universe," *New York Times*, Feb. 8, 2000.

75   J. N. Willford, "Sizing up the Cosmos: An Astronomer's Quest," *New York Times*, March 12, 1991, pg. B9. See also Vera Kistiakowsky, professor of physics at MIT: "There remains the question of how the Big Bang started, but it seems unlikely that science will be able to elucidate this...the exquisite order displayed by our scientific understanding of the physical world calls for the Divine." Quoted from Margenau and Varghese, *Cosmos, Bios, and Theos*, pg. 52.

76   George Greenstein, *The Symbiotic Universe: Life and Mind in the Cosmos* (1988), pgs. 26–27.

ORDER IN NATURE AND ITS RELIABILITY

The order in nature and its reliability is not one of the classical philosophical approaches to the Divine, but it contains important insight worthy of reflection. As a preface, consider the concept of laughing and the source of where laughter comes from. It is, in fact, no laughing matter. The idea of laughter is very telling of the existence of an internal, ordered system in the world. The secret of comedy is surprise. We tend to view the world as an ordered system. There are ways in which things are "supposed to go" in our minds. Laughter means that for a moment, something in reality is found outside of its usual place in the framework of the human experience. Our reality, the orderliness of how we perceive things, has been momentarily mocked. The joke or funny situation surprises us, it deviates from the norm, and we laugh. Where does this sense of normalcy and order come from so that deviation from it surprises us, making us laugh?

Most people are inherently certain that the order of things in the world around them is as it should be, and that there is an existential rhyme and reason for the way reality operates. The prevailing worldview of many is that there is a general fate of sorts and that "what goes around comes around." Additionally, humans have a tendency to feel that "everything is okay" and that their life has a purpose. When things get tough, there is an instinctive sense of hope that things will eventually work themselves out. In a haphazard, godless, and meaningless world, where does this sense of security and hope come from? In a world with no guiding force or inner structure, how does one confidently expect justice and realistically await better times?

Furthermore, there is an apparently baseless expectation that everything in nature will continue to act in the way in which it always has. Does anyone even entertain the idea that reality will ever change—that fire will pour down from the sky instead of rain, or that tomorrow the sun will not rise in the east and set in the west? Without the governance of a rational Being, is there any sound reason to assume the rationality of the universe—that reality should be regulated to fixed laws based on unchanging mathematics?

This order and structure is not something just imagined in the human mind, it is the actual reality of the way the universe operates. Science bases all of its formulas and conclusions on the assumption that matter, elements and atoms will operate today as they did yesterday, and that the forces in the universe will remain constant. Science can tell over what the rules of the universe are, but cannot explain *why* the universe continues to follow these rules with uncanny precision.[77] Joel Primack, cosmologist at the University of California, Santa Cruz, once posed the question to a colleague, Cambridge cosmologist Neil Turok: "What is it that makes the electrons continue to follow the laws?" Turok responded with a smile, saying "somebody has to do that. I've never understood the argument that starting the universe required a Creator but keeping it going did not."[78] Something seems to compel physical objects to obey the laws of nature. Ironically, neither compulsion nor obedience is a physical idea. Why, in fact, do the laws of nature operate with such precision?

Along the same lines, the deep structure and order present in nature is mathematically chartable; it is rational. This type of profound order is hard to dismiss as merely the result of a random primordial explosion. There is rationality in the world at large and a rationality and order to the human mind as well. The fact that the universe is at all understandable is perplexing, boggling even the great Albert Einstein, who wrote, "The eternal mystery of the world is its comprehensibility."[79]

How do mathematical structures that essentially exist within the human mind parallel the natural law-like behavior in the external physical universe? This concept was noticed by theoretical physicist John Polkinghorne, where he writes as follows:[80]

> We are so familiar with the fact that we can understand
> the world that most of the time we take it for granted.
> It is what makes science possible. Yet it could have been

77   Paraphrasing Shiller, *The Road Back*, pg. 133.

78   Alan Boyle, "Did the Cosmos Arise from Nothing?" NBCNews.com, April 15, 1999.

79   Albert Einstein, out of *My Later Years* (1950) ["Physics and Reality" (1936)], pg. 61.

80   All quoting from John Polkinghorne, *Science and Creation: The Search for Understanding* (2006), pgs. 29–31.

otherwise. The universe may have been a disorderly chaos, rather than an orderly cosmos. Or it might have had a rationality that was inaccessible to us.

He continues, "Our minds have shown themselves to be apt and adequate for the solution of all the problems that the physical world presents to us," adding that "there is congruence between our minds and the universe, between the rationality experienced within and the rationality observed without." He sees the congruence of rationality within the human mind and the congruence within the world as stemming from a profound state that unites the two, namely, the "Rationality of the Creator."

We have seen that human beings view their reality with a certain order and structure, and that the laws of nature themselves actually conform to order and structure. Likewise, the historical tendency of civilization has been to form ordered and value-symbolizing societies.[81] This is a logical and obvious outgrowth of an intrinsic sense of order and structure programmed within. Chaos and anarchy would be the logical result of the godless nonsense world. Why should mankind willingly subjugate his crass and pleasure-seeking tendencies in the name of building civility and refining himself? Why not just exist as the animals do, allowing only the fittest to survive? Perhaps this seemingly baseless propensity in society toward collective order is an extension of our intuitive perception of an existing Divine order. It seems reasonable that our perception or rationality and order in our worldly outlook, the actual existence of order in nature, and our propensity to form rationally functioning and orderly societies, emanates from a purposeful Source.

MORALITY

Almost all human beings acknowledge and strive to uphold some kind of morality and each person has at least a basic inherent understanding that some things are categorically wrong. Even those who claim that morality is relative usually believe in at least *some* absolute

---

81   See Eric Voegelin, *Order and History* (1969), pg. ix, cited in Schiller, *The Road Back*.

moral truth. That moral truth may be only that it is wrong to hurt others, cheat, or murder innocents. We know these truths deep inside of ourselves.

When the United States helped liberate the concentration camps in Nazi- occupied Europe, General Eisenhower made sure many photographs were taken to clearly display the magnitude of this unthinkable situation. When these photographs were published, the public was horrified. The Nazi camps were immediately and intuitively declared categorically wrong. Where does this intuitive knowledge come from?

Right and wrong cannot simply be decided by the "Law of the Land." In this case of the Holocaust, the death-camps were certainly within the bounds of the law. "Right" also cannot be defined in this case as a form of utilitarianism—"the greatest good for the greatest number"—as this would also be agreed on by the Nazi officers, who would say they were simply eliminating Jews and other minorities for the sake of the "greater majority" and with the majority's support.

The sane individual realizes what took place within the barbed wire of these camps was *absolutely* wrong. The sane individual says to himself that this was wrong, but not only wrong because *I* believe it to be wrong, or society believes it to be wrong. It was intrinsically wrong in the absolute sense of the word. This was a fact admitted by even one of the most famous atheist philosophers, Bertrand Russell, who wrote, "I cannot see how to refute the arguments for the subjectivity of ethical values, but I find myself incapable of believing that all that is wrong with wanton cruelty is that I don't like it."[82]

There are other situations and deeds that the reasonable person will classify as absolutely unacceptable and wrong. Where does this intuitive sense come from? It also seems that categorizing something as absolutely wrong implies an Absolute place from which this absolute concept was derived. It cannot be an individual or cultural thing, as these will always be subjective assessments. Large groups are still subjective. Consider the Nazi wave that swept across Europe. They

---

82   See Germaine Bree, *Camus and Sartre* (1972), pg. 15; "Notes on Philosophy, January 1960," *Philosophy* (April 1960), as quoted in *The Retreat to Commitment*, 2nd ed., pg. xxv (Preface).

believed what they were doing was right. If there is no objective or absolute wrong, who can authoritatively say that what took place was wrong in the truest sense of the word? What makes my subjective opinion of what is right better than their subjective opinion? Without an absolute defining mark, it remains my opinion and their opinion— which we are both entitled to. It would seem that one who acknowledges that there is *anything* that is absolutely wrong simultaneously acknowledges that there is an Absolute source for this stipulation.

An absolute moral truth must come from a source that is Absolute. Absolute denotes something not subject to change, something not subject to physical reality or the confines of time. The entirety of the moral approach can be summed up thusly: If G-d does not exist, absolute moral values do not exist. Objective moral values do exist; therefore, G-d exists.[83]

Dostoevsky wrote, "If there is no G-d, everything is permitted."[84] If man is a mere sophisticated animal, there should be no sense of right and wrong. When a lion preys a lamb, or kills another lion for that matter, he is not to be condemned, nor is his victim to be considered a martyr. The animal is simply following its nature. Why should murder of innocent people be regarded as any different? Why is it embedded in the human psyche that this is unacceptable? The problems of a society without Absolute morality are too numerous to enumerate in this work—and terrifying.[85]

---

83   This succinct summary of the moral approach parallels what is recorded in *Ethical Theory: An Anthology*, edited by Russ Shafer-Landau, pg. 226. A number of internationally renowned ethicists have defended the moral philosophical approach. See for example Robert Adams, *Finite and Infinite Goods* (2000); John Hare, "Is Moral Goodness without Belief in God Rationally Stable?" in *Is Goodness without God Good Enough? A Debate on Faith, Secularism, and Ethics*, ed. Nathan King and Robert Garcia (Lanham, MD: Rowman & Littlefield, 2008); C. Stephen Evans *Kierkegaard's Ethic of Love: Divine Commands and Moral Obligations* (2004).

84   Fyoder Dostoevsky's *The Brothers Karamazov*.

85   Perhaps the most extreme example is the words of Erik Von Kuehnelt-Leddihn in reference to secularism, that "there is no scientific reason why one should not make lampshades out of reactionaries. None whatsoever." See "Thoughts on the Faith of a Liberal," *Catholic World* (July 1946): pgs. 310–318. For further reading on the topic, see Lawrence Kelemen, *Permission to Believe* (1993).

CONCLUSION

In essence, the cosmological, teleological, order of Creation and moral arguments are some of the many approaches taken in both classical Jewish sources and more recent philosophical ponderings. These approaches are certainly conceptually more palatable than the juvenile "bearded old man"[86] in the sky that some have erroneously associated with G-d. All too often, the god that the atheist does *not* believe in is the same god that the believer does *not* believe in.

The conclusion of faith is formulated with a combination of reason, emotion, and willingness. There is no *one* approach to G-d's existence that will suffice; each should be taken as a piece of a collective unit. Just like we mentioned above, that Big Bang cosmology was not widely accepted until later confirming proofs were incorporated into the picture; so too here, it is important to take everything into account. Individually, and especially together, all of these avenues, when examined in balance and correct proportion, point to the existence of a Supreme Being and Creator—G-d. The more that one will delve into the classical Jewish sources, in particular amongst the great Jewish philosophical writings, the more apparent the reality of G-d becomes.

---

86   For an extreme example of how this premise was used to slander the concept of G-d, see Yemelyan Yaroslavsky, *The Bible for Believers and Non-Believers* (1958), cited from Davydov, *God Exists* (2000), pg. 91.

EVOLUTION:

Points To Ponder

The idea that there is a Creator who brought everything into existence is clear; however, the means by which this took place is less openly discernable. Evolution or changes *within* a species over time is clear, tested, and agreed upon by everyone, and hence *not* addressed in this work.[87] The discussion presented here concerns only the idea that living beings arose by chance and were perpetuated through random mutations—that one species over time eventually became another.[88]

A NATURALIST NECESSITY

Before addressing some of the points of contention, it is fitting to preface with a point made by the late Dr. A. Chaim Zimmerman. Everyone agrees that the world did not exist in its present form since

---

87 Evolution is typically taught in two different ways: I) Microevolution: small, observable changes that occur through natural selection, adaptation; II) Macroevolution: large, non-observable changes, from a single-celled organism eventually to mankind. Most textbooks and professors will not make a distinction between the two; instead, they show evidence for the small changes and use that to show that it also takes place on a grand scale as well.

88 In this section, evolution is being discussed in the neo-Darwinian sense. Neo-Darwinism describes the current modified theory of Darwinian evolution: living beings arose by chance and were expanded through random mutations and natural selection, combined with the later Mendelian genetic discoveries. (For a concise assessment of the difference between macroevolution and microevolution, see "Evolution: Myths and Facts," printed in Arnie Gotfryd, *Mind Over Matter* (2003), pgs. 410–420).

the beginning of time—it certainly has undergone major changes. How did this change happen? Dr. Zimmerman says that there are two possibilities: a) G-d created it, and put it into its form or b) it changed by itself naturally.

Actually a more accurate outlook is as follows:

For the believer in G-d, there are *two* possibilities:

- G-d created the universe in one "bang."
- He chose with His own will and reasons to create the world by an evolutionary process of time.

For the one who does *not* believe in G-d, there is only *one* possibility:

- The world progressed through some sort of evolutionary process.

For the believer, evolution may perhaps be a *possibility*, but for the non-believer it is a logical *necessity*. There is no other option. This is why, explains Dr. Zimmerman, the concept of evolution has in many ways become the backbone of secular academic knowledge—because there is no other option.[89] Acceptance of evolution does not necessarily result in atheism, but atheism *does necessarily* result in accepting an evolutionary process.

In sync with this logical introduction to the topic, some of the later Torah authorities have stated that even if certain aspects of evolution were true, they would still not negate the traditional Torah approach.[90] Notwithstanding, the section in this work looks at several components of the theory of evolution *without* assuming that any aspect of macro-evolution actually took place.

THE SOURCE OF CONTENTION

The modern theory of evolution began and grew in the eighteenth and nineteenth centuries. It was pioneered by Georges Buffon and Jean Lamarck, and most identified with Charles Darwin. Today, in

---

89   These are Dr. Zimmerman's thoughts, paraphrased from his work *Torah and Reason*, pgs. 52–54.

90   See Rabbi Shimshon Raphoel Hirsch, *Collected Writings*, 7:263–4; Hoffman, commentary on Genesis, vol. 1 (Bnei Brak, 1969), pgs. 9-52; Kook, *Oros HaKodesh*, pgs. 559, 565.

the scientific community, it is the predominant theory of the development of life, although there are differences of opinions about the facts and how to interpret them.

In 1859, Charles Darwin published his famous work *On the Origin of Species by Means of Natural Selection*. In it, he proposed that all higher life forms evolved from lower life forms and therefore all species have a common ancestor. He maintained that living systems owe their existence to chance and natural selection. Through this model, organisms with favorable traits are more likely to reproduce and pass these traits on to the next generation. Those with weaker traits than the competition eventually die out. This is referred to as "the survival of the fittest."

Since its inception, a corollary of the theory was an underlying tone of lack of purpose and meaning in the universe. Many people mistakenly associate this lack of purpose as something that is *scientifically* conclusive. Purpose and meaning, however, are theological concepts.[91] Any statements conveying lack of purpose are not derived from scientific inquiry itself, but are rather an unfortunate undertone expressed by some scientists.[92]

The scientific community in Darwin's day was quick to jump on the new idea. At the time, he had little tangible proof for his theory, but this did not stop the masses from endorsing his work as gospel. Other various theories and even forgeries quickly sprouted up to

---

91   In 1997, an argument took place at the National Association of Biology Teachers (NABT). The argument was over a vote that took place in 1995 incorporating the following statement on the teaching of evolution: "Evolution is an unsupervised, impersonal, unpredictable and natural process." After hours of arguments the words "unsupervised and impersonal" were removed from the statement. The executive director, who pushed for the change, did it in the name of good science, claiming that "to say that evolution is unsupervised is to make a theological statement." See E. J. Larson, and W. L. Larson, "Scientists and Religion in America," *Scientific American* (Sept. 1999): pgs. 88–93. Although many scientists would like to attach theological underpinnings to evolution, it is unnecessary and inappropriate.

92   This blunder is discussed and refuted by David Berlinski, a former research assistant in molecular biology at Columbia University, in his book *Devil's Delusion: Atheism and its Scientific Pretentions*. It is interesting that Berlinski is a staunch opponent of evolutionary conclusions, yet he considers himself an agnostic. This demonstrates that his deductions and critiques on evolution are not based on trying to defend religious belief, but rather on its own inherent flaws.

bolster Darwin's theory.[93] The theory was made during the Victorian era, which followed major religious puritan revivals in Europe and the Americas. Many philosophers at the time were trying to free themselves from biblical influence. Many scientists were antagonistic toward religion. Evolution became a flag under which to champion atheism and support for denying the supernatural. Soon after the theory became popular, tremendous hostility developed between the reaffirmed atheist scientists and the Church.

In reaction, the monotheistic religions passionately fought against anything that had to do with evolutionary theory.[94] Early on, and until this very day, many would-be challengers and contenders in the scientific community keep their silence in order to uphold their self-respect amongst their colleagues, who have overwhelmingly embraced the ideas.

Still today, there are quite a few significant challenges and glaring flaws in Darwin's theory.[95] The following are issues of consideration regarding neo-Darwinianism:

MUTATIONS

Within the nuclei of all cells are genes with programmed information, each one carrying the code for a specific trait in its living entity.[96]

---

93   The most famous paleontological forgery can be reviewed in Chris Stringer and Joseph S. Weiner, *The Piltdown Forgery: The Classic Account of the Most Famous and Successful Hoax in Science* (2003). See also E. Pennisi, "Haeckel's Embryos: Fraud Rediscovered," *Science* 277 (1997):1435. Forgeries are not limited to remote incidents of the past, even recently there have been big claims that have turned up to be fraudulent; see for example L. M. Simons, "Archaeoraptor Fossil Trail," *National Geographic* 198:4 (2000): 128–132.

94   See Avraham Steinberg, "Theory of Evolution—a Jewish Perspective," *Rambam Maimonides Medical Journal*, vol 1, issue 1 (2010). This article contains a wealth of information on the subject.

95   Michael Denton, *Evolution: A Theory in Crisis* (1986), pgs. 326–329. Of note is French biochemist and philosopher Pierre Lecomte du Noüy (*Human Destiny* 1947) who disagreed sharply with Darwin's conclusions. "He pointed out that the lowest forms of life found today can be found unchanged in the oldest fossil forms known. This implies that they have not altered their structures at all, and that they have survived under adverse conditions normally detrimental to the higher forms. According to the principle of natural selection, the lower forms alone should have survived." (See Paul Forchheimer, *Our Miraculous World* (1983), pg. 29).

96   Single traits are known to be spread across several genes. Also many single genes are known to affect several traits.

Plants and animals constantly renew and reproduce themselves through cell division, reproducing the entire genetic code. When the code is not copied correctly, the result is a mutation, which in turn can be passed on to offspring.

Current evolutionary theory proposes that species developed through a long series of positive mutations, which the environment inherently selected to survive. Over millions of years, these beneficial mutations supposedly formed completely new species.

The effects of mutations can be beneficial, harmful, or neutral, depending on their context or location. In the overwhelming number of cases, mutations are a step back or not a step at all. It is difficult to theorize that for billions of years most mutations were, instead, constructive and led to the development of new species over and over again. One thinker described it this way: "Mutations are thought to stem from random errors in copying the commands of the DNA's genetic code. To suppose that such a random event could reconstruct even a single complex organ like a liver or kidney is about as reasonable as to suppose that an improved watch can be designed by throwing an old one against a wall."[97]

One might suppose that with harmful mutations, their effect is only temporary. Maybe these initial genetic deformities could, over millions of years, become a new trait that would, in the end, be considered beneficial. For example, consider the wing of a bird. In a slow process of development over millions of years, the developing wing would have initially been a handicap for a long period of time, but eventually became a functional and beneficial appendage. However, were that the case, somewhere along the line natural selection would have eliminated the early version of the wing because natural selection only perpetuates the more superior specimens. The early wing stubs would have been a dangerous handicap to survival. How could natural

---

97   Phillip Johnson, *Darwin on Trial* (1991), pg. 37. Dr. Lee Spetner, biophysicist and former professor at Johns Hopkins University, says that "all point mutations that have been studied on the molecular level turn out to reduce the genetic information and not to increase it... information cannot be built up by mutations that lose it. A business cannot make money by losing a little bit at a time." See Dr. Lee Spetner, *Not by Chance* (1997), pg. 138.

selection determine from the outset which mutation is better if each creature's full development takes millions of years to complete?[98] It is a purely faith-based assumption that random mutations gradually move life forward and can produce new creatures.

Perhaps the most often cited proof of evolution is the study of the Peppered Moth in England. Originally the light-colored moths reproduced more successfully than the dark-colored ones because they could camouflage well with the light-colored tree trunks that they rested upon, however, the dark-colored ones could be easily identified by predators. After the Industrial Revolution, the smoke from factories darkened the tree trunk and over several decades the dark-colored moths instead became the majority. This is not an example of classic evolution, but merely adaptation, or what some would call "microevolution." There was no new species or even a new organ produced. It is simple adaptation within an already existing system. Doron Aurbach of Bar-Ilan University Chemistry Department said, "Mutations are not capable of developing a new capability or the formation of a new organ. At most they are responsible for a fine change in the existing functions, and in most cases it is a negative one."[99]

---

98   Additionally, natural selection does not just eliminate the "bad" traits, it eliminates the whole organism that obviously had a majority of "good" traits; otherwise it would not have survived up to that point. Natural selection is actually not a good way of selecting traits at all; it just eliminates the most extreme mutational cases. Minor mutations keep accumulating in the species. This is called "genetic load." And this means that all species are accumulating mutations (which are errors on the genetic code). This is referred to as "genetic entropy." All species are basically going toward genetic disorder, exactly the opposite from what is predicted by the evolutionary theory.

99   See Adi Cohen, *We Are Not Alone* (2009), pg. 124. Along the same lines, Dr. Gerald Schroeder writes that the only proof for evolution the Natural History Museum in London could come up with was "pink daisies evolving into blue daisies, little dogs evolving into big dogs, but they could not come up with one single morphological change clearly recorded in the fossil record." He continues that although the math clearly shows that evolution through random mutations cannot produce the significant changes in morphology, the theory of Darwinian evolution is likely to continue, despite the fact that it does not depict reality, given that the world is so steeped in physicality and materialism. See Gerald Schroeder, *The Hidden Face of God* (2001), pgs. 91, 107, 120.

COMMON DESIGNER, NOT COMMON ANCESTOR

Homology studies and compares shared anatomical, physiological, and genetic features in different organisms. It is often interpreted as evidence for evolution. There are similarities that exist between creatures. There are genetic similarities between human beings and other life forms, even in much lower organisms like worms or mice. This does not conflict with the biblical Creation account, as it seems sensible that G-d, who is described as the Architect of the world, would have used the molecular biology of DNA as His blueprint in planning the design of all His creatures. Those with a naturalist worldview interpret the similarities to be evidence of a common ancestor, yet it is just as cogent to attribute the similarities to a common designer.

This concept of a common designer, as opposed to a common ancestor, is not new. Before Darwin published *On the Origin of Species*, biologist Sir Richard Owen delivered a discourse at the meeting of the Royal Institution of Great Britain in which he proposed that shared anatomical features were evidence of an original archetypal pattern and not a common ancestor.[100]

Many cars share similar parts or have similar designs. This does not mean that one car is an evolved version of the other car; rather it implies that there was a similar blueprint being used. Consider the early Porsche and Volkswagen cars, for example, that shared many of the same parts and features. This could be expected since they were both designed by Ferdinand Porsche. If creatures across the world were all completely different, devoid of any similarities, this would naturally look as though they had more than one designer. The uniformity and similarities that are found among creatures are actually a natural hint to a single source—an original Designer. These remarkable similarities in DNA sequences between the human and many other organisms provide many benefits. This is especially true in the realm of research set to improve human health.[101] The knowledge and insights gained

---

100 Richard Owen, *On the Nature of Limbs: A Discourse* (2007), ed. Ron Amundson.
101 "Almost all drugs approved by the FDA undergo rigorous testing in animals before en-

from these similarities was purposefully embedded by the Creator for our benefit.

MISSING INFORMATION

Two major points of contention with the classic evolutionary approach are (a) the lack of evidence for the so-called "pre-biotic soup theory" that supposedly facilitated the origin of life, and (b) in the fossil record of how that life developed over time. Each will be briefly discussed below.

"Pre-biotic Soup Theory": The original focus of the theory of evolution was on how *already existing* life transformed over time, not on the origin of life itself. Darwin's students took his reasoning a step further and suggested that life itself had evolved into being from inanimate matter.[102] Following the findings of Louis Pasteur in the late nineteenth century, which refuted the theory of spontaneous generation, the question of *how* life began was at least passively included in evolutionary theory and discussions.

According to the pre-life soup theory, life first sprang up from non-life in a "soup" of various organic chemicals in the early Earth's water. Over an extended period of time, some of these chemicals gradually came together and formed molecular chains that would eventually form the first self-replicating primitive life forms.

The theory that there once existed some "pre-biotic soup" remains elusive, as there is no proof of its existence. In general, a major roadblock in assessing the Darwinian Theory, and in particular approaches to the origin of life, is that it is not provable. It is impossible to reproduce the conditions like the temperature and pressures of primeval

---

tering human trials. Scientists studying single-celled organisms, like bacteria and fungi, to more complex organisms, like mice or chimpanzees, have made monumental medical discoveries that directly apply to human beings. It would be irrational to experiment on mice to understand human diseases were it not for the biological and genetic threads that link mice to humans." This quote, as well as some other concepts addressed in this section, was gained from Loike and Tendler, "Molecular Genetics, Evolution, and Torah Principles," *The Torah u-Madda Journal* 14 (2006-07): pgs. 178–80.

102 Although Darwin himself never suggested that dead matter could evolve into live matter. See Lawrence Kelemen, *Permission to Believe* (1990), pg. 52.

existence, or the length of time, in a laboratory. Dr. Benjamin Fain, former professor-emeritus at Tel Aviv University School of Chemistry, gives examples as to why the theory of evolution is impossible to refute:[103]

> Imagine that a particular planet has similar conditions to those on Earth. Let us say, too, that life was formed there, a simple living organism appeared, and as a result of the evolution of life on that planet, large quantities of new species did not develop, but that only two bacteria developed. Would this disprove the theory of evolution? Absolutely not. The theory of evolution can easily explain this. We could say that all the organisms that came about as a result of mutation, only two survived because only they were sufficiently suited to the environment. In this way, the theory of evolution can explain every possible discovery anywhere in the world.

He then brings another theoretical example:

> In a laboratory, scientists manage to create conditions that will lead to the formation of life, and as a result, life forms develop that are entirely different from those that currently exist. Can this disprove the theory of evolution? Certainly not. It is always possible to claim that the environment in the experiment is not identical to that on Earth. Even if it is identical, then there are simply different mutants in this experiment. Since the formation of mutants is a random process, no experiment would be able to disprove the theory of evolution.

A theory that cannot be refuted by any conceivable event is, by definition, not scientific.[104]

---

103   Benjamin Fain, *Law and Providence* (2011), pgs. 255–256.
104   Sir Karl Popper, *Conjectures and Refutations: The Growth of Scientific Knowledge* (1963), pgs. 7–36. "Despite the fact that Darwin's theory of evolution has won wide acceptance, it is

Getting back to the topic at hand, about the primeval soup theory, which can never be proven, Sir Fred Hoyle remarked that scientists have replaced the religious mysteries that shrouded the question of the origin of life, with "equally mysterious scientific dogmas."[105]

There are several glaring points of contention with this theory of life's origin:

Needle in a Billion Haystacks?

Firstly, for example, Dr. Hoyle writes that the chance that even a *single* viable bacterium ever evolved on Earth is so outrageously small, calculated at a chance near one in 1,040,000, that is, a one with *forty thousand* zeroes. This is a number that "could not even be faced, even if the whole universe consisted of organic soup."[106] He explains that this one problem "...is big enough to bury Darwin and the whole theory of evolution." He vividly stresses the impossibility of life forming in this way by comparing it to 1,050 blind persons all *simultaneously* solving a Rubik's cube, and elsewhere to a whirlwind blowing through a junk-yard and assembling a ready-to-fly Boeing 747 with the pieces therein. Most researchers agree with Hoyle on this point.[107]

With more complex forms of life, the odds only become more exponentially slim. Experts vary in their estimation of the statistical calculation, but in all cases the likelihood is so ridiculously small that the human mind cannot even relate to it. Hoyle wrote that the chances of accidently forming the 25,000 enzymes contained in the human body are about one in 10,600,000. Even some of the more liberal estimates and optimistic assumptions equate it to the odds of pulling out one red marble from a mound of black marbles *trillions and trillions and*

---

nevertheless not experimentally demonstrable, and it is impossible to verify." See Aaron Katzir in *The Midst of the Scientific Revolution*, pg. 134.

105   Fred Hoyle and Chandra Wickramasinghe, *Lifecloud* (1978), pg. 26.

106   Fred Hoyle and Chandra Wickramasinghe, *Evolution from Space* (1981), pg. 24.

107   Hoyle, *The Intelligent Universe* (1983), pg. 19. The Boeing 747 metaphor is reported in *Nature* 294 (1981), pg. 10. Notably, *Scientific American* in February 1991 (pg. 102) reprinted Hoyle's comment and added that "most researchers agree with Hoyle on this point."

trillions of times larger than the entire universe on the first try.[108] These statistics show that the chances of life beginning spontaneously on Earth are unfathomably small.[109] That which is the basic assumed scientific theory has a lot of trouble even getting started.

Not Enough Time

Even if chemistry and blind chance could have produced something alive, it would have required *a lot* of time. Paleontologists claim to have the fossilized remains of living cells that are almost as old as the Earth. Between the start of the chemical process and the advent of life, there was simply not nearly enough time for "chance" to work.[110]

Impossible Oxygen

Many researchers are convinced that no evidence will ever be found for the "soup theory," and claim that such a scenario never could have existed. They point out that the pre-biotic soup would require an oxygen-free environment, as oxygen would react with and destroy the mixture's chemicals.[111] At the same time, an oxygen-free zone (i.e., no ozone layer) would leave the Earth unshielded from the sun's intense ultraviolet radiation. Any life that managed to survive would be mortally irradiated. Furthermore, such a soup would not last long, for it would need to contain complex organic compounds, which studies show are unstable, tending to quickly dissolve again into solution.[112]

---

108 The equations, along with the contemporary scholars who produced them, can all be found in Kelemen, *Permission*, pgs. 60–61.

109 Ilya Prigogine, who received the Nobel Prizes in chemistry: "The statistical probability that organic structures and the most precisely harmonized reactions that typify living organisms would be generated by accident is vanishingly small. The idea of spontaneous genesis of life in its present form is therefore highly improbable, even on the scale of billions of years..." I. Prigogine, G. Nicolis, and A. Babloyantz, *Physics Today* (November, 1972): pg. 23. Even the outspoken atheist Francis Crick cannot fathom the idea of life starting in this way (see *Life Itself* 1982); see also A. Simon, *Torah U'mada*, vol. 2 (Shvat 5732): pgs. 13–17.

110 See Gershon Robinson and Mordechai Steinman, *The Obvious Proof* (1993), pg. 97.

111 The evidence is actually otherwise. Oxygen has always been present in Earth's environment. (See Lauren Gravitz, "Early Breath of Fresh Air," *Discover* 23 (4) (April 2002): 11. There was no time when the "oxygen-free" environment existed.

112 See Robert Shapiro, *Origins* (1986), pgs. 112–113. Paraphrased from Kelemen, *Permission*, pg. 57.

NEWLY THEORIZED BEGINNINGS

Science has yet to answer the origin of life on this planet. The belief in spontaneous generation from non-living matter was shown to be scientifically impossible after careful experimentation.[113]

With the lack of evidence that any natural process can cause even the simplest life forms to originate from non-living matter, researchers posited another possibility for the origin of life on Earth. Knowing that the idea of life self-generating from a primordial soup lacks all foundation, and resisting the idea of a purposeful Creator, some prominent scientists actually subscribe to *panspermia*, the idea that life was brought to Earth by comets, meteors, or even extra terrestrial life. It is clear that life could not have spontaneously come about, so this is the most "logical" thing they could come up with!

The first modern scientist to propose this theory was Swedish chemist Svante Arrhenius in 1908.[114] For decades it lay at the wayside, but much later the theory gained support from Francis Crick, Thomas Watson and others.[115] Interestingly, these scientists are not bothered by the question of how life was started in space. In the end, they have not solved anything. It is doubtful whether they all even truly believe it.[116] In truth, biochemist Michael Denton describes it best, writing, "nothing illustrates more clearly just how intractable a

---

113 J. W. N. Sullivan, referred to by *Time Magazine* as "one of the world's four or five most brilliant interpreters of physics to the world of common men," said that as far as the evidence goes, the origin of life seems to lead back to some supernatural creative act. He continues, saying that since that is the case, it is a conclusion that scientific men find very difficult to accept. "It carries with it what are felt to be, in the present mental climate, undesirable philosophic implications, and it is opposed to the scientific desire for continuity. It introduces an unaccountable break in the chain of causation, and therefore cannot be admitted as part of science unless it is quite impossible to reject it. For that reason most scientific men prefer to believe that life arose, in some way not yet understood." Although these words were said decades ago, they are still affirmed today. J. W. N. Sullivan, *The Limitations of Science* (1933), pg. 94.

114 "Life," *Colliers Encyclopedia*, ed. W. Halsey and B. Johnson (1989) 14:622.

115 F. Crick and L. E. Orgel, "Directed Panspermia," *Icarus* 19 (1973), 341–46.

116 Francis Crick told Professor Robert Shapiro that he was just putting forth the theory in order that people forget the other failed hypotheses of life arising from inorganic matter. See Robert Shapiro, *Origins: A Skeptics Guide to the Creation of Life on Earth* (1986), pgs. 227–228, cited in Shmuel Waldman, *Beyond a Reasonable Doubt* (2002).

problem the origin of life has become than the fact that world authorities can seriously toy with the idea of panspermia," and further, "the failure to give a plausible evolutionary explanation for the origin of life casts a number of shadows over the whole field of evolutionary speculation."[117]

FOSSIL RECORD

There are many speculations, contradictions, and even forgeries surrounding fossils. For starters, the size, shape, or species of entire creatures have, at times, been recreated based upon negligible discoveries of finger or jawbone fragments. There is substantial proof that major mistakes have been made regarding fossil interpretation.[118]

Additionally, and perhaps more significantly, is the point that the oldest, lowest level of geological strata should show only the simplest organisms, and the higher (more recent) levels should become progressively more filled by complex life forms. While this may be somewhat true in general, many findings contradict this supposition.[119] There are mixtures of simple and complex organisms where only the simple should be.[120]

Most importantly: were the classical theory of evolution true, there should be millions of fossils in intermediate stages of transition between phyla and classes over an extended period of time. They should show the progression of each individual species' gradual evolution, and not just record of ancient ancestors. However, they do not.

---

117 Denton, *Theory in Crisis*, pg. 271; see there for more detail.

118 Mistakes have been seen particularly with regard to human-ape fossils. See Nathan Aviezer, *Fossils and Faith* (2001), pgs. 179-193, and "Misreading the Fossils: The Dark Side of Evolutionary Biology," *Jewish Action* 58 (2) (Winter 1997), for a look at the incorrect interpretations of hominid fossils, including Neanderthal Man, Piltdown Man and Hesperopithecus.

119 For example, the Seymuria, the supposed transition between amphibian and reptile, has been discovered in Permian formations, and earliest reptiles found in Pennsylvania formations, which according to geologists preceded the Permian by close to 20 million years. (G. Kerkut, *Implications of Evolution* (1960), cited in Allswang, *The Final Resolution* (1988), pg. 28.)

120 In some instances, scientists try to justify the findings by attributing it to volcanic activity or other natural disasters. Such speculations are not conclusive.

Creatures have always appeared suddenly and fully formed in the fossil record. Likewise, regarding human evolution, where are the hundreds of various species of sub-humans who did not develop into man? There is not a single sub-human "ape-man" or super-human alive or in a fossil state.[121] Neanderthal Man shows up in the fossil record and then abruptly disappears, and since then only modern man has appeared in the fossil record with no intermediary form. There is no proof that any of the ape-like man-creatures touted in textbooks and museum galleries are ancestors of modern humans. All of the so-called ape-human fossils have turned out to be fully ape or fully human.[122] Even if there would be an intermediary form, Jewish tradition has a more robust account of *devolving* humans, than of evolving apes.[123]

---

121 "We have all seen the canonical parade of apes, each one becoming more human. We know that as a depiction of evolution, this line-up is tosh [tidy, but sheer nonsense]. Yet we cling to it. Ideas of what human evolution ought to have been like still colour our debates... Almost every time someone claims to have found a new species of hominin, someone else refutes it. The species is said to be either a member of Homo sapiens but pathological, or an ape." See Henry Gee, "Craniums with Clout," *Nature*, Vol. 478, 6 (October 2011): pg. 34. "Fossil evidence of human evolutionary history is fragmentary and open to various interpretations. Fossil evidence of chimpanzee evolution is absent altogether." Henry Gee, "Return to the Planet of the Apes," *Nature*, Vol. 412 (July 12, 2001): pg. 131. See also Avigdor Miller, *Rejoice O Youth!* (1962), #39.

122 A wealth of information can be obtained in Miller, *Rejoice O Youth! Sing, You Righteous* (1973); and *Awake My Glory* (1980) in their relevant sections. The following is a sampling:
  Proconsul Africanus, described as progenitor of both apes and humans, was declared at London meeting of the Congress of Zoology to be nothing but an ape. The long-standing fable was demolished. It was based on a few bones found, however, once the head and forearm were eventually found, it was declared definitely an ape ("Science: Near-Men & Apes" *Time Magazine*, July 28, 1958, cited in *Rejoice*, #37)
  Neanderthaloid types found today among modern men (Ernest Elwood Stanford, *Man and the Living World*, pg. 648; cited in *Sing*, #180).
  Java Man and Peking Man declared humans (Franz Weidenreich, *Apes, Giants, and Man* (1946); cited in Miller ibid.).
  Cro-Magnon Man cited as fully developed and intelligent (Miller ibid., #186).

123 According to tradition, there were other sons of Adam besides Abel, Cain, and Seth (*Eruvin* 18b). Rav Sherira Gaon (as cited in the Radak) and the Rambam (*Guide to the Perplexed* 1:7) explain that some of the offspring were primates—half-human and half-animal. The primate animals have been said to be a product of the immoral and decadent generations of Enosh. As punishment for the actions of many humans at the time, their human appearance degenerated or devolved, and they instead became primates (*Bereishis Rabbah* 23:6). According to the Talmud (*Sanhedrin* 109a), the people of the Tower of Babel were punished in different ways: one group that wished to go to war with G-d had their

There are no links between Neanderthal Man and modern man. Professor Steven Stanley at Johns Hopkins University writes, "out of nowhere [modern man] appeared in the fossil record with particular features that are utterly unpredictable on the basis of what preceded them."[124] One should use caution before trying to contrast apes and men, either in form or in behaviors.[125] David Pilbeam, professor at Harvard University and leading paleoanthropologist at the Peabody Museum of Archaeology and Ethnology, writes:

> Our theories have often said far more about the theorists than they have about what actually happened... Virtually all our theories about human origins were relatively unconstrained by fossil data... Many evolutionary schemes were in fact dominated by theoretical assumptions that were largely divorced from data derived from actual fossils."[126]

"Divine Image" taken from them and were flung into the forests; among other things, these people devolved into apes (See Maharsha and Margaliyos Hayam. See also Maharal, *Chiddushei Aggados*, vol. III, pg. 260). For all of the aforementioned, see Elie Munk, *Kol HaTorah* (2003). Furthermore, the *Mileches Shlomo* (*Kilayim* 8:6) asks why the blessing, "Who diversifies the creations," is specifically recited upon seeing an ape (and two other animal species), but not on other strange creatures. He writes that the *bracha* can be translated as, "Who changes the creations," so it is appropriate for apes, since they were changed from humans into primates.

124   Stanley, *The New Evolutionary Timetable* (1981), pg. 151. See also "Modern apes, for instance, seem to have sprung out of nowhere. They have no yesterday, no fossil record. And the true origin of modern humans—of upright, naked, tool-making, big-brained beings—is, to be honest with ourselves, an equally mysterious matter." See Lyell Watson, "The Water People," *Science Digest* (May 1982), pg. 44.

125   "Any speculation and conclusions pertaining to human behaviour drawn on the basis of Darwinian evolutionary theories...must be treated with the greatest caution and reserve...a less discriminating section of the public may enjoy reading about comparisons between the behaviour of apes and man, but this approach—which, by the way, is neither new nor original—does not really lead us very far... Apes, after all, unlike man, have not produced great prophets, philosophers, mathematicians, writers, poets, composers, painters and scientists. They are not inspired by the Divine spark which manifests itself so evidently in the spiritual creation of man and which differentiates man from animals." Ernest Chain, *Social Responsibility and the Scientist in Modern Western Society* (1970), pg. 26.

126   David Pilbeam, "Current Argument on Early Man," in *Major Trends in Evolution* (1980), pgs. 262–67.

Darwin, on no less than seven occasions in his *Origin of the Species,* implores his reader to both ignore the evidence of the fossil record as a refutation of his concept of evolution, and to "use imagination to fill in the gaps."[127] He was sure that if the fossils would be searched for, they would surely be found, but over a century of worldwide digging has left paleontologists still without fossil support to Darwin's theory.[128] The idea that the theory is well-proven by the fossil record is an outright myth.[129] The absence of these fossils is a serious challenge to evolutionary theory. Once again, noted scholars contend that the gaps will never be filled. Professor N. Herbert-Nilsson of Lund University, Sweden, put it like this:

> The fossil material is now so complete that the lack of transitional series cannot be explained as scarcity of material...It is not even possible to make a caricature of evolution out of the palaeo-biological facts...The deficiencies are real, they will never be filled.[130]

Darwinism is based on hypothetical prototypes, and not on real creatures, as sound scientific theory would require.[131] Instead, the records show that species appeared abruptly. In some cases, the fossil record actually makes it easier to *disprove* evolution than to prove it.[132] This somewhat embarrassing announcement was made at the 1980 Conference on Macro-Evolution in Chicago. World-famous paleontologist Dr. Niles Eldridge stated that "the pattern that we

---

127   Schroeder, *The Science of God*, pg. 31.

128   Denton, *Theory in Crisis*, pg. 162.

129   *Evolution from Space*, pg. 147. See also Jeffrey Schwartz, *Sudden Origins* (1999), pg. 89.
         In addition, "Despite the bright promise that paleontology provides a means of "seeing" evolution, it has presented some nasty difficulties for evolutionists, the most notorious of which is the presence of gaps in the fossil record. Evolution requires intermediate forms between species and paleontology does not provide them..." from David B. Kitts, "Paleontology and Evolutionary Theory," *Evolution*, vol. 28 (1974): pg. 467.

130   Heribert-Nilsson, *Synthetische Artbildung* (1954), cited by Francis Hitching, *The Neck of the Giraffe: Where Darwin Went Wrong* (1982), pg. 22; See Kelemen, *Permission*, pg. 54, for several other citations from modern scholars.

131   L. Bounoure, *Recherche d'une Doctrine de la Vie*, (Paris 1964).

132   Stebbins in *Variation and Evolution in Plants*, pgs. 517–518; see Miller *Sing*, #192.

were told to find for the last one hundred and twenty years does not exist."[133]

The following chart displays the Darwinian prediction for the fossil record compared to the actual discoveries:

RESULTS IN DEVELOPMENT OF SPECIES:[134]

Darwinian Prediction:	Actual Discoveries:
Species appear gradually	Species appear suddenly
Species change constantly	Species show no significant change
Species disappear gradually	Species disappear suddenly
Missing links between major types will be filled in	The missing link problem more unresolved as time passes

With a lack of fossil record and the statistical impossibility of random mutations gradually forming into species, experts were forced to rethink the workings of the evolutionary process.

Dr. Stephen Jay Gould, for example, suggested that the evolutionary process takes place more suddenly and not in small increments as originally speculated. In other words, the vast majority of the time there are no changes in life forms; however, every so often, there are brief periods of drastic change. According to this theory of "punctuated equilibrium," it is for this reason why the transitions do not appear in the fossil record; transitions happened quickly and therefore there is no chartable trace of mutation.[135] This is very divergent from the Darwinian approach. Evolutionary biologist Steven Stanley said that Darwin would have been confounded by the fossil evidence.[136]

Although "punctuated equilibrium" seems interesting to imag-

---

133 See *The Neck of the Giraffe*, ibid.

134 Chart based on Dr. Arnie Gotfryd, *Mind Over Matter* (2003), (Shamir) pgs. 417–418.

135 "Organic Evolution," Colliers Encyclopedia, ed. W. Halsey and B. Johnson (1989) 9:481; S. J. Gould and N. Eldredge, "Punctuated Equilibrium: The Tempo and Mode of Evolution Reconsidered," *Paleobiology* 3 (1977):115.

136 Steven Stanley, *The New Evolutionary Timetable* (1981), pgs. xv–xvi.

ine, it seems more like an attempt at retroactive and hypothetical patchwork on a failed fossil record. In other words, based on the lack of intermediate fossils, a new theory within the same context of evolution was suggested to make the evidence fit. Scientists are, effectively, shooting an arrow at a tree and then painting the bulls-eye around it. There is never any explanation as to *why or how* a new species appears.[137]

CONCLUSION

With all of the aforementioned questions, what is it that keeps the idea of evolution from single-celled organism to human being still the widespread view?

The simple answer is worldview—the prevailing philosophical or sociological outlook. Naturalism is the current paradigm of how many scientists view the world. The widespread view is that within the context of science one must assume naturalism, despite any evidence to the contrary. If one assumes at the outset that there cannot be any involvement of a Creator, then one has no choice but to explain the origin and development of life in naturalistic terms. Professor Scott Todd of the Department of Biology at Kansas State University says, "even if all the data point to an intelligent designer, such a hypothesis is excluded from science because it is not naturalistic."[138]

The naturalistic worldview is additionally pleasing, because by rejecting the intervention of a Creator, there is less accountability for one's actions. In such a scenario, facts can be overlooked and reality skewed in order to subconsciously justify one's actions.[139] The naturalistic theory of evolution is maintained because the downfall would be too psychologically bothersome, and therefore, unacceptable.

In the past, many great names in science have had much contention

---

137   See Gotfryd, *Mind Over Matter*, ibid.
138   See Scott C. Todd, "A View from Kansas on the Evolution Debates," *Nature*, vol. 401 (September 30, 1999), pg. 423.
139   The idea of how human cognitive dissonance keeps people from accepting truth, especially in the matter of acknowledging a Creator, is the thesis of Gershon Robinson, in *The Obvious Proof* (1993). See there.

with the theory of evolution. British author and biochemist Michael Denton shares that "throughout the past century there has always existed a significant minority of first-rate biologists who have never been able to bring themselves to accept the validity of Darwinian claims. In fact, the number of biologists who have expressed some degree of disillusionment is practically endless." When Arthur Koestler organized the Alpbach Symposium[140]...for the express purpose of bringing together biologists critical of orthodox Darwinism, he was able to include in the list of participants many authorities of world stature, such as Swedish neurobiologist Holgar Hyden; zoologists Paul Weiss and W. H. Thorpe; linguist David McNeil; and child psychologist Jean Piaget.[141] At this symposium, some of the sociological aspects of Darwin's theory and its survival were discussed by biologists, statisticians, and others. One such point sums it up succinctly:

> I think that the fact that a theory so vague, so insufficiently verifiable, and so far from the criteria otherwise applied to "hard science" has become a dogma and can only be explained on sociological grounds.[142]

The theory is called a dogma. Along the same lines, Sir Fred Hoyle writes that "if one proceeds directly and straightforwardly in this matter, without being deflected by a fear of incurring the wrath of scientific opinion, one arrives at the conclusion that biomaterials with their amazing measure of order must be the outcome of intelligent design."[143] Hoyle concludes that the theory survives mainly because it is socially desirable.

Once an idea has become the working paradigm it is not easy to uproot. Dr. Max Whitten, professor of genetics at the University of Melbourne, professes that "biologists are simply naive when they talk about experiments designed to test the theory of evolution. It is not

---

140   This is an interdisciplinary international conference that takes place in Alpbach, Austria. The goal is to foster knowledge, prosperity, and peace in the world.

141   Denton, *A Theory in Crisis*, pgs. 327–328.

142   Arthur Koestler and John. R. Smythies, *Beyond Reductionism—New Perspectives in Life Sciences (The Alpbach Symposium)* (1969), pg. 66, cited in Robinson et. al., *The Obvious Proof*, pg. 87.

143   Hoyle, *Evolution from Space*, pgs. 27–28, 148.

testable. They may happen to stumble across facts that would seem to conflict with its predictions. These facts will invariably be ignored and their discoverers will undoubtedly be deprived of continuing research grants."[144] Whitten more recently expounded upon the difficulty of overcoming entrenched ideas in all forms of science:

> Despite what some scientists might think, very little biological research is designed to challenge the robustness of a prevailing world-view like evolution. Some biologists would claim that they are validating the theory of evolution on a daily basis. Not true. If something happens that is consistent with the theory, all is well and good. If it doesn't happen, we will likely find a satisfying explanation within our prevailing world-view...[145]

> It seems that since its inception, evolution has prevailed as an alternative religion of sorts—a dogma, rather than science.[146] Michael Ruse, a philosopher of science at Florida State University who specializes in the philosophy of biology, says that "evolution is promoted by its practitioners as more than mere science. Evolution is promulgated as an ideology, a secular religion—a full-fledged alternative... This was true of evolution in the beginning, and it is true of evolution still today."[147]

We have discussed several of the essential problems complicating the Darwinian Theory. There are certainly more points to ponder, and

---

144   Giving the Assembly Week address in 1980.

145   Max Whitten, "Facts Are Not Everything in Science," *Issues Magazine* (May 2008).

146   See also Henry Solomon Lipson, professor of physics at the University of Manchester, who writes: "In fact, evolution became in a sense a scientific religion; almost all scientists have accepted it and many are prepared to 'bend' their observations to fit in with it." See "A Physicist Looks at Evolution," *Physics Bulletin*, vol. 31 (1980): pg. 138. See also an example of a much older source but an interesting thought nonetheless: "The more one studies paleontology, the more certain one becomes that evolution is based on faith alone...exactly the same sort of faith which it is necessary to have when one encounters the great mysteries of religion." L. T. More, *The Dogma of Evolution* (1925), pg. 160.

147   See Michael Ruse, "Saving Darwinism from the Darwinians," *National Post*, May 13, 2000, pg. B-3.

the reader is encouraged to delve into other works for more depth.[148] While this section does not prove that the world was created by G-d, it does enable one to see that belief in Darwinian evolution appears to be a greater leap of faith than belief in a Creator.

---

148   Included are all of the above-sourced Jewish books, along with extensive research provided in Spetner, *Not By Chance*; Michael Behe, *Darwin's Black Box* (1996).

AGE OF THE UNIVERSE

The age of the world is commonly discussed in conjunction with the theory of evolution. In order to give time for evolution to occur, millions or even billions of years are required. The age of the world is used to support evolutionary theory, and evolutionary theory is used to support the age of the world.[149] A cursory look at the traditional teachings of Judaism suggests that the world is only six thousand years old. Truth be told, believing that the world is older than six thousand years is not one of the tenets of faith. In other words, one need not cast off belief in G-d or Torah because he finds it difficult to accept the notion of a fairly recent Creation. Notwithstanding, it is an important and fascinating subject, and one that people commonly inquire about.

BRIDGING THE GAP BETWEEN THOUSANDS AND BILLIONS

Although the Torah text and bulk of Talmudic and mystic writings suggest a world of six thousand years, there are other statements within Jewish tradition that some have cited to suggest other theories. Trying to bridge the gap between six thousand years and billions of years has been attempted in several ways in the past few generations. One school of thought is that the Torah was not truly understood until modern discoveries shed new light and the Torah really does agree that the world is billions of years old. Another approach is to say that science is wrong and should be completely rejected. Other approaches

---

149   Miller, *Sing You Righteous*, pg. 102.

suggest both are correct and are merely saying the same thing from a different vantage point.

Before briefly examining some of these suggested theories, it is important to point out that Jewish tradition counts the years from the creation of Adam and Eve, not from the creation of the world itself. The Torah records that Adam and Eve were created on the sixth day of G-d's creation process, thus the questions and commentaries on the topic of the age of the world are centered on discerning the length or meaning of those original six days.

SIX DAYS AS SIX EPOCHS

One proposed way to reconcile the meaning of the six days of Creation is to reinterpret the first few lines of the biblical text to mean that each of the six Creation days lasted much longer than twenty-four hours. According to this idea, the Torah was not fully understood until more recent scientific advances suggested that the world was much older. This theme of making the first six days longer than 24-hour periods is presented in various ways.

There may be some issue with this approach. The first thing discussed in the book of Genesis is G-d creating the world in six days. Later on in the Torah, the Sabbath is referred to as a sign between G-d and the Jewish people that Heaven and Earth were created in six days and that G-d rested on the seventh.[150] This fact is also regularly attested to in the liturgy of the weekly Sabbath prayers that the sages ordained. Being that the observance of the Sabbath is to commemorate the creation of Heaven and Earth in six days, it can be solidly concluded that the days being discussed are meant literally. There is no reason to assume that these days are meant as any other span of time. The Talmud records that from the first day of Creation the lengths of day and night were established so that together they would always form one *twenty-four hour period*,[151] implying that the word *yom*, or

---

150   *Shmos* [Exodus] 20:11; 31:17.
151   Rashi on *Chagigah* 12a. For further sources for a literal six-day Creation, see Ramban on *Bereishis* 1:3; Ibn Ezra. This also negates the suggestion that the counting of "days" as

day, should not be misconstrued into a figurative meaning, such as an "era" or "epoch." This form of apologetics does not seem to have any grounding in the classical Torah commentaries.

Another similar attempt for reconciliation is reading into the stage of *tohu va'vohu* [void and chaos] that the Torah describes existed at the beginning of Creation. There are those who try to suggest that this period lasted for large spans of time, however, nearly every classical Jewish biblical commentary agrees that this period ended on the first day.

SIX DAYS AS SABBATICAL CYCLES

Another attempt to reconcile the billions of years with the thousands of years of the Torah is based on certain cryptic statements made either in Torah verses or in the words of the early sages and mystics. These are statements that give the impression that Jewish tradition affirms that the world could be much older. Examples include statements in the Midrash that G-d "created many worlds before this current one and destroyed them,"[152] and various vague sentences in the *Zohar* about primordial man. These statements are taken in the literal sense, as if there were physical men and physical worlds that were later destroyed.[153]

Some describe these epochs of time as cosmic Sabbatical cycles.

---

they are known today only began after the fourth day—when the sun and moon were set in their place—as the precise length of time for each day was already determined on the first. Whatever the conditions that are necessary for the passage of time are, they were already working normally from the first day.

It is stated that twenty-four hours is the amount of time it takes the Earth to make a full rotation, regardless if the light of the sun and moon are present. The sun and the moon do not create a "day" or create "time," but are simply a means of measuring a certain amount of time much like a watch. After the fourth day, when the celestial lights were put in their places, the 24-hour spin of the Earth sphere included the effects of the light of the sun and moon. (See *Moreh Nevuchim* 2:30; Rabbeuinu Bachya and Ralbag on the beginning verses in the Torah. See also Abarbanel; Ralbag; Seforno; Bartenura; Rabbi Elchanon Wasserman commentary on *Pesachim* 2a, for related alternative explanations.)

152   *Bereishis Rabbah* 3:9. See also Ibn Ezra and Ramban to *Vayikra* 25:12.

153   This is an explanation offered in several places, especially among the early Kabbalists. See *Torah Shleima* on *Bereishis* 1:5, (pg. 422).

According to this line of thought, this current epoch is but one of several cycles destined for the world, and that previous creatures and civilizations have existed here in the past.[154] In fact, acclaimed modern day sage, Rabbi Israel Lipschitz *zt"l*, during the nineteenth century when dinosaur bones and mammoths were being unearthed, welcomed these findings, saying that they are modern confirmations of ancient Kabbalistic writings.[155] Later in the nineteenth century, the great Rabbi Shimshon Raphoel Hirsch *zt"l* avowed that "Judaism is not frightened even by the hundreds of thousands or millions of years... Our sages discuss the possibility that earlier worlds were brought into existence and later destroyed by the Creator before He made our own Earth in its present form and order."[156] Some contemporary scholars, based on these Sabbatical cycles and words of the early sages, have calculated that the world is in fact billions of years old.[157]

Despite the fact that these early statements about Sabbatical cycles exist in Jewish tradition, and the fact that these more recent scholars mentioned above presented them as authoritative, not all of the later sages embraced these ideas.[158] While acknowledging the greatness of Rabbi Lipschitz and Rabbi Hirsch both in righteousness

---

154   Alluded to in *Sanhedrin* 97a; Rabbeinu Bachya on *Vayikrah* 25:10, and also *Torah Shleima*, ibid.

155   After discussing the (then) recent findings of mammoths and dinosaur bones, he said: "From all this it is clear that everything that the kabbalists have told us for hundreds of years—that the world has already once existed and was then destroyed, and then it was reestablished...now in our time it has become clear in truth and righteousness." See *Derush Or HaChaim*, printed in *Mishnayos Yachin u-Boaz*, after tractate *Sanhedrin*.

156   Hirsch, *Collected Writings*, vol. II, pg. 265.

157   This idea was popularized by Rabbi Aryeh Kaplan in his posthumous book *Immortality, Resurrection and the Age of the Universe: A Kabbalistic View* (1993). In it, he quotes the Ramban and Rabbeinu Bachya who understand a physical or literal interpretation to the Midrash of 7 Sabbatical cycles to the world, of 7,000 years each. Rabbi Kaplan then quotes Rabbi Yitzchak of Acco, a student of the Ramban, who writes that each of those years is one year of G-d. He also writes that one day of G-d is 1,000 human years. This means that a year of G-d is approximately 365,250 human years. He concludes from here that the duration of the universe is 7 (Sabbatical cycles) x 7,000 (years each) x 365,250 (G-d years) = almost 18 billion years. It should be noted that there have been some strong questions raised on this view; see Ari Kahn, *Explorations* (2001).

158   See *Teshuvos Minchas Elazar*, vol. I, 64:2; *Haamek HaDavar* (Netziv) on *Bereishis* 7:23.

and scholarship, other great contemporary sages suggested that their words may not be as far-reaching as one may have initially thought.[159]

Furthermore, despite the intrigue of these considerations, the later sages and mystics generally regard these Sabbatical-years references as describing events that took place in the spiritual realms, and not prior physical worlds.[160] Indeed, Rabbi Isaac Luria, known as the Arizal, and accepted by world Jewry as the final authority on Kabbalah, maintained that any "worlds" mentioned in Jewish tradition that predate Adam were purely spiritual and did not exist on the physical plane.[161] Subsequently, the Kabbalists following the Arizal likewise rejected the concept of the Sabbatical years.[162] This is the commonly accepted approach.

TIME AND EXISTENCE BASED ON HUMAN OBSERVATION

Related to the above debate between the early Kabbalists, who said there were physical Sabbatical years, and the later Kabbalists, who said that these worlds were purely spiritual, there may actually be a way to reconcile both perspectives. Dr. Alexander Poltorak, former professor of biomathematics at Cornell University Medical College, is one of the

---

159   The Lubavitcher Rebbe says that their tone implies that these ideas were meant to open the minds of the secular world to other concepts within Jewish tradition, but not necessarily something meant to be applied as a mainstream idea; see *Iggros Kodesh*, vol. 7, pg. 133; vol. 15, pg. 60 and 133; vol. 19, pg. 144. See similarly Rabbi Chaim Kanievsky, *Kraina D'Igresa*, vol. 1, sec. 46.

160   Similar idea expressed in the *Anaf Yosef*, who writes that G-d merely "thought" about creating. When he "changed His mind," it is like they were destroyed.

161   See *Likkutei Torah* 51d. See also *Sha'ar Ma'amarei Rashbi* (Jerusalem, 1959), 46b. From then on it would seem that it is no longer possible to describe Creation in any other way, just as one cannot decide in any matter of Torah that he will hold like the "minority opinion."

162   Israel Weinstock, *Bema'agalei Hanigleh Vehanistar* (1969), p. 230. See Rabbi Neftali Bacharach's words: "This is contrary to those who hold that there were sabbatical worlds of kindness and now it is the sabbatical of strength. All this is untrue. They heard from their rabbis that G-d built previous worlds and destroyed them and they added to this the notion of the sabbaticals, but this is not true." See *Emek Hamelech* (2003) [Jerusalem], vol. 1, pgs. 58, 237. See article on this by Raphael Schuchat in *The Torah u-Madda Journal* (13/2005).

scientists who has attempted to reconcile these sources for spiritual or potential worlds using the nuances of Quantum Mechanics.

There is an old philosophical question: "If a tree falls in the woods, and nobody is around to witness it, does it make a sound?"

As various schools of thought have emerged in Quantum Mechanics, this question has gained more concrete and tangible meaning. Part of this developing approach to reality places a lot of emphasis on the human observer. In other words, it has been shown that subatomic particles act differently when observed by a human observer. Reality is actually different when it is being watched. In a certain sense, reality does not become actual reality until it has been been observed. The eminent physicist, John Wheeler, said that "the observer is as essential to the creation of the universe, as the universe is to the creation of the observer."[163] Wheeler also says that "acts of observer-participancy in turn give tangible reality to the universe not only now but back to the beginning."[164] A full description about how this theory works is beyond the scope of this work, yet it is worth noting how Dr. Poltorak uses this idea to reconcile the debate between the early and later Kabbalists. He writes that since the years in Judaism are counted from the creation of Adam, these worlds before Adam, or "prehistory," were a proto-physical existence before the first human observer, and then from Adam onward it became a tangible physical existence brought about by Adam and Eve, the first human observers.[165] In doing so, he suggests a fascinating and unique approach to resolving this apparent conflict of physical worlds versus spiritual worlds, and at the same time, reconciling biblical and contemporary cosmology.[166]

---

163 John Wheeler, "Genesis and Observership."

164 Wheeler, "Beyond the Black Hole" in *Some Strangeness in the Proportion: A Centennial Symposium to Celebrate the Achievements of Albert Einstein*, 1980.

165 Adam, being the first human observer, was responsible for the collapse of the wave function.

166 He writes as follows: "The history of the universe is comprised of two main periods: pre- and post-human. In the first period—before the first conscious human observer peered into the world—the universe was in an amorphous fuzzy state of linear superposition of all possible states of existence and non-existence. At this stage, the universe existed only mathematically as a distribution of probabilities as it is expressed by the global wave function. This period lasted approximately twelve to fifteen billion years. From the moment

The concept of the human observer's role suggested by Poltorak bears similarity to an earlier unique approach to solve the conflict between the Torah and scientific view of the age of the universe. Rabbi Shem Tov Gefen offers an approach, based somewhat on a principle from Kantian philosophy. The idea is that space and time do not have absolute existence but are instead merely entities that appear to us. He writes that "forms of time and space do not exist in the essence of things, by themselves, but are forms used by the person perceiving these objects, just like color, heat, cold and the like, for all these forms have no existence but in the human psyche which perceives them." He goes on to say that since the human being comes last in this progressive order of creation described by the Torah, all creations that preceded humanity had no temporal existence, for there cannot be a concept of time without human beings. The events of Creation happened without reference to time.[167]

SIX DAYS AS RELATIVE TIME, BASED ON LOCATION

One very recent attempt to bring together academia and Torah is found in the books of MIT physicist Gerald Schroeder. In his theory, time is relative and calculated differently based on where one is located in the universe. Einstein demonstrated that when a single event is viewed from two frames of reference, a thousand or even a billion years in one can indeed pass for days in the other. According to Schroeder, the six days at one vantage point were experienced as billions of years from Earth.[168] It appears that Rabbi Yisroel Belsky, in his commentary on the

the first human looked outward, they collapsed the world wave function and brought the universe into actual existence. From that point on, the Torah and humanity began counting the new age of the universe." See Poltorak, "On the Age of the Universe," *B'Or HaTorah* 13 (2002): pgs. 19–37. See also Poltorak, "The Age of the Universe: Many-Worlds Interpretation," *B'Or HaTorah* 18 (2008). See also Rabinowitz and Branover, "The Role of the Observer in Halakha," *Fusion*, 1990.

167 Geologists draw conclusions about the amount of time it should have taken for the events in this progression to happen, based on an analogy with events that they themselves have perceived, but this analogy is based on a fallacy. See Gefen, *Hamemadim, haNevuah, vehaAdmetanut*, pgs. 226–235. [Paraphrasing synopsis by Raphael Schuchat in *The Torah u-Madda Journal* (13/2005)].

168 See his *Genesis and the Big Bang* and *The Science of God*. A similar view can also be seen in

Torah, also suggests a similar possibility regarding the relativity of time in different frames of reference.[169]

All of the aforementioned ideas share the common goal of seeking to reconcile modern cosmology with Torah cosmology. Without casting any judgment on the value and usefulness of these approaches, and without seeking to negate how intriguing they might be, these forms of compromise are perhaps not even necessary.

THE MESORAH

The Talmud says that the world is destined to exist for six thousand years.[170] The *Seder Olam Rabbah* details the chronology from the beginning of Creation to the conquest of Persia by Alexander the Great, which—extending the calculations since then—amounts to nearly six thousand years at the present time. This was always viewed as a recognized fact amongst the Jewish people, as Rabbi Yehuda HaLevi said in the twelfth century: "There is no Jew anywhere [from Hodu to Kush] who contests that."[171]

Jewish tradition teaches that the Torah is not a book of history, culture, or even religion. It is referred to as the blueprint of Creation, the will and wisdom of G-d, the conduit with which He "gazed into and created the universe."[172] Few would dispute that the world *appears* older than six thousand years; however, the Jewish religion stands upon the unbroken tradition that the ancestors of all Jews experienced a revelation of the Torah by G-d at Sinai. The universe is comparable to a projector screen, manifesting that which is contained in the Torah. Things are not always as they seem in this world. If the Torah is a sort of "blueprint" of Creation, how can a scientific fact contradict a statement of the Torah?

One glaring cause for the discrepancy between Torah and the

Nathan Aviezer, *In the Beginning...Biblical Creation and Science* (1990).

169   Belsky, *Einei Yisroel* on *Bereishis* 1:1.

170   *Avoda Zara* 9a, corresponding to the six days of Creation.

171   *Kuzari* 1:45, and surrounding paragraphs. See similar in *Emunos V'Deos*, end of ch. 1.

172   *Bereishis Rabbah* 1:1; Also see *Zohar*, *Terumah* 161b and other places in that work; Rabbi Tzadok HaKohen in *Tzidkas HaTzadik* (Lublin, 1910), pg. 90; *Pirkei D'Rebbe Eliezer*, ch. 3.

conclusions of the scientific community is that the latter bases their conclusions on a steadfast rate of change using the conditions present today. This idea is known as uniformitarianism. This school of thought exists across a spectrum of scientific study. It negates catastrophic changes and assumes that conditions have always remained the same. The Torah, as elaborated upon in the cumulative body of Jewish tradition known as the Mesorah, describes how the first six days of Creation were completely different than anything the modern mind can relate to. The details of this will be examined below, but first it may be beneficial to preface with some background on the scientific community.

THE SCIENTIFIC COMMUNITY

It is well known that through various means of calculation, the scientific community as a whole concludes that the age of the Earth is around four-and-a-half billion years old and that the universe is several billion years older.

Many people think of scientific conclusions as infallible, and scientists as impartial robotic beings who serve merely as conduits to relay pure observation and systematic logic. This is far from the case. Scientific thought has trends that shape its conclusions, as well as societal norms of a given time that it conforms to. Scientists are human beings, immersed in culture, with their own preconceived perspectives and agendas as well.[173] Evolutionary biologist Stephen Jay Gould explains that "our ways of learning about the world are strongly influenced by the social preconceptions and biased modes of thinking that each scientist must apply to any problem. The stereotype of a fully rational and objective scientific method with individual scientists as logical (and interchangeable) robots is self-serving mythology."[174] Theoretical physicist John Polkinghorne says likewise that scientists assess their data through "(theoretical) spectacles behind the eyes," which may shape and color the results a certain way.[175] This is not to

---

173   Based on Steven J. Gould, *Time's Arrow, Time's Cycle* (1987), pgs. 6–7.

174   S. J. Gould, "In the Eye of the Beholder," *Natural History*, vol. 103 (Feb. 1994): pg. 14.

175   John Polkinghorne, *Science and Theology* (1998), pg. 10. This echoes what American

say that religion cannot color conclusions as well; it is just to emphasize that science, and more so *scientists,* are not immune to this as
is commonly thought. The facts being assessed remain the same, but
tend to be interpreted according to one's philosophical worldview.

Historically, new discoveries and changes to established cultural paradigms were often stunted because the previous worldview was deeply
embedded. It is interesting that many revolutionary discoveries were
made either by amateurs or younger researchers, specifically because
they had been less conditioned as to what the "correct" results that they
were "supposed to find" were. The advantage of youth allowed them to
think outside the box of what the intelligentsia of their day were conditioned to believe. Following the trend is not some conspiracy or dia-
bolic plan of deception or coercion; it is just human nature to follow the
crowd and go with the consensus opinion, a "groupthink" of sorts.[176]
It should be noted, however, that in many academic studies, there are
other factors such as nationalistic considerations, political scenarios,[177]

---

philosopher of science, Norwood Russell Hanson, wrote in his *Perception and Discovery:
An Introduction to Scientific Inquiry,* where he describes the "spectacles-behind-the-eyes."
In this work he suggested that scientific theory not only makes predictions that can be
tested but that it can also color the results. In other words, our expectations or worldview
will actually determine what is found. This concept is illustrated in a famous "duck-rabbit"
photo, where if one looks for a rabbit, he sees a rabbit in the picture; whereas if he looks
for a duck, he sees a duck.

176 In 1781, William Herschel detected the planet Uranus for the first time when gazing into
the night sky with his telescope. Upon further examination the planet had actually been
seen twenty times prior, but repeatedly misidentified as a star (*Scientific American*, Dec.
2004). The consensus of the time was that there could only be five other planets in the
solar system. Because Herschel was an amateur, it allowed him to think outside the box
of what the intelligentsia of his day were conditioned to believe. Additionally, Einstein
was only twenty-five years old when he published three papers that would revolution-
ize physics. Also, Werner Heisenberg and Paul Dirac were in there mid-twenties when
they were making major contributions to quantum mechanics. Another example is Kurt
Godel, who was in his mid-twenties when he published his greatest work on the logical
foundations of mathematics. These examples are all mentioned in the phenomenal work
by Yoram Bogacz, *Genesis and Genes* (2013); he is also to be credited with the "groupthink"
comparison.

177 Daniel Sarewitz is Professor of Science and Society at Arizona State University. He writes
that a March 2010 Gallup poll showed that 66 percent of Democrats (and 74 percent of
liberals) say the effects of global warming are already occurring, as opposed to 31 percent
of Republicans. Does that mean that Democrats are more than twice as likely to accept

and economic concerns (funding)[178] that can askew and shape conclusions—besides from the already mentioned ideological or philosophical preconceptions.

This statement does not in any way seek to discount the value of scientists and the worthy fields in which they study, but instead to clarify and distinguish between popular contemporary opinions and notions, and truth and objectively conclusive evidence. Popularity or general acceptance does not equal truth. The system and framework in which knowledge is acquired must, in and of itself, always be checked for accuracy.

Research, in whatever subject it may be, must always seek to ask the right questions and not assume information that ultimately leads to building theories on groundless foundations. Rabbi Yosef Reinman

---

and understand the scientific truth of the matter? And that Republicans are dominated by scientifically illiterate yahoos and corporate shills willing to sacrifice the planet for short-term economic and political gain? Or could it be that disagreements over climate change are essentially political—and that science is just carried along for the ride? For twenty years, evidence about global warming has been directly and explicitly linked to a set of policy responses demanding international governance regimes, large-scale social engineering, and the redistribution of wealth. These are the sort of things that most Democrats welcome, and most Republicans hate. No wonder the Republicans are suspicious of the science. Think about it: the results of climate science, delivered by scientists who are overwhelmingly Democratic, are used over a period of decades to advance a political agenda that happens to align precisely with the ideological preferences of Democrats. Coincidence—or causation? Now this would be a good case for Mythbusters (slate.com/articles/health_and_science/science/2010/12/lab_politics.html). Professor Sarewitz has several books and many articles on this topic. For further reading, see another interesting article: Daniel Sarewitz, "Science Must Be Seen to Bridge the Political Divide," *Nature*, vol. 493 (January 2, 2013).

178 The following examples were extracted from Bogacz (2013) ibid., pgs. 28 and 31: For decades, studies conducted by highly qualified and reputable scientists at reputable institutions could not find a link between smoking and emphysema, lung cancer, and addiction. Perhaps this may be in part due to the fact that these institutions and researchers were also being sponsored by Big Tobacco. There are also many examples there cited of "cash-for-science" practices between nutrition and drug companies and the academics that conduct their research. Another point to consider is that in 2012, a committee of the National Academy of Sciences heard testimony that scientific papers that had to be retracted increased more than tenfold over the last decade, while the number of papers rose only 44 percent. Ferric Fang of the University of Washington, speaking to the panel, said he blamed a hypercompetitive academic environment that fosters poor science and even fraud, as too many researchers are competing for diminishing funding.

tells an interesting anecdote about a question in history. He says that he was at one point curious about the accepted chronology of Egyptian Pharaohs. For example, Thutmose I is documented as reigning from 1493 BCE to 1481 BCE. Rabbi Reinman was very impressed by the apparent accuracy. He relates that he asked a friend of his who was a history professor at a New York university, "How do historians pin down such precise dates?" His friend responded to him that some academic takes a guess, and by the time it gets into the secondary and tertiary sources, it's just a fact. Who is going to check it out?[179]

Another example can be gleaned from the "well-established fact" that Native Americans migrated from Siberia to Alaska on a land bridge where the Bering Strait is at present. Everyone learns this in school, and it will probably be quite some time until it is stricken from the textbooks, even though this theory has been torn to shreds.[180]

It is not uncommon in history or science that a certain speculation gets around the block, becomes accepted, is assumed true, and never checked again. If one does question it, he is mocked for even bringing up the idea, irrespective of how concrete and conclusive his argument might be. Sometimes the idea is corrected right away, other times it can take quite some time to be overturned.

Children attending public school throughout the twentieth century were taught that when Columbus set sail in 1492 to find a new route to the East Indies, it was feared that he would fall off the edge of the Earth because people then thought the planet was flat.[181] This is incorrect. It is widely known that people have known that the Earth was round for a very long time, as far back as ancient Greece.[182] Educated people throughout medieval times knew that the world was

---

179 See Reinman, *One People, Two Worlds* (2002), pg. 184.

180 See Vine Deloria Jr., eminent Native American author in *Red Earth, White Lies* (example brought from Reinman, ibid.).

181 Valerie Strauss, "Christopher Columbus: Three Things You Think He Did that He Didn't," *The Washington Post*, Oct 14, 2013.

182 See D. R. Dicks, *Early Greek Astronomy to Aristotle* (1970), pgs. 72–198. Furthermore, Hellenistic astronomy (third century BCE) established the spherical shape of the Earth as a physical given. This idea spread gradually throughout the Old World during the Late Antiquity and the Middle Ages.

a sphere.[183] So where did this prevalent rumor of a flat Earth come from? Dr. James Hannam, a member of the British Society for the History of Science, wrote that the misconception that "the majority of the medieval world believed in a flat Earth" gained currency in the nineteenth century because of inaccurate histories. Some of these inaccurate histories were from prominent antagonists of religion.[184] They used these imaginary generalizations in an effort to prove that science and religion are locked in an eternal conflict. Dr. Christine Garwood of the University of Hertfordshire seems to concur with this, saying that some prominent nineteenth century writers exaggerated the number and significance of medieval flat-Earthers to support the model of warfare between "oppressive-dogmatic" theology and scientific progress.[185] Despite the fact that Columbus discovering the round Earth was untrue, and many sources confirmed it, it was the accepted approach in society and that is what was taught in the schools.

Interestingly enough, even the flat Earth myth has a connection to the discussion at hand. According to Dr. Jeffrey Burton Russell, professor of history at the University of California, the myth that "most medieval people believed in a flat Earth" became widely publicized after 1870, and had to do with ideological struggles over evolution. He again echoes the idea that the flat-Earth myth became popular as a means of showing that religion is against science—it was a means to impugn religion. Russell examined a large selection of textbooks and found those written before 1870 usually included the correct account—that most educated people knew the Earth was round beginning from the ancient Greek period, but most textbooks written

---

183   Eustace Mandeville Wetenhall Tillyard was a British classical scholar and literary scholar. In his work *The Elizabethan World Picture*, he extensively discusses how the educated classes in Renaissance and medieval times knew the world was round. Professor Louise Bishop of the University of Oregon says that virtually every thinker and writer of the thousand-year medieval period affirmed the spherical shape of the Earth. See Louise M. Bishop, "The Myth of the Flat Earth," in Stephen J. Harris, and Bryon Lee Grigsby, *Misconceptions about the Middle Ages* (2008), pg. 99.

184   For example: John William Draper's *History of the Conflict between Religion and Science* (1874) and Andrew Dickson White's *A History of the Warfare of Science with Theology in Christendom* (1896).

185   Christine Garwood, *Flat Earth: The History of an Infamous Idea* (2007), pg. 12–13.

after 1880 uncritically repeated the erroneous claims of prominent religious antagonists.[186] The myth that "most people before Columbus thought that the Earth was flat" is still taught in some schools.[187]

In an earlier chapter, we discussed the shift from the long-standing belief in an eternal universe to Big Bang cosmology in the mid-twentieth century. This theory was initially not very well-received because of its religious implications, yet it has become the mainstream perspective. This should not come as too much of a surprise, as it is not uncommon for widespread, long-standing ideas across the spectrum of scientific or historical thought to be overturned. This has certainly taken place throughout the twentieth century as well.[188] Sometimes though, even after evidence exists to modify or reject a long-standing theory, it is met with resistance for various reasons.

When it comes to the age of the world, many have a hard time accepting the possibility that it may be a lot younger than previous-

---

186   See Jeffrey Russel, *Inventing the Flat Earth* (1991).

187   Additionally, not surprisingly, individuals today who question an age of the world of billions of years are often looked upon scornfully and derogatorily lumped together with "flat-earthers."

188   Just the tip of the iceberg of long-standing beliefs that were clearly discredited in the twentieth century alone include: 1) Physics: Newtonian physics was superseded by relativistic physics and quantum physics. Luminiferous aether was also replaced in modern physics by the theory of relativity and quantum theory. 2) Geology/geophysics: Prior to the middle of the twentieth century, scientists believed the Earth's continents were stable and did not move. This began to change with continental drift theory, and further developed with the theory of plate tectonics during the 1950s and 1960s. 3) Climate study: Many people believed, and it was a popular topic published in the press during the 1970s, that the Earth was cooling. 4) Medicine: Humorism was a theory of the makeup and workings of the human body adopted by ancient Greek and Roman physicians and philosophers. The theory dominated medical thinking until at least the middle of the twentieth century (see humorism.askdefine.com). 5) Psychology: Most of the work of Freud has been discredited. Psychology as a whole is constantly being reassessed, discredited, and revamped. Sometimes it can take a while for old theories to be universally scrapped. Take, for example, Rorschach blots, which were once thought very effective and widely used, but have come under heavy question. Scott Lilienfeld, an associate professor of psychology at Emory University, after surveying fifty years of Rorschach research evidence says that many psychologists concluded that its accuracy is "weak at best and nonexistent at worst." (See Lilienfeld, *What's Wrong with the Rorschach?* (2003)) 6) History/Anthropology: Out of Asia Theory—most anthropologists until the mid-twentieth century saw Asia as the continent where the first hominids evolved. The currently preferred theory sets the origin of modern man in Africa. The list is nearly endless.

ly assumed. This is what they have been taught in school and what is seemingly accepted by everyone. It is important to realize that results and conclusions are not the product of unbiased or transparent lab results, but are filtered (perhaps even unknowingly) to conform with certain agreed-upon premises or with an established social framework.

Notwithstanding, the truth is that even if full credence and infallibility were granted to the dating methods themselves, their ultimate validity still rests upon the assumption that all conditions have remained exactly the same and that all things change at a steady step-by-step rate over the immeasurable periods of billions of years.

In one of his letters, the Lubavitcher Rebbe zt"l emphasized the difference between empirical and experimental science.[189] It is important to distinguish between things that are observable phenomena and speculative unknown phenomena that often cannot be duplicated in a laboratory. When approaching the latter, scientists can only infer from known facts and apply them to the unknown. The Rebbe continues, saying that there are two general modes of deducing the unknown: interpolation and extrapolation.

- **Interpolation:** By knowing the results at two extremes, one can predict what the results will be in the middle.
- **Extrapolation:** Trying to infer beyond the known range, based on the variables within the known range.

The Rebbe gives an example: Suppose one knows the variables of a certain element within a temperature range from 0 to 100. Extrapolation would be estimating the results at 101 degrees and up or 0 degrees and down. The farther one strays from the known variables, the more the uncertainty increases. Needless to say, estimates on the age of the Earth are of the weaker method of extrapolation. Furthermore,

---

189   This is just a brief summary of the Rebbe's famous letter that has been printed in numerous places. It does not do justice to the Rebbe's full approach. What is extracted here is only in relation to how extrapolation works. For further reading on this topic, see the full print in Dr. Arnie Gotfryd, *Mind Over Matter* (2003), and *Challenge: Torah Views on Science and Its Problems*.

it is even more speculative when inferring from a known result back to an unknown antecedent.

Conclusions extended to unknown areas can have validity only on the assumption that all prevailing conditions have remained the same. If it cannot be concluded that certain variations and changes did not occur at some point, then such conclusions or inferences are most probably flawed. The Rebbe summarizes some of the holes in scientific conjecture about the age of the world as follows:

- These conclusions were advanced on the basis of observable data during a relatively short period of time—several decades or, at best, not more than a few centuries.
- On the basis of such a relatively small range of known data, scientists venture to build theories by the weak method of extrapolation, and from the consequent to the antecedent, extending to many thousands of years.
- In advancing such theories, they blithely disregard factors universally admitted by all scientists, namely, that in the initial period of the "birth" of the universe, conditions of temperature, atmospheric pressure, radioactivity, and a host of other catalyst factors, were totally different from those existing in the present state of the universe.

The concept of backwards extrapolation under uniform conditions that exist today is the foundation of all conclusions on the age of the world, be they cosmological, geological, or the like.

It is quite possible that the conditions either on the Earth or in the universe were different at points in the past. The assumption that the laws of nature have been constant since the beginning of time has been questioned by prominent scientists. Nobel Prize-winning physicist Paul Dirac wrote, "At the beginning of time the laws of nature were probably very different from what they are now. Thus, we should consider the laws of nature as continually changing within the epoch, instead of holding uniformly throughout space-time."[190] Following the

---

190   Paul Dirac, "The relationship between mathematics and physics," *Proceedings of the Royal*

uncertainty principle established by Heisenberg, prominent physicist John Wheeler wrote likewise: "There is no law except the law that there is no law."[191] Within the last decade, an international team of astrophysicists has discovered that within the basic laws of nature, certain constants regarded as immutable may have in fact changed over the history of the cosmos.[192] Granted, these statements and ideas do not in themselves make the universe young, yet they do shed light that perhaps certain variables assumed to be scientific axioms are not as fixed and uniform as previously assumed.

GEOLOGY

Classical discussions in the field of geology may provide insight on the age of the Earth. There has been extensive discourse as to how the world came to look the way that it does. The discrepancy in perspective is whether the current geological features on the Earth are the result of uniformitarianism—slow, uniform, incremental changes—or whether they were caused by periods of sudden catastrophic transformation. It is likely that the Earth has undergone drastic and swift changes at various times in the past. Meteor strikes are one catalyst that could have triggered rapid changes in temperature and atmosphere and could have caused upheavals in the landmasses. The changes would have been so large that, despite the accuracy of the scientific tools of measure, the conclusions wind up being meaningless because they are based on assumptions of slow gradual change. The current working paradigm seems to be the uniformitarian outlook. However, it is important to consider how this worldview developed, and if there are challenges to it.[193]

Society, v. 59 (1939), pgs. 122–129.

191   F. Wolf, *Taking the Quantum Leap: The New Physics for Non-Scientists* (1989), pg. 116.

192   "When we refer to the laws of nature, what we are really talking about is a particular set of ideas that are striking in their simplicity, that appear to be universal and have been verified by experiment. It is thus human beings who declare that a scientific theory is a law of nature—and human beings are quite often wrong." John Webb, "Are the Laws of Nature Changing with Time?" *Physics World*, April 2003; also Glanz and Overbye, "Anything Can Change, It Seems, Even an Immutable Law of Nature," *New York Times*, August 15, 2001, pg. A1.

193   A good summary of this topic can be found in Yaacov Hanoka, "Dating the Earth," *B'Or HaTorah* 17 (2007): pg. 49–55, from where this author obtained some source information.

CATASTROPHISM VS. UNIFORMITARIANISM

The study of geology became more popular in Europe toward the end of the 1600s, and quickly picked up steam through the eighteenth and nineteenth centuries. Interestingly, early geologists like Nicolaus Steno, John Ray, and John Woodward, were also clergymen. They saw no conflict between the Bible and geology, and attributed rock formations and geological phenomena to the worldwide flood in the days of Noah. Steno wrote in his *Forerunner* that the world was around 6,000 years old and fossils were remnants of the flood. Woodward and others echoed that idea as well. Later, Reverend William Buckland, the first professor of geology at Oxford University, wrote that rock formations were "*Reliquiae Diluvianae* attesting the action of a universal Deluge."[194] These early geologists, who accepted the premise of a universal flood, became classified as "catastrophists." Simply put, catastrophism stipulated that the history of the Earth has been interrupted or greatly influenced by natural catastrophes occurring on a very extensive scale.[195] Although not all catastrophists were biblical literalists, they were seen as belonging to the same group.

Even before Buckland's works, the original theory began coming under fire. Perhaps the strongest critic was James Hutton, an eighteenth century Scottish geologist, who rejected the idea of a universal flood. In his research, he found no beginning in the rock record and proposed that the Earth was much older than originally thought. This eventually became the dominant scientific approach, and Hutton is recognized as the father of modern geology.

A further blow to the catastrophists came when Charles Lyell, a lawyer and former student of Reverend Buckland, published an influential three-volume work entitled *Principles of Geology*. In it, he resurrected Hutton's propositions and insisted that the history of the Earth is best interpreted in terms of *what is known about the present*. In other words, the geological process of change has been uniform throughout history; what it is today—is how it has always been. For

194   *Reliquiae Diluvianae*, Latin for "Relics of the Flood."
195   See William Lee Stokes, *Essentials of Earth History* (1982).

example, rivers at present erode valleys very slowly, so valleys or canyons seen today must have been eroded slowly and gradually over millions of years. Sediments nowadays are deposited in lakes and seas very slowly, and likewise sedimentary rocks seen today must have been built up slowly, over eons of time. This approach was eventually termed "uniformitarianism."

Lyell was a contemporary and friend of Charles Darwin, and, not surprisingly, played a major role in Darwin's conclusions. Lyell's work convinced Darwin, who was more of a geologist than a biologist at the time. Darwin later linked Lyell's gradual geological processes with gradual biological processes. Darwin wrote, "I always feel as if my books came half out of Lyell's brains..."[196] The tremendous influence that Lyell's writings had on Charles Darwin is summed up by Janet Browne, professor of "The History of Science" at Harvard University: "... without Lyell there would have been no Darwin."[197] By the end of the nineteenth century, in conjunction with, and because of, the popularity of Darwinism, the uniformitarian school of thought became the standard in geology. This also automatically meant that the Earth was estimated to be at least hundreds of millions of years old.[198] Lyell and Darwin brought the "old Earth" and evolutionary framework into vogue. Once accepted in academia, all subsequent discoveries were examined through this lens, without questioning the original conclusions.

The lengthy ages of the evolutionary process are invoked to make the miraculous leaps of development from the first random particles to modern-day humans seem feasible. Time becomes the god through which anything can be accomplished—just give it enough time. George Wald said, "Time is the hero of the plot... Given so much time, the impossible becomes possible, the possible probable, and the probable

---

196   Charles Darwin, "Letter to Leonard Horner," August 29, 1844. The influence of Lyell's thinking on Darwin was immense. Discussing his famous voyage on the Beagle, he wrote, "I had brought with me the first volume of Lyell's *Principles of Geology*, which I studied attentively; and this book was of the highest service to me in many ways. Nora Barlow, *The Autobiography of Charles Darwin* (1958), pg. 77.

197   E. Janet Browne, *Charles Darwin: Voyaging* (2003), pg. 186.

198   Tarbuck and Litgens, *Earth Science* (2003), pg. 288.

virtually certain. One only has to wait; time itself will perform the miracles."[199]

Rabbi Avigdor Miller *zt"l* also emphasizes the correlation between the age of the world and evolution that developed through Lyell and Darwinism. Likewise, he points out that any obstacles to evolution are simply swept under the rug and attributed to endless ages:

> The age of the Earth is supposedly demonstrated by the argument that in order to accomplish the development of life from lower forms, eons of time were necessary. The theory of evolution stands on this doctrine; and because the theory required millions of years, therefore the millions of years were created on the bases of pure imagination. Thus (i) the age of the Earth is "proven" by evolution, which needed such time periods, and (ii) evolution is supported by the imaginary age of the Earth. In this fantasy of circular logic, one non-existent fact is cited to support the other. Each of these two elements individually is not supported by the least evidence, and together they equal the sum of two zeros.[200]

In the twentieth century, however, some cracks began to appear in strict uniformitarianism. Certain major scientific discoveries and recent theories have been based on dramatic and cataclysmic changes on the Earth. There seems to be a bit of resurgence in the idea of catastrophism. Some examples:

CONTINENTAL DRIFT

The idea of the continents originally being one landmass and later splitting into seven was first proposed several hundred years ago, but became more fully developed through German meteorologist Alfred Wegener in the early twentieth century. Aside from the way that the

---

199   "The Origin of Life," *Scientific American* (Aug. 1954): pg. 48.
200   Miller, *Sing You Righteous*, pg. 102.

continents seem to fit so perfectly together,[201] and the discovery of the Mid-Atlantic Ridge,[202] similar rock formations, plant life, fossils, and even living creatures are found on opposite continents.

Geologists in the early twentieth century had strong objections to the theory of continental drift, including Charles Schuchert, the foremost historical geologist in America. Why did Schuchert reject it so strongly? Did he find something irrefutable that disproved the theory of continental drift?

No. Schuchert felt that continental drift was incompatible with the uniformitarian school of thought, and that it smelled of catastrophism,[203] and therefore was unacceptable.

Alfred Wegener's original observations paved the way for the modern theory of plate tectonics. Plate tectonics in geology is a theory that explains the distribution of continents, earthquakes, volcanoes, mountains, and other geologic phenomena in terms of the formation and movement of tectonic plates. These plates move in response to forces deep within the earth, and earthquakes and volcanoes tend to occur at the boundaries between plates. Today, the theory of plate tectonics is widely accepted, despite the fact that it involves catastrophism.

CHICXULUB CRATER—THE METEOR THAT DESTROYED DINOSAURS

According to the fossil record, the dinosaurs had a sudden and unexpected extinction. Popular scientific opinion suggests that the dinosaurs became extinct through a major catastrophe, not natural selection. It has been suggested in the last few decades that the abrupt disappearance was caused by a meteor striking the Earth, propelling a dust cloud into the atmosphere that blocked the sun and triggered

---

201   The continental shelves of South America and Africa seem to fit. Antarctica and Australia would also fit with Africa and Asia. See "Microcontinents Sought," *Science Newsletter* (Oct. 9, 1965): pg. A3; and (Feb. 28, 1970): pg. 229.

202   The Mid-Atlantic Ridge is a large underwater mountain range where seafloor spreading takes place in the middle of the Atlantic Ocean. The existence of the ridge was confirmed with sonar in 1925.

203   Naomi Oreskes, *The Rejection of Continental Drift* (1999), pgs. 178, 207.

earthquakes, volcanic eruptions, and tsunamis for a significant amount of time. The theory asserts that the change in climate, disastrous upheavals, and devastating ongoing natural calamities caused the dinosaurs—along with many other creatures—to perish. While it was initially somewhat controversial, it has become widely accepted, and taught as a given in schools.

The theory was proposed by Luis Alvarez, one of the most brilliant experimental physicists of the twentieth century, which likely contributes to its wide acceptance. The meteor was said to be approximately ten kilometers in diameter, weighed billions upon billions of tons, and hit the Earth at nearly 45,000 miles per hour, seven times faster than a speeding bullet, making a collision with Earth equivalent to one hundred trillion tons of exploding TNT.[204] It is hard to imagine a more catastrophic event.

The main critics of this theory, at least at its inception, were, of course, those who could not reach beyond the box of staunch uniformitarianism. An early supporter of Alvarez was geologist Kenneth Hsu of the University of Colorado. He believed that it was a comet that hit the Earth and published other geochemical evidence to support his claim.[205] Hsu did not have issue with upholding the catastrophist approach to Earth history.[206] After Alvarez's passing, strong evidence pointed to the Chicxulub Crater in the Yucatan Peninsula as the scar of this cataclysmic event. In 2010, forty-one experts from across the scientific spectrum concluded that Chicxulub was the site of the collision that led to the mass extinction.[207] There is also evidence of a large meteor that hit near India that may have helped finish the job. This evidence furthered the acceptance of this catastrophist idea.

204 Kring and Durda, "The Day the World Burned," *Scientific American* 289 (2003): pgs. 98–105.

205 Kenneth J. Hsu, "Terrestrial Catastrophe Caused by Cometary Impact at the End of Cretaceous," *Nature* 285 (May 22, 1980): 201–203.

206 For example, from an expedition of the Mediterranean, he concluded that the sea had gone under catastrophic desiccation [extreme dryness] and that it can dry out very rapidly, as opposed to others who insist that it must be a gradual and long process. See *The Mediterranean Was a Desert, A Voyage of the Glomar Challenger* (1983).

207 Peter Schulte, "The Chicxulub Asteroid Impact and Mass Extinction at the Cretaceous-Paleogene Boundary," *Science* 327 (5970) (March 5, 2010): pgs. 1214–1218.

CATASTROPHIC FLOODING IN THE SCABLANDS

The Channeled Scablands are a barren landscape in eastern Washington State. Channels and steep rectangular canyons run through the hard basalt rock throughout the Scablands. Uniformitarian school of thought would suggest rounded, gradually sloping sides. How did these features develop the way that they did?

American geologist Harlen Bretz first recognized evidence of the catastrophic floods, which he called the Spokane Floods, in the 1920s. He proposed that these calamitous floods shaped the entire area in a very short period of time. Along with geologist Joseph Pardee, they concluded after many years that Lake Missoula in Montana was the source of this great flood.[208] Estimates place the flow of water at ten times the flow of all of the rivers on the planet combined.[209] Needless to say, a thousand feet of water moving at around sixty miles per hour can drastically and instantaneously transform the geography of a given area.

Bretz's view was originally and predictably discarded because it argued for a catastrophic explanation of geology, which was once again counter to the prevailing view of uniformitarianism. Much later, satellite images confirmed his conclusions. He was awarded the prestigious Penrose medal for his discovery, and the telegram attached by the prize committee closed with the vivid and ironic words of "we are all catastrophists now."

REEVALUATING UNIFORMITARIAN THINKING

Geological transformations are very much affected by the prevailing atmospheric conditions. Rabbi Eliyahu Eliezer Dessler *zt"l* compares this idea to cooking: Several conditions would alter the time it would take to cook a piece of meat. If the pot is uncovered it takes so much

---

208 Bretz, "The Channeled Scabland of the Columbia Plateau," *Journal of Geology*, v. 31 (1923): pgs. 617–649.

209 Bruce Bjornstad, *On the Trail of the Ice Age Floods* (2006), pg. 2; U.S. Department of the Interior, National Park Service, www.cr.nps.gov/history/online_books/geology/publications/inf/72-2/Sec5.htm

time, if covered it takes less time, and if sealed in a pressure cooker it takes merely a fraction of the original time.[210] Likewise, depending on atmospheric conditions at a given time in history, the rate of change in Earth's topography would have been different as well. What today, when measuring, may appear like it took many years, could be because current atmospheric conditions produce one result—slow change; whereas in days gone by, under different prevailing conditions, things could have changed at a much more rapid rate.

In truth, there is much evidence that different atmospheric conditions and cataclysmic upheavals have caused significant sudden transformations in a region or even globally.[211] Beginning in the nineteenth century, a huge number of mammoths were discovered entombed in Siberian permafrost. The amount is estimated in the millions. Flesh of frozen mammoths was later eaten with no harm coming to the animals that ate it,[212] suggesting that whatever killed them also quick-froze them as well. It also suggests that they never thawed until the day of their discovery, for had they defrosted, their meat would have rotted.[213]

These mammoths have been very challenging to explain according to the uniformitarian worldview. Charles Darwin, who as mentioned above rejected the idea of catastrophic changes in the past, confessed in a letter to Sir Henry Howorth that the perfectly preserved mammoths in the north were to him an inexplicable conundrum.[214] Additionally, why would these masses of mammoths and other animals

---

210   Dessler, *Sefer HaZikaron LiBaal Michtav Me'Eliyahu*, Institute for the Dissemination of Torah and Mussar 1994, Collected Letters, pg. 108.

211   Some of the following examples are mentioned by Rabbi Yosef Reinman in his *One People, Two Worlds*, pg. 196. Here they are noted in the original sources that they are mentioned.

212   In 1797, the body of a mammoth with flesh, skin, and hair was found in northeastern Siberia, and since then bodies of other frozen mammoths have been unearthed from that region. The flesh appeared as freshly frozen beef and was eaten by wolves and dogs without harm; see Digby and Bassett, *The Mammoth and Mammoth Hunting in North-East Siberia* (1926), pg. 9.

213   Dessler, ibid. Also D. Gath Whitley, "The Ivory Islands in the Arctic Ocean," *Journal of the Philosophical Society of Great Britain* 12 (1910): pg. 35.

214   See Whitley, ibid., pg. 56. Also George F. Kunz, *Ivory and the Elephant in Art, in Archaeology, and in Science* (1916), pg. 237.

migrate to Siberia in the first place? What could they possibly eat? Why are there no signs of Ice Age glaciers in Siberia, currently one of the coldest places on Earth? Such extreme changes in atmosphere must have also changed atmospheric pressure. If so, how can the duration of geological changes be measured by current atmospheric conditions?

Furthermore, consider the fact that there is a deserted but well-preserved city located two-and-a-half miles above sea level in the Andes Mountains.[215] It is far above where anything grows and the air is hard to breathe, suggesting that the mountains rose in the historical era after the city had already been built. Interestingly, Helmut de Terra of the Carnegie Institute and Thomas T. Paterson of Harvard concluded that the Himalayas reached their current height during the historical period.[216]

All of the aforementioned cataclysms, from continental drift, meteor impacts, and other rapid catastrophic upheavals and climate shifts, have notable parallels in the writings of the sages concerning the flood and similar cataclysms in early Earth history.[217] This perspective

---

215   This is a reference to Tiwanaku in Western Bolivia.

216   *Studies on the Ice Age and Associated Human Cultures* (1939), pg. 223. See also Heim and Gausser, *The Throne of the Gods: an Account of the First Swiss Expedition to the Himalayas* (1939), pg. 218.

217   In the days of Enosh the ocean rose and engulfed much of the Earth (Rashi on *Bereishis* 6:4). At the creation of the world, mountains were not created. After many years of storms and geological upheavals including the flood, the mountains and hills were formed (Maharatz Chayos on *Niddah* 23a). The complete overturn of the natural order in the times of the flood is elaborated upon by the sages. The sun and moon functioned differently (*Avos DiRebbe Nosson* 32; *Sanhedrin* 108a; *Yalkut Reuveni*, Noach). The constellations did not function (Hirsch on *Bereishis* 8:22). The Midrash (*Bereishis Rabbah* 34) says that before the flood there was constant springtime, people only needed to cultivate their fields once in forty years, people had much longer life spans, and that the Earth was one landmass that could be traveled across uninterrupted by ocean. The Talmud (*Brachos* 58a and *Rosh Hashana* 11b) says that G-d "took two stars from Kima and brought a flood upon the world." Rashi and Tosofos say that Kima refers to the tail of Aries. It has been suggested that perhaps these were the two asteroid impacts that triggered the global upheavals that split the continents, and so forth (see Yaacov Hanoka, "Continental Drift, Asteroid Impacts, and the Flood," *B'Or HaTorah* 13 (2002), pgs. 87–93). Furthermore, the sages say that during this time the Earth got its 23.5 degree tilt, creating sudden climate changes and initiating seasons (Malbim and Seforno on *Bereishis* 8:22; see also Netziv on *Bereishis* 7:20).

answers many of the mysteries concerning the development of the planet. The issue is not with the scientists, or the tests that they are performing, which may be completely accurate; rather the concern is primarily focused on the assumption of uniform conditions.

So with all of this to ponder, scientists are still often unwilling to further the possibility of historical catastrophes because, without eons of time, evolution falls apart. That option is not on the table for discussion.

Rabbi Miller writes:

> When a world catastrophe is postulated to explain the phenomena used as proof of the Earth's age, they reject it by claiming that the history of nature is uniform, and what is now has always been. On the basis of uniformity they exclude any possibility of the great upheaval caused by the flood, which explains many of the Earth's riddles. Yet, when needed to serve their own ends, they do not disdain the theories of countless recurrent global upheavals, such as the extraordinary heat followed by suddenly extraordinary cold, which is essential for the Ice Age theory, and which their theory requires that it happened many times.[218]

New technological advances may help validate a young world as well. The Los Alamos National Laboratory in New Mexico is one of the most prestigious research institutes in the United States. The facility is home to a unique and sophisticated computer program called TERRA that models plate tectonics. The program was developed by John Baumgardner, the preeminent expert in the design of computer models for geophysical convection.[219]

TERRA takes the spatial volume of the Earth's mantle and imagines it as ten million 3-D cells. The mantle rock is mostly in a solid state, but it is so hot that over time it moves and flows, behaving as if it

---

218 Miller, *Sing You Righteous*, pg. 94.
219 Information on John Baumgardner obtained and extracted from Chandler Burr, "The Geophysics of God," *U.S. News and World Report*, (June 16, 1997), pgs. 55–58.

were a fluid, not a solid. The mantle rock churns or makes convection. Convection in the mantle is the same as convection in a pot of water on a stove: cooler, heavier material on top sinks while hotter material nearest the heat source is lighter and rises.

TERRA divides the mantle into hexagonal cells, assigning each one a value for heat, direction, velocity, and other unknowns, as if creating ten million small blocks to make up an immense, three-dimensional Rubik's cube. It then "runs" each piece through time and watches where each will go. Add all the pieces together and TERRA gives you a 3-D map of a huge mass convecting through time.

Interestingly, Baumgardner is a believer in the Bible. His research has furthered his conviction that the Earth and universe as a whole are only several thousand years old. He also describes details about how he sees the flood of Noah play out. He says an enormous blob of hot mantle material came rushing up at an incredible velocity through the underwater mid-ocean ridges. The material ballooned, displacing a tidal wave of seawater over the continents. Then, after 150 days, the bubble retreated with equal speed into the Earth, and the continents began re-emerging above the water, sending the runoff back to the oceans at around 100 miles an hour. Baumgardner says that this runoff would have been sufficient to create the Grand Canyon and other massive geologic features and to deposit the various sedimentary layers in about one week.

Almost all physicists calculate the age of the Earth at 4.6 billion years because they assume, for example, that the liquid-like mantle flow and speed of tectonic plates has been consistent throughout time. They use the value that applies today. However, Baumgardner says that if one will factor in a flood and catastrophes, which are evident everywhere in the geological record, then it is very possible to have a young Earth. "If you look at the geological record," he insists, "there are fingerprints of catastrophe everywhere one looks." Most interesting is that the entire process can be watched first-hand on Baumgardner's TERRA program. "In my opinion, the present is emphatically not the key to the past as far as the geological record goes," Baumgardner says.

Baumgardner is a very well-respected and well-qualified scientist.

He is seen as one of the world leaders in numerical models of mantle convection and, as mentioned, is creator of one of the most useful and powerful geological tools in existence. Gerald Schubert of the UCLA Earth and Space Sciences said that "as far as the computer program code goes, Baumgardner is a world-class scientist." It is worth noting that even MIT geophysicist Brad Hager has praised Baumgardner's program, although he disagrees with some of his conclusions.[220]

DATING METHODS

Over the last two centuries, there have been various methods used to date the Earth that have since been discounted. Techniques included rates of salt washed into oceans, sedimentation, and the time it takes for the Earth to cool from a molten state. There were so many unknowns in these calculations that they became completely discounted.[221]

The current, and considered the most reliable, method is radioactive dating. Some atoms are radioactive. These atoms decay within a characteristic time period into a different atom. The period of time in which half of the "parent" atom transforms into its new "daughter" atom is known as the half-life. By measuring the amounts of the original atom and the new one formed by the decay, *and assuming uniform conditions* over millions or billions of years, it is thought possible to extrapolate and date a rock from the time of its formation.

Dating an object is not quite like people imagine. Many envision some sort of machine into which one inserts a rock or bone, which is then scanned, and the computer screen displays that this object is such and such years old. In reality, when measuring and calculating the ratio of parent and daughter atoms, it must be emphasized that all of the dating methods rely on a variety of assumptions, such as:[222]

---

220 His contention lies in "thermal diffusivity," the rate at which rocks conduct heat. Hager does admit, however, that if the diffusivity of the Earth was different before we learned to measure it, then you could speed up these calculations.

221 Ruth Moore, *Man, Time, and Fossils* (1953), pg. 317.

222 There are many references available, see for example Aitkin, *Physics and Archeology* (1961), pg. 101.

(a) What the initial amount of the parent atoms was when the rock formed, and (b) that the original composition of the rock contained no daughter atoms. Why would there be no daughter elements present when the rock formed? It is favorable for the theorists to assume that none of the daughter products were present in the object in the beginning, as this will yield the most massive age.[223] This issue alone puts into question the validity of the calculations for the age of the world based on mineral radiometric dating methods.

Furthermore, one must assume that the decay rate from parent atom to daughter atom has always remained uniform. This notion could be problematic in acquiring accurate data. For instance, basalt is a common rock formed from volcanic activity. In many basalts, radioactive potassium metal decays into argon gas. Measuring the potassium-argon ratios helps researchers estimate the age of the basalt. Once again, this assumes a closed system, in which all factors have remained the same since the rock formed. What if, for example, the temperature was different at certain periods of time? If it was hotter, the argon gas could have dispersed out of the rock more quickly than usual, leaving a low amount of remaining argon, and thus appearing much younger than in actuality.

Temperature or other factors can cause the same effect in the other direction as well. One such example can be found with volcanic rocks produced by lava flows in Hawaii in the early nineteenth century. These were dated by the potassium-argon method as ranging from 160 million to nearly 3 billion years old. Similar modern rocks formed in 1801 near Hualalai, Hawaii, gave similar grossly inaccurate results.[224]

---

223   Miller, *Awake My Glory*, #172.

224   See John Funkhouser and John Naughton, "Radiogenic Helium and Argon in Ultramafic Inclusions from Hawaii," *Journal of Geophysical Research*, Vol. 73, No. 14 (July 15, 1968): pgs. 4601–4607. Other rocks that were dated with potassium-argon method showed ages up to twenty-one million years on rocks that were known to be around 200 years old. (See Noble and Naughton, "Deep-Ocean Basalts: Inert Gas Content and Uncertainties in Age Dating," *Science*, Vol. 162, No. 3850 (October 11, 1968): pgs. 265–266).

   Sometimes, reports come back that the rock is dated older than 4.5 billion years, which is the alleged age of the Earth! It is explained that in these cases an external source of argon found its way somehow into the rock making it appear older than it was, however, this shows that the experiments are not done in a closed system from the get-go.

British author Richard Milton, after extensive research among various scientific disciplines, writes that the ways in which the scientific community commonly estimates the age of the Earth, by measuring the half-life of the uranium or potassium isotope, or any of the other methods, are far from accurate and cannot be accepted as scientifically conclusive. He writes: "The chief tool employed to harmonize discordant dates is the simple device of labeling unexpected ages as anomalous and, in the future, discarding those rock samples that will lead to the 'anomalous' dates. This practice is the explanation of why many dating results seem to support each other—because all samples that give ages other than expected values are rejected as being 'unsuitable' for dating."[225] He continues: "Thus the published dating figures always conform to preconceived dates and never contradict those dates. If all the rejected dates were retrieved from the wastebasket and added to the published dates, the combined results would show that the dates produced are the scatter that one would expect by chance alone."[226] Because Milton does not toe the party line, he is dismissed or labeled a creationist—which he adamantly denies. In fact, what is perhaps most uniquely interesting about Milton is that he identifies as an agnostic. His conclusions are free of any hidden agendas to prove biblical authenticity.[227]

In essence, virtually all of the dating techniques are based on the assumption of uniform change. Notwithstanding, it is universally accepted that there have been several known catastrophic events that have drastically changed the entire planet. Is it still viable to say that

---

It is further worth considering that if major cataclysms happened in the Earth's past, such as the Chicxulub meteor, much rock that seems older would have been molten and solidified at that time. Potassium-argon results would be fruitless as there would be no way of knowing what the original potassium and argon values were, especially given the enormity of the catastrophes that went into their formation. Much source material for the potassium-argon discussion was gleaned from Yaacov Hanoka, "Continental Drift, Asteroid Impacts, and the Flood," *B'Or HaTorah* 13 (2002): pgs. 87–93. Potassium-argon is only one dating method, but similar difficulties are found in the others as well.

225   Milton, *Shattering the Myths of Darwinism*, pg. 49.

226   Ibid., pg. 51.

227   Not everything in Milton's aforementioned book is in sync with a Torah outlook; nevertheless, those parts that overlap become much more intriguing when established by someone without religion.

the conclusions of radiometric dating based on faulty premises can be accurate?[228] With the catastrophes suggested by Alverez above, connected with the sudden demise of the dinosaurs, the entire structure of the planet would have been altered beyond comprehension.[229] Even the 2004 tsunami in Southeast Asia, which pales in comparison with the infamous Alverez meteor, caused the island of Sumatra to move nearly two meters and the North Pole to shift about an inch.[230] In truth, all earthquakes have some affect on Earth's rotation, planet shape, and North Pole; however, they are usually barely noticeable.[231]

The upheavals on the planet, changes in atmosphere, temperature, and so forth, which were triggered by the Chicxulub meteor, created an impact equivalent to a billion bombs like those that were dropped on Hiroshima and Nagasaki. Is it not fair to conclude, along with the many world-class scientists that have been quoted, that dating based on uniform backward extrapolation is not reliable?[232]

As new information surfaces in connection with dating techniques, previous estimates are constantly being reassessed. One example of drastic reevaluation can be found in the study of the Wabar craters in the Arabian Desert by famed geophysicists Gene Shoemaker and Jeffrey Wynn. Originally, fission-track analysis of glass fragments by the British Museum suggested the Wabar impact took place several thousand years ago. Later luminescence studies by John Prescott attest to an impact of around 250 years ago. Field evidence related by Shoemaker and Wyatt show an impact even more recent.[233]

---

228   Radiometric dating is used to determine the date when materials were formed. This is done by analyzing the decay of radioactive isotopes that were incorporated into the material when it was created and that presumably have not diffused out.

229   Water and change in pressure and temperature cause major changes in the amounts of both daughter and initial concentrations of the elemental types.

230   Michael Kanellos, "Asian Quake Moved Islands, Shortened Days," accessed January 14, 2005, http://news.cnet.com/Tsunami-moves-North-Pole,-shortens-day-time/2100-1008_3-5536983.html.

231   Dr. Richard Gross of NASA's Jet Propulsion Laboratory, Pasadena, CA, and Dr. Benjamin Fong Chao, of NASA's Goddard Space Flight Center, Greenbelt, MD.

232   The strength of the electromagnetic field of the Earth could affect the speed of radioactive decay. The rest affect the initial concentrations.

233   J. R. Prescott, G. B. Robertson, C. Shoemaker, E. M. Shoemaker, and J. Wynn, "Luminescence dating of the Wabar Meteorite Craters, Saudi Arabia," *Journal of Geophysical*

Uniformitarian ideology contributes significantly to viewing the world as extremely old, perhaps older than it actually is, by assuming that the Earth and everything in it reached its current state slowly and gradually, rather than by undergoing rapid changes at some points in history. It is refreshing to see that in contemporary studies, the staunch uniformitarian perspective has made some room for the possibility of fast-changing catastrophic periods. It seems that most of the supposed contradictions regarding Torah and science are really issues within science itself, whether they are actual limitations of science or because of the perspective or framework set up by the scientific community.

THE MYSTERY OF THE FIRST SIX DAYS

Even if every dating method was correct, and the results they produced were perfect, Jewish tradition describes a very different state of existence during the first six days of Creation that would drastically alter scientific speculation.

One of the most fundamental beliefs in Judaism is that G-d created the world from nothing, *creatio ex nihilo*.[234] Creation clearly does not follow natural law, as there is nothing that can *naturally* come into existence from total non-existence. In other words, creation, by definition, defies the laws of nature. The universe's apparent age of billions of years is based on observations made after the laws of nature were set in place, and then applied backwards to nature as it existed during the days of Creation. These conclusions, however, are flawed according to Jewish tradition. The Talmudic sages teach that the world was created in a mature and functioning state. Additionally, there are many sources indicating that during Creation the laws of nature operated at a faster pace and that time itself functioned in a different way.

Research 109 (2004); Also J. C. Wynn and E. M. Shoemaker, "The Day the Sands Caught Fire," *Scientific American* 279 (1998): pgs. 36–45.

234 Ramban on *Bereishis* 1:1. See also *Emunos V'Deos*, 1; *HaIkkarim*, 1, 12, 27; Rashbatz in his introduction to the book of *Iyov*; *Chovos HaLevavos*, Sha'ar HaYichud 6.

YOUNG BUT CREATED WITH HISTORY

The Talmud says that when G-d created the world, He created everything in "full form and stature."[235] The medieval sages explain that when G-d created fruit-bearing trees, they were created complete, with fruit already growing,[236] and all creatures were made in their final form.[237] Adam, the first human, was created as a twenty-year-old man.[238] This means that although Adam was, in reality, only a few hours old, he appeared as a man of twenty years.

Everything was created already in the state needed to begin carrying out its purpose. The first trees, although only brought into existence a few days prior, were not saplings, but instead full and lush with trunks likely full of rings, as if they had been growing for decades. The first chicken was not created as an egg or a chick, but instead as a fully mature chicken. Even animals that survive on the carcasses of other animals likely had dead carcasses created just for them to eat. The world was complete—it had a built-in history. Any history that was *needed* for each part of Creation to begin to fulfill its purpose was created and built into the structure of the universe when it was brought into existence. Thus, if G-d needed Abraham (twenty generations after Adam) to be able to gaze to the stars, He created them in a way that their light would be visible to him, even though they are at a distance from which the light should not have reached Earth yet.

Looking at the newly created Earth would show Creation with the appearance of age. A modern example of how to imagine such a phenomenon can be seen in aged cheese. Some cheeses are ripened to produce an enhanced flavor, texture, and appearance. In the past, cellars or caves were used to ripen cheeses. Today, with technology and advanced machinery, temperature and humidity can be precisely controlled and combined with knowledge of enzymes. The cheese

---

235   *Rosh Hashana* 11a, *Chullin* 60a. See also *Bamidbar Rabbah* 12:8.
236   Rashi on *Rosh Hashana* loc. cit. This fact is even alluded to in the Torah text itself; see *Bereishis* [Genesis] 1:11–12.
237   Tosofos on *Chullin* loc. cit.
238   *Bereishis Rabbah* 14:7.

manufacturer can produce "aged-cheese" right away. To all external appearances the cheese would appear as if it had taken months to ripen, though it had actually taken significantly less time. In a similar way, the world appeared and appears old because it was created complete and fully functional.

REALITY DIFFERENT DURING THE SIX DAYS

The sages teach that before the sin of Adam, the entire structure of the universe, including the laws of nature, operated completely differently compared to the way they do today. Adam, the first man, and subsequently all of humankind, is known in Jewish literature as an *olam katan*, a universe in microcosm.[239] His actions affect the entire Creation, for better or worse.[240] The *Zohar* relates that when G-d created man, the Heavens and Earth trembled. It is explained that this was out of fear that man, the microcosm, would do something that would harm the entire universe.[241] According to Jewish tradition, this indeed took place, most significantly after the sin of Adam. Following the transgression of Adam and Eve, physical existence began to function in a totally new way, including a change in how time operates, the movement of the celestial objects, and a drastic change in the physical world.

LAWS OF NATURE NOT FULLY IN PLACE

The Talmud explains that all of the laws of nature that are in place today were first set into course at the end of the six-day period beginning with the first Sabbath. The Talmud states that when G-d created the world, "it continued to expand like two clues of warp until G-d rebuked it and brought it to a standstill."[242] Until this point there were no boundaries in the laws of nature, and the universe

---

239 *Midrash Tanchuma*, Parshas Pekudei, sec. 3; *Kuzari* 4:3.
240 *Mesilas Yesharim* 1:1.
241 *Tiferes Levi Yitzchok*, Bereishis 28.
242 See *Chagiga* 12a. Woof and Warp: The threads in a woven fabric. The warp (threads running lengthwise) and woof (threads running crosswise) to create the texture of the fabric.

functioned completely differently than experienced today. Once G-d said "enough," the boundaries of all forces in Creation were set. Parenthetically, it is through the establishment of these fixed laws that G-d expresses Himself as Master of the universe.[243]

Rabbi Dessler explains that the workings of time were also different during the first six days. The perception of reality that we identify with is fragmented and broken up into past, present, and future. The human definition of time is rooted in the framework of the consecutive order of perceptions. The human perception of time is subjective, and as modern physics demonstrates, time is relative, varying based on certain considerations.

In the spiritual realm, from the vantage point of ultimate truth and true reality, there is no such thing as time. Much like everything else in Creation, time is a constriction, limitation, and a veil, but *not* a necessity and an absolute, as was once thought. G-d created time, and is above it.[244] In spiritual terms, past, present, and future are an illusion, and reality truly exists in a simultaneously existing eternal present. The human mind does not currently perceive this. Jewish tradition teaches that in the hereafter, the soul will be able to experience reality beyond the veil of time.[245]

Before the sin of Adam, time functioned differently. The world was in sync with the heights of spirituality—a unified world, where

---

243 The name of G-d pronounced "Shad-ai" means Al-mighty, as in *Bereishis* 35:11. It indicates this phrase that Hashem said in *Chagiga* 12a: "*Ani hu* she'*amarti l'olam* dai," which means "I am the one who has instructed My world [during Creation], enough." With the word "*dai*" (enough), G-d fixed the measure of all objects and the boundaries of forces. If G-d did not order "*dai*," the heavens and Earth would continue expanding and developing, as though the product of blind physical forces. Through the establishment of fixed laws in the universe to protect the integrity of Creation as He intended it to be, G-d revealed Himself in His Attribute of Shad-ai, the Omnipotent Al-mighty Master of the universe. (See Rav Shimshon Raphoel Hirsch, quoted from Munk, *Wisdom of the Hebrew Alphabet* (1983), pg. 203.)

244 G-d has many Names that He is called by. The Great Name, is sometimes called the Tetragrammaton, and in its very letters indicates His Oneness and transcendence of time and space. It is composed of four letters: *yud* and *hei*, with a *vav* and *hei*. The word itself is also a contraction of three words that can be spelled from it: past (*hayah*), present (*hoveh*) and can be adjusted to make it future (*yihiyeh*).

245 *Michtav Me'Eliyahu* 2: 150-154.

even time functioned in a unified present. After the sin, reality was coarsened to the depths of corporeality, which resulted in a world of division and fragmentation, in which time also took on its perceived current gradual progression.

Time as experienced by Adam was completely different than what the perception of time is today. If Adam had not sinned, Moshiach would have come that day, and all of the revelations that were destined to happen over the course of history before Moshiach arrived would have happened during that one day, the Friday when Adam was formed. When Adam sinned, time became fragmented into many days, and the revelations instead needed to wait many years before they would happen.

In the current workings of nature, just as more than one object cannot simultaneously occupy the same space, so too, time is perceived as progression. Two moments cannot exist simultaneously. During the first week of Creation, the laws of nature were completely different than anything known at present. This does not mean to say that there were more than six 24-hour days, or that days or hours were longer than they are now, as we have discussed. Rather, it means that the essence of time functioned qualitatively differently during that period. The laws of nature as a whole, and the dynamics between time and space, were not set in place the way that they are at present.[246]

A CHANGE IN MATTER

Additionally, matter and the laws of nature in the universe itself changed.

For instance, before the sin of the Tree of Knowledge, the Midrash says that the constellations moved faster.[247] Based on this, Rabbi Chaim Halberstam of Sanz, known as the Divrei Chaim, elaborates about a star that scientists discovered whose orbit takes 36,000 years. Being that the Talmud says that this world will only last for 6,000

---

246   See *Michtav Me'Eliyahu* 2: 150-152, including his explanation to the Gra in his *Likutim* at the end of *Sifra D'tzniusa*.
247   *Midrash Rabbah* 10:4.

years, one could have the question why this star was created to begin with? The Divrei Chaim responds with an answer brought from the days of the Arizal:

> It is known that the universe was once in its most perfect state, but Adam corrupted it and weakened the entire Creation. Therefore, at the time of Creation, if not for the sin of our father Adam, the first human being, the movement would have been fast, but now because of the flaw caused by the sin of Adam, the orbit has to wait 36,000 years..."[248]

This line of thought is likewise described elsewhere in Jewish tradition.[249] It would seem from here that Creation as a whole functioned in a "healthier" or supercharged way; created perfectly and energized but subsequently blemished and weakened through the erring of man. It would seem that as time progressed and humanity headed down the wrong path, the "infection" or "spiritual pollution" spread. After all, people lived longer and had perfect weather year round until the days of the flood. It is perhaps fair to say that as the generations subsequently spiraled downward, so did the status and construct of the Earth and universe at large slow down and deteriorate.

YOU'RE A SMALL WORLD AFTER ALL

Rabbi Moshe Chaim Luzzatto, known as the Ramchal, says that "the structure and makeup of Heaven and Earth is much like the makeup of the human being, as the two are analogous to each other on various levels."[250] Along those lines, it may be appropriate to suggest an analogy: that the history and development of the world resembles that of a human being, with rapid changes in the beginning of life, only to later gradually and drastically slow down.

Consider the following: If one had only seen a baby in his life, never

---

248   *Divrei Chaim al HaTorah*, Chanukah, pg. 90.
249   *Yaaros Dvash* vol. 1:1 and 15; see *Divrei Yoel*, Simchas Torah, pg. 613.
250   *Da'as Tevunos*, Section 2, ch. 9:1.

once having seen an adult, one would error tremendously with future growth predictions. Imagine tracking the height of the baby through his early years of childhood with pencil marks on the wall. Based on the limited scope of information available while looking at his rate of growth, one may predict that the child will grow to be seventeen feet tall. This is because the child grows extremely quickly in his earlier years of life.

Now consider the opposite scenario: one has *never* seen a baby, he has instead seen only a fully grown seventy-five-year-old man. Without knowing his age, using only the rate of change in his body in his later years, try to guess how long ago it was when this older gentleman was a baby. The changes that the human body undergoes between age 70 and 75 are negligible. 65-70 is also insignificant. Measuring only at that infinitesimal and uniform rate of change would suggest that this man of seventy-five was really much older, because there are several rapid or catastrophic changes that take place in the human body in the earlier stages of life. Without knowing that, one assumes a uniform change in this man and estimates that he is several hundred years old. As mentioned above, there is an enormous and rapid metamorphosis in the early years that transform a human being from a newborn to an infant, to a baby, to a toddler, to a child, to an adolescent, and so forth. The early years occupy the same five-year increments on the timeline, yet are a world of difference developmentally when compared to later in life, in the 70–75 year span of time.

A very similar approach can be seen in the development of the world, not just in geology as seen above, but rather an overall outlook across the spectrum of the universe. It is baseless to assume that all of the current rates of change in the world today were always operating as they are at present, and that there were no earlier periods of rapid and drastic changes. Moreover, one cannot ascertain that the beginning point or Creation itself, likened perhaps to the gestation period of the universe, also fits the conditions of today.[251] "Indeed, a scientifically

---

251   After writing this analogy, this author later noticed that the former Chief Rabbi of Uruguay, Rabbi Yosef Bitton, writes a similar analogy in his recent work *Awesome Creation*. He takes the parable a step further to the point of birth. He gives an enlightening parable

based theory of cosmology is an oxymoron. To 'prove' a theory of cosmology, one would have to presuppose that the present state of the universe is analogous to its initial stages, in which case, cosmology will be indistinguishable from physics and not a topic of its own."[252]

CONTEMPORARY CRYSTALLIZATION OF THE ABOVE APPROACHES

Rabbi Shimon Schwab zt"l, a contemporary sage, has said that there is no contradiction between the Torah and scientific measure of the age of the world.[253] Firstly, he explores the concept of the light and darkness created on the first day of Creation. This was, from the start, the gauge that marked the beginning and end of a day. The light and darkness that come about from daylight and nighttime are only paralleling coarse manifestations of the "Creation light." The Creation light is spiritual in nature and something that is currently concealed, yet its full rotation of light-to-darkness-to-light is twenty-four hours.

He writes that "billions of years during the era of Creation are equal to six regular days today." In other words, he writes that the first six days of Creation were regular 24-hour periods, measured by the "Creation light," yet at the same time contained within them all of the physical changes that appear as billions of years. This means that all of the history and upheavals on Earth and in the universe at large took place in the first six days at a much accelerated speed.

Rabbi Schwab uses the example of two clocks. The first clock ticks accurately, measured with a never-failing, scientifically controlled

---

that the Rambam writes in *Moreh Nevuchim* 2:21: A child who was abandoned on a deserted island at birth and had never seen a woman could not figure out on his own how he was born. He would never be able to come up with the idea that human beings are conceived as they in fact are. All he can go by are the facts that he is familiar with, and from that perspective, he could not possibly know, deduce, or imagine the processes of conception, pregnancy, or birth. So too, with the universe, one is extremely limited on the information that is available to him—only that of the present—and cannot make assumptions projecting these preconceived notions to the beginning or times passed.

252 Jose Faur, *Homo Mysticus: A Guide to Maimonides's Guide for the Perplexed* (1998), pg. 117–18, source provided from Bitton, *Amazing Creation*.

253 See his "How Old is the Universe," *Challenge: Torah Views on Science and Its Problems*, pgs. 165–174.

device. The hands of the second clock are manipulated by an individual. The individual can spin his clock many full times around. With enough effort he can mark several weeks on his clock, while the first clock only registers a few minutes. When the individual decides to stop, the two clocks can move in complete synchronism, registering the exact same time from then on. Up until the end of the sixth day, which was measured by the "Creation light," the Creator was manipulating the second clock, meaning all of the events of Creation were happening millions of times faster than they operate today. It is similar to playing a video in super fast-forward, where all of the events and story line of a two-hour movie happen in a matter of seconds. One who has ever watched time-lapse photography, which compresses longer events like a blossoming flower or the construction of a building into a few moments, has an idea of what could have taken place. Following the sixth day, when G-d rested, the Earth began to rotate around its axis slowly, exactly the amount of time that it takes for the appearance of the Creation light.

Rabbi Schwab cautions the reader to realize that these words of a "sped-up Creation" are to be taken more metaphorically. Clearly, "if all motion were uniformly multiplied, all radiation, for instance, would become lethal. The accelerated rate would turn every particle into a deadly missile." Instead, he continues, "it should be thought of as a uniform nexus of change in the entire system of the natural order as known today, a variance in all functions within the framework of natural law in conformity with the new universal velocity, not upsetting the intricate balance of all physical phenomena and the orderly cooperation of all parts with the whole."

Had G-d created a universe resembling ours, but where every aspect of it pointed to a young age, and by default to the ever-presence and omnipotence of G-d, it would completely eliminate human free choice. As Rabbi Schwab says, "the immediate proximity of the Creator would overshadow all our thoughts and emotions." It is only through the apparent gradual development from chaos to order that enables free choice to exist. The Jew knows that this transition from chaos to order, though, actually took place over the course of six literal days.

Much more could be said about the age of the world to further explain points of contention. We have simply seen a taste of the Torah sources on the unique nature of the Creation days, as well as the disagreements and faulty assumptions and conclusions in the academic arena. Readers are encouraged to do further investigation in reconciling Torah and science, which will only further enlighten the reader's appreciation of the magnificent insights of Torah and Creation.

FREE WILL AND DIVINE KNOWLEDGE

T here is an age-old question regarding the apparent paradox between two fundamental religious principles: the omniscience of G-d,[254] and the fact that human beings are granted free will.[255] The philosophical quandary goes as follows: If G-d's knowledge is absolute, then it is seemingly impossible for free will to exist, for G-d *already knew* what the individual would choose.

Free will is essential to Judaism. One of the Thirteen Principles of Faith is that G-d rewards good and punishes evil.[256] If a person's deeds are predetermined, how then could one be rewarded or held accountable for his actions?[257] On the other hand, if freedom of choice is a reality, and a person can truly do something entirely of his own volition, then G-d's foreknowledge is seemingly not absolute.

This topic is addressed from various angles in the classic works of the sages and major rabbinic philosophers throughout the generations. It is a very deep subject, one that countless volumes could be dedicated to and still only scratch the surface. Its full answer is described as "longer than the measure of the land and broader than the oceans."[258] That being said, this section seeks to merely highlight

---

254 See Rambam, *Yesodei HaTorah* 2:9.
255 *Devarim* [Deuteronomy] 30:15. Rambam, *Teshuvah* 5:3-4; Commentary to Mishnah, *Shemoneh Perakim*, ch. 8.
256 Rambam, Principle 11. See also *HaIkkarim* 3:12; *Shir HaShirim Rabbah* 1:45; *Zohar* 1:10b.
257 *HaIkkarim* 4:1.
258 Rambam, *Teshuva* 5:5, wording borrowed from *Iyov* [Job] 11:9.

some of the traditional and contemporary approaches taken on this dilemma.

ONE-SIDED RECONCILIATION APPROACHES

With a cursory examination of the issue, some of the early sages seem to reconcile the paradox of Divine foreknowledge and free will by putting limitations on one of the axioms.[259]

NO FOREKNOWLEDGE FOR FUTURE HUMAN CHOICES

The Ralbag says that G-d cannot know how a man will behave in the future.[260] He can know beforehand the effects of all causes, and since everything that will ever happen is dependent on causes, He knows the future in this way. Human beings have free choice, which essentially is the ability to move outside the realm of cause and effect. Hence, the Ralbag explains, G-d cannot know what they will eventually choose, since He cannot rely on the causes to determine that.

It is likely that the Ralbag does not intend to limit G-d's ability to foresee the future, but more probable that he holds that future does not exist in the present and therefore *cannot* be known.

This is similar to the age-old riddle of G-d's omnipotence, which asks: "Can G-d make a rock that is so heavy that He cannot lift it?" The answer to this question is that the rock *cannot* exist, because G-d can lift all rocks. This does not limit G-d's capabilities, for omnipotence is only in the category of those things that *can* exist.

In a similar way, a possible approach to understanding the Ralbag is that he holds that G-d's lack of ability to know the future does not limit His omniscience. Omniscience only refers to those things that are possible to know. The future does not yet exist, even "in the future."

---

259 These are not the finalized mainstream views, but some perspectives that put limit on either human free will or Divine knowledge.

260 *Milchamos Hashem*, 3:6

NO REAL FREE CHOICE

On the opposite side of the spectrum one finds those early philosophers who limit the free choice of the human being in order to uphold Divine omniscience. Perhaps the leading sage sharing this view is Rabbi Hasdai Crescas. Rabbi Crescas differentiates between fatalism, which stresses that future events are entirely inevitable, and determinism, which says that everything is based on cause and effect.[261] For the determinist, different past events would produce different present situations, whereas the fatalist would say that no alternative past, present, or future is possible.

Rabbi Crescas is not a fatalist. He would more appropriately fall into what modern philosophical jargon dubs "soft determinism" or "compatibilism." G-d's foreknowledge is of the choices that man actually makes of his own free will. Since man's choices are, in a sense, determined by G-d's foreknowledge, man is not truly free. Other sages fall philosophically somewhere in between.

PERCEIVED PARADOX

Upon further examination, the world contains many apparent paradoxes. The sages refer to G-d as "He who carries opposites,"[262] or as the "Paradox of Paradoxes."[263] The enigmatic nature of exactly how G-d interacts with Creation is likewise described allegorically as "He is the place of the world, but the world is not His place,"[264] and as "present yet not present."[265]

As a preface, it is important to realize that the *perceived* contradiction of free will and Divine foreknowledge exists only because the human mind is totally incapable of grasping the reality and totality of G-d. The problem exists from our vantage point alone, based on mankind's mental deficiency, and ultimately is not a true

---

261 *Ohr Hashem* 2:5:3.
262 *Likkutei Torah* 3:68.
263 *Teshuvos HaRashba* 18.
264 *Bereishis Rabbah* 68:9.
265 *Sefer HaMama'arim* 5679, pg. 237.

inconsistency.[266] This idea of the Rambam will be elaborated upon below.

Many of the infamous philosophical quandaries that have been pondered since time immemorial exist because there are, in essence, two ever-present frameworks or perceptions of reality: human and Divine. For example, one famous paradox in Judaism is the unchanging oneness and unity of G-d *alongside* His concealment and apparent "withdrawal" in creating a universe. Which is the true reality? In some sense, it depends upon which vantage point one is looking from.

The human sense of reality is limited to the perception and processing of the five senses. Just as one who is lacking the means to experience one of the five senses has a limited experience of the situation at hand, how much more can this be said about aspects of reality that are beyond all of the five senses. The human mind cannot conceive of anything beyond the joined signals of the five senses, and is therefore left in a state of confusion when trying to envision ultimate truth—the vantage point of the upper world.

From the higher vantage point, the flow of time and the multiple dimensions of space cease to exist, while from the lower vantage point the human eye views the multifarious "otherness" of the universe as reality. Because the higher vantage point transcends the grasp of the human being, it cannot be fully reconciled from the human vantage point and is perceived as a paradox.

Likewise, Divine knowledge and free choice are not contradictions, but belong to two distinct vantage points. Freedom of choice is a perception from the lower, human vantage point; whereas Divine knowledge is something far beyond the grasp of the human being. The human conclusion of what is Divine knowledge is only a projection of what he knows knowledge to be, not what it is in essence.

---

266   See *Moreh Nevuchim* 3:20.

HUMAN LACK OF KNOWLEDGE ABOUT DIVINE KNOWLEDGE

This point is elaborated upon by the Rambam. The expression of qualities attributed to G-d is only according to our perceptual capabilities and not reflective of the essential being of G-d. Thus, conceptual traits of "kindness," "anger," "compassion," or "knowledge" are terms that human beings associate with G-d because *we* do them. It is from the lower vantage point that these traits are perceived in this way, yet they are not intrinsic to His Being. It is likewise erroneous to think that His traits, which are ostensibly referred to as "kindness" or "knowledge," bear any qualitative semblance to that which human beings call "kindness" or "knowledge." In reality, there are no "characteristics" or "attributes"; there is only G-d's relationship with a human situation, which, from the perspective of the human being, *resembles* a human attribute.

In the case at hand, the fact that human knowledge of the future poses a potential contradiction to free will in no way indicates that the same thing would be true of G-d's "knowledge," as the human mind cannot even begin to fathom what G-d's "processing knowledge" means.[267] In other words, the human being cannot even pose the question of G-dly foreknowledge versus human free choice because the human mind "lacks the ability to know in what manner G-d knows all of Creation and their activities."[268]

PLAUSIBLE APPROACHES

KNOWLEDGE NOT COERCION

First, let it be simply stated that there is no conflict between the foreknowledge of G-d and the free choice of human beings. The only thing that could be a contradiction would be coercion—where one is

---

267   *HaIkkarim* 4:3. See also Rabbi Chaim Friedlander, *Sifsei Chaim*, Emunah and Hashgacha, vol. 1, pg. 329.

268   *Kesef Mishnah* on *Teshuvah* 5:5.

forced to act in a certain way, not mere knowledge of a future event. For example, if a prophet or clairvoyant knows all of the activities that a certain individual will engage in tomorrow, that in no way compels them to actually do them. In other words, the forecaster's knowledge allows him to know how the other person will freely choose. The knowledge is dependent on the result of the choice.[269]

BEYOND THE REALM OF TIME

Perhaps an even deeper approach is one that is a bit difficult for human beings to really wrap our minds around since we are under the jurisdiction of time. The paradox of Divine knowledge and free will can only be questioned in a time-bound world.

The sages have said that the concept of time began with, and is part and parcel of, the creation of the physical world.[270] Within the past hundred years, it has become more clearly understood in the scientific arena that time is a dimension of matter.[271] Just like the measurements of length, width, and height make up the three dimensions of reality, time—the measure of change—is the fourth dimension.[272] Notably, the sages write that the word *shanah*, used to describe the dimension of time, is related to the word *shinui*, which means "change."[273]

The Theory of Relativity shows that time is relative and not absolute. The facts indicate that time, like everything else in Creation, is a constriction, a limitation, and a veil, and *not* a necessity and an absolute, as was once thought. In the physical world, where progression of time is an inescapable reality, there is a contradiction between future

---

269 Summaries of this approach, and the ones that follow, can be found in *Iggros Kodesh*, vol. 3, letters beginning on pgs. 40 and 48. See also *Letters From the Rebbe*, vol. 1 (Otzar Sifrei Lubavitch, 1998), pgs. 57–58, 161–162, 218.

270 Seforno and Malbim, *Bereishis* 1:1; Ramban, *Bereishis* 1:4.

271 See for example Sir Arthur Stanley Eddington, *The Nature of the Physical World* (1929).

272 The Maharal of Prague explains that time is created through changes in reality, and evolves through movement. This is something only connected to the physical world (see *Ohr Chadash*, *Gevuros Hashem* 46). The spiritual realm is not subject to the illusion of time (see Maharal, *Tiferes Yisrael* 14, 25).

273 Although *shanah* literally means "year", in *Sefer Yetzirah*, an ancient work, it is the term used to describe the changes of time in general.

knowledge and present free choice; however, in essence, time is an illusion.

Notably, Jewish tradition teaches that in the hereafter, the soul will be able to experience reality beyond the veil of time. Rabbi Dessler writes:

> When a person is born, he is placed under the concealment of time. After his passing the concealment of time will be removed...and he will view everything simultaneously; he will see that time is a veil, since everything was really one reality appearing all together.[274]

Science tends to see time as somewhat of an illusion as well. Einstein captured this idea when writing a letter to the family of his friend Michele Besso, following Besso's death: "Now Besso has departed from this strange world a little ahead of me. That means nothing. People like us, who believe in physics, know that the distinction between past, present, and future is only a stubbornly persistent illusion."[275] Interestingly enough, patients who recall events from a near-death experience also describe their view of the world, while in that state, as such that they realized that time was merely a guise.[276]

VISUALIZING TIMELESSNESS

The spiritual realm is beyond time, existing above its limitations. From the Divine vantage point, everything is foreseen and overseen—in every place and throughout time—in a single glance. Rabbi Dessler compares the human perception of time to looking at a map through a card with a small hole in it. One can move the hole from city to city. The onlooker perceives these places in sequence, but that progression is a product of his view of the map, not the map itself. If the card is removed, the entire map is seen in one glance.

---

274   *Michtav Me'Eliyahu* 2: 150-154.
275   Pierre Speziali ed., *Albert Einstein and Michele Besso Correspondence 1903–1955* (1972), pg. 215.
276   See Dr. Raymond Moody, *Life After Life*.

Another metaphor: Imagine a man riding on a train that makes ten stops. He begins at the first stop, and then travels to the next stop, then the following stop, ultimately arriving at his final destination at the tenth stop. To the passenger, each stop is experienced in sequence— the current stop, the past stops, and the upcoming stops. However, if someone was standing on a nearby mountain overlooking the entire city and the full route of the train, he would be able to see in one single, sweeping glance what the passenger perceives as a progression.[277]

Likewise, what is perceived as sequence below, in the physical world, is seen at once—past, present, and future—on High. Just as knowledge of a certain event in the past, or seeing an action in the present, does not rob the doer of his free choice, so too with G-d's knowledge of the future, which is the *same* as His knowledge of the past and present, the individual is not robbed of their free choice.[278]

For G-d, past, present, and future are all one and the same, existing as an "eternal present."

A FURTHER QUESTION

There is a further question addressed in the discourses of Chassidic thought: How is it possible that the knowledge of the Creator, that brings into being and maintains the existence of all the created beings, does not influence them at all?[279]

The answer is that such knowledge only affects created beings in a

---

277 Compare these analogies of Rabbi Dessler *zt"l* to the words of Paul Davies, professor of natural philosophy at the University of Adelaide: "Physicists prefer to think of time as laid out in its entirety—a timescape, analogous to a landscape—with all past and future events located there together... Completely absent from this description of nature is anything that singles out a privileged special moment as the present or any process that would systematically turn future events into the present, then past, events. In short, the time of the physicist does not pass or flow." In the same article he writes: "A clock measures durations between events much as a measuring tape measures distance between places; it does not measure the 'speed' with which one moment succeeds another." See Paul Davies, "That Mysterious Flow," *Scientific American* (Sept. 2002): pg. 40.

278 See Midrash Shmuel, Tosofos Yom Tov, Tiferes Yisrael on *Avos* 3:15. See also *Michtav Me'Eliyahu* 3:262.

279 Question presented and answered with further sources in *Iggros Kodesh*, vol. 3, letter beginning pg. 48.

transcendent manner, and not in an imminent and internalized way. As a result, this knowledge on High does not cause a person to change at all; whatever the person chooses is by his own will, without coercion from Above.

Moreover, G-d is not only omniscient but also omnipotent; He can do anything He desires. That being said, He can prevent His foreknowledge from affecting His creatures. This is indeed what happens; He prevents His foresight from impinging on free will.[280]

---

280   See *Likkutei Sichos* vol. 5, pg. 66 and the sources mentioned there. *Tzemach Tzedek, Sefer HaLikkutim*, Bechira pg. 72–73. See related idea of how G-d somehow restricts His knowledge of the future in order to give man free will in *Ohr HaChaim* on *Bereishis* 6:2; *Meshech Chochmah, Bereishis* 1:26.

THE PROBLEM OF EVIL AND SUFFERING

The belief in Divine justice is a foundation of the Jewish faith. The question of evil and suffering in the world is perhaps the most prevalent argument against a belief in G-d. After all, how can there be room for evil in a world created and overseen by He who is described as the quintessence of goodness and kindness? Why do the righteous suffer while evildoers are abundant and prosper?[281] Supreme justice and order seem to come into question with these considerations. If G-d is described as being completely good and powerful, why is there so much suffering?

It is important to preface this section with a disclaimer and an analogy. One who has suffered, or knows someone else who has experienced excruciating hardships, witnessed a natural disaster, or studied troubling situations in world affairs both past and present, can rest assured that any distress they may have felt is legitimate and not something that should be minimized. The objective of the discussion here is surely not to minimize the hurt, or the reality of the anguish felt by individuals in their own life experiences. Rather, these words seek to broaden the perspective of considerations.

The Mishnah instructs, "Do not try to comfort the mourner while his deceased is still before him."[282] There are no rationales that can address suffering and pain that are emotional expressions of the heart. The heart and mind operate on completely different planes.

---

281   *Shmos Rabbah* 45:6; *Zohar* 2:117b, 3:168a.
282   *Avos* 4:23.

To clarify: G-d created the human being with both intellectual capabilities and emotional potentials. Both are good and legitimate tools, yet at the same time have completely different functions. Just as a chainsaw and a wrench are both tools, but their uses cannot be interchanged, so too one looking for *emotional* support, reassurance, and pain relief will never be satisfied with an *intellectual* proof, validation, or rationalization. Ultimately, the only appropriate response to an emotional need would be an emotional response, such as a hug. No matter how well an answer suits the question or fits the situation, it will be unsatisfactory for one requiring emotional support. The same holds true the other way around as well. One who seeks intellectual satisfaction will not find "feel-good" responses meaningful.

This being said, it must be stressed once again that this segment and the contents contained herein do not seek to dismiss any emotional pain one has had in response to challenging times. Instead, we are trying to appeal to the intellect, seeking to give the mind some food for thought.

GOOD AND EVIL

The first details that must be clarified are the terms themselves. What is meant by a good person? What defines him? How about "bad" things? What makes something a "bad thing"? Good, evil, and suffering are used colloquially in subjective contexts. The expressions may not be true in the absolute sense, but instead borrowed terms describing a matter of perception.

For an extreme, yet fitting example, consider any number of tyrannical dictators of recent history. These oppressive, murderous tormentors were often seen by their followers as heroic saviors, gallant commanders, and quasi-messianic supermen. Millions of people may have regarded these wicked, malicious, and immoral figures as upright and virtuous. In the ultimate or absolute sense, though, are these ruthless men good? Do they somehow become good because so many viewed them as such?

On the opposite extreme, leaders like George Washington and Thomas Jefferson were considered by Britain as outlaws, interested in stealing land and instigating rebellion. Is this who they really were, and what they stood for? What makes someone "good" in a more definitive sense?

It is apparent that a good person or evil person cannot truly be judged based on majority perception. In Western society, good and evil are loosely defined, hinged upon whatever is in vogue at a given time. Right and wrong, or good and evil, cannot be subject to electability, terms that are subject to the whims of a fickle society. It seems more reasonable that what defines a good person be judged upon more objective criteria.

Furthermore, reward and punishment are also not absolute in the grand scheme. Just as what one person considers trash is a treasure to another, so too what is considered by some to be a blessing is looked upon quite differently by another. Consider the lifestyles of the rich and famous. Seemingly they have all of the best that life has to offer: fancy cars, beautiful homes, and a lot of fans. An onlooker sees these things as blessings, something to be envious of. However, a considerable number of celebrities are constantly depressed; despite their beautiful homes, they have no personal lives, and despite their abundance of fans, they suffer from severe loneliness. These woes frequently lead them to drug abuse, unstable relationships, and thousands of dollars in therapy—hardly the coveted existence.[283] Is their life situation equated with blessing or suffering?

The same applies to less extreme scenarios. "Bad things" happening to "good people" are very subjective classifications. The challenge is that it is nearly impossible to see the *absolute* definition of a person or an event when viewing from the limited vantage point of a human being.[284]

THE REAL ISSUE

The real issue that the human mind questions is not the concept of suffering itself, but instead its seemingly immoral nature. The human mind is not bothered by the fact that "bad things" happen, only that

---

283   This is common knowledge; still for example see Maria Puente, "Celebrity Addicts: Who Dies and Who Survives?" *USA Today*, Mar. 26, 2012, 01D.
284   Based on Kelemen, *Permission to Believe* (1990), pg. 93.

they happen to "good" people for no apparent reason. Everyone believes in justice—something that the Torah is based on as well. Bad circumstances are only regarded as "bad" if the person did not deserve it. If on the other hand it was deserved, then the same occurrence is seen as fair and justice was simply carried out.

Determining what is good and evil or what is a reward and what is a punishment are commonly decided upon by a subjective observer. In other words, when we ask why "bad" things happen to "good" people, these are somewhat subjective assumptions. Who says, in the grand scheme, that this situation is a bad thing? However, one cannot truly ask this question without having an objective or absolute view of the situation.

As mentioned in a previous chapter, it is sensible that absolute truth, good and evil in the objective sense, comes from a source that is absolute. Absolute implies something not subject to change, ultimately meaning something not subject to physical reality or the confines of time. In other words, G-d is the only entity that can fit the criteria. Ironically, then, by citing the existence of evil to question the existence of G-d, the questioner is simultaneously silently acknowledging His existence, by agreeing that there are absolute standards in the universe.

Furthermore, G-d either exists or He does not. Either He created the universe or He did not. The fact that the universe does not look the way one might want it to look does not play any part in determining whether G-d exists or not. The truth of His existence or non-existence is completely independent of any subjective reactions about the vicissitudes of life. His existence does not depend on personal agreement with how the world is run. Such a perspective is comparable to having negative feelings about how a corporation is run, and thereby concluding that the CEO must not exist. The reality of suffering may interfere with *our relationship* with an existent G-d, but does not determine or negate His existence.[285]

---

285   Paraphrased from Moshe Averick, *Nonsense of a Higher Order* (2010), pgs. 231–232.

BEYOND HUMAN REASONING

It is completely logical that some things that are a part of Divine reasoning will be higher than the comprehension of what man is able to grasp.[286] The biblical prophet Isaiah elaborates, "For My thoughts are not your thoughts, neither are your ways My ways, says G-d. For as the heavens are higher than the Earth, so are My ways higher than your ways, and My thoughts higher than your thoughts."[287] After all, we are mere mortals.

British philosopher Colin McGinn, former professor at Oxford and Princeton University, writes in a similar fashion that monkeys may be able to understand certain basics of electricity, like touching an electric fence is bad and painful, but are not cognitively capable of grasping the concept of an electron as a human does.[288] Similarly, in infinitely greater proportions, the human mind cannot fathom the true reasoning of G-d.

The sages addressed this idea as well. Rabbi Yannai, teaching in the Mishnaic volume *Ethics of our Fathers*, says, "It is not within our power to explain either the tranquility of the wicked or the suffering of the righteous."[289] The Mishnah does not even attempt to answer this question, as any answer will not give due justice. Rabbi Yannai is stressing that some things are just impossible to be grasped by the human mind.[290] There is a reason for it, but the matter is not comprehensible.[291]

In truth, better a G-d that the human mind *cannot* fully understand than a god that can be fully understood. What kind of god would it be if the human mind could understand the full depths of his wisdom? Is the human mind on par with G-d?[292] Since no man shares G-d's absolute knowledge, no one is qualified to question His judgment.[293]

---

286   *Bereishis Rabbah* 65:7; *Koheles Rabbah* 11:9.

287   *Yeshayahu* [Isaiah] 55:8-9.

288   Colin McGinn, "Can We Solve the Mind-Body Problem?" *Mind* 98, no. 391 (July 1989): pgs. 349–366, brought down in Bitton, *The Awesome Creation* (2013), pg. 17.

289   *Avos* 4:19.

290   Commentary of the Meiri.

291   Rabbeinu Yonah, *Avos* ibid.

292   See similar concept in *Likkutei Moharan* 2:62.

293   *Shmos Rabbah* 6:1; Rashi on *Iyov* 23:13.

The issue of Divine justice is the only philosophical problem formally raised in the Torah. This inability to understand the ways of G-d perplexed even the greatest of prophets and sages, including David, Solomon, Jeremiah, Malachi, and Habbakuk.[294] Moses himself, the greatest of all prophets, could not understand the suffering of the righteous. He asked G-d, "Show me Your glory,"[295] which the Talmud explains is really an allusion to the grand question, "Why do the wicked prosper and the righteous suffer?"[296] It is of no surprise that when Moses had the opportunity to ask G-d any question, this was one that he chose, as it touches the very root of faith upon which the Torah rests.[297]

The Torah says that G-d responded by saying: "You will not be able to see My face," meaning that no mortal can gain the unadulterated perception of G-d Himself while alive. Even a man of the spiritual caliber of Moses was unable to experience this level of G-dly insight. G-d instead showed Moses His "back." The Chasam Sofer explains that "My back you will see" means that sometimes one can understand G-d's ways in retrospect, but one cannot see His Face as the events are unfolding. Sometimes a person is privy to sense the Divine Providence in a series of difficult events when looking back, but in the moment it is never possible.[298]

Rashi explains that G-d showing His "back" meant the "knot of His tefillin." There are a variety of explanations for what this means. One interesting idea is that when one gazes at the knot on the back of the head tefillin, he sees two straps extending and then disappearing to the front of the head. Just from that angle, it is difficult to understand what these straps are needed for, as they apparently lead to nowhere. If he sees the front of the head, he sees that they were attached to the boxes of the glorious head tefillin. When trying to understand Divine stewardship of the world, all one can view is the knot of the tefillin, a

---

294   See *HaIkkarim* 4:14.

295   *Shmos* [Exodus] 33:13.

296   *Brachos* 7a.

297   Ramban, commentary on *Iyov*.

298   See the introduction to the *Teshuvot Kol Aryeh*.

glimmer of the essence, which seems to lead to nowhere. In the World to Come, one will be able to see things from the front and clearly connect the dots of cause and effect in the universe.[299]

Rabbi Yissachar Frand, a contemporary scholar, comments on this using the analogy of a needlepoint work. The back looks like an unattractive mass of random knots, but the front is a beautiful work of art. Either way, "you shall not see My face," means that it is inherently impossible for a living mortal to see the full cosmic beauty being formed, and instead one can only see the "back," i.e., the apparently random, tumultuous, crisscrossing occurrences.

It was this dilemma of the suffering of the righteous that is grappled with throughout the book of Job. It is perhaps the most philosophical book of the Bible and essentially dedicated to this question. It is interesting, and yet of no surprise, that according to most opinions, this book was authored by Moses himself.[300] There is no real resolution in the book. However, the realization that there *is* a hidden answer, a rhyme and reason to how G-d orchestrates the world, was itself comforting to Job. The Ramchal writes that part of the reward that awaits one in the World to Come is the revelation of meaning to all of the suffering one endured during one's lifetime.[301]

LIMITED PERSPECTIVE

The idea that the human mind is only privy to a very limited perspective cannot be stressed enough. When situations seem one way, they can be quite another.

The Talmud says that Rabbi Yehoshua ben Levi would have frequent encounters with Elijah the Prophet.[302] On one such meeting there is a fascinating story that really demonstrates how limited the human perspective can be:[303]

---

299 Answer brought down by Dov Moshe Lipman, *Discover* (2006), pg. 112.
300 *Bava Basra* 14. Malbim, introduction to the book of Job, writes that Moses wrote it in order to console the enslaved Jewish nation. There are opinions that put the book of Iyov at a later date, see *Bava Basra* 15a; *Yerushalmi, Sotah* 5:6.
301 Theme in *Da'as Tevunos.*
302 *Sanhedrin* 98a.
303 *Yalkut Sippurim,* Parshas Vayeira 18; *Seder HaDoros,* Rabbi Yehoshua ben Levi, sec. 4, p.

Once, Rabbi Yehoshua ben Levi asked Elijah if he could accompany him on his way to learn from his conduct. Elijah refused him, saying that his mortal mind would raise too many questions and that there would be no time for explanations. Rabbi Yehoshua promised that he would not ask any questions. Elijah reluctantly agreed on the condition that if Rabbi Yehoshua would begin to ask questions, they would part ways.

They set off. Late in the day, they reached an old hut. An elderly couple was sitting outside. They were very poor, but also very welcoming of these guests, eagerly inviting them into their home. They could not offer much, but whatever they did have they earnestly and enthusiastically shared.

In the morning the couple bid their two guests farewell. Shortly after they had departed, Rabbi Yehoshua overheard Elijah praying that the only thing of value that this couple owned, their thin cow, should die. Rabbi Yehoshua was shocked, but kept to his agreement.

The following night they came to a beautiful mansion. The owner was very wealthy but very cold to them. He reluctantly let them in to spend the night, but did not feed them and barely spoke to them. The next morning Rabbi Yehoshua overheard Elijah praying that a wall in the mansion that was cracked should be quickly repaired and should remain strong and solid. Rabbi Yehoshua was baffled, yet stuck to their pact.

The following night they reached a wealthy neighborhood with a beautiful synagogue. Despite the affluence, nobody invited them home, and they had to sleep in the synagogue without eating that night. In the morning, when they were leaving, Elijah blessed the inhabitants of the city that they should all become leaders. Once again, Rabbi Yehoshua was left dumbfounded.

On the final night they reached a quainter synagogue. The

192.

people were warm and hospitable. Before leaving in the morning, Elijah blessed that only one of them becomes a leader.

Rabbi Yehoshua could no longer contain his curiosity. He told Elijah, that despite the consequences, he must know the rationale behind these strange behaviors. Elijah explained that the first elderly couple always performed acts of kindness. It was destined for the woman to pass away that day. By hosting them, she merited that the decree was almost entirely lifted. Elijah thus prayed that their cow should die instead. The death of the cow would really be a blessing for them.

In the mansion, the cracked wall had a great treasure buried inside. Because he was miserly, Elijah prayed that the wall should become strong so that he would not be able to benefit from the treasure.

In the affluent city, the idea that they should all become leaders in the city is not a blessing. The most destructive thing that can happen in a city is that everybody becomes a leader. In the other city, where the people were kind, they were given a genuine blessing that only one of them becomes a true leader.

At first, all of the blessings seemed unfounded and perplexing, yet when the perspective was broadened, all was fitting. There is a similar account related by the students of Rabbi Dov Ber, the Chassidic master known as the Maggid of Mezritch. During his lifetime, Rabbi Dov Ber, like his teacher the Baal Shem Tov, persistently prayed for the Jewish community. When he foresaw trouble on the horizon through his Divine intuition, he fervently prayed to annul the decrees on High against the community. After Rabbi Dov Ber passed away, he appeared to his students in a dream. They inquired as to why it seemed that he stopped praying on their behalf while he was in Heaven during their time of great need? He responded: "In Heaven we see that all that seems evil to you is a work of mercy."[304] From

---

304   Shlomo Zevin, *A Treasury of Chassidic Tales* (1981).

the heavenly vantage point, all that takes place in this world is seen clearly and objectively.

BEYOND WHAT THE EYE SEES

It has been said that the one who believes in G-d must explain the existence of evil; however, the non-believer has to explain the existence of everything else. How does a believer deal with the issue of theodicy?[305] Do men of faith simply ignore the suffering that takes place in the world?

The answer, of course, is no. To the believer, the visible world only represents part of the picture. The Jew sees a person as an entire spiritual continuum. The soul is an eternal entity, housed in the spiritual realms until its time to descend to the world.[306] The time that is spent in the material world in a physical body is just incidental to an eternal soul. Thus, there are two segments of life: the stage in which the soul is housed in the confines and restrictions of the body, and the stage where the soul experiences the infinity of the afterlife. Death is the portal from one state of being and the next.

Judaism views suffering not as random occurrences, but instead as systematic Divinely orchestrated challenges for the benefit of mankind. Torah literature takes into account the absolute meaning of good and evil, pain and suffering, considering the full person, body and soul, and the full experience of life in this world and the next. Jewish tradition mentions some key reasons as to why, in general, suffering and adversity occur, however it must be kept in mind that the practical application of these ideas cannot be applied to any particular case.

JUSTICE FOR ALL

G-d, being the source of true justice, rewards every good deed done by whoever does it, and punishes the evil deeds as well. G-d does not deny, even the wicked, compensation for their good deeds.[307]

---

305 Theodicy: Reconciling G-d's goodness and omnipotence in view of the existence of evil.
306 See for instance Rashi on *Yevamos* 63b (s.v. *guf*).
307 *Pesachim* 118a; *Bava Kamma* 38b; *Horayos* 10b.

The Divine system is just, and even logical: The evil person is rewarded for *any* good that he may have done, while living in this physical world,[308] and receives punishment for his wickedness only later on—losing out in the afterlife experience.[309] In the same way that a free ticket to a concert is meaningless to the one who does not appreciate music, someone who is immersed in wickedness will not apprehend or appreciate the spiritual bliss in the hereafter.[310] On the other hand, the righteous person experiences his punishments while in the temporary physical existence, and reaps his true reward in the everlasting afterlife, which is, qualitatively, far superior.[311]

In the grand scheme, the good person obtains the ultimate good, namely, in a way that will be experienced forever. The wicked, on the other hand, receives only a fleeting reward relegated exclusively to the passing pleasures of the physical world. In the long run, the good person really winds up with good and reward and the wicked suffer the consequences of their actions.

These are general guidelines. One should not assume that if someone has it good in *this* world, then that must mean that he is wicked and will not have reward in the afterlife. The opposite is also true—one should not assume that the person who appears to have the most struggles in this world must be righteous and getting his reward in the afterlife. The main thing is to realize that there is more to reality than meets the eye. The other important idea to keep in mind is that each person is judged according to his own unique upbringing, life situation, environment, influences, and potential. Only G-d, Who can know an individual in the absolute sense, with all of these factors considered, has the right and the ability to judge them.

---

308   *Kiddushin* 39a; *Sanhedrin* 111a; *Midrash Tehillim* 17:11, 86:7, 103:11, 119:8; *Derech Hashem* 2:2:6.

309   *Midrash Tehillim* 73:1; *Yalkut Shimoni* 2:808.

310   Someone immersed in worldly pleasures and lusts and the other falsities of life will not appreciate the G-dly radiance that the next world has to offer. This does not necessitate that the person is excluded forever from the afterlife, but may require some purging beforehand. Also a person's overall assessment of righteous or wicked is dependent on many things—some of which will be addressed in the main text.

311   *Kiddushin* 40b; *Bereishis Rabbah* 33:1; *Chovos HaLevavos* 4:3.

ATONEMENT FOR SINS

In this sense, suffering in this world for a righteous individual can serve as a means of atonement. At times, in order to achieve atonement for a certain misdeed, there must be a fitting degree of suffering.[312] In the big picture, this suffering is an act of kindness, insuring that the individual will easily acquire his share in the afterlife.[313] Through suffering one loses his drive toward materialism, which is often the cause of sin.[314] In this state of mind he can also assess his deeds, refocus on the spiritual, and be inspired to amend his ways. In this way, the previously soiled soul can be cleansed of misdeeds and not need purification in the next world. Thus the purpose of suffering, as it relates to atonement, are twofold: to galvanize an individual to return to G-d, or to spare him some of the cleansing process upon entrance into the next world.

AFFLICTIONS OF LOVE

Another appropriate comparison to the human perception of suffering is the parent who chastises his child who is playing with matches or who runs into the street. The slap is not a punishment for its own sake; it is a correction agent done only out of love for the well-being of the child. It is likewise necessary to view every affliction in life as a correction agent performed for the benefit of the person.[315] Interestingly, even in English the word *pain* has to do with purification. *Pain* derives from the Latin *poena* (punishment), and likewise to the Sanskrit root *pu* meaning purification.[316]

A related concept is the idea of *yissurim shel ahavah*, or afflictions of love. There are a variety of approaches to this idea in Jewish tradition.[317] The purpose of experiencing these afflictions is in order to

---

312   See *Brachos* 5a; *Mechilta, Shmos* 20:20; *Derech Hashem* 2:2:5.

313   See *Shmos Rabbah* 1:1; *Tanya, Iggeres HaTeshuva* 12.

314   *Shelah, B'asara Ma'amaros* 1:85a.

315   See *Devarim* [Deuteronomy] 8:8. Also *Michtav Me'Eliyahu* 1:21.

316   Kenneth L. Vaux, "Pain," in *Encyclopedia of Health Services Research*, edited by Ross M. Mullner (Thousand Oaks, CA: SAGE Publications, Inc., 2009), pgs. 890–91.

317   See *Brachos* 5a, and Rashi and *Pnei Yehoshua* there. Also see, Rabbeinu Bachya, *Shmos*

enhance the experience in the next world and it also serves as a means for personal growth.

The Midrash teaches that the human experience can, in some ways, be compared to an olive.[318] The essence of the olive, found in its oil, can only be extracted through squeezing or crushing; likewise, the essence of the person, found in his soul, can only be brought out and revealed through experiencing pressures and difficulties. It is these challenges that enable the innate potential, usually hidden within an individual, to surface. It is only through this crushing that the person will realize how much potential he has. These afflictions of love are the only means of extracting those unknown gifts.

Furthermore, sometimes what appears to be detrimental and painful is actually the very force that is helpful. Not that the anguish *leads to* healing, but that the misery itself *is* the healing. For example, when the body has a virus, the bacteria thrive at normal body temperature. In order to prevent the virus from spreading, the body turns up its heat, killing the bacteria. This heated temperature is what causes a fever. Most people look at a fever as a curse, when in reality it is the actual healing agent.

The Talmud hints that one should not be sad on cloudy days. "When the clouds are darker, the rain will be heavier."[319] Dark clouds bring about the promise of red apples and yellow bananas. We are often not able to know what is happening to us on a daily basis. Rain can serve as a lesson that G-d desires to provide with good, even though we may not understand the whole process.[320]

Another example could be pain in the body. Pain lets one know that something is wrong. One would not know to go the dentist to prevent his tooth from rotting away if one did not have a toothache. Thorns are the agent that protect the rose and allow it to grow; and likewise the stinger of the bee protects the honey of the hive.

Sometimes one is privy to see, in retrospect, how a challenging time in one's life was actually a healing agent. There are countless stories

---

5:22; Malbim, *Mishlei* 3:11; *Shelah, B'Asarah Ma'amaros* 5; *Derashos HaRan* 10.

318 *Yalkut Shimoni, Yirmiyahu*, 289.

319 *Taanis* 10a.

320 Based on Rabbi Avigdor Miller, *Praise My Soul*, #496.

of people getting laid off from a long-time job, only to get hired in a better place that enables them to express their talents and receive higher salary than their initial job. In the moment, the act of being fired seemed terrible and very challenging, but in the end was an agent that brought about a much more rewarding job situation. Other times one is not privy to see the ultimate good that has taken place. One must remember that the challenging situation itself is often the healing agent. Just like a fever, where one feels miserable, suffering can cause the same feeling, yet it must always be remembered that the distress is actually purifying.

G-d says in the book of Exodus: "All the diseases that I placed on Egypt, I will not place on you. I am G-d your Healer."[321] The verse, at first glance, seems contradictory. First G-d says that sickness will not come, but concludes the verse "I am G-d, your Healer," implying that sickness may indeed come and He will heal it!

The ambiguity can be explained as follows: When G-d brought the plagues to Egypt, He did so as a punishment for transgression. G-d informs the Jewish people that afflictions that come upon them will be of a different nature. The afflictions will not be punishments per se; they will instead be curative wounds.[322]

Consider a surgeon performing an operation. Although the doctor holds a knife in his hand, cuts flesh with it, and reveals blood, it can hardly be said that he is hurting the patient. All of the actions he is taking are clearly for the good of the patient. However, to an unknowing onlooker who never saw a surgical procedure before, this would indeed appear very cruel.[323] The same knife and same blood, when seen in their proper context, become a source of healing.

The same idea takes place when a child has his first cavity. He is strapped to the dentist chair, prodded with drills, scrapers, and suction machine, and is in excruciating pain. When he looks to his nearby

---

321   *Shmos* [Exodus] 15:26.

322   See explanations of verse by Rabbi Tzadok HaKohen *zt"l*, and essay of Rabbi Simcha Zissel Ziv *zt"l*.

323   Analogy brought down by the Lubavitcher Rebbe, *Iggros Kodesh* vol. 13, pg. 171. See also *Nachalas Yaakov*, commentary on the verse.

parent for support, not only is he not rescued from this cruelty, but his parent helps the dentist hold him down in order to keep him still. As the blood, saliva, and tears drip down his face he cannot imagine why he has been forsaken. The parent is willing to carry out this necessary evil in order to help the child. All of the actions in the dentist chair appear to the child to be an affliction, but are in reality a healing. He views his parents as cruel at the moment, whereas in reality they are being kind. The same way the parent is acting in the best interest of the child, likewise with the actions of our Father in Heaven.

REINCARNATION

The soul is one immortal continuum. The soul can be reincarnated several times in order to correct blemishes from its previous lifetime,[324] or to perfect something that it left unperfected in its mission.[325] The act of reincarnation is an act of benevolence, where G-d allows a second chance for the refinement of the soul. Purging and uplifting through challenges in life can also be the results of previous incarnations.

Rabbi Israel Meir Kagan zt"l, known as the Chofetz Chaim, told a parable as to why one individual might be poor and the other rich. He compares the plight of these people to a man visiting a synagogue: Upon entering the morning service the visitor sees many people being honored to read from the Torah scroll, seemingly at random. One after the other, they are called up from all different sides of the room. After the service, the visitor confronts the sexton and inquires about the order that these people were called up in. The sexton told him that because he was from out of town it must have appeared as if there was no rhyme or reason as to who was being called up and in what order they were following. The sexton then went on to explain to him the exact reasoning as to why these people were called up, and in

---

324   See Ramak (*Shiur Komah* 84, *Erech Gilgul*); Vilna Gaon on *Mishlei* 14:25; Chofetz Chaim (*Sfas Tamim*, ch. 4) who gives the example of reincarnation to return an object that was stolen, as well as several other examples.

325   "Every soul of Israel needs to be reincarnated many times in order to fulfill all 613 commandments of the Torah in thought, speech, and action." (*Tanya, Iggeres HaKodesh* 7, 29.)

that particular order. The Chofetz Chaim explained that since in this world we have such a limited scope of the full reality, we are here for a limited amount of time, and we are confined by what the senses can perceive, our initial assumption is that one being rich and the other poor is injustice; meanwhile, we do not realize that in the previous life, the soul of the rich was poor, and the poor one was rich. They faced and overcame those challenges already, and are now perfecting other challenges.[326]

When Moses requested from G-d to behold His face or full glory, he was told that no human being could grasp the Divine orchestration of the universe while living, and instead G-d showed Moses His back. The Midrash elaborates that G-d actually did reveal to Moses a clue of how things work, and why the righteous seem to suffer. The secret was reincarnation. Moses was shown the following scene:

> A prince, who was passing a river on horseback, stopped to drink and accidently dropped his bag of money. He then galloped away. Soon after, a poor boy and his mother, who were enslaved to a wicked lord, found this bag of money. The boy took the money and redeemed himself and his mother from slavery, and lived happily ever after. Not long after this, an old man chanced upon that same river spot. He took a drink and lay down to rest. In the meanwhile, the prince realized that he had dropped his purse at that spot and returned to search for it. Unable to find it, he awoke the old man, who swore he knew nothing of the bag of money. The prince did not believe him, and slew him.

> Upon seeing this, Moses was dumbfounded. Where was the Divine justice? G-d showed Moses another scene: A father and son, after amassing a small fortune for themselves, were happily walking on their way. All of a sudden a man with a sword appeared. He took the money and killed the father. All the while, a prince stood to the side witnessing the event, but did nothing to help.

---

326   Based on Yoel Shwartz, *Shoah: A Jewish Perspective on Tragedy in the Context of the Holocaust* (1990), pgs. 44–45.

G-d explained that the old man in the first story, who seemed perfectly innocent, was a reincarnation of the man who killed the father and stole the money in the second story. The child who struck it rich, by finding the bag of money, in the first story, was a reincarnation of the child who had his money taken in the second story. The prince, who in the second story did not help the father and son, was penalized in his next incarnation, described in the first story, by losing his money. He also kills the old man, whom he should have killed in the second story when he was negligent in helping. Moses then saw that the way G-d runs the world is beyond reproach, and carried out measure for measure.[327]

In essence, Jewish tradition teaches that many of the most difficult situations in life can be viewed as one part in an ongoing chain of reincarnation.[328] There is discussion in Jewish tradition that the deaths of young children, stillbirths, disabilities, or disease are rooted in the secret of reincarnation. In other words these souls often come from lofty sources on high and only need limited time or limited abilities in order to refine and uplift the aspect of their soul that needs correcting.[329] Suffering without purpose is very lonely and disheartening. Having general guidelines to the significance inherent in some of the most difficult situations may not take away the

---

327 See Yitzchok Fingerer, *Search Judaism* (2009), pgs. 264–266.

328 *Nishmas Chaim* 4:11.

329 For example, it is known that the Steipler Gaon and the Chazon Ish would stand in reverence in front of the disabled, believing them to be pure souls, who needed very limited abilities in this world in order to accomplish their soul's mission. The Chazon Ish would say that they were exempt from the commandments because the Al-mighty found within their souls a purity that did not need the perfection and discipline of the mitzvos. See, for example, Jonathan Sacks, *Faith in the Future* (1997), pg. 219; Avraham J. Twerski, *Positive Parenting: Developing Your Child's Potential* (2004), pgs. 33–34.

The Lubavitcher Rebbe also answered in this light, when asked about the passing of a young girl; see *Toras Menachem*, Menachem Tzion II (1995), pg. 568. It is also known that the Baal Shem Tov would comfort the parents of children who had passed away young by explaining that their child had a very lofty soul sent down to live for a very short time just in order to complete the original mission that the soul had been sent for. For an alternative view as to how reincarnation plays a role of completion in these difficult life scenarios, see *Nishmas Chaim* 4:11; Maharal, *Tiferes Yisrael* 63.

emotional hardship, but certainly brings meaning, relevance, and perhaps peace of mind.

PRESERVING FREE WILL

An additional reason why G-d must, at times, inflict suffering in the world is connected with preserving human free will. Most evils that occur in the world are the result of human beings. G-d grants free will.[330] Without free will a human being would no longer be human, becoming instead a puppet or robot. Human beings were created with free will in order to give them reward for doing the right things. Without free will there could be no credit given nor would anything ever truly be accomplished. The existence of evil is the price paid for human freedom.

Furthermore, if sinners would always be immediately punished, and the wicked would be in a visibly worse-off situation in the world, there would be little temptation to sin. The choice between good and evil would be too clear and no longer a choice. G-d, therefore, allows evil to look alluring and accessible, in order to keep His key element of free will in play.[331]

G-d created the world for the purpose of bestowing on His creations the greatest possible good.[332] Not only to receive the greatest possible good, but also to get it in the greatest possible way. In order to fully appreciate the good they are receiving, they must earn the reward, for undeserved reward does not bring the same pleasure.[333] The reason that G-d allows for the existence of evil in the world is so that a person should have the opportunity and temptation to do the wrong deeds and instead choose the right deeds, thereby *deserving* G-d's bounty.

The whole nature of the human being means responsibility for his decisions. This involves being free to act wrongly or to act rightly. There can be no advanced guarantee that a truly free being will never

---

330   *Brachos* 5a; Rambam, *Teshuva*, ch. 5.
331   *Sha'ar HaShamayim* 1:22; *Michtav Me'Eliyahu* 1:18–21.
332   See *Derech Hashem* 1:2.
333   Gaining from something not earned is termed "shameful bread" in many places in Jewish tradition. See *Maggid Meisharim, Bereishis*; and the beginning of *Da'as Tevunos* of the Ramchal.

choose incorrectly. The idea that G-d should have created beings that would not have the desire to sin is tantamount to saying that He should not have created people.[334] The necessary evil that comes along with the ability to choose is the necessity of evil to exist.

What about suffering in the world? Although the bulk of human pain can be attributed to misused human free will, there are still causes of pain that are independent of human will, like famine, flooding, and other natural disasters. The boundary, though, between the suffering caused by human folly and that which falls upon mankind from without, can often be blurred.

To illustrate: There is a hunger problem in many areas of the globe. At first glance, this seems like a problem that has befallen the region from the outside; however, these days, food shortages are often brought about by human hands, be it via political strife or legal concerns. This unfortunately causes food to go to waste, instead of into the mouths of the hungry. Furthermore, the term "natural disaster" can often be a means to skirt the blame onto nature for something that was poor human planning. Wherever so-called natural disasters like floods exist around the world, there are frequently people who have cut down the forests that buffer rainfall, paved the grasslands that allow rain to soak into the soil, and built their homes right in the middle of gullies and natural drainage channels. Damaging river banks, altering natural waterways, and creating poor drainage patterns in urban areas can directly cause floods that would not have otherwise occurred. Instead of blaming themselves for building their homes in the middle of a flash-flood zone, they instead cry out to the heavens, questioning why their home was destroyed.

Obviously, not all floods are the fault of the people affected by them. In 2011, there were large floods happening in Brisbane, Australia, that seemed completely out of character for the region there. While the residents cannot be blamed for being caught up in this flooding, ironically, many Australians will rebuild their homes right back in the

---

334   While G-d is certainly capable of creating any kind of beings He desires, He did not do so, because they would be lacking the ability of entering into a personal relationship with Him by a free and uncompelled response to His love.

same locations devastated by this flood. The same can be said about rebuilding the low-lying regions of New Orleans after Hurricane Katrina. It is extremely likely that sometime in the future another strong hurricane will impact the same regions affected the first time in this geographically unfortunate area. The question is not so much *if* the area will be affected again, but *when*. The same idea can be said about people who build their homes next to large forests that inevitably catch fire every few decades. Many times the resonant "why" question, uttered by the person undergoing the suffering caused by natural disasters, would be better addressed instead at himself or his fellow, rather than at his Maker.[335]

Additionally, unwise agricultural practices and deforestation certainly intensify the effects of a drought, and likewise, although humans do not cause tornados or hurricanes, their activities in an area can make the effect of these natural disasters worse. While natural disasters certainly do exist, a significant majority can instead be classified as human initiated or exacerbated.

Parenthetically, it is worth at least mentioning the perceived suffering of animals as well. They have no free will. Why would a Merciful G-d allow predatory animals to so gruesomely devour their prey? The animal ecosystem must be balanced for it to properly continue. Every ecosystem has some sort of predators. Regarding deer, for example, many local government municipalities will reintroduce predators back into the wild in their area because the absence of these predators leads to deer overpopulation, as there is nothing to cull the vulnerable prey. The next step with the overabundance of animals is that they overgraze and end up dying of starvation, not to mention the negative result of deforestation that comes with it. By controlling the size of prey populations, predators also help slow down the spread of disease. In these situations, the presence of the predators ironically enhances the overall survivability of the herds on which they have preyed. In order to perpetuate a world that

---

335 Natural disaster information gleaned from: Mike Adams, "Why Most Natural Disasters Aren't Natural at All," NaturalNews.com, January 16, 2011.

functions under established laws of nature, the predator and prey relationship is essential.

"Natural" suffering, whether it is caused by humans or external factors, is inextricably mingled together in the human experience and built into the very structure of the world. It is not possible to show how each item of human pain serves the ultimate Divine purpose of good, but it can be shown in a general sense that the Divine purpose of the world, as expounded upon in Judaism, could not be carried out in a world designed as a paradise.[336]

FREE WILL WITHOUT PAIN?

If people would have free will, meaning that they could choose to do wrong, yet the world was a place without the possibility of experiencing any sort of pain or suffering, the consequences would be very far-reaching. John Hick, professor of philosophy at the University of Birmingham, introduces this thought-provoking situation in his counterfactual hypothesis:

> For example, no one could ever injure anyone else: the murderer's knife would turn to paper or his bullets to thin air; the bank safe, robbed of a million dollars, would miraculously become filled with another million dollars; fraud, deceit, conspiracy, and treason would somehow always leave the fabric of society undamaged. Again, no one would ever be injured by accident: the mountain-climber, steeplejack, or playing child falling from a height would float unharmed to the ground; the reckless driver would never meet with disaster. There would be no need to work, since no harm could result from avoiding work; there would be no call to be concerned for others in time of need or danger, for in such a world there could be no real needs or dangers. To make possible this continual

---

336   Much of the discussion in this section brought from John Hick, *Philosophy of Religion* (1973).

series of individual adjustments, nature would have to work by "special providences" instead of running according to general laws which men must learn to respect on penalty of pain or death. The laws of nature would have to be extremely flexible: sometimes gravity would operate, sometimes not; sometimes an object would be hard and solid, sometimes soft. There could be no sciences, for there would be no enduring world structure to investigate. In eliminating the problems and hardships of an objective environment, with its own laws, life would become like a dream in which, delightfully but aimlessly, we would float and drift at ease.

It is evident that our present ethical concepts would have no meaning in such a world. He continues:

If the notion of harming someone is an essential element in the concept of a wrong action, in our hedonistic paradise there could be neither wrong actions nor any right actions in distinction from wrong. Courage and fortitude would have no point in an environment in which there is, by definition, no danger or difficulty. Generosity, kindness, the agape aspect of love, prudence, unselfishness, and all other ethical notions which presuppose life in a stable environment, could not even be formed. Consequently, such a world, however well it might promote pleasure, would be very ill-adapted for the development of the moral qualities of human personality. In relation to this purpose it would be the worst of all possible worlds.

He concludes that it seems that in order to create an environment intended to make possible the growth in free beings of the finest characteristics of personal life, it must have a lot in common with our present world. It must operate according to general and dependable laws; and it must involve real dangers, difficulties, problems, obstacles, and possibilities of pain, failure, sorrow, frustration, and defeat.

This world, with all of its heartaches and challenges, is quite well-attuned to the goal of developing righteousness in individuals.

NATIONAL TRAGEDIES

Sometimes, as a punishment for the collective sins of the Jewish people, G-d hides His face. When the Jewish people abandon G-d and turn to alien worship, G-d likewise "abandons" them to the natural order. In other words, the world is perceived as a series of random occurrences. These "natural events" develop into tragedies. Notwithstanding, each event has its purpose in the Divine plan.[337]

One Piece of the Cosmic Puzzle

As in the above allegories of the surgical observation or the child with the cavity, the human being must always consider everything that takes place in the world as one piece of a cosmic puzzle. It is presumptuous to try and pinpoint why there appears to be challenges in his life or in the world when he only has access to one piece in this puzzle. Would anyone try to give an assessment of characters and events in a film that he had only seen a few minutes of?

It must be remembered that even a work of art can look like an abstruse and unattractive mass of strokes and colors shortly before its completion. Human history is the masterpiece of G-d. It is quite audacious to critique the greatest artist before the masterpiece is complete—even though at this point it seems like history is fraught with suffering and injustice.[338]

THE HOLOCAUST

No discussion about suffering or national tragedy would be complete without mentioning our six million brothers and sisters who were murdered at the hands of the vicious Nazis. No matter of words could appropriately begin to justify how such an event could occur. Louis Shifier, a gentile who was an inmate in a concentration camp,

---

337   For deeper insight into this topic see, Rashi, *Chullin* 139b, in regard to Esther and the story of Purim; *Meshech Chochmah*, *Devarim* 31:17.

338   Based on the commentary of Rabbi Avraham Chaim Feuer on *Tehillim* 92.

said that "one can write about war, even if he has not participated in it, but it is impossible to write about concentration camps unless one has lived in one."[339]

INCOMPREHENSIBLE

To try and assemble reasons for why this horror of horrors took place is futile, especially in a generation so closely affected by it, where survivors and children of survivors are many. None of the above-mentioned perspectives properly capture the enormity of both the cruelty demonstrated by the Nazis, and the number of innocents killed. The inner reasons of why this event had to take place must be dismissed as completely beyond the grasp of what the human being is able to comprehend. The acclaimed psychiatrist and survivor of the Holocaust, Viktor Frankl, posed the following thought-provoking question to a group:

> [He asked:] Could a certain ape that was being prodded with needles for medicinal development purposes ever understand the reason for its suffering? The group replied that it would not because of its limited intelligence. He then asked: "Is it not conceivable that there is still another dimension, a world beyond man's world; a world in which the question of an ultimate meaning of human suffering would find an answer?[340]

Rabbi Elchonon Wasserman *zt"l*, who was killed at the hands of the Nazis, told a parable that illustrates the inability of human beings to comprehend the Divine plan, yet emphasizes that there is plan and purpose. The story was told in response to the events surrounding the Holocaust, explaining why they were happening:

> *Once there was a city-dweller who came to a farmer to learn about farming. The farmer stressed to the visitor that the key*

---

339 Shabbatai, *As Sheep to the Slaughter* (1963), pg. 46.
340 In his *Man in Search for Meaning*, pg. 186.

to faming was patience, and that appreciation about what a farmer does can only really be seen at the end of his work.

The visitor saw a beautiful and attractive piece of land filled with grass. The visitor stood in horror as the farmer plowed up the grass and turned the beautiful green field into a mass of brown ditches. Then the farmer showed him a sack full of plump kernels of wheat, nutritious grain, and seemingly wastefully dropped the kernels into the open ground, and covered them up with soil. The city-dweller was mortified.

A few months passed, and the farmer took the man into the field where the stalks were fully grown. The city-dweller was relieved that there had been good made from the destruction. No sooner could he breathe a sigh of relief before the farmer came with his sickle and chopped them all down. The visitor watched in shock as the farmer once again destroyed his beautiful scene. Then the farmer took his bundles and crushed them until they became a mass of straw and loose kernels. He pulverized the kernels until they were dust-like. He mixed the dust with water, formed the shape of a loaf, and baked it into bread. The visitor saw that all of his previous worry and frustration at each step of the process were unfounded, for he now realized the purpose of each step.

Hashem is the farmer, and human beings are the fools who do not begin to understand His ways or the outcome of His plan. Only when the process is complete will all the Jewish people know why all this happened. Then, when Moshiach has finally come, we will know why all of this had to be. Until then we must be patient and have faith that everything, even when it seems destructive and painful, is part of the process that will produce goodness and beauty.[341]

There was a similar answer given to someone who questioned G-d

---

341   Simcha Wasserman, *Reb Elchonon: The Life and Ideals of Rabbi Elchonon Bunim Wasserman of Baranovich* (1984).

while speaking to Rabbi Avrohom Yeshaya Karelitz zt"l, the Chazon Ish. He responded: The simple person gets upset when he sees a tailor cutting good material. He is too ignorant to understand that the tailor is making a new garment. We are, likewise, too small and puny to understand the ways of G-d, but we must recognize that even the most incomprehensible eras of history are a part of the Divine plan. If we could see the complete design, we would understand each of its parts.[342]

These stories illustrate that the Holocaust must simply be considered beyond human grasp. At the same time, it may not be dismissed as without purpose and reason—just not a purpose and reason that humankind is privy to at this point. As Rabbi Shem Klingberg, the Zaloshitzer Rebbe, said when he was conducting the third Sabbath meal in the Plaszow Concentration Camp near Cracow: "The Holocaust is completely incomprehensible to the human mind. When Moshiach comes, only then will it be revealed to mankind the course of history."[343]

Along those lines, many Chassidic masters and mystics saw a glimmer of light in the darkness that was the Holocaust. Before the world takes on the novelty and beauty that is the world of Moshiach, it must purge out all negativity. This was the last straw. According to what they believed, all of this pain was the birth pangs or expected suffering before Moshiach comes.[344]

The Holocaust also does not disprove the existence of G-d, or His Providence, in any way. The specific inner reasons of how it was allowed on High, or its meaning in the grand scheme of things, may never be fully grasped by human beings[345]—but that does not negate

---

342 Parable brought down in many places; see, for one, Nachman Bulman, *Longing for Dawn: Inspiration and Consolation* (1995), pg. 34.

343 See Menashe Unger, *Sefer Kedoshim* (1967), pg. 151.

344 See Ehrenberg, *Artzei Levanon*, pg. 171. Also *Sefer Kedoshim*, pg. 110.

345 It is common that when a national calamity takes place, the sages of the time reveal some of the potential reasons for the occurrences. This is done so that the people of the time can know where to properly do *teshuva*, retrace their steps and make amends accordingly. This is something practiced throughout Jewish history. The Talmud (*Yoma* 4b) relates that the First Temple in Jerusalem was destroyed because of prevalent idol-worship, sexual

G-d. In some ways, it may even strengthen the need for an Absolute authority in the world. In those days, the German people were considered the apex of culture and morality, yet these same people committed perhaps the worst atrocities in human history. One key lesson from the Holocaust is that morality and civilized existence is possible only through the acceptance of Divine authority.[346]

---

immorality, and bloodshed. The Second Temple was destroyed because of baseless hatred, among other things (*Yerushalmi, Yoma* 1:1; *Bavli, Yoma* 9a-b). The Chasid Yavetz was a part of the Spanish Expulsion and wrote *Ohr HaChaim*, in which he partially attributed its cause to Spanish Jewry's putting a central focus on philosophy and secular knowledge in lieu of Torah knowledge.

Some contemporary sages have ascribed at least peripheral reasons for the catastrophic events of the Holocaust as being chastisement for assimilation and the effort to secularize Judaism. In 1927, twelve years prior to the Second World War, Rabbi Meir Simcha HaCohen of Dvinsk *zt"l*, famously and eerily wrote in his *Meshech Chochma* (Bechukosai) about the last stage before the destruction of the generation that "thinks of Berlin as his Jerusalem." He added, "The fierce storm of destruction will emanate from Berlin and leave but a scant remnant." See likewise the Maggid of Kelm quoted in Rabbi Wasserman's *Ichvisa Dimeshicha* (1942), pg. 61; Introduction to *Teshuvos Achiezer*, vol. 3; Steipler, *Chayey Olam*, pg. 37.

Many people in Europe, and Germany in particular, sought to leave the "antiquated" laws and values of traditional Judaism and instead give full allegiance to their host country. They exchanged the eternal longing to return and rebuild Jerusalem with the complacency and pseudo-comfort of life in exile. One such example, Rabbi Shimshon Raphoel Hirsch *zt"l*, in his *Judaism Eternal*, describes Tisha B'Av night in 1828 Germany when the clergyman of a new temple in Hamburg condemned the mourning of the Holy Temple. He said that crying over a Jewish homeland is treason against the Fatherland. Instead he said, "Germany is our Palestine, Hamburg is our Jerusalem, and this temple is our Holy Temple."

Not all contemporary sages agree that one can pinpoint specific sins that resulted in the Holocaust. For instance, the Lubavitcher Rebbe rejects that specific sins could be the real inner meaning behind the events of the Holocaust, stating: "The destruction of six million Jews in such a horrific manner that surpassed the cruelty of all previous generations could not possibly be because of a punishment for sins. Even the Satan himself could not possibly find a sufficient number of sins that would warrant such genocide! There is absolutely no rationalistic explanation for the Holocaust except for the fact that it was a Divine decree...why it happened is above human comprehension, but it is definitely not because of punishment for sin." See *Sefer HaSichos* 5751 Vol. 1, pg. 233. The Rebbe adds, "On the contrary: All those who were murdered in the Holocaust are called holy ones since they were murdered in sanctification of G-d's name."

346   See *Likkutei Sichos*, vol. 33, pg. 260. In other words, if not for the existence of an Absolute law in the world that "murdering innocents is absolutely wrong," then (to play devil's advocate) who's to say that what the Nazi's did was inherently wrong? Maybe it was just subjectively wrong—meaning that I think it is wrong, and others like me think that it's

SPIRITUAL UNDERPINNINGS

In every synagogue, on any given week, the same segment of the Torah is being read. The full text of the Torah is divided up into fifty-four portions that are completed over the course of a year. In two portions in particular, the Torah speaks about extreme punishments that will befall the Jewish people in the future. These sections are called the *tochacha* or chastisement. The names of these portions are *Bechukosai* and *Ki Savo*.[347] There is perhaps no more mysterious a concept, and challenge to faith, than the atrocities that are foretold in these portions to happen to the Jewish nation in the future. At the same time, the chilling accuracy of the horrific retribution spelled out so clearly, affirm its Divine origin. The commentaries mention that the fact that the events will line up so exactly with the descriptions in the Torah, one will have no choice but to see that this was under Divine decree and not by chance.[348]

One such correlation is found in the writings of Rabbi Eliyahu Kremer *zt"l*, known as the Vilna Gaon, who lived in the eighteenth century. He maintained that all of the events that would befall the Jewish people throughout history are hinted at in the Torah, and that all of the events of the sixth millennium are found in the book of Deuteronomy.[349] In other words, the ten Torah portions that split up the book of Deuteronomy correspond to the ten centuries in that millennium.[350] The seventh century during the sixth millennium, which incorporates the years of the Holocaust, corresponds with

---

wrong. But why is my subjective outlook of its "wrongness" any more empirically true or valuable than the vast majority of the people of the time who thought it was not wrong? Without absolute "rights" and "wrongs," one can only claim it was wrong in the subjective sense. The issue with that is: Of what value is calling something (subjectively) wrong? For why is any person's assessment more correct than another's? Absolute morality, by definition, cannot be man-made, as anything man-made is inherently subjective. If one can utter the words that the events that took place were "absolutely wrong," then they, of necessity, must have an "Absolute" [non-human] source.

347   *Vayikra* [Leviticus] 26:14; *Devarim* [Deuteronomy] 28:15-68.

348   See for example the commentary of the Ramban in these sections.

349   Years 5000–5999 according to the Jewish calendar, from Adam, the first man.

350   Netzavim and Vayeilach are counted as one.

the Torah portion of *Ki Savo*, which contains all of the curses and suffering.[351]

Rabbi Eliyahu Dessler *zt"l* relates that even the whole episode about how Hitler took power in Germany is historically mind-boggling. He writes that the way of the world is that talent and abilities facilitate one to the position of leadership. Yet out of nowhere, this lunatic and his cohorts, may their names be obliterated, all of a sudden rose from their insignificant works and ascended quickly to become the absolute rulers of the German state. Hitler was a very poor, crude, paranoid, narcissistic, anxious, depressed, uneducated paper-hanger,[352] yet in no time became like a supreme being to the German people.[353]

One can certainly see parallel in the Nazis with the archetypal enemy of the Jewish people—the nation of Amalek. This was a people that embodied evil. The Torah describes the boundless, baseless hatred of the Amalekites on the Jewish people. The Jew is obligated to "remember what this nation did."[354] When any nation throughout history attempts to wipe out the Jewish people they can be considered, at least symbolically, the modern manifestation of Amalek.[355] Haman, who sought to destroy the Jewish nation, as told over in the book of Esther and commemorated on Purim, was a descendant of Amalek. In the Passover Haggadah, Jews recite, "In every generation they rise up to destroy us," which refers to Amalek who each time are embodied in a different nation.[356]

Nazi Germany may have an even more inherent connection with the nation of Amalek. There is an eerie statement recorded in the Talmud. It says that "Jacob said before G-d: 'Master of the universe, do not grant to Esau the wicked, the desire of heart, draw not out his bit,' this refers to Germamia of Edom, for should they go forth, they would

---

351   Rabbi Yissachar Dov Rubin, *Talelei Oros* (2002), *Devarim*, pgs. 4–5.

352   Dr. Fritz Redlich, professor emeritus of psychiatry at both Yale University and the University of California at Los Angeles, in his recent work *Hitler: Diagnosis of a Destructive Prophet*.

353   *Michtav Me'Eliyahu*, vol. 1, pg. 204.

354   *Devarim* [Deuteronomy] 25:17.

355   See *Ish Ha'emunah*, pgs. 101–102.

356   See *Yalkut Me'am Loez, Devarim*, part 3, pg. 977.

destroy the entire world."[357] Rashi comments that Germamia is "the name of a monarchy from the kingdom of Edom." Rabbi Yaakov Emden *zt"l* comments on this Rashi, as the Vilna Gaon comments on the word Germamia as well, that it refers to "Germania" or Germany.

The Talmud continues that there are 300 crowned heads in Germamia of Edom and 365 chieftains in Rome, and that every day one set goes forth to meet the other and one of them is killed, and they have all the trouble of appointing a king again. In other words, Germany does not rise to power because its kingship is scattered and is in constant struggle with Rome. Germany is divided into "300 heads." Notably, after the middle ages, which saw a unified Britain and France, Germany remained a crazy patchwork of some *three hundred* individual states.[358] It appears that the Jewish sages, quite a few generations before the Second World War, foresaw that a modern Amalek would show itself as Germany.[359] Remarkably, when Hitler came to power, his strength was gained after *unifying* the German people, and *aligning* itself with Italy (Rome), as opposed to conflicting with it, just as the Talmud relates.[360]

There are many fascinating parallels discussed that link the Nazi war criminals that were executed in the Nuremberg Trials and the ten sons of Haman executed in the book of Esther. Usually verses in the Torah or Megillah are written uninterrupted. When the format is different, there is a lesson to be learned. For thousands of years, in every scroll of the book of Esther, the ten sons of Haman who were hanged were

---

357 *Megillah* 6b.

358 William L. Shirer, *The Rise and Fall of the Third Reich* (1990), pg. 91. See also Hebrew Encyclopedia, "Germany."

359 There is a known story that Rabbi Yosef Chaim Sonnenfeld *zt"l* would not participate in the reception of Kaiser Wilhelm II of Germany when he visited Jerusalem in November of 1898, as he had a tradition from the Vilna Gaon that Germany was connected with Amalek (see *Mara De'Ara D'Yisrael*, part I, pg. 200). See also Sonnenfeld, *The Man on the Wall* [Hebrew](1976), pg. 108.

   Furthermore, the Bobover Rebbe, Rabbi Ben Zion Halberstam *zt"l* was killed by the Nazis in 1941. He wrote that the number 7 represents holiness in Judaism. He connected the fact that the number 7 in Germany is written with a line through it, with how Amalek is always trying to strike out and eradicate holiness. (See *Hamelakeit*, cited from Dovid Meisels, *Shabbos Secrets* (2003), pg. 148.)

360 The Germans also did not lose the war until after Italy fell to the Allies.

always written in a column, and have a large space to the left, followed by the word "and." See below:

וְאֵת | פַּרְשַׁנְדָּ֫תָא
וְאֵת | דַּלְפוֹן
וְאֵת | אַסְפָּתָא:
וְאֵת | פּוֹרָתָא
וְאֵת | אֲדַלְיָא
וְאֵת | אֲרִידָתָא:
וְאֵת | פַּרְמַשְׁתָּא
וְאֵת | אֲרִיסַי
וְאֵת | אֲרִידַי
עֲשֶׂרֶת   וַיְזָתָא:

According to the sages, the large space and the word "and" on the left-hand column denotes replication, meaning that there is "another ten" going to be hanged in addition to the ten sons of Haman.[361] It is interesting that exactly ten Nazi leaders were executed on October 16, 1946, and specifically through the means of hanging, which was obscure and not practiced at the time, especially in a military tribunal. There was supposed to be an eleventh person killed, Herman Goering, but he committed suicide. Paralleling that, the Midrash says that Haman had a daughter who committed suicide. Furthermore, in the Megillah text, as depicted in the above image, there are three letters that are exceptionally smaller: *tav, shin, zayin*; and an exceptionally large *vav*. *Vav* has the numeric equivalent of six. The large *vav* corresponds to the sixth millennium, which began at the year 5000 on the Jewish calendar. The small *tav, shin, zayin* have a numerical value of 707, all together equaling 5707. Astonishingly, 5707 on the Jewish calendar corresponds with the secular year 1946, which was when

---

361   See *Me'am Loez*, Esther (Or Hadas, 5734), pg. 237.

these men were hung. Perhaps even more captivating, is that according to the eyewitnesses present, Julius Streicher, with the noose around his neck, moments before he was hanged shouted out, "Purim Fest 1946!"[362] The last riveting detail is that the date of the hanging, October 16, 1946, was the Jewish festival of Hoshana Rabbah, which tradition teaches is the day of final judgment.[363]

The similarities are quite gripping. Hitler and head Nazi officials knew about Purim and sought to halt its observance. Hitler banned the reading of the book of Esther and ordered that all synagogues be closed and barred on Purim day. He also said that "unless Germany is victorious, Jewry could then celebrate the destruction of Europe by a second triumphant Purim Festival."[364] The point is that although nobody can pinpoint the reasons for the events of the Holocaust, there is more to the picture than meets the eye.

Despite the broadened perspective laid out above with analogies from Holocaust survivors and parallels of those events found in Scripture and commentaries, questions still remain. Questions are perfectly legitimate, but should be asked from the right internal place. The believer knows that G-d created the human being with a mind to be inquisitive. The believer may turn to G-d and say, "I know You are there, and I know You are kind, this makes no sense to me, why does it have to be this way?"

During the Holocaust, many Jews chose to abandon their faith, while many others steadfastly clung to theirs. The difference between the two was not that one group had unanswered questions, and the other group had answers to their questions—neither had answers. Perhaps the difference is whether or not the faith was solidified beforehand or not. That would affect what one does with questions on faith.

There is a powerful lesson taught in the play *The Trial of G-d* written by Holocaust survivor Elie Wiesel. He writes about an event that he

---

362   *New York Herald Tribune*, Oct. 16, 1946; *Newsweek*, Oct. 28, 1946, "Foreign Affairs," pg. 45. See also Burton Andrus, *I Was the Nuremberg Jailer* (1970), pg. 197.
363   See *Yerushalmi, Rosh Hashana* 84:8; *Zohar*, Tzav 32.
364   Elliot Horowitz, *Reckless Rites: Purim and the Legacy of Jewish Violence* (2006), pg. 91; *New York Times*, January 31, 1944.

witnessed in Auschwitz. There were three Jewish scholars, who were also in the camp, holding a mock trial, a rabbinic court of law to indict the Al-mighty. The following is a small caption:

> The trial lasted several nights. Witnesses were heard, evidence was gathered, conclusions were drawn, all of which issue finally in a verdict: the Lord G-d Al-mighty, Creator of Heaven and Earth, was found *guilty* of crimes against Creation and humankind. And then, after what Wiesel describes as an "infinity of silence," the Talmudic scholar looked at the sky and said, "It's time for evening prayers," and the members of the tribunal recited *Maariv*, the evening service.[365]

In other words, questions may exist, and from the human standpoint there does not seem to be any way to make sense of anything, and it's nighttime and it's dark, but serving G-d is still a must. Questions are appropriate, but it must not detract from the unwavering commitment to Judaism.

The most important thing, at the end of the day, is not how to understand the Holocaust, but what to do in reaction to it. If pain and despair disheartens people, and as a result the new generation of Jews is not raised with a strong commitment to their Jewish identities, then Nazism has indeed accomplished its goal. If, instead, the nation rises as a proud generation committed to their Jewish spiritual growth, then the Jewish nation has truly been victorious. As Israeli historian Mordechai Bar-On once wrote, "I belong to the generation which was born without faith. When I read the literature about the Holocaust my reaction is, 'I shall not die, but live.' I say to myself, what can I do in response to this horrible act? My answer is to strengthen my faith in, and my attachment to, Judaism."[366]

---

365   All from Robert McAfree Brown, *Introduction to The Trial of God* (1986), pg. vii.
366   *Pehatim*, Elul 5727.

FINAL WORDS

In essence, this section has gone through the perspectives of the greatest prophets and sages up to the present, with different insights into human suffering. While the specifics have not been answered, and cannot be answered, one can at least gain from an enhanced understanding about the general principles of how suffering fits in the Divine plan. May it be that we all witness very soon that "G-d will wipe away the tears from every face," speedily in our days.[367]

---

367   *Yeshayahu* [Isaiah] 25:8.

TORAH

It is logical that G-d created the world with a purpose. What does He want? What is the purpose? For thousands of years, Jews have believed that the Torah was given by G-d at Mount Sinai. Is that a reasonable belief? What is the Oral Torah, and why is it necessary? Did the Talmudic sages have any special intuitive insights? What about the Bible critics? Do contemporary discoveries prove—or disprove—the Torah?

Let's begin to explore.

REASONABLE APPROACH TO THE DIVINE ORIGIN OF THE TORAH

I t is logical that the Creator would provide a manual on how to function in the world that He created. Every car manufacturer provides a manual on how to operate the car he has created. Every appliance and electronic gadget has instructions on how to put it together properly. Every game has rules that make it into the game that it is. Likewise, common sense dictates that G-d provided a manual for human beings to know what to do in life. The Torah is the manual for life that was given to the Jewish people.

NATIONAL REVELATION

The founding of the Jewish religion is counted from the giving of the Torah at Mount Sinai. Even though Abraham, Isaac, and Jacob lived several generations earlier and their descendants were considered Jews, it was not until the giving of the Torah that all of the responsibilities of the Jewish people became binding. Judaism makes an assertion about its founding that is unique compared to every other religion that ever was. Virtually every religion is founded upon the lone testimony of a single individual.[368] This person claims to experience a revelation, receiving Divine information from above, and then proceeds to inform the world of this encounter. Even religions that do not believe in an omnipotent deity still usually claim that their

---

368 Or at best a small group of people.

secret spiritual insights were attained by a single person who then teaches others the path. The details of these encounters are typically found in the professed holy books of each religious group. The story line of where this special information came from can be described as the faith's own "revelation narrative."

How Other Faiths Form

- Christianity essentially begins when Paul encounters Jesus after his death while on the road to Damascus.[369] He then pursues telling the masses of his newfound truth.
- The Latter-Day Saints begin with the Angel Moroni, the guardian of the golden plates (the source of the Book of Mormon), revealing himself to Joseph Smith Jr., who then shares his findings.
- Buddhism begins when Prince Siddhartha Gautama settles beneath a Bodhi tree to put himself into a trance. He passes through the eight stages of Transic Insight, and becomes a Buddha.[370] He got up from that lone experience and began teaching.
- When Muhammad was forty years old, Muslims claim that the angel Gabriel appeared to him in a cave where he was meditating, and, over the next twenty-three years, revealed to him messages from heaven. These messages were compiled into the Quran.

Every other religion, both ancient and modern, begins with the same premise: one lone testimony.[371] These narratives have little objective credibility as they can only be as reliable as their founders. In all of these cases, where there is a claim of only a single witness to the Divine revelation, there is much potential for unintentional error,

---

369 New Testament, Acts ch. 9 and other places.

370 Asvaghosa, *The Buddhacarita*, (second-century Buddhist narrative), reprinted in Smart and Hecht, *Sacred Texts of the World: A Universal Anthology* (1982), pgs. 233–4.

371 For further elaboration and many more examples, see Lawrence Kelemen, *Permission to Receive* (1996), pgs. 50–51. Some of the information presented about other religions was gleaned from this monumental work.

purposeful untruths, hallucinations, or later changes and corruptions by others.[372]

NATIONAL REVELATION IS UNIQUE

Judaism, on the other hand, is the lone faith that makes the claim of a national revelation, where G-d appeared in front of the *entire nation* at one time. The Jewish people's assurance in the public revelation of the Torah given by G-d at Sinai is founded upon an unbroken tradition and pragmatic assessment of facts. The entire nation saw G-d reveal Himself, give His instructions, and designate Moses as the conduit for recording His Torah. The Torah was dictated to Moses by G-d, and Moses wrote it down "like a scribe writing dictation."[373]

The Torah, the book of instructions, is what defines Judaism, and it was therefore at this Sinai event—where the Jewish people received the Torah—that Judaism began. Many Jewish people today may be unaware that a national revelation is the traditional Jewish position. Countless Jews, often with very limited formal Jewish education, assume Cecil DeMille's *The Ten Commandments* movie to be an accurate depiction of the Sinai experience, where the lone Moses ascends the mountain while the rest of the newfound nation awaits encamped. While often regarded as one of the classics, its account of biblical happenings is painfully inaccurate. Zeroing in specifically on the Sinai experience, the Torah is explicit numerous times that everyone present heard G-d speak the Law. In the book of Exodus, all of the details of the Sinai event are laid out. G-d says to Moses:

> Behold I will come to you in the thick cloud so that *the nation* will hear when I speak to you, and in you they will trust forever... Go to the people, and sanctify them today and tomorrow. Let them immerse their clothing. They

---

372 See Sa'adia Gaon, *Emunos v'Deos* 3:6.

373 Rambam, Commentary to Mishnah: Introduction to *Sanhedrin* 10:8. See also *Bava Basra* 14b, *Yerushalmi, Sotah* 5:8. The rest of the books of the Hebrew Bible are seen as written with a "human element" yet still Divinely inspired.

will then be ready for the third day, for on the third day, G-d will descend on Mt. Sinai *in sight of all the people*.[374]

The Jewish nation was enumerated as 600,000 able-bodied men between the ages of twenty and sixty.[375] In addition, it can be assumed that they had their wives, minors, and senior citizens as well—an estimated total of three million people.[376] The Jewish people are enjoined to have faith in G-d, accept His commands, and pass the Torah and commandments on to the next generation on the basis of this historical experience. In order to avoid doubts being raised, G-d chose to elevate the entire nation, allowing all to witness Moses as the agent with whom G-d is presenting them the Torah.[377] The Sinai event is something that no one in Jewish history questioned, even the fringe dissenters and detractors like the Sadducees and early Christians who would have benefited from denying that it happened. It was something so clearly affixed in people's minds—a fact methodically handed down from parents to children and teacher to students as something that all of our ancestors witnessed.[378]

PARENTS DO NOT TEACH UNTRUTHS

Rabbi Moshe ben Nachman, the Ramban, explains that if the initial parents did not witness first-hand the cataclysmic Sinai event of G-d speaking and giving instruction to the entire nation, they would never have believed it and would not have collectively passed it on to their children as a fact.[379] It is possible for parents to pass on false legends or ideals that they believe to be true, like Communism for example. However, they will not tell over to their children things *as facts* that

---

374 *Shmos* [Exodus] 19:9-11, emphasis added.

375 The Torah enumerates those who were capable in those times for military service, i.e., males between twenty and sixty.

376 *Shmos* [Exodus] 12:37; *Bamidbar* [Numbers] 2:32.

377 See Malbim on *Shmos* 19:9.

378 In the words of the historian Josephus (*Against Apion* 1:8): "All Jews imbibe with their mother's milk the belief that these books are Divine origin, as well as the resolve to remain faithful to them, and willingly, if need be die for them."

379 Ramban, *Devarim* [Deuteronomy] 4:9.

they know to be utterly false. James Michener, acclaimed American author, writes that students were the ones who began the Hungarian Revolution in 1956. The students revolted because even though they heard the false Communist ideals and history in school, their parents taught them the truth at home. This contradiction inspired them to revolt.[380]

NATIONAL REVELATION CANNOT BE FABRICATED

The giving of the Torah at the Sinai event is rationally pleasing. The public observation of the Sinai event, with consistent reports among diverse observers, preserved in an unbroken chain of tradition throughout time and across the globe, gives us sound reason to believe in the Divine origin of the Torah.

The fact that this claim of national revelation has never been attempted again by another religious group is puzzling, as this would seemingly be the greatest way to start a religion—to claim as many witnesses to the Divine revelation as possible, rather than just one. The reason why it has never been duplicated is because national revelation is something that *cannot* be fabricated. The Torah even implies that other nations will not be able to successfully claim national revelation. The book of Deuteronomy says clearly:

> You might inquire about times long past, from the day that G-d created man on Earth, [exploring] one end of Heaven to the other. Has there ever been anything like this great thing or has anything like it been heard? Has a people *ever heard the voice of G-d speaking from the midst of the fires as you have heard, and survived?*[381]

The Torah is teaching that no other nation will claim that masses of people witnessed *G-d speak His instructions to them and lived to tell about it.* The claim is not merely that a large amount of people saw

---

380   James Michener, *The Bridge at Andau* (1957), pg. 186, cited in Yosef Eisen, *The Miraculous Journey* (2004), pg. 23.

381   *Devarim* [Deuteronomy] 4:32–33.

some spectacular event; it is that they all witnessed Divine instruction.[382] The Torah is the only revelation of Divine instruction given over in this most public way.[383]

---

382 Fantastic occurrences without specific instructions being publically given over can be attributed to hallucination, delusion, charlatanry, or a myriad of other factors. Just for clarity, let us emphasize once again the claim of national revelation. Large groups are certainly able to witness abnormal occurrences. If groups of several thousands of people witness a UFO at one time, this does not prove the existence of alien life; it merely shows that a group of people saw some lights, and were not quite sure of its source. If the same group said that an extraterrestrial beamed itself down, introduced itself to all of them and spoke about its planet, and the people present and their descendants upheld the details of the story, and based everything in their life upon this event, then there might be something to talk about. Short of that, it is just unidentified lights.

Similarly, miracle claims are rampant around the world, in some religious traditions more than others. Popular claims found on nearly every continent to this very day are claims of Mary apparitions. Sometimes hundreds or even thousands of people witness these occurrences. The apparitions are usually vague or bright lights and not mass revelations where there are instructions given over in front of everyone. Some of the most famous claims of this kind were in Fatima, Portugal and Zeitoun, Egypt.

In 1917, at Fatima, three shepherd children claimed to have seen an apparition and had interaction with Mary. They were the only ones to have any claimed interaction with Mary. They predicted that Mary would appear in a field several days later. The large crowd of witnesses said that on that day, after the rain and the dark clouds broke, the sun appeared as a spinning disc in the sky. This event was considered to be a sign by believers. No voice was publicly heard or instructions given, just some obscure astronomical event.

Similarly, between April 1968 and May 1971, thousands of people, sometimes at one time in a large group, reported seeing light "apparitions" over a Coptic Orthodox Church in the impoverished town of Zeitoun, Egypt. When photographed, these phenomena appeared as irregular blobs of light. People who revered Mary assumed it was Mary. Incidentally, even in the Christian world, this is only identified as a miracle by the Coptic Church. It is unknown for sure what exactly caused these lights. There is one well-known hypothesis by J. S. Derr and M. A. Persinger, associating anomalous, terrain-related, luminous phenomena with tectonic strains. Once again, no instructions were given, no life-altering laws to follow, just lights. These cannot be considered national revelations.

383 Lawrence Kelemen mentions that there is a tradition among some Indian groups that the god Krishna revealed himself to the entire nation in a historic battle. However, nobody survived from the battle. The only way they know that the event supposedly occurred is because Krishna revealed himself to someone (one man's lone testimony) later in history and told him the story. So even with this claim of "national revelation," the source of that historical event is claimed through a single individual at a later point in history.

Some have suggested that the Aztec narrative was also a national revelation. It seems upon further examination that this is not the case. Among other issues with their sto-

There is a single written Torah that has been passed down for over three thousand years, exactly the same, word for word, the world over. Significantly, not one letter in a Torah scroll is allowed to be written from memory. The text must be copied from a kosher scroll to ensure perfect accuracy and transmission.[384]

The Sinai account could not have been made up at a later date. Jewish people by nature have trouble agreeing on anything. Is it reasonable to say that they could somehow all conspire together at a later date about a national event that never happened, not to mention an event that would regulate and shape every aspect of their lives forever, and then transcribe it in a way that everyone agreed to?[385]

The Torah commands the people to *remember* some of the other more significant events that they witnessed.[386] It is not reasonable that a nation would accept upon itself what it allegedly saw and experienced

---

ry, it seems that the god-figure only revealed himself to the high priests in the form of dreams, so once again the revelation is lone man/small group testimony. See Manuel Aguilar-Moreno, *Handbook to Life in the Aztec World* (2006), pg. 32. Also see Leonidas Le Cenci Hamilto, *Border States of Mexico: Sonora, Chihuahua and Durango with a General Sketch* (1881), pg. 140. Both of these sources come from Rabbi Dovid Gottlieb [blog. dovidgottlieb.com/2012/11/aztec-national-revelation-in-past-i.html].

It is impossible to address every revelation story, but they will all presumably fit into one of these categories: (i) not a revelation at all, because no commandments, instructions, or information were actually given, as in the case of the UFO, Mary apparitions, etc. (ii) not a national revelation because the story is introduced by one person or a small group. The Torah remains distinct in that several million people witnessed G-d speak, on a specific date in the year 2448 on the Jewish calendar, and that He gave very specific instructions that dictate a lifestyle and curtail literally every aspect of life. This event was also apparently so convincing that all of their children and children's children for the past 3000 years, until this very day, have accepted and adapted their life to that message accordingly.

384 *Yoreh Deah* 274; Rambam, *Tefillin, Mezuzah, and Sefer Torah* 1:12. Adding or subtracting even a single letter renders the entire Torah scroll invalid (ch. 10).

385 "It is utterly out of the question that a body of laws, never before heard of, could be imposed upon the people as though they had been given by Moses centuries before; and that they could have been accepted and obeyed by them, notwithstanding the fact that these laws imposed new and serious burdens, set aside established usages to which the people were devotedly attached, and conflicted with the interests of powerful classes of the people." (W. H. Green in J. H. Hertz, *The Pentateuch and the Haftorahs* (1978), pg. 555.)

386 The Slavery and Exodus from Egypt (*Devarim* [Deuteronomy] 8:18–19, 16:2–3); Receiving the Torah (ibid., 4:9–10); Amalek (ibid., 25:17–19); Sojourn in the Wilderness (8:2).

if these events had not really taken place.[387] Neither the Jews nor any other people could concoct such an outrageous lie.

Furthermore, Jewish history is completely accounted for, as is the historical dissemination of Torah knowledge. This detailed transmission is unique to the Jewish people.[388] In fact, many prominent rabbis can trace themselves very precisely, teacher to student, all the way back to Moses at Sinai. In other words they can confirm who their teacher was, their teacher's teacher, and so forth, until they reach the original source at Sinai. It is an effort in futility to maintain that such a living and detailed tradition is merely the product of the imagination of later generations.

A charismatic Moses could come along and convince people that G-d revealed Himself to him in private. However, if a charismatic Moses came along and said that the instructions that are recorded in his book were given by G-d to all of the ancestors of the Jewish people sometime in the past, the Jewish people of his day would question him as to why he is the only one who has heard about it. The national revelation idea could not have been made up at a later time, and invoked retroactively, as nobody would have accepted it in such a way.

Invoking national revelation retroactively to past ancestors might not work, but perhaps Moses was a very convincing person who was somehow able to persuade the masses in his own day to believe that G-d was speaking to them directly. However, if Moses was able to somehow charismatically convince the Jewish people

---

387   Sutton, ibid., brought down in Benzion Allswang, *The Final Resolution* (1988), pg. 40. Rabbi Allswang's book helped shape the style and provided source material for some of the ensuing sections.

388   Abraham Malamat, professor emeritus of Jewish history at the Hebrew University of Jerusalem, writes: "The early history of every nation is shrouded in mystery. Only the faint memories of minimal historical value have succeeded in reaching us through the corridors of history. The Nation of Israel is unique among all the nations...in preserving a complex organic transmission, contained in the books of Pentateuch and Joshua, concerning its origins and development before it emerged onto the horizon of history as a defined national entity...no other nation of the biblical period has reached us which compares to that of the biblical account of the patriarchs, the Exodus, or the conquering of the Land." A. Malamat, *A History of the Jewish People* (1976), pg. 33.

that they all heard G-d, it would make more sense to try to make a quick reference to it and not dwell upon this lie over and over as the Torah does.[389]

Additionally, the Torah itself speaks on occasion disparagingly about Moses. Why would Moses, on his own accord, trying to persuade a nation to follow him, include his sins and punishment of not being allowed to lead the nation into the Promised Land in his Torah that he invented? Furthermore, it is impossible to think that he would be able to convince the people to accept some of the more challenging precepts of the Torah without each one of them being sure that they actually heard G-d as claimed.[390] This logic of the Torah's authenticity was already brought out by the sages.[391]

Besides the traditional approach to the Sinai event's validity, it is worthwhile to mention some other anomalies unique to the Torah, as well as information contained within it that could not have been thought of and promulgated by a human mind.

OBJECTIONABLE LANGUAGE

The Hebrew Bible is unmatched in documents of national history in its objectivity and impartiality toward the very people that accepted it.[392] Typically, the annals of a nation's development are biased and subjective, bent on glorifying its people and past leaders. Histories often served as propaganda tools of sorts to venerate the monarchy and instill a sense of pride or elitism in its people. Anything that could be

---

389 *Shmos* [Exodus] 19:1–25, 20:1–9, 24:1–18, 34:27–35; *Devarim* [Deuteronomy] 4:9–15, 4:32–40, 5:1–30, 9:8–29, 10:1–11, 18:15–22.

390 While it is true that people are gullible, and can even be coerced into things that are self-destructive; however, this is only when the lie is not checkable. Cults, for example, are able to make outlandish claims and convince their followers to do the unthinkable, but only when the cult leader bases his claim on something that cannot be checked. If it can be checked, and found to be a lie, nobody would subject themselves to the harmful behavior. In the case of Judaism, there is the *bris milah*, Sabbatical years, financial commitments, and other issues of detriment that will be elaborated upon further; all dependent on "you just heard G-d speak," something verifiable, see Kelemen, ibid.

391 *Kuzari* 1:87.

392 There is a section that also mentions this fact in the *New World Encyclopedia*, quoted in Allswang, ibid.

viewed as even remotely humiliating or condemning was conveniently left out, hidden, or obliterated.[393]

The Hebrew Bible is uncomplimentary and replete with criticism of the ancient Israelites. They are constantly described as a "stiff-necked,"[394] argumentative, stubborn, and divisive people; a nation of whiners, doubters, and rebels who have their roots in slavery.[395] Their recurring falls into the barbarism, paganism, and moral degradation of their neighbors is repeatedly and openly recorded and reprimanded. These are hardly alluring traits to attract potential members. Is it possible that the entire Jewish nation would accept upon itself an invented Torah, written by unknown authors at a later date, with these denigrating descriptions of themselves and their ancestors? Is it possible that writers, trying to dream up the Jewish nation's history and gain acceptance abroad, would mention its people in such unflattering terms?

Furthermore, and perhaps more surprising and novel, is the open mention of the blemishes, faults, and shortcomings of Judaism's founders and prominent leaders.[396] Abraham and Isaac both have rebellious and wicked children. Jacob steals his father's blessing from his brother Esau, is forced to flee from his attacks, and spends twenty years with Laban, the idol-worshipping swindler, eventually marrying two of *his* daughters.[397] Jacob's sons, founders of the twelve tribes of Israel, wish to kill their brother Joseph and then concede to "only"

---

393   The Egyptian historians avoided reporting anything embarrassing, as did the Assyrians. (See Alfred Jerimias, *The Old Testament in Light of the Ancient East* [In German] (1930), pg. 392. For more examples, see the notes cited in Phillip Biberfeld, *Universal Jewish History* (1948), pgs. 24–27. See also Avraham Sutton and others, *Pathways to the Torah* (1985), pg. E8.

394   *Shmos* [Exodus] 32:9, *Bamidbar* [Numbers] 14:11, *Devarim* [Deuteronomy] 9:13, and many more places.

395   No nation, unless compelled by overwhelming facts, would have ascribed to its forefathers such humiliation. See Hertz, *The Pentateuch* (1950), pg. 396; Rudolf Kittel, *Geschichte des Volkes Israel* (1932), pgs. 341, 365–66.

396   The following paragraph is a summary of Shmuel Waldman, *Beyond a Reasonable Doubt* (2002), pgs. 93-96. It is important to bear in mind that the Oral Tradition describes how all of the so-called "slipups" of the righteous forefathers and prophets are much deeper than would seem with just a superficial look at the written text.

397   *Bereishis* [Genesis] ch. 27–29.

sell him.[398] Other questionable episodes are mentioned with Jacob's children, for example the incidents with Dinah, Judah and Tamar, and Reuben and Bilhah. Moses, Judaism's most well-known figure and greatest leader, is not allowed to enter the Holy Land because of a sin.[399] Aaron, future High Priest and brother of Moses, is associated with the construction of the Golden Calf. The illustrious King David has an episode with Bathsheba.[400] Why would the hypothetical author(s) of the Torah and books of the Prophets not omit the blunders of its most celebrated figureheads, as was common in all ancient documents of the near East and universally practiced until this very day?[401]

UNFEASIBLE PROMISES

Another objective approach pointing to the Torah's authenticity is the commandments that contain elements not possible for a human being to promise. No human ruler could ever contemplate introducing these ordinances, nor could one impose them with forcefulness.

THE SABBATICAL YEAR

The first example is the law of the Sabbatical year, known as *shmittah*, which forbids usage of the entire Land of Israel for a full year out of every seven years. In other words, the sixth year's yield would need to be enough to last its owner for the sixth, seventh, and even the eighth years—until there are crops to harvest again. Furthermore, after seven cycles of the *shmittah* years there is the Jubilee, or *yovel* year, in which the land must also be left alone.[402] After leaving the fields in the seventh year of the seventh cycle (i.e., the forty-ninth year), the fiftieth year, or *yovel* year, it must be left unsown again. That is now two years in a row of unplanted fields.

The Israelites were commanded to begin doing this around 1200 BCE

---

398   *Bereishis* [Genesis] ch. 34.

399   *Bamidbar* [Numbers] 20:12.

400   *Shmuel* II, [II Samuel] ch. 11–12.

401   Even in the United States, children are educated in the "saintliness" of the founding fathers and other significant historical figures.

402   *Vayikra* [Leviticus] 25:8–24.

when everything was dependant on harvest. If crops grew, people ate; if there was not enough, people starved. Additionally, the frequent droughts made it often difficult to produce enough food for their immediate needs, let alone to salvage anything for the future.

In addition, it is known that naturally every year the harvest of the field becomes weaker, meaning that the first year in counting would be the best yield and the sixth year the worst. Sensing that the people may question where they will procure food from in those years, the Torah promises that in the sixth year, the G-d Who they heard speak would grant them a surplus, allowing them to make it through the Sabbatical year unharmed.[403] Is it even conceivable that a human being could have devised such an absurdity, an ordinance doomed to fail the first time the sixth year came without a double crop? A human being would not guarantee that which defies the laws of nature. Only G-d could devise such an ordinance as only He could honor such a promise.[404]

TRI-ANNUAL PILGRIMAGES

The Torah obligates all able-bodied men to come to Jerusalem on the three designated festivals of Pesach, Shavuos, and Sukkos every year.[405] While there, they would participate in festivities and worship. This was practiced nationwide until the destruction of the Holy Temple in Jerusalem.[406]

This command leaves all of the borders of the Land of Israel abandoned, and puts the women and children who remained home in constant danger of attack. As is the case today, the land was surrounded by enemy nations. In their days, the neighboring Moabites, Ammonites, Philistines, and Amalekites were waiting for any opportunity to invade. The Torah assures the people that "no one will be envious of your land when you go to be seen in G-d's presence three times a year."[407]

---

403 *Vayikra* [Leviticus] 25:20–22.
404 See Chasam Sofer on Behar.
405 *Shmos* [Exodus] 34:23–24; *Devarim* [Deuteronomy] 16:16–17.
406 There is ample proof that the Jewish people kept this commandment. (See Safari, "HaAliyah L'Regel During the Second Commonwealth," in Waldman, ibid., pg. 84.)
407 *Shmos*, ibid.

It is unfeasible for a lawmaker or human author of the Torah to make such a grandiose promise that all women and children left unguarded will continually be safe and secure until the men return; the first time the remaining family members encounter calamity, the Torah's credibility is lost forever. Only Hashem can make such a promise.

PREPARATION FOR WAR

The Torah relates that when the Jewish people take the field against their enemies, and see horses and chariots that are much larger than their forces, they should not fear for G-d is with them.[408] Before actually engaging in battle the army officials are to make a bizarre announcement exonerating certain people:

1. Anyone who built a house and has not lived in it yet may return home, lest he die in battle and be unable to live in it.
2. Anyone who planted a vineyard and has not yet rendered it fit for use may return, lest he die and someone else make use of it.
3. Anyone who betrothed a woman but had not yet married her may return, lest he die and someone else marry her.
4. Anyone who is afraid or fainthearted may return home.[409]

After all of these groups have left the battlefield, there may only be a fraction of the original enlisted men. Is there a monarch or human general who could grant such freedom to soldiers in a time of war and still expect to win? Moreover, it is extraordinary that in a time of primitive warfare, the Torah alone showed concern for seemingly irrelevant problems. Only G-d would have the ability to establish victory with such diminished forces.

---

408   This and the following paragraph can be found in *Devarim* 20:1-8. This is brought as a proof of the Torah's Divine origin in Eli Gottlieb, *The Inescapable Truth* (1971), pgs. 132–34.

409   The sages debate the meaning of being afraid. Rabbi Akiva says it is literal, while Rabbi Yossi says that he is scared of retribution because of his sins. (See *Sotah* 44b.)

THE SOTAH

The Torah speaks of the *sotah*, a woman suspected of committing adultery based on her seclusion with a man whom her husband had suspicions about.[410] She was taken through a whole ordeal to prove whether she is innocent or guilty of the alleged adultery. This process concludes with her drinking the "bitter waters," an elixir that revealed her fate. The Torah promises that if she is guilty, and did commit adultery, then these waters would cause her belly to blow up and her organs to rupture, killing her and her "partner in crime."[411] If she is innocent, she is compensated for her strife—had she been barren, she would give birth; if she had children already, the next ones would be of an even higher caliber.[412]

Yet again, the Torah presents a case which would be nonsensical and self-defeating for a mortal to promise. Why would anyone assure a supernatural occurrence that could be openly refuted when it failed?

AHEAD OF ITS TIME

The Torah is out of sync with the era in which it came about, many of the commandments showing a drastically different approach to the lifestyle, ethic, and outlook of the time. In fact, it is because of these more advanced ideas of civilized society that are found in the Torah that the critics insist that it must have been written at a later time, rather than accept the Divine authorship. Some examples:[413]

- Belief in One, non-physical, personal G-d compared to the prevalent idolatries of the time
- A day of rest in the way of the Sabbath
- The rights of slaves who are treated on par with the owner,

---

410   *Bamidbar* [Numbers] 5:11–30.
411   *Sotah* 27b.
412   For instance if she previously gave birth with difficulty, she will now give birth with ease or give birth to children with a more desirable complexion (*Sotah* 26a).
413   See Simcha Cohen, "Divine Origin of the Torah," in *Return to the Source* (1984), pg. 159–160. See also Hertz, ibid., pgs. 403–406, for an overview in comparison with the Code of Hammurabi. This is merely one example of ancient legal codes.

compared to the oppression of their neighboring nations

- Loving even the stranger,[414] compared to the barbarism of the time
- Overcoming base animalistic urges and instincts, as compared to the more common pleasure-seeking and self-gratification
- Equitable relation between a crime and its punishment, compared to the widespread bribery and injustice
- Limitation on the wives and wealth of the king
- Insuring protection and mercy to the widow and orphan

DIVINE FOREKNOWLEDGE

HISTORY OF THE JEWISH PEOPLE

The Hebrew Bible professes that the Jews will be an eternal nation:

> Thus says G-d, "Who establishes the sun to light the day, the laws of the moon and stars to light the night, Who stirs up the sea into roaring waves, Whose name is the L-rd of Hosts? If these natural laws should ever give away before Me," says G-d, "only then shall the offspring of Israel cease to be a nation before me for all time."[415]

Jewish history and destiny is one of the strongest evidences of the Torah's Divine origin and general existence of G-d and His Divine providence.[416] The difficulty of remaining an eternal nation becomes more difficult when the nation is forcibly separated and scattered throughout the world. The Bible itself warns that this is what is going to befall the nation "when I scatter them among the nations and disperse them over foreign lands."[417]

The Torah describes there and elsewhere, in no uncertain terms, that the Jewish people will be dispersed throughout the world at the

---

414   *Vayikra* [Leviticus] 18:34.
415   *Yirmiyahu* [Jeremiah] 31:34–36.
416   See *Aruch Hashulchan* on *Orach Chaim* 1:10.
417   *Yechezkel* [Ezekiel] 12:15.

aggressive hand of all of the nations and face constant persecution. "Among the nations, you shall find no respite; no rest for your foot, for there the L-rd will give you an anguished heart and wasted eyes and a dismayed spirit. You will live in constant suspense, and stand in dread, both by day and by night, never sure of your existence."[418] The Torah also relates that they will remain small in number, saying, "You will remain few in number, whereas you could have become as numerous as the stars of the heavens, because you would not obey the voice of G-d, your L-rd."[419] It stresses that the Jews will persevere despite the overwhelming odds against them, that they will continue to have attachment to the Land of Israel throughout their dispersal, and that they will one day ultimately return to their homeland.[420] There could not be a more accurate depiction of how Jewish history has played out.

The biblical vision takes it a step further, saying that while the Jews are away from their homeland the land will lie desolate,[421] and no kingdom will ever be able to build it up.[422] When Mark Twain visited Ottoman-ruled Palestine (Israel) in 1867 he described it as a wasteland.[423] Professor Sir John William Dawson, Canadian geologist, wrote: "Until today, no people has succeeded in establishing national dominion in the Land of Israel...The mixed multitude of itinerant tribes that managed to settle there did so on lease, as temporary residents. It seems

---

418   *Devarim* [Deuteronomy] 28:65–67.

419   *Devarim* [Deuteronomy] 4:27.

420   See *Vayikra* [Leviticus] ch. 26, and *Devarim* [Deuteronomy] ch. 28.

421   *Yechezkel* 33:28–29.

422   *Vayikra* 26:32–33.

423   Mark Twain, *The Innocents Abroad* (1869). Consider the following excerpts: "Stirring senses...occur in this [Jezreel] valley no more. There is not a solitary village throughout its whole extent—not for thirty miles in either direction. There are two or three clusters of Bedouin tents, but not a single permanent habitation. One may ride ten miles, hereabouts, and not see ten human beings." Also his 1867 description of the Galilee: "These unpeopled deserts, these rusty mounds of bareness that never, never, never, do shake the glare from their harsh outlines...that melancholy ruin of Capernaum: this stupid village of Tiberias, slumbering under six funereal palms... A desolation is here that not even imagination can grace with the pomp of life and action... We reached [Mount] Tabor safely... We never saw a human being on the whole route."

that they await the return of the permanent residents of the land."[424] The astounding precision of how history will play out is uncanny, undeniably written with Divine foresight.

The survival of the Jewish people, while incessantly up against dreadful conditions and arduous antagonism, is a mystery that defies all rational explanation. Rabbi Yaakov Emden *zt"l* says that it is the greatest miracle, even more wondrous than the splitting of the sea.[425] Russian political philosopher Nikolai Berdyaev summed it up well, saying, "[The Jews'] destiny is too imbued with the metaphysical to be explained in either material or historical terms."[426] This fact is well known and has been stated countless times throughout history. Over three hundred years ago, Blaise Pascal told King Louis XIV of France that the survival of the Jews was nothing short of a miracle.[427] Only a Divine document could predict so perfectly the continued existence and detailed history of the Jewish nation.

THE WONDROUS WESTERN WALL

Related to the survival of the Jewish nation is the prophetic survival of the Western Wall in Jerusalem. The Wall is a remnant of the ancient walls that surrounded the Temple courtyard and currently the most holy site in the world for the Jewish people. A prophecy is uttered about it, not in the Five Books of Moses, but later on in the Bible, in the Song of Songs. The verse reads, "Behold He stands behind our wall."[428] It is related in many places in ancient Jewish literature that this "refers to the Western Wall which G-d vowed would never be destroyed."[429] Throughout Jewish history, Jerusalem has unfortunately been the scene of great battles, and utterly destroyed and rebuilt at least nine times. Nevertheless, throughout the centuries it has remained intact.

---

424   Dawson, *Modern Science in Bible Lands* (1888), pg. 450.

425   See introduction to his *siddur*.

426   Beryaev, *The Meaning of History* (1936), pg. 86.

427   Pensees, paragraph 620, pg. 285.

428   *Shir haShirim* [Song of Songs] 2:9.

429   See *Midrash Tanchuma, Shmos* 10. Similarly in *Midrash Rabbah, Shmos* 2, *Bamidbar* 11, *Shir HaShirim* 2, *Eichah* 1; *Yalkut Shimoni, Melachim* 196; *Zohar, Shmos* 5b.

MOSES THE ZOOLOGIST?

The Torah lays out signs that help discern kosher animals from those that are not. A land animal is considered kosher if two factors are present: it has split hooves *and* chews its cud (ruminates).[430] Both of these signs must be present to render the animal kosher. The Torah then specifies four animals that only display one of the signs: the camel,[431] *shafan* [hyrax],[432] and *arnevet* [hare][433] because they chew their cud but do not have (completely) split hooves, and the pig, which has split hooves but does not chew its cud.

The Torah could have listed only the kosher characteristics, and yet it goes out of its way and lists four categories of animals that have only one of the signs. The Talmud states that these four are the *only*

---

430   *Vayikra* [Leviticus] 11:3–8.

431   The Torah mentions the main animals that have these characteristics. The camel also represents the llama, which chews its cud and does not have split hooves. Likewise with the pig, it includes the wild boar, etc.

432   As it is commonly translated. It is bracketed because we have no tradition identifying this creature. It may be extinct. The translations are modern Hebrew adaptations that bear no connection to the biblical meaning. It does not ruminate in the usual sense, but has minor regurgitation. Also it has ruminant-like chewing movements.

433   As it is commonly translated. It is bracketed because we have no tradition identifying this creature. It may be extinct. The translations are modern Hebrew adaptations that bear no connection to the biblical meaning.

    At any rate, the Torah's classification of animals may at times differ from the groupings in modern zoological taxonomy. The *shafan* and the *arnevet* are puzzling to some because they do not "chew their cud" in the same way as kosher animals do, as contemporary science has pointed out. Instead they practice caecotrophy, a type of coprophagy, where its body produces fecal pellets that are then ingested. The fact that these animals may only "appear" to ruminate, but technically do not according to the current scientific outlook, is immaterial, as the Torah could have used a different benchmark when categorizing the animals. Moreover, this process is considered vital, and similar to cud-chewing. If "cud" refers to food that has been chewed and swallowed, this act truly is "chewing the cud." It should be noted in any event that the hyrax displays several signs of resemblance to typical cud-chewing animals. (For further details see "Mammals: Major Mammal Orders: Lagomorpha," Encyclopedia Britannica Deluxe Ed. 2004, CD-ROM, cited in Levi, *Torah and Science* (2006), pg. 210; see also Amitai ben David, *Sichat Chullin al Masechet Chullin*, pg. 410.)

    Additionally, translation or changes in terminology over the years may also play a factor in the perceived discrepancy. For example, Rabbi Shimshon Raphoel Hirsch *zt"l* suggests the possibility that the animal referred to in the Torah may be a completely different (perhaps extinct) animal to what we call a *shafan* or *arnevet* today.

animals in the world that have only one of the two signs.[434] So, for example, if one chanced upon an unknown species that had split hooves and is definitely not a pig, it would be permitted because the **only** animal that has split hooves and does not chew its cud is the pig. The author of the Torah limited his credibility. Australia, the Americas, Antarctica, and the vast majority of the other continents had not yet been discovered, let alone explored, when the Torah was given. The sages asked rhetorically, "Was Moses an expert hunter [and knew so much about animals]?" Rather this was written to answer anyone who might claim that the Torah is not from Heaven, as the One who rules the world knows all of its creatures.[435]

People are constantly exploring new locations and discovering creatures unknown to earlier generations, yet never have they found a single exception to the four animals with only one kosher characteristic. This is beyond the capability of any human being.[436]

Recently, Dr. Yitzchak Betech, a prominent Mexican physician, had extensive correspondence with Dr. Esther van Praag, a Swiss expert in rabbit biology and medicine. The nature of their discussions was centered on the contemporary identification of the biblical *shafan* and the other biblical animals. Their extensive conclusions were recently published. Regarding their research, Dr. Van Praag remarked that "it was exciting to discover that detailed scientific and medical knowledge related to rabbits and hares are found in the Torah."[437]

There is a similar phenomenon found regarding kosher fish. In order for a fish to be classified as kosher, it must possess both fins and scales.[438] The Mishnah puts its integrity on the line and writes "**every fish that has scales has fins**; but there are those that have fins but no scales."[439] Thus, if the fins were removed, or one only had a section of the fish without the fins, it can still be established as a kosher fish—

---

434   See *Chullin* 59a; See also Malbim to *Vayikra* [Leviticus] 11:4.

435   See *Chullin* 60b; *Sifri, Devarim* 14:97.

436   *Maharatz Chayos, Chullin* 59a; *Torah Temimah, Vayikra* 11:17; *Rashbatz, Magen Avos,* sec. 2, ch. 3.

437   See her approbation to Yitzchak Betech, *The Enigma of the Biblical Shafan* (2013) on pg. 33.

438   *Vayikra* [Leviticus] 11:9; *Devarim* [Deuteronomy] 14:9.

439   See *Niddah* 51b; *Chullin* 66b. See also *Taz, Yoreh Deah* 83:3.

because we *know* that it indeed had fins. Thousands of fish have been discovered since this statement was written down by the sages, yet no fish to date with scales and no fins.[440] Where did this information come from? Both of these biblical descriptions have withstood the test of time and the discovery of thousands of new species.[441]

CIRCUMCISION ON THE EIGHTH DAY

One of the most well-known commandments of the Jewish people is the Torah's command to circumcise sons on the eighth day after birth.[442] The Torah specifies the exact day, not before and not after, but on the *eighth* day for a newborn healthy boy.

This commandment is classified as one of the Torah's obligations that are beyond human understanding. While it would be presumptuous and even absurd for anyone to assume a full understanding of this obligation, it is certainly interesting to see some of the recent

---

440 The Torah's classifications may at times differ from the groupings in modern zoological taxonomy. Parenthetically, the *Ma'adanei Yom Tov* (*Chullin*, Rosh section, 67:5) tells how he was brought a "fish" called *Stincus marinus*, which had scales and no fins, but four animal-like legs. He answers that the two Torah verses, *Vayikra* [Leviticus] 11:9 and 10, distinguish between fish that live in the water from other creatures that live there. All fish have both scales and fins; but there may be other creatures that live in the water that only have scales. The Chasam Sofer also writes that the stincus is not even a fish but some sort of creature closer resembling a lizard or frog. Additionally, even if it had the status of fish, it may not even be included in the sages' general statement because it is a poisonous fish that nobody would wish to eat anyway (see *Mishulchan Gavoha*).

There are others who try to refute the claim by using the *Monopterus cuchia* that lives in the Indian Ocean, claiming that it has scales and no fins. Even if this creature is classified as a fish according to the Torah, just breaking down the name shows that this claim is inaccurate. *Mono* means one, and *pterus* means wing. This creature is said to have a rudimentary dorsal fin.

As an aside, Rabbi Yonoson Eybeshutz (*Kereisi u'Pleisi, Yoreh Deah* 83) says that the Mishnah is speaking about the majority of fish, and so even if one day there theoretically was such a fish found, it would still be in sync. Even in such a case the point of Divine authorship would still hold strong, for how would a writer from the biblical era know anything about the "majority" of fish?

441 There has been a lot of discussion about these animals, both the land and sea, over the past few years. See Betech, *The Enigma of the Biblical Shafan*, for a comprehensive assessment and defense of the Divinity of the written and oral Torah, through explaining the parameters of these animals.

442 *Vayikra* [Leviticus] 12:2–3.

discoveries about the eighth day following birth in the medical field.

It has become more evident through medical research in the more recent generations that the eighth day is the earliest advisable time to perform a circumcision. The major clotting agents, prothrombin and vitamin K, do not reach peak levels in the blood until the eighth day of life. Vitamin K forms between the fifth and seventh day, and prothrombin levels are normal at birth, drop to very low levels in the next few days, and after the eighth day reach their average of 100%. Furthermore, on the eighth day—and only on the eighth day—prothrombin levels are at 110 percent, more than any other day in a boy's entire life. "From the consideration of vitamin K and prothrombin determinations, the perfect day to perform a circumcision is on the eighth day."[443] Coincidence? Dr. Armand James Quick, former head of the department of biochemistry at Marquette University, does not seem to think so, asserting "that it hardly seems accidental that the rite of circumcision was postponed until the eighth day by the Mosaic Law."[444]

The Israelites were not the only ancient people that observed the rite of circumcision, yet the Torah's directive describes the details of the performance in perfect harmony with man's nature.

PRIESTLY DNA

WHO IS A PRIEST (KOHEN) AND WHAT DOES THAT MEAN?

The Torah bestows a special responsibility on Aaron, brother of Moses, and his progeny—serving as a *Kohen*, or priest.[445] Their duties included carrying out the priestly service in the Tabernacle, and later on in the Holy Temple, which also included sacrificial offerings and blessing the Jewish people. They were given added sanctity restrictions regarding marriage and burial, but were given privileges like receiving gifts and tithes designated for the priestly class. The *Kohen* status is

---

443   Dr. Sim McMillen, *None of These Diseases*, pgs. 21–23.
444   Quick, *Hemorrhagic Diseases and Thrombosis* (1966), pg. 109.
445   *Shmos* [Exodus] 28, and many other places.

transferred from father to son, and to this day tradition holds that the *Kohanim* are the descendants of Aaron.

CAN THIS BE TRACED?

In recent years, Dr. Karl Skorecki, director of nephrology and molecular medicine at the Technion Faculty of Medicine, teamed up with other researchers and decided to put the tradition to the test and see if self-identified *Kohanim* have a common set of genetic markers revealing a common ancestry.[446] *Kohanim* were tested from a wide range of Jewish communities the world over. A particular genetic marker was found in an astounding 98.5 percent of the *Kohanim*, and a significantly lower percentage in non-*Kohanim*.[447] These exciting results were published in several prestigious science journals.[448]

In a further study, they found that a particular array of six chromosomal markers was found in 97 out of the 106 *Kohanim* tested. The high frequency of common genetic markers in both Ashkenazi and Sefardi *Kohanim* worldwide indicates an origin pre-dating the separation of the two communities around a thousand years ago. Date calculation for the ancestral founder of the line, based on the variation of mutations among *Kohanim* today, amounts to a time frame of 106 generations, around 3,300 years, which is approximately the same time of Aaron, Moses, and the exodus from Egypt. Professor Skorecki excitedly summarizes the conclusions of this research, saying, "The scientific information confirms that the majority of contemporary *Kohanim* are descended from a common male ancestor who founded a patrilineal dynasty consistent with the Jewish priesthood."[449] He compares its significance to finding an ancient piece of the original garb worn by Aaron, the first priest.

---

446   Most of the source information for this section can be found in Rabbi Yaakov Kleinman, *DNA and Tradition* (2004), or in abridged form: "The DNA Chain of Tradition," *Jewish Action* (Winter 5760/1999).

447   K. Skorecki and others, "Y Chromosomes of Jewish Priests," *Nature* 385 [6611](1997): 32. Articles also printed in *Discover* 18 (April 1997) 24; *Science News* 154 (October 3): 218.

448   See other footnotes for this section for exact locations.

449   P. Hirschberg, "Decoding the Priesthood," *Jerusalem Report*, May 10, 1999.

In reaction to these fascinating results, Dr. David Goldstein, molecular geneticist at Oxford University, said: "It looks like this chromosomal type was a constituent of the ancestral Hebrew population. It was incredibly exciting to find something that could trace paternally-inherited traits over (one hundred) generations, three or four thousand years of history."[450]

In conclusion, Dr. Abraham Amar, a senior scientist at the Tissue Typing Laboratory of Ein-Kerem Medical Center, summarizes the research as follows: "Anyone who refuses to believe in the tradition of the Jewish people must bow his head before scientific evidence proving the truth and authority of the Torah's tradition as it has been passed down precisely from generation to generation."[451]

---

450   J. Travis, "The Priests' Chromosome? DNA Analysis Supports the Biblical Story of the Jewish Priesthood," *Science News*, October 3, 1998.

451   Zamir Cohen, *The Coming Revolution* (2008), pg. 184.

THE ORAL TRADITION

One of the major tenets of Judaism is that the Torah, revealed at Sinai by G-d, is of a dual nature. There is a written Torah that is recorded in the Five Books of Moses and includes the Prophets and Writings, as well as an oral tradition to be memorized and transmitted by the sages of every generation.[452] Accepting the veracity of the written text demands that one also accept the accompanying oral tradition. By way of analogy, the written Torah functions as the outline or shorthand notes of a lecture, and the oral Torah is the lecture itself. Only one who has heard the full talk from the orator can make sense of the written outline, while others are left merely guessing. These two aspects of the Torah working together help form the Mesorah,[453] which is the base of the Jewish religion and how it is applied.

AMBIGUITY OF THE WRITTEN LAW

There are instances where the written text alludes directly to the oral law,[454] however, in most cases, the existence of the oral tradition can be deduced through a logical necessity—elaboration upon the vague nature of the written text. In truth, there is not a single commandment

---

452 Rambam, Number Eight of the Thirteen Principles of Faith.
453 *Mesorah* is the precise transmission of the Torah.
454 "I shall give you the tablets of stone, and the Torah, and the commandment which I have written..." (*Shmos* [Exodus] 24:12; see *Brachos* 5a). Another example is the verse: "These are the *chukim*, the *mishpatim*, and the Toros which G-d established between Himself and the children of Israel..." (*Vayikra* [Leviticus] 26:46). The word *Toros* in the plural can be understood as meaning a second Torah—or Oral Torah.

in the written Torah that can be fully understood without the guidance of the oral tradition.

TEFILLIN

The Torah commands one to "bind them as a sign upon your arm and be for *totafos* between your eyes."[455] This is the source for the mitzvah of tefillin, but the uninitiated reader is left unaware as to what the precept is all about. What are supposed to be tied to the arm? With what do we tie it? What are *totafos*? Those who reject the oral tradition claim that this sign is meant figuratively; however, this is out of sync with the rest of the Torah.[456] Significantly, throughout all known history, all Jews the world over have affixed the same black boxes, containing the same four Torah passages, with black leather straps, along with dozens of other details, to fulfill the mitzvah of tefillin. How could world Jewry come to these identical conclusions, solely based on the Torah's ambiguous written instruction? It is clear that there was oral instruction as well.[457] The same ambiguity is found in the command of affixing tzitzis to a garment,[458] and other common mitzvos.

RITUAL SLAUGHTER

An even more clear reference to the oral tradition in the written text can be seen in the obligation of *shechita*, or ritual slaughter of animals

---

455   *Devarim* [Deuteronomy] 6:8.

456   The word for "a sign" that is used is the Hebrew word "אות" Throughout the Torah that word is only used to describe a visible sign. For example, the same word is used to describe the mark of Cain, the rainbow of Noah, the *bris milah*, G-d's visible miracles in Egypt, the Sabbath day, the mark of the letter *tav* on the forehead in the days of Yechezkel [Ezekiel] 9:4, etc. Furthermore, it does not make sense that the word *totafos* (*Shmos* [Exodus] 13:16; *Devarim* [Deuteronomy] 6:8; 11; 18), which is used to describe the "head ornament," is figurative. Why use a peculiar, non-Hebrew word if it is figurative? The obscure word choice instead suggests a tangible object known to the generation that left Egypt.

457   Also, what to do to make tefillin was not voted upon or decided on at a later date. The oldest tefillin ever found date from the time of the second Temple in Jerusalem, around 2,100 years old. The details that make tefillin what they were were only mentioned in the oral tradition. These tefillin predate the Mishnah by several hundred years.

458   *Bamidbar* [Numbers] 15:38.

one wishes to eat. G-d instructs the nation to "slaughter from your herd and from your flock *as I have commanded you.*"[459] The text says to slaughter the animal in the way G-d has commanded, yet a search of the entire written text of the Bible shows no mention of how to slaughter an animal. What tool does one use to slaughter? Where on the animal does one make the cut? The details of kosher slaughter are extremely tedious and complicated, yet everyone does it the *exact same way* and always has. It is thus very apparent that there were further instructions orally related.

Parenthetically, in the days of King Saul, many centuries before the oral Torah began to be compiled in the Mishnah, he refreshed the people on some of the oral laws that were beginning to be neglected in the laws of *shechita*. King Saul says, "Slaughter *with this (ba-zeh)* and eat."[460] The words "with this" show that Saul was visually showing a specific point about the utensil used for slaughter. The Talmud relates that Saul was clarifying how a knife was properly checked for its sharpness.[461] The sharp knife is imperative to be sure that the animal did not die by another nick or poke rather than the smooth action of the slaughter itself. The object of the knife and its specifications are not mentioned in the written Torah, yet King Saul was refreshing the people on an idea that they had already practiced. Moreover, in Hebrew, the word *ba-zeh* can only be in reference to a specific object.[462]

---

459   Ibid. 12:21, see Rashi.
460   *Shmuel* I [Samuel I] 14:34.
461   *Chullin* 17b.
462   In case one wanted to theorize that the *ba* prefix of a word can mean "upon" as well, making the verse say instead: "Slaughter upon this." However, the word used for "on" in the Torah is nearly always the word *al* (e.g., "Upon the Earth" *Bereishis* [Genesis] 1:11; "Upon the ground" *Bereishis* [Genesis] 7:8; "Upon the altar" *Bereishis* [Genesis] 22:9; "Upon his head" *Bamidbar* [Numbers] 6:5). So it is clearly not speaking about a "place." Instead, the *be* or *ba* prefix is used to describe the use of an implement (e.g., Jacob says that he crossed the river be-*makli* (with my staff); Jacob tells Joseph on his deathbed that he had taken the city of Shechem be-*harbi u*-be-*kashti* (with my sword, and with my bow).

JEWISH HOLIDAYS

Along the same lines, the major commandments required to be performed on the Jewish holidays are unclearly hinted at in the written text. Regarding Yom Kippur, the Torah charges the people to "afflict your souls."[463] This is the only detail uniquely commanded for the Day of Atonement that everyone is required to do. It is from this passage that the Jewish people learn to fast on this day; however, where is that derived from, as "affliction" can mean different things to different people? For some people affliction might mean to spend the entire day at the opera or get a root canal surgery, but it has been universally performed in the same way by all Jews, of all places, and at all times in the exact same way—fasting.

Likewise, for the holiday of Sukkos, the yellow citron fruit, or *esrog*, is described in the written Torah as the "fruit of the beautiful tree."[464] Why is it that a lemon, mango, or orange tree is not considered beautiful? The fact that everybody agrees that this fruit can only be the *esrog*, with absolutely no record of anyone ever using a different fruit in its place, once again shows the presence of an oral tradition. The mitzvos of all of the other holidays on the Jewish calendar are equally elusive in the written text. Furthermore, the backbone of the Jewish religion, keeping the Sabbath—one of the Ten Commandments—has no description in the written text of *how* to keep it. All of its laws are expounded only in the oral tradition. What is classified as "forbidden work"? What exactly are the details? This is extremely important, given that the consequence for purposely and rebelliously breaking the Sabbath can warrant capital punishment. Yet no information is given in the Written Torah.

TRANSLATION AND PRONUNCIATION

In addition to the particulars of the commandments, the oral tradition is also the only source of translation and vocalization of the

---

463   *Vayikra* [Leviticus] 23:27.
464   *Vayikra* [Leviticus] 23:40.

written text. The Hebrew alphabet does not have vowels, and therefore every Torah scroll is written without vowels. For this reason, anyone who has ever read from the Torah knows that it takes much practice beforehand to learn the pronunciation and cantillation. Bible scribes did not begin adding vowels to outside study texts until beginning in the sixth century CE.

This is where the oral tradition comes in. Most Jewish people are aware that the Torah forbids eating milk and meat together, or as the Torah says, not to cook meat in חלב, or *cholov,* meaning milk.[465] These three letters, *chet, lamed, beis*, with different vowels can also be read as *cheilev*, meaning fat—or "do not cook meat in fat." Without the oral tradition, it would be a mystery here, and in countless other places in the written text, as to what the law actually is.

Torah is also not full of commas and semicolons. Punctuation, for all practical purposes, is non-existent in the Torah scroll text. Only the oral tradition informs the reader which verses are grouped together, and how verses should be read and emphasized, and likewise key information about context. A simple change in punctuation can make a world of difference in meaning. As this popular parody phrase found on t-shirts and bumper stickers demonstrates all too well:

"Let's eat grandma!"
"Let's eat, grandma."
Punctuation saves lives.

The first phrase is a cannibal's mealtime call, whereas the second is merely an invitation to eat. In this case, "punctuation saves lives." Although this is only meant as a cute joke, it very clearly and accurately pinpoints the importance of correct punctuation and context, which in the Torah is only accomplished through the oral tradition. In light of the above, the oral Torah can be considered even more important than the written text, as next to nothing could be understood properly without it.

---

465   *Shmos* [Exodus] 23:19; 34:26; *Devarim* [Deuteronomy] 14:21.

WHY NOT WRITE EVERYTHING DOWN?

There are several key reasons why the entire content of the Torah was not to be written, and that the vast majority of Torah depth was to remain oral.

Firstly, the Torah is deemed by the Jewish people as the word and will of G-d. If the entirety of the law were written, it would not promote assiduous study; instead, the Torah would be a tool of reference that would collect dust among the other books on the shelf. With an oral aspect, every individual engages in scouring the depths of every matter and compels the Torah student to seek out learned rabbis for guidance needed to thoroughly understand Jewish law and philosophy. Ironically, because the written text is not so clear, the entire religion becomes stronger.

Nearly every realm of society transmits its knowledge, at least partly, through written text and oral supplement in conjunction. To truly acquire the knowledge, and enable it to become a tangible sensory knowledge, ideally one must have the "book smarts" and "street smarts" of a given subject matter. Only through the balance of both can one fully trust that the individual knows how to apply the knowledge.

Would anyone take lessons in karate from an instructor who only learned his techniques from a book? The answer is a categorical—no. To really acquire the knowledge, one must be under the leadership of a good sensei, who likewise spent time under another master sensei.

Likewise, nobody would ever consider seeing a doctor who did really well on his tests in his medical books but never learned under the direction of senior doctors or professors in residency. The apprenticeship or internship system is set up in virtually every professional field because the reality is that without the hands-on experience, which comes through discussion, questioning, and wise guidance, it is virtually impossible to really know something in its depth.

This constant interaction between teachers and their students ensures Jewish continuity and the accurate transmission of the Torah tradition, for whenever a text is written down, it is always subject to misinterpretation.[466] In other words, without the oral tradition, anyone would be able to interpret the text as he desired, in effect destroying the Torah as the revelation of G-d's will and altering it into the construed desires of man. This outcome is common in the world, as some non-Jewish religions accept the Jewish Bible as sacred, yet without the oral tradition they are forced to interpret the terse wording and nebulous phraseology of the written text based on mere whims. An outcome of this can be that verses meant to be taken literally are taken figuratively, and those meant figuratively are taken literally.

One glaring example of this might be the concept of "an eye for an eye."[467] It is a well-known excerpt from a verse, yet it is commonly misconstrued to mean that one is punished with exactly what one inflicts on another. So someone who damages another person's eye will have his eye damaged as punishment. This system would likewise apply with any other body part. However, the oral tradition understood that "an eye for an eye" means that someone who damages an eye must pay the *value* of that eye.[468] In other words, an eye's worth for an eye. So when Mahatma Gandhi said that "an eye for an eye ends up making the whole world blind," he is correct—in a world without the oral tradition. Yet, for the Jewish nation who carefully transmitted the oral law, it was always known to be adhered to figuratively.[469]

---

466 A very real example of this is the constant debates as to how to interpret the United States Constitution. See also Rambam, Introduction to his commentary on the Mishnah; *Moreh Nevuchim* 1:7.

467 *Shmos* [Exodus] 21:23-24.

468 *Mechilta*, *Shmos* [Exodus] 21:24; *Kesuvos* 32b and *Bava Kamma* 83b. Notably, the Lubavitcher Rebbe points out that the Torah of kindness would never give a punishment that would fully hinder a person from completing his mission in the world; see *Sichos Kodesh* 5736, vol. 1, Purim.

469 Some are under the misimpression that the verse really is speaking literally, but as the generations progressed, and people became more "enlightened," the rabbis decided it was too barbaric and modified it to suit the trends of society. This is simply not the case. Firstly, the Torah elsewhere gives indication that monetary compensation is given for damage caused. See *Shmos* [Exodus] 21:18–19, "If men quarrel and one strikes the other with a stone or fist...he shall pay for idleness and medical costs." In other words, the consequence is compensation, not retaliation. The Hebrew words used are *ayin tachas ayin*, an "eye for an eye," but a similar pattern is also seen in *Vayikra* [Leviticus] 24:18, "One

The oral Torah preserves Judaism as unique and our tradition as the correct reading and unchanged meaning since it was given at Sinai.[470]

Finally, the Torah is an eternal pact documenting G-d's will in all situations and at all times. A solely written Torah could not answer the question of whether one could turn on an electric light switch on Sabbath, nor any other future discovery, because those things had not been invented when the Torah was written. The oral tradition contains the ground rules for determining any newly arising circumstance throughout the course of history. Only through assiduous study, debating, questioning, seeking, and cross-referencing over the course of years, even decades, can a person possibly reach the appropriate knowledge to know the underpinnings of all of these ground rules and have the proper sensory knowledge to be able to rule accurately on how to deal with nuances in the world from a Torah perspective. The authority to make these calls has been bestowed amongst the modern *poskim*, rabbis who are proficient in the written and oral law and the decisions of earlier authorities on Jewish law. Such a person, and only such a person, can then be entrusted to ascertain G-d's will in all

---

who slays an animal [of another] shall pay for it: a life for a life." Here, the same Hebrew word *tachas* in "life for a life" is meant as financial compensation. So in "an eye for an eye," the word *tachas* means payment "in lieu of" the damage. One of the early post-Talmudic sages, Rabbi Sa'adia Gaon, says that logically it cannot mean equal retaliation. He says that suppose one hit another in the eye and impaired one third of his vision. How will one logically be able to inflict the same damage, no more or less, on the perpetrator? Maybe the victim will fully blind the perpetrator and that is not equal justice. Logically, it could never have been literal; cited in Ibn Ezra on *Shmos* 21:24.

Parenthetically, there is a hint to monetary compensation encoded in the wording of the verse itself. Rabbi Eliyahu, the Gaon of Vilna, questions why the Torah did not use the more appropriate *ayin* baad (for) *ayin*" instead of "*ayin* tachas (in lieu of) *ayin*." He answers that *tachas* also literally means "underneath." He notes that the three Hebrew letters that make up the word "eye" (ayin) are *ayin*, *yud*, and *nun*. The letters that are *tachas* (literally underneath) them, meaning directly beneath them in the Hebrew alphabet, are *fei*, *kaf*, and *samech*. These letters form the word *kesef*, which means money. The Torah is hinting that for an *ayin* you should pay that which is *tachas ayin* namely *kesef*. See the *Kol Eliyahu*, *Mishpatim*.

470 *Hoshea* 8:12. If G-d would have written the majority of the Torah, then Israel "would be counted the same as strangers." *Gittin* 60b relates that in the future, all the nations will write down the Torah for themselves. Were the oral Torah written, they would write it down for themselves as well. In that case, the Jews would no longer be the sole possessors of the oral Torah and will be like strangers to it.

situations and at all times, because this information has been delved into in an unbroken chain in the same format all the way back to Sinai. In this way, when the modern Torah authorities (and there are very few in a generation who have reached the depths of knowledge and experience to properly be called one) rule, for example, that one may not turn on electric lights on Sabbath, it is not simply "their opinion or perspective," but is rooted in and contains the authority of that which was received at Sinai.

In the face of Jewish persecution and dispersal to many foreign lands, significant content of the oral tradition was written down to insure it would be preserved.[471] Its teachings are encompassed in the Mishnah, Talmud, Midrashim, and cryptic books of Kabbalah. Contained within this tradition is the very fiber of Judaism, the method of correct biblical interpretation and transmission, something that cannot and will not ever be forgotten. It is up to every individual Jew to keep its preservation alive through engaging in assiduous study, living according to its ethos, and imparting it to the next generation.[472]

---

471 This was no simple matter. A legal dispensation was enacted by the sages to allow it to be written down lest it be lost forever; see Rashi, *Gittin* 60b; *Tosefta*, *Eduyos* 1:1. This monumental change became necessary by the destruction of the Second Holy Temple and the dispersion of the Jewish people (*Temurah* 14b).

472 A full analysis of the history and transmission of the oral law is beyond the scope of this work.

THE FORESIGHT OF THE SAGES

J ewish tradition looks at the Torah and the universe as two masterpieces composed by the same Author. According to Jewish
mysticism, they may be more appropriately deemed two different manifestations of the same thing. The *Zohar* teaches that
G‑d "gazed into the Torah, and created the universe."[473] The Torah is
not merely a book of instructions but the very "blueprint" of the universe—the will and wisdom of the Al-mighty. It dictated what should
be created and how the world looks and functions. Only those items
and situations needed to fulfill the Torah were brought into existence.
In other words, the physical world is merely a personification of the
Divine blueprint.

It is taught in the Hebrew Bible that "there is nothing new under the
sun."[474] The same tools and circumstances experienced in the modern era
have existed since the beginning of time. The sages relate that the Torah
contains everything.[475] Everything that ever was, is, and will be, even the
minute details of all subject matters, are alluded to in the Torah.[476] At
times, this exclusive information is stated outright, and other times it is
up to the sage to delve into the inner meaning of the Torah, and through
that he is clued in to events, discoveries, and scientific insights of the future. The following are some examples of the foreknowledge of the sages:

---

473   *Zohar*, Terumah 161.
474   *Koheles* [Ecclesiastes] 1:9.
475   *Avos* 5:22.
476   Gaon of Vilna, *Book of Concealment*.

NEW DISCOVERIES

The nineteenth-century dean of the Volozhin Yeshiva was named Rabbi Naftali Zvi Yehuda Berlin *zt"l*, and known as the Netziv. He was once asked how it could be said so many years ago, in biblical times, that "there is nothing new under the sun," when many things had not yet been invented. He replied that everything always existed in potential, even the newest inventions and devices. He mentioned a telescope, lightning rod, and phonograph in the classic works of the sages.

A type of telescope was used in the Talmud.[477] Rabban Gamliel had a hollow tube that he was able to sight a distance of two-thousand cubits on land and sea. A long hollow tube narrows and shortens the viewer's range.

He also mentions use of a lightning rod from the Tosefta.[478] The Tosefta there is discussing differences between two types of tools: those used in supernatural phenomena, which lack logical explanation and are deemed superstitious or of witchcraft, and other tools attributed to natural causes. The Tosefta prohibits an iron rod from being placed among chickens to ensure that they develop healthily, because this act has no natural explanation and is thus classified as superstitious or witchcraft. However, it is permissible to place a metal rod among chickens to save them from lightning, because there is a natural explanation for the phenomenon. The lightning rod would not be invented by Benjamin Franklin until 1752. When Rabbi Saul ben Joseph Katzenellenbogen of Vilna[479] heard about Franklin's experiments, he was unsurprised and unimpressed, saying that the discovery was nothing new, as it had already been in Jewish tradition for over 1,200 years.[480] A type of phonograph is also mentioned as used by the early sages.[481]

---

477 *Eruvin* 43b. The lenses were innovated into the telescope 1,400 years later.
478 *Tosefta, Shabbos* 7:10. The Tosefta is a supplement of the Mishnah, and is a compilation of Jewish Oral Law.
479 A disciple of Rabbi Eliyahu, the Gaon of Vilna.
480 See The Jewish Chautauqua Society's *The Menorah*, volume 36, pg. 85.
481 *Mechilta*, Yisro 18:19. Story about the Netziv printed in R. David Koppelman, *Glimpses of Greatness* (1994).

The foresight of the sages in not limited to inventions. Much of the wisdom that science has only relatively recently discovered was in many instances already addressed by the sages.

Dr. Louis Pasteur, French chemist and microbiologist, is most remembered for his breakthroughs in disease prevention. His novel conclusions attempt to cure diseases using the same bacteria that cause them. In 1885, Rabbi Israel Michel Rabinowitz, who was a close friend of Pasteur, was translating pages of the Talmud into French. One of the translated pages spoke about treating a victim who was attacked by a rabid dog.[482] Pasteur got a hold of this page and it inspired his work to discover the key to artificial immunization.[483]

TALMUDIC ASTRONOMY

THE LUNAR MONTH

Rabban Gamliel said, "I have received tradition from my father that the moon will renew no sooner than twenty-nine days and a half, two-thirds of an hour, and seventy-three parts of an hour."[484] The Rambam comments that a full hour has 1,080 parts. After writing out the above statement in decimal form, the result is 29.53059 days.

NASA only recently discovered the precise time that the lunar cycle begins and ends. Carl Sagan, renowned cosmologist and physicist who was chief scientist at NASA, writes that scientists calculated the length of a lunar month, the time from new moon to new moon.[485] It was calculated by reflecting a laser beam back to Earth from a glass prism placed on the moon by American astronauts. With the aid of powerful telescopes connected to an automatic clock, they have computed a time of 29.530388 days.

As astonishingly close as these numbers already are, Dr. Hugo

---

482   *Yoma* 84a.

483   *Mevo She'arim* quotes reliable witnesses who heard from Rabbi Rabinowitz that Pasteur discovered the basis for his research from the Talmud. See Aaron Parry, *The Complete Idiot's Guide to the Talmud* (2004), pg. 199.

484   *Rosh Hashana* 25a.

485   Carl Sagan, *Broca's Brain: Reflections on the Romance of Science* (1979), pg. 157.

Mandelbaum, a noted mathematics professor at Wayne State University, said that upon further mathematical assessment, the prediction of the sages and that of NASA are actually the exact same number.[486]

NUMBER OF STARS

The Talmud writes that the Congregation of Israel complained to G-d for having forsaken her. To this G-d responded: "My daughter, twelve constellations [*mazalos*] I created in the firmament, and in every constellation I created for it thirty hosts and for every host I created for it thirty Legions and for every Legion I created for it thirty cohorts and for every cohort I created for it thirty Karton and for every Karton I created for it thirty camps and for every camp I suspended in it 365 thousands of myriads [3,650,000,000] of stars corresponding to the days of the Solar year, all of them I created only for your sake."[487]

According to the Talmud the number of stars would be:

$12 \times 30 \times 30 \times 30 \times 30 \times 30 \times 365{,}000 \times 10{,}000 = 1.06 \times 10^{18}$.

This number is unfathomably large. These are the cosmic objects defined by the sages as stars. Interestingly enough, this calculation fits in line with the modern calculations.[488] Also evident from the Talmud's language is that the distribution of stars is neither even

---

486   Hugo Mandelbaum, "Proceedings of the Association of Orthodox Jewish Scientists," vol. 3–4.

487   *Brachos* 32b.

488   One example that puts the number of stars at around 1018 is from Arizona State University (see http://eagle.la.asu.edu/openhouse/faq.html). Granted this is a relatively low estimate in comparison to others. In general, current research estimates the amount of stars in the universe to be closer to 10^{22}–10^{24}. It is likely that the figure will fluctuate up and down in future years. Additionally, researchers obviously do not count each star individually, but make their estimates based on a survey from a strip of sky. It is also important to consider that the number in the Talmud also does not factor in the many non-zodiac constellations; it refers only to a special status connected to the zodiac constellations. Including these stars and clusters would also significantly raise the total number of stars in the universe.

   In any event, the Torah's calculation is an estimate much greater than that which can be seen by the unaided eye. Even under ideal conditions, a person can only see around 3,000 stars with the naked eye, or maybe a bit more if he has really good vision. Abraham was blessed that his descendants would be like the stars in the heavens. Living in the time before telescopes, this was hardly a blessing. The Giver of the Torah knew that there were more than what was then humanly perceived.

nor random. Rather, they are grouped together in what are presumably called galaxies today. Galaxies are also grouped in clusters, and a group of clusters forms a super-cluster. The description of clusters and super-clusters are very recent discoveries and impossible to know about without the aid of the most powerful telescopes. Moreover, interestingly there are about **thirty** galaxies in the Local Group that the Milky Way is a part of, just as the Talmud states.[489]

The Talmud says that the stars and their positioning are for our sake as well. Although the Talmud has spiritual implications in writing this, it is fascinating that contemporary research shows that there is even a physical correlation. Dr. Nathan Aviezer, former Chairman of the Physics Department at Bar-Ilan University writes: "Recent advances in astronomy have revealed a remarkable link between life on Earth and the distant stars. In fact, it is no exaggeration to say that without the stars, life on Earth would have been impossible."[490]

INHABITABLE PLANETS

Of the greatest medieval sages who served as a teacher for many of the sages who wrote the Tosofos commentary to the Talmud, was Rabbi Yehuda Bar Barzilli. He writes in one of his Kabbalistic commentaries, quoting the Talmud, that there are many planets in the universe where people can live.[491] He writes that he is unclear as to whether there actually are "people" living there, as it was not something stated clearly by the Talmudic sages; however, this concept was well ahead of its time.

---

489   See Richard Matzner (ed.), "Local Group," *Dictionary of Geophysics, Astrophysics, and Astronomy* (2001), pg. 283. This is one estimate, and thirty is an average number mentioned in many contemporary books. Astronomers have different ways of categorizing and counting the exact number of galaxies in the local cluster. Some count nearly double this number because they are classified differently. For instance, if two galaxies are passing through each other, should they be counted as one as they exist now, or as two independent ones? Some galaxies are small but grouped close to one another; should they be classified as individuals or as their own miniature group? This author finds it fascinating that a passive Talmudic statement corresponds with any contemporary viewpoint.

490   Nathan Aviezer, *Modern Science and Ancient Faith* (2013), pg. 64; see also his *In the Beginning* (1990), pg. 107.

491   *Sefer Pirush, Sefer Yetzira*, pg. 172, quoting the Talmud in *Avoda Zara*.

RECURRING COMETS

In 1705, Edmond Halley thought that he was the first to discover that a certain comet appears in the sky roughly every seventy-five years. The comet later bore his name and was called Halley's Comet. There is record of this comet documented by early Chinese and Babylonian astronomers even before the Common Era, but it was not recognized as the recurring emergence of the same object until Halley, who insisted on receiving the credit for discovering its reappearance.

What Halley did not know is that the Jewish sages Rabban Gamliel and Rabbi Yehoshua had a conversation about "a certain star [that] rises once in seventy years and leads the sailors astray,"[492] which has been identified in modern times as referring to Halley's Comet.[493] It is significant that the Rabbi Yehoshua whom the Talmud quotes knew about *recurring* comets around 1,600 years before the rest of the world.

REFLECTED PLANETARY LIGHT

Until a few hundred years ago, scientists thought that light shining from a planet was inherent light, rather than a reflection from the light of the sun. In the days of Galileo, he showed that the light emanating from Venus was merely reflected light.[494] What is interesting is that two thousand years ago the sages referred to planet Venus as *nogah*, which means "shining."[495] The word *nogah* expresses an object that does not possess inherent light but rather emits a reflected light, similar to the moon.[496] The sages clearly understood that the planets

---

492 *Horayos* 10a.

493 S. Brodetsky, "Astronomy in the Babylonian Talmud," *Jewish Review* (May 1911), pg. 60. Some suggest that it was not actually Halley's Comet, based on the fact that Halley's Comet appeared in the year 66 CE when Rabban Gamliel was only in his twenties and perhaps too young to have students, as the Talmud further records. This argument is somewhat weak, but nonetheless, what has significance is the knowledge of the recurrence of any comet, not which particular comet it was.

494 See I. Bernard Cohen, *The Birth of a New Physics* (1985), pg. 72; however, really any book about the discoveries of Galileo will attest to this.

495 *Shabbos* 156a, as opposed to the word *ohr*, which means "light."

496 See Malbim and Gra (*Aderes Eliyahu*) on *Chavakuk* 3:4, "And *nogah* will be similar to *ohr*."

were a reflection of the sun's light, as opposed to luminaries in their own right, thousands of years before the rest of the world.

THE ROUND, ROTATING PLANET

There is biblical allusion to a round Earth. Naturally, the wisdom of the sages reflects this tradition. The Mishnah says that a statue holding a globe in its hand is considered an idol.[497] The Talmud elucidates that this is because "the world is shaped like a globe."[498] The Hebrew word for "earth" is *eretz*, which comes from the word *ratz*, meaning "moving" or "running." Rabbi Aviad Sar-Shalom Basilea in the seventeenth century writes that the fact that the Earth is round and rotates on its axis is something accepted by the Talmudic sages.[499] He also quotes the *Zohar* that says that the Earth turns around like a ball, and that the settlement changes from down to up and up to down. There are places where in one place it is light, and in another place it is dark. There are places where it is day for a long time, and almost no night, and vice versa.[500]

KOSHER ANIMALS

INSIGHT INTO KOSHER SLAUGHTER

One of the benefits (not reasons) of kosher slaughter of animals is that it is painless to the animal. *Shechita* requires one swift movement across the throat with a very sharp knife in which the animal dies instantaneously. There is a fascinating phenomenon recently discovered as being unique to kosher animals. Kosher animals are physiologically different than non-kosher animals. During the *shechita* process, the carotid artery, which connects with the brain, is severed upon the knife sliding across the throat. There is another artery that

---

497   *Avoda Zara* 3a.

498   See *Yerushalmi, Avoda Zara* 3a. Likewise see *Bereishis Rabbah* 13:14; and Rabbeinu Chananel and Tosofos to *Avoda Zara* 41a.

499   In his *Emunas Chachamim*, ch. 5.

500   See *Zohar*, part III, 10a.

runs through the vertebrae, connecting to a part of the brain known as the Rete Mirabile.

It has been claimed that during kosher slaughter, only the front carotid artery is actually severed, however, the vertebral artery in back of the neck still gives blood flow to the brain. This would make a prolonged suffering for the animal that is being kept alive by this blood flow. Remarkably, it has been discovered that in kosher animals, and only kosher animals, the carotid and vertebral arteries actually merge, so the *shechita* cuts off all blood flow to the brain, allowing the animal to die immediately and painlessly.[501]

KOSHER HONEY

The Mishnah cites a general rule when it comes to kosher foods: "That which comes from something which is not kosher—is not kosher, and that which comes from something which is kosher—is kosher."[502] For example, the milk of a pig or eggs of a vulture are not kosher, just as the pig and the vulture are not kosher. There is one seeming exception to this rule: the honey from bees is kosher, while bees are not. Why are bees different?

The Rambam writes that honey is permitted because "honey is not extracted from their bodies; instead, they gather it from the plants into their mouths and spit it out in the hive."[503]

According to modern understanding, honey is made in the following way:

Bees store and transport collected nectar to the honeycomb. While inside the bee, the nectar is transformed into honey by enzymes within the bee, however, it is never digested by the bee; it is expelled as is. Ergo, honey is not a product of the bee itself in the way that milk

---

501 S. D. Rosen, "Physiological Insights into Shechita," *The Veterinary Record* (June 2004) 154: pgs. 759–765; C. J. G. Wensing, *Essentials of Bovine Anatomy* (1971). For a full treatment on the subject, as well as in-depth information of just how painless kosher slaughter is because of the above and other factors, see Rabbi Dr. Yisrael Meir Levinger, *Jewish Ritual Slaughtering and the Suffering of Animals* (2004), in Heb.

502 *Bechoros* 5b, also see 7b.

503 Rambam, *Ma'achalos Assuros* 3:3.

is, honey is merely temporarily stored inside the bee. It is quite interesting that the sages knew bee anatomy and this difference in animal "by-products" close to two thousand years ago.

ANIMAL WITHOUT KIDNEYS

In the realm of *kashrus*, there is another interesting law that seems ahead of its time. A *treifa*, which literally means torn or mortally wounded, is one of the categories of non-kosher meat. The Torah writes, "Do not eat meat from an animal torn (*treifa*) in the field."[504]

The sages explained that an animal may qualify as a *treifa* if it has a birth defect, has a diseased or inflicted wound, suffers from a mortally defective organ or limb, or is close to death. So even though it may be a kosher animal and is slaughtered in the proper way, the meat could still be considered non-kosher if certain defects are found, including: lesions, lacerations, broken limbs, missing or punctured organs.

Interestingly, in Jewish law the rule is that an animal whose kidneys are missing is not considered a *treifa*, and is healthy enough to be ritually slaughtered.[505] This law seems puzzling, for how can an animal live without functioning kidneys? There was a Dutch study in the 1970s where cows had their kidneys surgically removed and surprisingly survived. It seems that ruminants (kosher animals) possess an automatic mechanism that causes the rumen to compensate for a loss of kidney function by filtering toxins.[506] Jewish law codified this secret of nature thousands of years before it was discovered by science.

---

504   *Shmos* [Exodus] 22:30.

505   *Shulchan Aruch*, *Yoreh Deah* 54:1; see also *Chullin* 54a.

506   Rabbi Dr. Levinger, cited in Rabbi Yaakov Dovid Lach, *Chullin Illuminated* (2005), pg. 182. See Rabbi Moshe T. Schuchman, "A Cut Above: Shechita in the Crosshairs, Again," *Kashrut Kurrents*, star-k.org.

CONCLUSION

In truth, there are hundreds of examples of the foresight in the To-rah and that which was revealed through the sages. In a world where Torah and science are so widely thought to be mutually exclusive, it is fascinating to see when the knowledge of the sages actually pre-dates a modern scientific discovery. It appears as thought there was an other-worldly wisdom passed down and guarded throughout the generations that enabled these concepts to be known long before the invention of the sophisticated tools in the modern era. The above is simply a starting point, but the wonders will continue to boggle the mind of the individual who wishes to seek out further examples.

BIBLICAL CRITICISM

A significant number of modern secular scholars reject the claim of the Torah's Divine origin, and even its historicity. Social scientists are often reluctant in investigating biblical history in great detail because of this consensus. The more universally accepted the background assumptions of any discipline, the less likely they are to ever be questioned. In the case at hand, suggesting single authorship of the Torah, and needless to say Divine authorship of the Torah, can be considered in academic circles as a sort of unacceptable or fringe ideology.

However, this perspective among the secular academic world is tenuous at its foundations. It is a result of a grossly biased system called "Biblical Criticism," which became widely popular in late nineteenth-century Germany. The original critics baselessly dismissed many components of the Bible as myth.[507] They then proceeded to concoct a whimsical system, rooted in Hegelian philosophy, of how Judaism must have evolved from primitive idolatry to sophisticated monotheism.[508] Little did they dream that

---

507 "The late Professor Leo Strauss, in his *Philosophy and Law*, made the very telling point that the Enlightenment, in its assault on religious traditions, generally and biblical faith specifically, never truly engaged with the concept of revelation. It merely took its non-existence as given and proceeded to interpret the Bible accordingly, as if it had proved what in fact it had merely assumed. The traditional belief in revelation, meanwhile, was neither refuted nor refutable. For that reason, Orthodoxy, unchanged in its essence, was able to outlast the attack of the Enlightenment and all later attacks and retreats." Cited from Jonathan Sacks, "Fundamentalism Reconsidered," in *The Jewish Action Reader* (1996), pg. 258.

508 Georg Hegel was a German philosopher. He was a primary force in popularizing the overarching idea of "progress." The buzzword in nineteenth-century philosophy was evo-

new discoveries would eventually be made that would shatter their foundations and declare these assumptions to be both unscientific and obsolete.[509]

The origin and intentions of the Bible critics were nothing new. Greek writers and historians nearly two millennia ago would have competitions as to who could find more libelous assertions about the Jewish people. At that time, the primary focus they sought was to deny the antiquity of the Jewish nation and eradicate the concept of being a people "chosen" by G-d. One need look no further than the work *Against Apian* by Josephus to see the anti-Semite Apian and how outlandish the slanderous vile against the Jews would go. Their efforts were fruitless, and today even anti-Semites do not deny the significant role that the Jewish people played in the ancient world. Since the provokers' original quest of rejecting Jewish historicity failed, they attacked that which goes hand in hand with the Jewish people, namely, their Torah. Since the assailants could not claim that the Jewish people began at the latter half of Second Temple times, a bit over two thousand years ago, they claimed instead that this was when the Torah originated.[510]

---

lution. Evolution was thought to occur in all institutions: economics, sociology, etc. In this system, civilization develops from simplicity to complexity, and from primitive to enlightened. In this context Hegelian philosophy assumed that monotheism was a later development than when the Torah claims to have been written. Monotheism was seen to be a peak that progressed from paganism. If the Bible was written at the time that it claimed, monotheism could not have existed yet. Ergo, the Torah must be more recent according to this philosophy. The monotheism that the Torah is known for must have been written into older, evolving texts at a later date.

This philosophy has been shown false across the board. One glaring example of the non-existent "evolution" and "progress" in the societal sense can be gleaned from the twentieth century. The scholar and philosopher, Isaiah Berlin, wrote that the brutal leaders of the past century—Lenin, Stalin, and Hitler—returned the world to barbarism; according to the nineteenth century's theories of progress, this would have been impossible; see Berlin, *The Sense of Reality: Studies in Ideas and Their History* (1996), pgs. 30–31.

509   For example, see the recently published work: Eyal Rav-Noy and Gil Weinreich, *Who Really Wrote the Bible?* (2010), for a systematic, meticulous, and complete assessment of the myth of multiple authorships. J. H. Hertz, *The Pentateuch and the Haftorahs* (1961), pg. 398, is also a classic on this topic.

510   Paragraph paraphrased from Chaim Zimmerman, *Torah and Existence* (1986), pgs. 410–11.

The theory of the more modern Bible critics has been called the "Documentary Hypothesis," which assumes the Torah, and by extension the entire Hebrew Bible, to be the compilation of previous literary works. Early Bible critics, including Englishman Thomas Hobbes and Dutch Jew Benedictus Spinoza, began by denying Mosaic authorship and conceived of a Bible written much later than it claimed. Later, French physician Jean Astruc became the "Father of the Documentary Hypothesis" by proposing that the various names ascribed to G-d, especially in the first two books of the Bible, suggested different authors. In other words, the Tetragrammaton (Y-H-V-H usually rendered Jeho-vah) was ascribed to the anonymous writer dubbed the "J source," and the Name *Elokim* to the "E source." He also noted perceived repetitions or redundancies in the text. Later German academics added additional authors. There was the "P" or Priestly source, who supposedly wrote the parts in the Torah that deal with the laws and customs of the priests, Levites, and Temple service, and the "D source" that authored the book of Deuteronomy. There was also thought to be a Redactor who edited the Bible into its current form. In the late 1800s, Julius Wellhausen, a German professor of theology and oriental studies, formalized and popularized the theory of multiple authorship, canonizing it into its current prominence in the academic world.

Wellhausen's popularizing the Documentary Hypothesis did not exist in a vacuum. Just as when it comes to the development of life, the individual who cannot accept the supernatural must accept the notion of an unguided gradual evolutionary process, so too the one who rejects the possibility of a "Divine Will" in the form of laws must confine themselves to an "evolving" scripture that came together by natural means. As will be discussed in a later chapter, the trend in the late nineteenth century was to see "evolution" in everything: economics, sociology, anthropology, and history, in addition to the widely known biological evolution of life. The popularity that the Documentary Hypothesis gained during that era is expected.[511]

---

511   Even prior to the late nineteenth century, there were also trends that helped bolster the

CONTENTION WITH THE DOCUMENTARY HYPOTHESIS

Aside from the fact that there is not a shred of archeological evidence of pre-redacted Torah scrolls, the Documentary Hypothesis faces some serious problems.[512] It is known that Christian scholars of the time, in trying to make their New Testament seem more significant, sought to minimize the authority of the Hebrew Scriptures.[513] This, coupled with strong sentiments of anti-Semitism in Europe, assisted in igniting and sustaining Higher Criticism,[514] catapulting it into its spot as the backbone of secular biblical scholarship. Historian Paul Johnson writes that Bible Criticism was "tinged with anti-Semitism."[515] Wellhausen himself certainly had an affinity to anti-Semitism.[516] As anti-Semitism mounted just prior to the Second World War, Germans found themselves believing that anything non-German was worthless. "When Friedrich Delitzch delivered a lecture called 'Babel und Bibel,' in which the Hebrew Bible was considered devoid of any religious or moral value, Kaiser Wilhelm congratulated him for helping 'to dissipate

---

Documentary Hypothesis's evolving philosophy of Scripture. For example, it was popular in the eighteenth century to question whether the Iliad and the Odyssey were really written by one man, Homer, or whether it was in reality derived from previous documents. A French dilettante, Abbe d'Aubignac, who is considered the father of the Homer problem, put forth his ideas in *Conjectures academiques: ou, dissertation sur l'Iiad*. John Astruc's critique on the Bible called *Conjectures sur les memoires originaux don't il parait que Moise s'est servi pour compusor le livre de la Genese*, has a remarkably similar name. This is not a coincidence.

512 It is also significant that the Samaritans, a group who broke off from the mainstream of the Jewish people very early in Jewish history, endorse the idea of Mosaic single authorship and possess a Samaritan Pentateuch that is incredibly similar to the standard Jewish Torah scroll.

513 See Weinfeld, *Deuteronomy and the Deuteronomic School* (1972), pg. 5.

514 A "scholarly" approach to Bible study seeking to establish authorship and date of composition.

515 Paul Johnson, *A History of the Jews* (1988), pg. 6.

516 In a nineteenth century volume of Encyclopedia Britannica, Wellhausen's entry on Israel contained strong antagonism against Judaism. He said that Judaism "takes the soul out of religion and spoils morality." See Moshe Weinfeld, *Getting at the Roots of Wellhausen's Understanding of the Law of Israel, On the 100th Anniversary of the Prologomena* (1979), no. 14:4–5.

the nimbus of the Chosen People.'"[517] Some referred to Higher Criticism as "higher anti-Semitism."[518]

Although, for the most part, Wellhausen's contemporaries blindly accepted his conclusions, not all were so quick to jump on the bandwagon. Famed Irish historian William Lecky criticized Wellhausen's lack of evidence, and the Earl of Halsbury—an excellent judge of evidence—was even harsher referring to his conclusions as "great rubbish."[519]

Wellhausen based himself on many premises that turned out later to be proven false.[520] He assumed that Moses could not have been the original writer because the time of Moses predated writing itself. This has shown to be inaccurate. Phoenetic script has its origins at around 1500 BCE. Archaeological evidence indicates that the original Hebrew script is related to the Phoenician script.[521] Therefore, "there is no reason whatsoever to deny the biblical text which ascribes to Moses the writing of events and the laws of the nation of Israel. Nevertheless, with the change of attitude toward the script, there was no parallel change towards the biblical text, still considered to be a collection of orally transmitted sayings."[522] The style of writing itself also implies ancient authorship, and not an evolving tradition that was compiled at a late historical period. Alan Millard, professor emeritus of Hebrew and ancient Semitic languages at the University of Liverpool, says that the Torah is remarkably free of Persian and Greek or even the grammatical influences of that period. The linguistic purity attests to a Torah written before Persia and Greece became world powers.[523]

Wellhausen also presumed that ancient people had only simple rit-

---

517   See essay entitled "On Bible Criticism and Its Counterarguments" in Nathan Cardozo, *Between Silence and Speech* (1995), where some of the facts were obtained for this section.

518   Solomon Schechter, "Higher Criticism—Higher Anti-Semitism," *Seminary Address and Other Papers* (1975), pgs. 35–39.

519   Hertz, ibid., pg. 199.

520   Umberto Cassuto, *The Documentary Hypothesis and Composition of the Pentateuch* (1941). Although Cassuto does not accept the Torah's view of complete Mosaic authorship, he has toppled many of the presuppositions that the Critical theory was founded upon.

521   See Robertson, *The First Six Days* (2007), pg. 90.

522   Ganor, *Who Were the Phoenicians?* (1985), pg. 224.

523   Alan Millard, "How Reliable is the Exodus," *BAR* (July 2000): pgs. 51–57.

uals and that more intricate ones must have come later. Evidence has shown that this is not the case.[524] Despite these discoveries, there has been no change in perspective by the academics. As one former Bible professor at Hebrew University in Jerusalem classically said,

> Biblical criticism finds itself today in a unique situation. There is a dominant theory, yet no one knows why it dominates. In the history of ideas, theories or concepts based on certain accepted principles often enjoy a disembodied existence long after those principles have been discredited...Wellhausen...based his theories on an interlocking system of proofs that seemed to complement each other...In the meantime, however, these foundations disintegrated one by one...The scholars of the Wellhausen School were forced to admit that most of the proofs do not hold up under scrutiny. Nonetheless, they did not abandon the conclusions.[525]

As far as the use of different Divine names in the Torah text, the significance of each has already been dealt with by the Jewish sages.[526] Likewise, biblical scholar Umberto Cassuto showed that each of

---

524 William Albright, *From Stone Age to Christianity* (1957), pgs. 118-119. M. H. Segal, *Masoreth Ubikoreth* (1955). See the section of this work that deals with biblical archaeology for further detail.

525 See Yehezkel Kaufmann, in *The Religion of Israel: from Its Beginnings to the Babylonian Exile* [Heb]. Roland Harrison, former professor of Old Testament studies at several universities, phrased it this way in his *Introduction to the Old Testament* (1969), pg 81: "Wellhausen's arguments complemented each other nicely, and offered what seemed to be a solid foundation upon which to build the house of biblical criticism. Since then, however, both the evidence and the arguments supporting the structure have been called into question and, to some extent, even rejected. Yet biblical scholarship, while admitting that the grounds have crumbled away, nevertheless continues to adhere to the conclusions."

526 The name *Elokim* refers to G-d as the Ruler of Creation. It shows how he oversees, governs, and guides the laws of nature. When the name *Elokim* is used, it shows G-d acting in justice, a methodical tick for tack in the natural system which He created (*Mechilta, Shmos* 15:2; *Yalkut Shimoni* 1:242).

The Tetragrammaton is the proper name of G-d, referring to Him as the Source of everything and above the laws of nature (*Tanya, Sha'ar HaYichud V'Emunah* 4; *Moreh Nevuchim* 1:61). Therefore when used in relation to mankind it indicates mercy—that G-d is dealing with the situation above the laws of nature or cause and effect (Ramban, *Devarim* 3:24).

the names is meant to bring out a different aspect of G-d's character, and that there is no basis for the hypothesis that they indicate multiple authors.[527] In addition, renowned Egyptologist Kenneth Kitchen cites many examples of Egyptian texts that refer to a single god with many different names, and emphasizes that Egyptologists would not use different names as a question of multiple authorship.[528] Even a superficial perusal beyond the first few chapters of Genesis and the name speculation crumbles with obtrusive inconsistencies. One finds the J and E names in repeatedly mixed orders even within a single chapter. The fallacy of this premise has been comprehensively and methodically shown time and again.[529]

Furthermore, the critics associate the book of Deuteronomy with a discovery that occurred in the days of King Josiah. In his time, the people had slipped into idolatry and were renovating the Temple, as it had been turned into a pagan house of worship by his predecessors. A scroll containing blessings and curses was found in the Temple that inspired King Josiah to cleanse the land from idolatry. The book of Deuteronomy contains a long section of blessings and curses, so the Bible critics concluded that this story describes its origin. This is just glaringly poor scholarship, as the truth of what this scroll was and what caused the commotion is stated explicitly in the text and elaborated upon by the sages. Jewish tradition, based on the text,[530] explain

---

527   Cassuto, ibid., pgs. 15–41.

528   Kenneth Kitchen, *Ancient Orient and Old Testament* (1966), pgs. 121–23.

529   See Rav-Noy and Weinreich, ibid.

530   During the reign of Achaz, many Torah scrolls, people, and other things of holiness were being destroyed (Rashi, *Melachim* II 22:8). Because of this, the Jewish priests hid the Torah scroll written by Moses to preserve it (*Metzudos Dovid*, ibid.). The definite article (letter *heh*) in the original Hebrew text (22:8) implies that this was a well-known, unique scroll. This scroll that was found was always kept in the Holy of Holies and rolled to the beginning (see commentaries to *Melachim* I [Kings I] 8:9). Later, during the reign of King Josiah, this Torah scroll was found hidden in the Temple, as it says, "Chilkiah the Kohen found the book of G-d's Torah, in Moses' hand" (*Divrei HaYomim* II [Chronicles II] 34:14). The joy of finding this priceless treasure was soon turned to fear as it was rolled to the Torah portion that discusses all of the admonitions, foreboding troubling times ahead. The discovery of the scroll and its ominous message helped catapult the Jews of the time back into Torah observance, which had been largely disrupted by Josiah's father and grandfather.

   Parenthetically, King Hezekiah, Josiah's great-grandfather, followed the Torah and

that this was *the* Torah scroll that was written by Moses himself.[531]

All supposed contradictions and redundancies that the critics imagined that they had nuanced have also been explained extensively in innumerable places in Jewish tradition. Alleged stylistic variations in the biblical text are highly subjective, demanding that a researcher look at two sections and deduce whether they come from the same source or not. In the last few decades, computer technology was even used to try and shed some light on the Torah's literary consistency.[532]

---

was considered a righteous person (see *Divrei Hayomin* II [Chronincles II] 30). Torah was strong in his generation. Menasseh, Josiah's grandfather, was wicked and led the nation astray. He ruled fifty-five years. Amon, Josiah's father, was also wicked and said to have burned Torah scrolls. He ruled for two years. This makes fifty-seven years between Hezekiah's death until Josiah's reign. When Josiah became king, many people were likely still alive who remembered the righteous King Hezekiah. Furthermore, King Menasseh returned to Torah at the end of his life (*Divrei Hayomim* II [Chronicles II] 33:16). Josiah became king only two years later. Even considering the opinions that it took a number of years for Josiah to return to the ways of G-d, it had not been that many years, and seems highly unlikely that Torah concepts and observance would have been completely abandoned and unknown to the Jewish people at the time of Josiah. For a further wealth of information concerning both the antiquity and continuity of the Torah in relation to this incident, see Hertz, *Pentateuch and Haftorahs*, pgs. 937–941; Miller, *Rejoice O Youth*, beginning at #106.

531   Moreover, King Solomon, who predates Josiah, clearly paraphrases and uses descriptions from Deuteronomy when dedicating the Temple, which would be impossible according to the Documentary Hypothesis.

532   Yehuda T. Radday, professor emeritus of biblical studies at the Technion, Israel's institute of technology in Haifa, conducted a study of the book of Genesis. The computer concluded that there was an 82% chance that the J and E sources were actually the same author. What makes this more interesting is that the same study was done with the works of German philosopher Kant and poet Goethe. The chances that they had each written their works independently were 8 and 22 percent. (See "Computer Points to Single Author For Genesis," *New York Times*, Nov. 8, 1981. See also Yehuda Radday, "Genesis, Wellhausen and the Computer," *Zeitschrift fur die Alttestamentliche Wissenschaft*, April 1982.) Even before this computer experiment, Goethe was already used as a comparison of multiple styles of writing within a single work: "Imagine a Higher Critic analyzing Goethe's *Faust*, which was written by a single human being in the course of sixty years...Where do we find more inconsistencies in style and thought and plan: in Goethe's *Faust* or in the Five Books of Moses?" (Walter Kaufmann, *Critique of Religion and Philosophy* (1978), pg. 377).

In a different study in 2011, Professor Moshe Koppel, on the faculty of the Computer Science Department at Bar-Ilan University, conducted an experiment on linguistics that involved the biblical text. News articles were all too excited to quickly over-glorify the results and proclaim that researchers have proven multiple authors. The truth does not nearly match up to the hype generated. The software recognizes repeated word selections

Different styles do not mean different authors. Many celebrated writers, both current and classic, had the ability to solely construct masterpieces that reflected a variety of literary genres and styles. Styles reflect the material that is trying to be conveyed. Being that the Bible contains different types of materials, different styles can be expected; they do not mandate multiple authors.[533]

The Torah text can only be fairly evaluated with in-depth Jewish theological understanding. The pilot manual for an F-15 is not meant for the uninitiated reader to peruse and shortly thereafter attempt to fly an F-15. The manual has certain assumptions about the knowledge and training of the reader. Without this previous background, it is simply impossible to try and make sense of how the manual works and what it is meant to accomplish. Just as the reader of the F-15 manual cannot get anywhere by whimsically determining what the manual means to him, so too Judaism has its own, very specific guidelines and traditions regarding the study, interpretation, and applications of the Torah. Any explanations of Torah made outside of these parameters, no matter how appealing or creative they may be, are outside the realm of Judaism and its Torah.[534]

One of the pillars of the Jewish faith is that G-d gave both the written and oral laws at Sinai, as was discussed in an earlier chapter. This was

---

and their synonyms in separate segments that it determines are from different authors. The study simply shows that similar language is used in distinct sections of the Torah text, which is what the Bible critics always pointed out—nothing new. The study does not show whether literary reasons or deeper elucidations exist for the different language choices. Furthermore, the method they used does not determine the number of authors. Rather, one decides in advance how many families you want and the method finds the optimal split of the text into that number. If you ask it to split Moby Dick into two or four or thirteen parts, it will do so. So the fact that they split the Torah into two shows absolutely nothing about the actual number of authors. The only real discovery that came about was that the program's results overlapped with some of the findings of higher Bible criticism regarding possible boundaries between distinct stylistic threads in the Torah. Professor Koppel writes clearly and specifically that "there is nothing in these results that should cause those committed to the traditional belief in Divine authorship of the Torah to doubt that belief." This information was paraphrased from Koppel's essay here: seforim.blogspot.com/2011/07/attribution-and-misattribution-on.html.

533   See Herman Wouk, *This is My God* (1973), pg. 291.

534   Paraphrased from Moshe Averick, *Nonsense of a Higher Order* (2010), pgs. 29–30.

accompanied with the formula in which to interpret the Scripture. The terse wording of the written text is not truly understandable without undergoing intense study in the oral tradition and proficiency in how the established recipes of interpretation work. It is all too easy to look at the vague wording of the written text and then, several thousands of years later, retroactively project capricious meanings and interpretations of what the text means. The written text is written in the succinct way that it is because it assumes prior and accompanying knowledge.

These are just the most basic issues with biblical criticism; many more thorough analyses have been published.[535] One can certainly add the genetic discoveries in Jewish priests that were discussed earlier to the classical contentions with the Documentary Hypothesis as well. The final issue to be addressed should be the subject of biblical authenticity in light of recent archaeological and other scientifically relevant discoveries. This furthers the blow to biblical criticism as many of the biblical traditions and the archaeological evidence relate with striking accuracy. The details of these discoveries, along with the breakdown of how they are viewed by contemporary researchers, will be discussed in the upcoming chapter.[536]

---

535 For example, Eyal Rav-Noy and Gil Weinreich, *Who Really Wrote the Bible* (2010); Feldman, "Changing Patterns in Biblical Criticism" in Carmell and Domb, *Challenge* (1976), pg. 432; Elihu Schatz, *Proof of the Accuracy of the Bible* (1973); Kapusten, "Biblical Criticism: A Traditionalist View," *Tradition* 7:4 (Winter 1965).

536 Although not a recent statement, Dr. Yohanan Aharoni, former chairman of the Institute of Archeology at Tel-Aviv University, strongly defended the traditionalist view, saying, "Recent archaeological discoveries have decisively changed the entire approach of the Bible critics. They now appreciate the Torah as a historical document of the highest caliber. The approach of the Bible critics has…been altered because parallel documents have been found which describe the same events, told in biblical narratives, from the perspective of the Egyptians, the Assyrians, or ancient Canaanites…We are familiar with customs and laws described in the biblical narratives, as well as the people and places mentioned…No author or 'editors' could have put together or invented these stories hundreds of years after they happened. No serious Bible scholar remains who can argue with the fact that these historical events were transmitted with incredible historical accuracy from generation to generation, until our time." See his *Canaanite Israel During the Period of Israeli Occupation* (1959), pgs. 2–3.

TORAH IN LIGHT OF CONTEMPORARY DISCOVERIES

Creation

For centuries, the academic world thought the universe to be eternal.[537] Even as late as the 1960s, when evidence was rapidly piling up to the contrary, two-thirds of leading surveyed U.S. scientists believed it.[538] The theory of an eternal universe likely remained popular for so long because, in the words of theoretical physicist Steven Weinberg, it avoids the "problem of Genesis."[539]

Today in the scientific world, it is a given that the universe had a beginning. Professor Brian Greene of Columbia University writes that "the accepted scientific theory of Creation is often referred to as the standard model of cosmology."[540] The term "creation" has left the private domain of biblical scholarship and entered the lexicon of science. Dr. Gerald Schroeder, formerly on staff at the MIT Physics

---

537   Heraclitus of Ephesus (535-475 BCE): "This cosmos, the same for all, was neither made by G-d nor man, but was, is, and always will be"; see Simon Singh, *Big Bang: The Origin of the Universe* (2005), pg. 79. While the later Greek philosopher Aristotle believed in a deity, he also believed that the universe was eternal. This set the trend for centuries of secular academic thinking.

538   S. Brush, "How Cosmology Became Science," *Scientific American* (Aug. 1992).

539   Steven Weinberg, *The First Three Minutes* (1993), pg. 154. Similar statement can be found by Steven Hawking in *A Brief History of Time* (1988), pg. 46.

540   Brian Greene, *The Elegant Universe* (1999), pgs. 345–346.

Department and member of the United States Atomic Energy Commission, writes, "this shift in scientific opinion, after millennia of opposition, represents the most significant change science can ever make toward biblical philosophy...for a beginning does not confirm the existence of a Beginner, but it does open the way to that possibility."[541] Along the same lines, Dr. Arno Penzias, one of three Nobel Prize recipients for identifying the "background radiation" that led to the Big Bang theory, writes "science has finally vindicated Moses and Maimonides over Aristotle."[542]

THE DETAILS OF THE BEGINNING

Besides the mere fact of there being a beginning, many of the latest discoveries in science about the details surrounding the beginning also have parallels in the Torah tradition. The Creation, in Jewish literature, was not a one-time occurrence, but instead an ongoing reality. G-d is continuously renewing Creation at every moment.[543] As Morris Engelson, a former professor at Oregon State University, points out, "According to quantum mechanics, fundamental particles like the electron are made to disappear, and instantaneously an identical version reappears. This happens all the time, everywhere." He writes that in effect "the universe is being perpetually renewed," just as the Torah tradition teaches.[544]

Another example is as follows: The first thing that G-d created in

---

541   Gerald Schroeder, *The Science of God* (1997), pg. 22.

542   "Creation is Supported by All the Data So Far," in Margenau and Varghese, *Cosmos Bios, Theos* (1992), pg. 78. He also writes: "The best data that we have concerning the Big Bang are exactly what I would have predicted, had I nothing to go on but the five books of Moses, the Psalms, the Bible as a whole."

543   See *Likkutei Amarim, Tanya, Shaar Hayichud Veha'emunah*, ch. 2, which says that G-d must keep re-creating the world constantly in order for it to remain in existence. In the daily prayer liturgy it says, "He renews each day, continuously, the work of Creation." The renewal is actually continuously at every moment. "Each day" is written because the renewal of Creation becomes apparent through the daily cycle of our existence; see *Likkutei Torah, Vayikra* 26a. See also *Sfas Emes*, Ki Savo, 5631, and many more places.

544   See Morris Engelson, *The Heavenly Time Machine* (2001), pg. 63. He also brings a quote from Rabbi Eliezer Eliyahu Dessler *zt"l*, who compares the Torah and science: "When we observe an object which appears to persist in the same form over a period of time, we certainly think that today we see the identitical object that we saw yesterday. But it is not so...Hashem re-creates for us momentary sections of existence..."

the Creation account is light, as in "Let there be light."[545] This light is said to be very powerful; nothing could withstand it. It is said that G-d decided to conceal this light and hide it away for the righteous in the hereafter.[546] People often ask about this light source, questioning where it came from, as the sun was not put in its place until the fourth day in the Torah account. While it is true that this Divine light of Creation is usually discussed in its more esoteric context, modern cosmology may also provide another tangible aspect of understanding. Professor Steven Weinberg, in his book *The First Three Minutes*, describes what was taking place in the early universe just after the Big Bang. He writes that at that point the universe was "filled with light" that was indeed very bright. There is a consensus about the existence of this light among physicists.[547] The Torah describes how the initial Creation light was put away, and the missing light was replaced with the radiation of the luminaries, albeit a light with much less intensity.[548]

SIMILAR HISTORIES FROM DIFFERENT CIVILIZATIONS

Dozens of civilizations have accounts of Creation very similar to that of the Bible, indicating that the stories come about from an actual experience. The similarities are found in cultures that are extremely distant and had no contact where they could have adapted the story of the other. There are various differences in story line, compared to that of the Torah, because the other nations had exclusively oral transmissions of their history for a long time before the stories were recorded. However, in some cases there are still enough similarities with the Bible to derive common origin.

---

545 *Bereishis* [Genesis] 1:3.

546 *Chagiga* 12a.

547 Weinberg, *The First Three Minutes* (1993), pgs. 5–6. See also Adam Frank, "The First Billion Years," *Astronomy* 34/6 (June 2006): 30–35.

548 The wording of the Torah points to this fact. With the original Creation light, G-d says, "Let there be light" or *ohr* in Hebrew. When G-d eventually says, "Let there be luminaries in the heaven" (*Bereishis* [Genesis] 1:14–15), the Torah spells "luminaries," or *ma'oros*, without a *vav*, i. e., incomplete. This teaching expresses that the light of these celestial bodies was not equal to the quality of the original Creation light; see Munk, *The Wisdom of the Hebrew Letters* (1983), pg. 100.

Some examples are as follows:

- The idea that water preceded all things is found all over the world, both in Mesopotamian nations and as far-flung as Native Americans and African tribes.
- The separation of Heaven from Earth is found in the Mesopotamian Epic of Creation, the Hittite story of Ullikummi, Egyptian myths, the Maoris of New Zealand, and the Bihors of India. It is also found in parts of Western Africa, Chinese folklore, the Pacific region, and Japan.
- The creation of man from earth or clay is found in Mesopotamian, Babylonian, Egyptian, Greek, native Australian, New Zealand, Tahiti, Melanesia, and Native American literature.
- There are likewise numerous sources for legends about a garden with special foods and four streams emanating from a central river.[549]

Secular scholars have tried to draw parallels between the Genesis account and other Middle Eastern accounts of the creation of the world. They claim that the other Creation stories served as the inspiration for the biblical narrative. These parallels are, at best, a figment of these scholars' imagination. The other narratives of the pagans all contain references to graphic and obscene circumstances by gods who were debased, irrational, and malicious. Gods birthing other gods and their physical relation to the world is found in all civilizations except for the Hebrew one. The Hebrew Bible is a much closer parallel to the Creation account across the globe by the nomadic Aborigines of Australia, whose primitive writing style avoided the corruption of Mesopotamia.[550] Dr. Leah Bronner, former professor of Bible and Jewish History at the University of the Witwaterstrand in Johannesburg, has eloquently described the contrast between the biblical and pagan creation accounts, saying, "the points of resemblance concern

---

549   See Theodore Gaster, *Myth, Legend and Custom in the Old Testament* (1969), pgs. xxvi–xxxiii, 3–35, cited almost verbatim from Elihu Schatz, *Proof of the Accuracy of the Bible* (1973), pg. 22.

550   Dr. David Medved, *Hidden Light* (2008), pg. 8–9.

matters of detail, and the points of difference, matters of principle. The ancient cosmogonies are crude and primitive, while the Genesis version is simple and sublime."[551]

COMMON ANCESTRY AND EARLY CIVILIZATION

THE THREE-AGE SYSTEM

The predominant secular view of historical development is similar to biological evolution. Just as life forms progressed from primitive organisms all the way up to mankind through millions of unlikely mutations, so too, human history must have advanced from the most primitive lifestyles to the most advanced urban society. The view of every aspect of life having an evolving development was very popular in the nineteenth century.

The origin of classifying human development into a three-age system of Stone Age, Bronze Age, and Iron Age is from a Danish archaeologist named Christian Jürgensen Thomsen. In the early 1800s, he placed tools and other artifacts present in the Museum of Northern Antiquities in what he determined to be chronological order. The Stone Age eventually became associated with a large span of time, beginning from the earliest beings that could be classified as human, and extended all the way until between 6000 BCE and 2000 BCE. It is called the Stone Age because stone was widely used to make tools in that time period. According to this view, when the ancestors of the human being began to stand upright, they began to work with their hands, building with stones and stone tools. During this period, only wood and stone were used by humans. A few million years later, with the advent of metalwork, the Stone Age period was followed by the Bronze Age and the Iron Age as civilization became more technologically developed. The artistic reconstruction of times passed displayed proudly in museums lay out a "just so" historical progression of civilization development.

Findings since the nineteenth century have been interpreted

---

551   Bronner, *Biblical Personalities and Archaeology* (1974), pg. 29.

according to the three-age system. The exclusivity of stone-tool use in the Stone Age era seems puzzling because researchers have found very well-defined and shaped stone implements that are identified as hundreds of thousands of years old. The intricacy involved seems tough to accomplish with just stone tools.[552] Additionally, the Iron Age is said to be the third Age because iron implements are dated most recently in archaeological findings. However, perhaps the iron utensils that are found are more recent than the bronze utensils, not because they belong to a different era, but because bronze takes longer to decay than other metals. With this consideration, it seems fairly predictable that iron utensils that are found would be more recent than the bronze utensils.

The evolution of civilization was thought to parallel the biological evolution of man; however, this does not seem to be the case.[553] What appears more likely is that throughout history, some nations or groups have lived more primitively, while other societies were simultaneously living civilized lives. Just like in our day, the world's technological leaders have the ability to launch men into space, while villages in some other areas are technologically backward.[554] These situations all exist simultaneously. They indicate differences in cultures and civilizations, not the evolution of societies.

British archaeologist Paul Bahn, in one of his books, touches on the concept of the essentially unknown development of human history, despite how authoritatively it is often displayed.[555] Quoting Professor Stephen Jay Gould, he writes that the traditional scenario of human

---

552   Stone on stone carving seems unlikely to carve the same symmetry, smoothness, and design details that are found on utensils classified as from the Stone Age. Making beautiful carvings of animals, for example, would be nearly impossible using only stone tools.

553   "In fact, concrete evidence of the inadequacy of the Darwinian hypothesis is to be found in the archeological record. If the Darwinian package were correct, then we would expect to see the simultaneous appearance in the archeological and fossil records of evidence for bipedalism, technology, and increased brain size. We don't. Just one aspect of the prehistoric record is sufficient to show that the hypothesis is wrong: the record of stone tools." See Richard Leakey, *The Origin of Humankind* (1994), pg. 12.

554   Ancient Egypt, for example, was a more sophisticated civilization than some of these present-day cultures.

555   In the introduction to his *Archaeology: A Very Short Introduction* (1997).

societal evolution from primitive to modern is merely a story.[556] He adds that much of science proceeds in this way, namely, as a story. He lists the traditional attributes of the so-called human societal evolution: tales of the hunt, cooking and campfires, dark caves, rituals, etc. He questions how much of these suppositions are based on bones and actual remains, and how much on literary criteria. Bahn also assures the reader that the same is true in historical archaeology. He continues onward, saying that since nobody knows what happened in the past (even the recent past), archeological research will always be ongoing. He explains that theories come and go through general repetition and widespread acceptance. Quoting Max Planck, he writes: "A scientific truth does not triumph by convincing its opponents and making them see the light, but rather because its opponents die and a new generation grows up that is familiar with it."

An interesting point to ponder, as well, is: What remnants of today's civilization will be around in several thousand years from now? Of the little that will be remaining from our era, how will future archaeologists interpret life in the age in which we live? In our modern age, we have much more capability to document our lifestyle—through books and videos—but even still, will their conclusions be accurate? So, getting back to the topic at hand, looking back thousands of years at the bone samples, tools, and other artifacts discovered—how accurate is our picture?

---

556 A related thought is brought out by Nigel Brush, assistant professor of geology at Ashland University in Ohio, saying: "The story of human evolution has great literary appeal because we've been telling stories to our children for generations. The usual basic plots are found in folktales around the world. The appearance of common story motifs and plots in scientific accounts of human evolution should warn us that we are not being given 'just the facts.' The 'facts' in evolutionary reconstructions have been selected and standardized from a much larger body of data and have been organized in such a way that they tell a logical, pleasing story. Discrepancies or missing data are often ignored in the interest of telling a story that is complete and that flows smoothly from one point to the next." See Nigel Brush, *The Limitations of Scientific Truth: Why Science Can't Answer Life's Ultimate Questions* (2005), pgs. 107–108.

THE HISTORICAL RECORD AND THE BIBLICAL "BEGINNING"

According to the biblical record, mankind as known today was created as intelligent, sentient beings approximately six thousand years ago. Right away, the Bible reader discovers the ancients using tools capable of building arks and towers. The necessities of an early society were developed and the groundwork for future generations was laid in the form of writing and art, philosophy, and technology.

Recorded history begins just several thousand years ago. It is at this time when significant human achievements are said to have developed. This timeline corresponds perfectly with when the biblical timeline says that civilized man came into being. According to everyone, language is only a few thousand years old,[557] as are most other remnants of ancient civilization like buildings and ruins, cemeteries or tombstones. Key inventions, like the wheel, are traced to around 3000 BCE, as well. Modern research also validates that the geographic region in which civilization sprouted from is also in sync with the Bible.

The claim of mankind's development from savage cave-people seems somewhat unconvincing as well. The supposition is that for hundreds of thousands of years, mankind shows virtually no signs of real intelligence, living more or less like animals, and then in the blink of an eye, around the same time as biblical Adam, wakes up with enlightenment and creativity and begins the ancient civilizations. Upon closer examination, it was not just language and tools that "sprung up" around the time of biblical Adam, but considerably more sophisticated feats that seem to develop out of thin air.

Consider the profound knowledge that went into building the

---

557 Writing, which is imperative to deem something historical, is notably traced back about 5,000 years by modern scholars ([C. B. Walker, *Reading the Past: Cuneiform* (1989)]. There is debate as to what is the oldest alphabet, but Hebrew is one of the primary considerations. [*Panim el Panim*, No. 367 (May 13, 1966): pg. 14]. The order of the Hebrew letters is, nonetheless, deemed the oldest. "Alphabets," *Encyclopedia Britannica* (Deluxe Ed. 2004-CD ROM).

megalith rock formations that are sprinkled across the ancient world.[558] The stone blocks in these monuments often weigh more than a ton and were transported significant distances. To this day they are considered engineering mysteries. These monuments need tremendous amounts of planning, possibly error-free drawings for accuracy, and impeccable communication skills that can accurately convey the intent to all those involved in the project. There is clear evidence in these structures of the ancients' knowledge of mathematics and geometry. Many of the structures are also aligned with astronomical phenomena, which would mean a familiarity with astronomy as well. Furthermore, they had the technology to transport construction materials from far away. It would seem impossible to do all of this with only primitive tools, manpower, and knowledge. The pyramids of Egypt, which came later, would be difficult even for modern men to duplicate.[559] Additionally, ancient Egypt was also known for its sophisticated methods of embalming the dead, textiles, and a deep grasp of art, science, and medicine.

The secular academic view of when and where civilization began coincides well with the timing and location of biblical Adam and his descendants. The intelligence and technological advancement of different peoples also seems to be in line with the way the peoples of the Torah are described. It is interesting, to say the least, that in a fifteen-billion-year-old world, all recorded knowledge only begins when the Torah tradition says civilization began.

---

558 Some of the most famous megaliths are Newgrange and Stonehenge. Newgrange is a monumental grave near Dublin, Ireland, assumed to have been built around 3200 BCE, see *The Archaeology Coursebook* (2008), pg. 159. Its builders had a thorough knowledge of engineering and architecture. Stonehenge is a monument in Wiltshire, England, that is dated between 3000–2000 BCE. Each of the blocks in the formation is around fifteen feet tall and weighs over twenty tons. The bluestones used in the monument were imported from the Preseli Mountains, which is over two hundred miles away. Its exact purpose is subject to debate, although its builders certainly seem to be much more technologically savvy than commonly assumed. They were also familiar with astronomy.

559 The earliest Egyptian pyramids are dated around 4,500 years old. Others were built later.

TORAH APPROACH: COMMON ANCESTRY AND COMMON TRADITION

The Mishnah explains that mankind was created from common parents so one man will never say "my father is greater than yours."[560] Although people would eventually be divided into nations and social classes, that single origin is a unifying element designed to tame provocations among people. More than one origin would have likely led to increased divisiveness and jealousy.

According to the Torah view, Adam and some righteous descendants of his communicated with G-d, and everyone initially believed in and worshipped Him. Although the Torah did not become obligatory until Sinai, much of its spiritual wisdom and legal precepts were conceptually well-known and taught by mankind, beginning with Adam.[561] There was one unified Torah-based tradition in humanity before any religion, as known today, was founded.

All of the ancient legal codes of the Near East, including that of Hammurabi, are warped outgrowths of early Torah knowledge.[562] The Torah names Methuselah, Shem, and Eber as examples of ancient prophets and spiritual giants, who were upright and served G-d through the conceptual Torah tradition. Certainly their achievements had influence on their surrounding neighbors and brought similarities into the surrounding ethical codes.[563]

---

560 *Sanhedrin* 4:5.

561 Mankind at the time was only responsible for the Seven Laws of Noah, yet Adam learned Torah in the Garden of Eden (*Pirkei D'Rebbe Eliezer* ch. 8). Noah distinguishes between taking seven of each kosher animal and only two of every non-kosher animal onto the ark around 700 years before the Torah was given (*Bereishis* [Genesis] 7:2). Shem and Eber had an ongoing *yeshiva*, and the forefathers actually kept the entire Torah before it was given. (See *Yoma* 28b; Rashi, *Bereishis* 26:5, 32:5 for just some of many examples.)

562 As far as the Torah's legal codes, one of the Seven Universal Laws is not to steal. Not stealing seems like an obvious obligation for a functioning society, but the precise details of what is considered stealing or deception are elaborated upon in the oral tradition. It would be sensible that many of the Talmud's descriptive laws of property and damages would be learned in passed-down oral traditions by the ancients, accounting for much of the similarity in the ancient legal codes. Interestingly, it has been said in the name of Rabbi Simcha Wasserman that Hammurabi was likely a dropout of the academy of Shem and Eber; see ohr.edu/ask_db/ask_main.php/92/Q1/.

563 See Kook, *Eder ha-Yakar*, pg. 42.

Jewish tradition teaches that the universal truths of Torah were truly the origin of nearly everything known today in ethics, spirituality, and philosophy. It has been traced as the origin of the Eastern religions,[564] and even the ancient wisdom of the Greek philosophers,[565] including

---

564   As far as spiritual knowledge and practice, it is quite interesting to consider how the wisdom of the East arose. Chinese history begins with the five emperors between 4000–5000 years ago. Their wisdom is also attributed to [spiritual] "giants" from afar. In the Torah, the children that Abraham had with concubines after Isaac, are given "gifts" and sent to the East (*Bereishis* [Genesis] 25:1–6). The Talmud (*Sanhedrin* 91a) teaches that these "gifts" that he gave them were the impure Divine names. In other words, he gave them some spiritual secrets that did not require ritual purity and described the manipulation of energy in nature. Unfortunately, as time progressed, the teachings and healing practices became completely corrupted with idolatrous associations. It is significant that the highest social class in India, who do not intermarry with "lower" classes are called "Brahmins"; adding an "A" makes Abrahmins, perhaps suggesting a relationship between those ancient spiritual giants sent by Abraham. See *Zohar* 99b–100b; *Nishmas Chaim*, sect. 4, ch. 21.

     Additionally, there are some word root similarities between Hebrew and the ancient world, which are interesting to say the least. For example, *Hindu* means "from the river (Indus)." Abraham was called a *hebrew*, which means "from over the river." *Vedas* is "knowledge" in Eastern philosophy, related to the Hebrew word *da'as*, which also means "knowledge." Furthermore, one of the concubine children sent to the East was named *Avee-da*. A "camp" in Hinduism is called an *ashram*. According to Rashi, one of the sons name means "a camp"; he is named *A-shurim*. There are many more that could be said as well.

     Furthermore, there has recently been a link discovered between body contact points of tefillin and ancient Chinese acupuncture points for spirituality and purified thought (see Steven Schram, "Tefillin: An Ancient Acupuncture Point Prescription for Mental Clarity," *Journal of Chinese Medicine* 70, Oct. 2002)

565   Megasthenes was a Greek ethnographer, explorer, and an ambassador of Seleucus I. He reported that "all that has been written on natural science by the old Greek philosophers may be found in philosophers outside of Greece, such as the Hindu Brahmins and the so-called Jews of Syria"; see Max Radin, *The Jews Among the Greeks and Romans* (1915), pg. 86. Also Josephus wrote, "Our earliest imitators were the Greek philosophers, who, though ostensibly observing the laws of their own countries, yet in their own conduct and philosophy were Moses' disciples..." see *Against Apion* 2.281.

     "Many intellectual Greeks were ripe to discard the plethora of traditional gods and myths in favor of a unitary creative force, and were open to the democratic precepts inherent in Judaic law. These Greeks were impressed with the universal literacy promulgated by the Jews and were intrigued by the atmosphere of inquiry that attended Jewish studies." Samuel Kurinsky, *The Eighth Day: The Hidden History of Jewish Contribution to Civilization* (1994), pgs. 293–294.

Pythagoras,[566] Socrates,[567] Plato,[568] and Aristotle.[569,570]

ONE G-D AND ONE TRADITION BECOME MANY

The development of idolatry is one example of how pure theology slowly became tainted. The Rambam explains that all started off from a pure beginning, relating to One, invisible, omniscient, unified G-d. As the generations progressed many people began to err, first using the sun, moon, and celestial bodies as go-betweens to get to G-d.[571]

---

566   See *Against Apion*, book 1, ch. 22, in *The Complete Works of Josephus* (1981), pg. 614. There he cites Hermippus of Smyrna, who accused Pythagoras of doing "things imitating and transferring to himself the opinions of the Jews." (See also Origen, *Contra Celsum* I:15. Also Porphyry of Tyre, *Life of Pythagoras* 11). Iamblichus, in his *Life of Pythagoras*, explained that he "conversed with the prophets who were the descendants of Moses the physiologist." See also Menashe ben Israel, *Nishmas Chaim, ma'amar* 4, ch. 21 who writes that Pythagoras's belief in reincarnation came from the early Jewish prophets.

567   See Rabbi Yechiel Halperin, *Seder HaDoros*: "3385: Plato received wisdom from the prophets, and Socrates studied from Achitofel and Assaf HaKarchi." See also Rama, *Toras HaOlah*, vol. 1:11.

568   *Nishmas Chaim, ma'amar* 2, ch. 10. He writes that it was well known, even amongst the writings of the ancient Greeks, that after the prophet Jeremiah was exiled to Egypt, he taught Plato the teachings of Torah, which is why many of his teachings are in sync with the Torah. See also related: Rama, *Toras HaOlah*, quoted in *Lev Eliyahu*, Vol 1 pg. 292; and Abarbanel in *Mifalot Elokim*. Numenius of Apomea, a disciple of Plato, said "For what is Plato but Moses speaking in Attic"; see Clemens Alexandrinus, *Stromata*, 1.22.150–154 and in Eusebius, *Praeparatio Evangelica*, 11.10.14. Sir Isaac Newton also writes in one of his manuscripts that "Plato, travelling into Egypt when the Jews were numerous in that country, learnt there his metaphysical opinions about the superior beings and formal causes of all things, which he calls ideas and which the Kabbalists call Sefirot." (See Yahuda MS, 15.7, pg. 137v. The National Library's collection of the Newton Papers is now available in digital format and this citation can be viewed here: newtonproject.sussex. ac.uk/view/texts/normalized/THEM00237).

569   Legend is that he received the teachings from Jewish sources; see Rabbi Meir Aldebi, *Shevilei Emunah*. It is related: "When Alexander [the Great] went to Jerusalem, he gave his teacher Aristotle control over King Solomon's books. He plagiarized his philosophies from there, and called them by his own name..." [In *Sheva HaChachmot* by Dov Rafel (Jerusalem, (5750), chapter 3), he cites many sources, both Jewish and non-Jewish, which mention these traditions.]; also *Nishmas Chaim, ma'amar* 4, ch. 21. There are even sources in Jewish tradition that Aristotle was either born a Jew (see *Derech Emunah* 2:303) or that he converted at the end of his life (see Introduction to *Sefer HaMidos*).

570   Be that as it may, this does not lend license to study Eastern religions or Greek philosophy, thinking that it coincides completely with Torah, as over the years the concepts have veered from their original state.

571   This began in the generation of Enosh, the grandson of Adam; see *Targum Yonason* on *Bereishis* 4:26.

Eventually, G-d was dropped altogether and these intermediaries became the center of worship.[572] This was long before Abraham and Judaism came to the world. Abraham did not invent monotheism per se; rather, he reawakened and publicized the idea that had long since been abandoned by all but a handful in the previous generations.

The idea that religion gradually evolved from barbarism to an eventual monotheism is an outlook that essentially became widespread and dominant concurrently to and as an outgrowth of the Darwinian theory of evolution.[573] At the turn of the twentieth century there emerged compelling evidence that monotheism preceded polytheism.

---

572   See Rambam, *Avodas Kochavim*, ch. 1.

573   Beginning around a hundred and fifty years ago, around the same time that Darwin published his *Origin of Species*, some thinkers started assuming that every event in human history and every aspect of human knowledge was founded upon an evolutionary pattern. Everything could be viewed as originating in a primitive stage and gradually advancing toward perfection.

Karl Marx, a contemporary of Darwin, premised his ideology with an evolutionary development of economic systems. He surmised that over the course of history, superior economic systems would replace inferior ones. Marx's layout says that feudalism was replaced by capitalism, which would eventually be superseded by socialism. However, Marx's scheme did not reflect reality. See Gregory and Stuart, *Comparing Economic Systems in the Twenty-First Century* (2005).

Sigmund Freud, in the realm of psychoanalysis, said that human beings were a very highly evolved species but that psychologically, their actions were still motivated by the same base drives as their primitive ancestors had been. Freud's overall suppositions are regarded as incorrect and obsolete.

Likewise, sociology, anthropology, history, and even religion have also been erroneously framed in the evolutionary format. Herbert Spencer, who was a very prominent English sociologist and anthropologist, was a heavy contributor in shaping the evolutionary mindset in these fields. Spencer also happened to be a good friend of Charles Darwin. Some anthropologists opine that religion started with worship of the dead. Others believe that it began with the worship of nature. From these starting points, humanity "evolved" to polytheism and culminated with monotheism. Parenthetically, it is of no surprise, that many of the "New Atheists" posit that their belief in "no god" is the last rung on the human evolutionary ladder.

There is adequate historical evidence that shows contrary to what these nineteenth century thinkers have proposed. People have believed in one G-d since the earliest of times. That is not to say that there were only monotheists in ancient times. Certainly there were many polytheists, and other deviant ideas to the One G-d, but there was no gradual evolution from barbarism to monotheism; they all existed and continue to exist simultaneously. Also today there are people who believe in G-d and there are also those who worship idols of wood and stone, or corruptions of monotheism.

Wilhelm Schmidt in *The Origin and Growth of Religion* conclusively disproves the widely accepted evolutionary development of religion from fetishism to polytheism to monotheism. Throughout the world, primitive peoples have preserved, behind their idols, the idea of an all powerful "Great Spirit" who created the world. Anthropologists refer to this god as the "Sky-god" but the more common term used by the peoples are "Father" or "Creator." His form cannot be represented physically and there are almost never idols of him. He is universally recognized as all-good and all-knowing, a judge following a person's death, and that some misdeed in the ancient past has kept humanity separate from him. Schmidt found that the early religions created idols to be "more accessible" gods. Schmidt says that there are still remnants of the invisible "Sky-god" in most early cultures, although artifacts are uncommon, as no physical representations were made of him.[574]

The use of the seven-day week by many ancient peoples, and the use of the number seven for mystic significance, point to the pre-Torah tradition of mankind, in which the seventh day was known as the end of the Creation.[575] Also mysteriously, the images of star constellations

---

574   See Nathan Robertson, *The First Six Days* (2007), pgs. 88–89. See also William Foxwell Albright, *From Stone Age to Christianity*, pg. 124, 171. Stephen Langdon of Oxford wrote, "The history of the oldest civilization of man is a rapid decline from monotheism to extreme polytheism and widespread belief in evil spirits." His work was essentially a study of the Sumerians and Babylonians; see Langdon, "Semitic Mythology," *Mythology of All Races*, Archaeology Institute of America, Vol. V (1931), pg. xviii. He writes elsewhere, "The history of the Sumerian religion, which was the most powerful cultural influence in the ancient world, could be traced by means of pictographic inscriptions almost to the earliest religious concepts of man. The evidence points unmistakably to an original monotheism, the inscriptions and literary remains of the oldest Semitic peoples also indicate a primitive monotheism, and the totemistic origin of Hebrew and other Semitic religions is now entirely discredited." See *The Scotsman*, November 18, 1936. The same conclusions were reached by other scholars for Semites and the Chinese; see James Meek, *Hebrew Origins* (1960), pgs. 188–189. Similarly, anthropologist and former professor emeritus of the history and philosophy of religion at the University of London, Edwin Oliver James, in his work *The Ancient Gods*, protests the idea that mankind reached monotheism by progressing through primitive polytheism.

575   Quoting from Miller, *Rejoice O Youth!* #125. The fact that the civilized world has adopted a week of seven days since antiquity attests to the veracity of the Torah—in the sense of knowledge coming from one original tradition (*Kuzari* 1:57; Ibn Ezra, *Shmos* 16:1;

were almost universally accepted, and nobody can say for certain their source or the means of how they were disseminated globally. Most ancient cultures also share similar personification stories about them, despite great distances between these nations. While it is possible that some of the characteristics and powers attributed to the constellations were stumbled upon by these nations on their own, Torah sources suggest that they were likely passed down from Abraham. The Talmud teaches that Abraham had an unparalleled knowledge of the stars, to the point where the kings from around the world would come to learn from his wisdom.[576] It is interesting that outside sources point to astrology originating in Babylon around the time of Abraham. Jewish mysticism is replete with astrological wisdom, attributed as early perhaps as Adam, and the signs of the zodiac have even been said to be connected with and testimony of many major events in Jewish history.[577,578]

Many concepts and stories about ancient events are strikingly similar among both the current and long-extinct religions of the world. It is sensible that this is because of an initial common source.[579]

---

and Rambam, *Moreh Nevuchim* 3:43). As far as the number seven's mystical significance, Annemarie Schimmel, a professor at Harvard University and acclaimed scholar of the Near East, in her book *The Mystery of Numbers* (1993), pg. 127, writes: "The number seven has fascinated humankind since time immemorial." One of the scholars from whom she obtains her information was Johannes Hehn. He wrote a book at the turn of the century explaining in great detail its universal significance since the earliest times. It always represented the Creator and the universe, and referred to the universal G-d, the Creator of Heaven and Earth. This is further indication that in early cultures the gods were originally just a manifestation of G-d the Creator. See Johannes Hehn, *Seibenzahl und Sabbath bei den Babyloniern und im A.T.*, Leipziger Semitische Studien II (1905).

576 *Tosefta* to *Kiddushin* 5:17. *Bava Basra* 16b: "Hashem blessed Abraham *b'chol*": he had great astrology (*istagninus*) in his heart, and all of the kings would come to Abraham to look at the constellations for them. This should not be confused with modern newspaper horoscopes. Much of the ancient wisdom has been lost or corrupted.

577 For further reading into this fascinating subject, see Ari Storch, *The Secrets of the Stars* (2011).

578 Parenthetically, it should be noted that contemporary astrology and horoscope readings are not endorsed, as they are considered corruptions of the ancient wisdom. If one is not worthy of Divine intuition, which these days is hard to come by, the only way to make an accurate astrological prediction is by using occult arts, which is prohibited in Jewish law; see HaKotev on *Ein Yaakov, Shabbos* 156a. See also *Shulchan Aruch, Yoreh Deah* 179:1.

579 Once idolatry became common, their "religious" practices became corrupted. Perhaps the

Furthermore, it is logical that the Torah tradition is that original source.[580]

GENETIC ADAM AND EVE

MITOCHONDRIAL DNA

Living things contain tiny strands of coded information called DNA. DNA directs the cell's operation. Much of one's appearance and personality is determined by the DNA that he or she inherited from his parents. Half come from the mother and half from the father, and they are mixed.

Most of the DNA in a human cell is contained in the nucleus. Outside the nucleus, there are small components that convert "food" into energy called mitochondria. The mitochondria each contain a strand of DNA. The mitochondrial DNA is genetic material that is inherited only from the mother. It is passed down through generations, unmixed with the paternal genes, and therefore easy to trace.

---

clearest example would be the universal use of animal sacrifices in the ancient world. In Jewish tradition, sacrifices are traced all the way back to Adam (*Avoda Zara* 8a; *Shabbos* 28b). As idolatry became widespread, the rites became more absurd and debased, in some places even leading to human sacrifice. It is interesting, however, that certain details from the original pure source were retained, for example: it was typical throughout Western Asia to eat the foreleg of a sacrificed animal (Albright, ibid., pg.179; *Bamidbar* [Numbers] 6:19) Furthermore, the distinction between pure and impure animals, which were not fitting for sacrifice, remained; see Rabbi Shimshon Raphoel Hirsch, *Bereishis* 7:2. Further sources can be obtained in Biberfeld, ibid., pg. 56.

580   In staunch contrast to many modern secular scholars who claim that the Bible is a revised monotheistic adaptation of the many pagan renditions of ancient traditions like the creation of man, the great flood, and the Tower of Babel. The trend is that the earlier the version that the story is, the account is noticeably purer and loftier both in general concepts and literary forms. "It would be impossible for any unprejudiced reader to contend that such corrupted traditions could have been the source of the biblical record... assuming that out of such monstrous and gruesome stupidities the majestic words of the Bible [were formed]." See Biberfeld, ibid., pgs. 47–48, 76–77 for much added detail.

COMMON HUMAN ANCESTOR

Over the past few decades, advances in genetics have further opened doors to estimate the origin of mankind through analyzing and comparing variations in mitochondrial DNA. In the late 1980s, a team led by molecular biologist Dr. Allan C. Wilson of Berkeley examined the mitochondrial DNA in the blood of living people of different races and continents. They published a report that all mankind descended from a single woman—referred to as "Mitochondrial Eve," who was of African origin.[581] Many of Wilson's contemporaries reviewed his work and found possible non-African roots for Eve as well.[582] Notably, archeology, as well, uncovers that the Chinese and Hindus point west as the beginning of their ancestry, whereas the ancient Europeans point east.[583]

WHEN DID MITOCHONDRIAL EVE LIVE?

To figure this out, one must know how frequently mutations occur in mitochondrial DNA. Based on certain preliminary assumptions,[584] she was first said to have lived between 100,000 and 200,000 years ago. Estimates have varied over the past few decades. Dr. Wilson later estimated that Mitochondrial Eve lived around 75,000 years ago,[585]

---

581   *Newsweek*, Jan. 11, 1988. It should be known that "Mitochondrial Eve" does not mean that there was only one woman alive at a specific point in the past. At the very least though, she is the only one of the early population in whose offspring there has been continuous female descendants in every generation. This is not a proof per se of the biblical Eve, but the research is certainly consistent with the idea that mankind descends from a common mother.

582   Among them: Drs. David Alan Templeton of Washington University, David Maddison of University of Arizona. See also Marcia Barniga, "African Eve Backers Beat a Retreat," *Science*, vol. 255, 7 (Feb. 1992): pgs. 686–7. Much of this paragraph's source information can also be found in *Permission to Receive*, beginning on pg. 84.

583   Reuben Parsons, *Universal History*, vol.1, pg. 8.

584   Researchers assumed that humans and chimpanzees had a common ancestor around five million years ago, and based on the differences in mitochondrial DNA between them, calculated the rate of mutation based on this.

585   Phillip E. Ross, "Crossed Lines," *Scientific American* (Oct. 1991): pg. 18; Stoneking, Sherry, Redd, and Vigilant, "New Approaches to Dating Suggest a Recent Age for the Human mtDNA Ancestor" (1992). This is down from an original estimate of about 200,000 years.

but also stipulated that if prehistoric birthrates or mutation rates exceeded what was estimated, that number could drop significantly. Researchers only disagree with *when* and *where*, but most agree that modern humans inherited their mitochondrial DNA from one common female ancestor.[586]

In the early 1990s, a French research team tracking variations in the Y-chromosome, which only men have, found the "Genetic Adam" using techniques similar to Wilson mentioned above. Since 1995 it has been confirmed that all modern men descend from one recent common ancestor, presumably in proximity to Africa. Conclusions vary, but research out of Cambridge University determined this Genetic Adam to be between 37,000 and 49,000 years old.[587] The dates given by these genetic studies are based on many assumptions, and with a change in certain variables factored in, the dates could be subject to change as well. What is most significant is that the genetic analysis shows that everyone alive today is the descendant of one man and one woman.

Interestingly, originally it was thought that Mitochondrial Eve and Genetic Adam lived tens of thousands of years apart, but more recent studies show that "they may have lived around the same time after all."[588]

---

586   Ann Gibbons and Alex Dorozynski, "Looking for the Father of Us All." *Science* (January 25, 1991): pg. 378.

587   John Noble Wilford, "Genetic Sleuths Follow Clues to Elusive Ancestral Adam," *New York Times*, Nov. 23, 1995: A28; Whitfiled, Suston, and Goodfellow, "Sequence Variations of the Human Y Chromosome," *Nature* 378 (1995), pgs. 379–380.

588   The common marker that they are placed is between around 100,000 and 200,000 years ago. See Ewen Callaway, "Genetic Adam and Eve did not live too far apart in time," *Nature News*, August 6, 2013. See also G. Davit Poznik, "Sequencing Y Chromosomes Resolves Discrepancy in Time to Common Ancestor of Males Versus Females," *Science* 341 (6145) (August 6, 2013): pgs. 562–565. It should be noted that these findings are still theoretically consistent with Torah, even if the most recent common female ancestor predates the male, because the most recent woman that all are descended from is Eve, however the most recent man would be Noah, who came many generations later.

EXTREME LONGEVITY IN EARLY GENERATIONS

According to the Torah, man was originally created as an immortal creature.[589] After the sin of the Tree of Knowledge, a "biological clock," using modern terminology, was set in the body and it would eventually be overtaken by death.[590] Nevertheless, when the Torah chronicles the pre-Noah generations, one will notice that the persons mentioned enjoy what would be regarded today as extreme longevity, on average living between 600–900 years and fathering their first children at 100–130. The oldest person recorded in the Torah is Methuselah, who lived to be 969 years, and fathered his first child at age 187. One of the "younger" people mentioned is Enoch who lived to 365 years and first fathered a child at 65. The Torah commentaries take these age figures as literal, twelve-month years. Although these numbers sound anomalous compared to the modern lifespan, trying to divide biblical years up into smaller units just causes anomaly in the other direction. For example, saying that early biblical years were counted only as 1/10th of the way we currently count years, then Enoch lives to be 36.5 years old but also has children at age six—also anomalous by today's standards.[591] After the biblical flood, the average life spans are drastically reduced.

In classic Jewish texts, reasons are given for their extended lives. First, they were closer to the initial creation of man and thus closer to the initial perfection of Divine handiwork.[592] This may be similar to making copies of other copies in a Xerox machine; one gradually loses the quality of the original. Alternatively, they had a different diet and metabolism that did not weaken their constitution.[593] Additionally, the Midrash says that they were bestowed long life spans to have a

---

589   *Avoda Zara* 5a; *Bereishis Rabbah*16:6.

590   Ramban, *Bereishis* 2:17.

591   Gleaned from Aryeh Kaplan, *Immortality, Resurrection and the Age of the Universe: A Kabbalistic View* (1993), pgs. 17–19; further information can be obtained there. This non-answer of year modification is mentioned elsewhere, even in non-Jewish biblical commentaries.

592   See Ramban, *Bereishis* 5:4.

593   Rambam, *Moreh Nevuchim* 2:47.

foundation in astronomy and other mysteries. Without extended years, they would not have been able to make these long-term observations.[594] After they left Eden, Adam and Eve were also exposed to outside causes of death, like accidents and diseases.[595] Many early historians and traditions speak of people having extreme longevity.[596]

In the biblical chronology there is a clear gap in longevity following the flood of Noah. Following this worldwide catastrophe, the average lifespan fell enormously, until eventually lowering to life spans that fit closer to what is known today. One suggested approach as to how the flood adversely affected lifespan was that:

> It caused the replication of microfungi, which produced highly toxic mycotoxins that affected the longevity of people after the flood. Mycotoxins are responsible for various diseases and disorders, including cancers and other diseases involving gene mutations. Molds have always existed, but only produce their mycotoxins in suitable conditions such as high humidity. The flood provided conditions suitable for the growth of mycofungi, which, when airborne, polluted the air inhaled as well as contaminating foods and drinks. The adverse health effects caused by mycotoxins would have impacted not only those who lived through the flood, but

---

594 *Bereishis Rabbah* 26:5.

595 Nathan Aviezer, "The Extreme Longevity of the Early Generations in Genesis," *B'Or HaTorah* vol. 14 (2004): pgs. 73–80.

596 Consider for examples: "All those that have written Antiquities, both among the Greeks and barbarians; for even Manetho, who wrote the Egyptian History, and Berosus, who collected the Chaldean Monuments, Mochus, Hestieus, Hieronymus the Egyptian, and those who composed the Phoenician History, agree to what I here say: Hesiod also, and Hecatseus, Hellanicus, and Acusilaus; and, Ephorus and Nicolaus relate that the ancients lived a thousand years." (*Antiquities of the Jews* 1:3:9) A Transylvanian gypsy tradition relates that "there was a time when men lived forever and when neither worry nor sickness troubled them." This all took place prior to a great flood; see A. Rehwinkel, *The Flood* (1951), pg.140; and also Sir James G. Frazer, *Folk-Lore in the Old Testament* (1919), vol. 1, pgs. 177–178.

the generations thereafter, hence shortening the lifespan of their descendants.[597]

Another approach is suggested by Dr. Gerald Schroeder. He writes that each species is genetically programmed to live for an approximate amount of years. He gives the examples that fleas live around five years, dogs around fifteen years, and humans around seventy years. Fleas never reach seventy years old, as they are not genetically programmed to do so. He continues, "There are terrible mutations that upset the delicate aging process. Progeria speeds up the aging process almost tenfold, causing a teenager to die with the body of an old person. Within the realm of possibilities is the reverse process, slowing aging tenfold. It would be surprising but not inconceivable that manipulation of a flea's genome might allow it to live ten times longer than normal, thus reaching the age of fifty years. After all, several animal species live even longer than fifty years. The fact that no animals currently reach the long ages associated with pre-Noah biblical persons does not preclude the possibility that this potential exists within our genome." He adds a point about the fossil record, saying that "if human metabolism was slower and life spans were longer during the pre-Noah period, fossils would not indicate this. The slower metabolisms would result in fossils that appear to have formed from younger individuals."[598]

Furthermore, in light of modern research, the figures given for life spans in Genesis seem feasible and even achievable perhaps in the not-too-distant future. There is growing scientific consensus that the cause of all aging processes is genetic.[599] In other words, the body itself does not wear out. Instead, it possesses defective genes that produce the characteristics of aging. Experts optimistically predict that if these defects could be identified and modified through genetic engineering, the human lifespan could be significantly extended. Given

---

597 R. Schoental, "Mycotoxins, the flood, and human lifespan in the Bible," *Korot* 9 (5–6) (Spring 1987): pgs. 503–6, cited in Rachel Blinick, "Aging and Longevity in Science and Tanach," *Derech HaTeva*, pg. 14–16.

598 Schroeder, *The Science of God*, pgs. 202–203.

599 R. Ricklefs and C. Finch, *Aging* (1995), pg. 176.

perfect conditions, explains Professor Caleb Finch of the University of Southern California's School of Gerontology, the average human lifespan, barring outside factors like accidents or disease, would be about 1,300 years. Chronologically, people would age, yet biologically remain young-looking, vigorous, and able to reproduce. It has been proposed that Adam and Eve did not have the genetic defects that cause aging, allotting them extreme longevity. At the time of Noah, the genes of aging were introduced into the human gene pool, and took several generations to make their way through the entire human population. This is evident in the gradual decrease of life spans after Noah's time.[600] In light of these ideas, the biblical numbers become easier to fathom. If today the genes were manually adjusted, humanity would perhaps enjoy the same amount of extended years.

NOAH AND THE FLOOD

Perhaps one of the most famous and interesting events recorded in the Bible is the flood of Noah. This story has captured the attention of young and old, scholar and layperson, faithful and humanist.

Scientists who have explored the flood topic have suggested subterranean volcanic shifting, or gasses covering the Earth's surface that turned into droplets of water, as the source of the massive amount of water for the flood. The melting of glaciers has also been a working option.

FINDING THE ARK

The ancient historian in Roman times, Josephus, writes that the ark existed. Many people have also attempted finding Noah's ark.[601] Marco Polo also wrote about how it was on a mountain top in Armenia.[602] In 1887 two Persian princes reported that they had seen Noah's ark on one of the mountains of Ararat, and in 1916 two Russian pilots claimed to

---

600   For citation and further information on the topic of extreme longevity, see Nathan Aviezer, *Fossils and Faith* (2001), pgs. 143-154, where some of this section's information was gleaned from.

601   *Antiquities*, Book 1, Chapter 3, sections 5-7.

602   In his *The Travels of Marco Polo*.

have seen it from the air. Since then dozens of similar reports have been published.[603]

ANCIENT FLOOD TRADITIONS

Traditions of an ancient and massive flood are found in nearly all cultures of the human family. Researchers estimate at least two hundred,[604] and perhaps as many as five hundred,[605] cultures worldwide that have a similar flood story. Surely such universal and concurring accounts must be reminiscent of an actual event.[606] Some of the ancient societies with record include Australia, Polynesia, Tibet, and Lithuania,[607] along with India, China, American Indian, and Mayan.[608] The biblical flood is recorded as taking place in the year 1656 from Adam, corresponding to around 2100 BCE. Interestingly enough, the Greek tradition's flood is dated 2376 BCE, the Chinese at around 2200 BCE,[609] and in India it began a new era, the "Silver Age," in 2204 BCE,[610] all in very close proximity to the Torah. The Bible lists the flood as happening ten generations after the first couple, as do the extra-biblical historical lists available.[611] The Sumerian king list chronicles eight pre-flood kings and states, "the flood then swept

603   See Bruce Feiler, *Walking the Bible* (2001).

604   See for example C. Sellier and D. Balsinger, *In Search of Noah's Ark* (1976).

605   Robert Schoch, *Voyages of the Pyramid Builders: The True Origins of the Pyramids from Lost Egypt to Ancient America* (2003), pg. 249.

606   W. H. Boulton, *Babylon, Assyria and Israel* (1924). pg. 60; Reuben Parsons, *Universal History* (1904), pg. 6; Albright, *From Stone Age to Christianity*, pg. 128.

607   Keller, *The Bible as History* (1980), pg. 43.

608   Biberfeld, *Universal Jewish History*, beginning on pg. 73.

609   Georges Cuvier, *Discourse on the Revolutions of the Surface of the Globe*, pg. 108, 134. Noted here as well is that the Chinese "Noah" (Yao) marks the beginning of history in the most ancient book of Chinese history. In addition to the other common similarities of a flood, ark, dove, etc., Yao, like the biblical Noah, is also the first to use fermented liquor. (See Parsons, *Universal History*, vol. I, pg. 45) Further information; see Harrison Forman, *Changing China* (1948), pg. 12.

610   Parsons, pg. 31. There is incredible similarity in Satyavrata's (Indian "Noah") sons' names to the biblical Noah: Shema (Shem), Charma (Cham), and Yapati (Yephet) (pg. 30).

611   Albert Clay, *The Origin of Biblical Traditions* (1923), pg. 125; Sydney Smith, *Early History of Assyria to 1000 BC* (1928), pgs. 17–18.

over the land. After the flood kingship came from Heaven."[612] Significantly, there is still in existence a place adjacent to Ararat called Nakhchivan, which means "first landing" or "first descent," and its establishment is ascribed to Noah in ancient Armenian tradition.[613]

The best known flood account, after the Bible, is the Babylonian Gilgamesh Epic. In 1853, tablets were found in excavations of ancient Nineveh where the story was detailed. In this rendition, Utnapishtim (Noah) and his wife are the lone survivors of a great flood. Notably, kofer was used to waterproof their ship, and the craft had a window, as it is in the book of Genesis. Eventually, they land on a mountain top and send out a dove and raven to ascertain when dry land is available. Many of the details and actual phrasing are strikingly similar to the biblical account.[614] Several other texts and fragments have also been gathered that tell the stories of some of the above-mentioned cultures. The oldest find to date is a Babylonian tablet from the ancient city of Nippur, dated around 4,000 years ago, right around the time of the biblical flood.

After these discoveries, rather than accepting the Torah's account, it was claimed that the Bible simply adapted and amended the ancient legends. It is significant that the earlier versions of the flood story contain hints of purity and refinement in their concepts. For example, the earlier Nippur tablet explains that their Noah-like figure was very pious and saved because of his righteousness, whereas later renditions show coarser reasons for the gods favoring and sparing the Noah character. These hints reveal a pure and original source that was gradually corrupted over time and stylistically suited to different

---

612   Samuel Kramer, *The Sumerians, Their History, Culture, and Character* (1963), pg. 328.

613   See Cuvier ibid., pg. 132. Discussed by ancient historians such as Josephus, Moses Chorenesis (Armenian), and Nicolaus of Damascus (Greek), see *Antiquities of the Jews* I, 3:5–6; as well as the writings of modern Armenian historians, see Suren Yeremyan, *Soviet Armenian Encyclopedia*, vol.8, pgs. 166–167. The Armenian traditions assign as their ancestor a man named Haik who, they claim, was the "son of Targom, a grandson of Noah"; see Moses Chorenensis, *Historia Armenae* (London, 1736), 1.4, section 9–11.

614   Sir Charles Leonard Wooley in Abraham, *Recent Discoveries and Hebrew Origins*, pg. 169. Although the name "Noah" is not seen in the Babylonian tradition, it is significant that in a Hurrian fragment the hero is named "Nahomoliel" (see Woolley, 175). In Hebrew, Noah is *noach*, which means "comfort," as does *nocham*.

cultures.[615] Professor Kenneth Kitchen of the University of Liverpool writes, "The common assumption that the Hebrew account is simply a purged and simplified version of the Babylonian legend (applied also to the Flood stories) is fallacious on methodological grounds. In the Ancient Near East, the rule is that simple accounts or traditions may give rise (by accretion and embellishment) to elaborate legends, but not vice versa. In the Ancient Orient, legends were not simplified or turned into pseudo-history (historicized) as has been assumed for early Genesis."[616]

Along those lines, Dr. J. A. Thompson, director of the Australian Institute of Archeology, writes, "It is more likely these stories reach back to an original event than that the Hebrew story is a modification of ancient myth,"[617] and it is likewise historically conclusive that some kind of massive flood did occur.[618]

TRACES IN THE ROCKS

There may even be some physical indicators of a large flood as well. In North America alone, whale skeletons have been found in Michigan, Vermont, and near Montreal.[619] In Alabama, farmers complained about the abundance of whale bones in their fields, and likewise walrus bones in Georgia.[620] Additionally, worldwide atop high mountain ranges one finds deep-sea fish remains, making it obvious that these areas were once under water. Even atop Mount Everest, the highest mountain in the world, there are marine crinoid fossils in limestone.[621] Both secular and religious scholars agree that these areas were once

---

615 See Biberfeld, *Universal Biblical History*, for extensive evidence of these trends.

616 Kenneth Kitchen, *Ancient Orient and the Old Testament* (1966), pg. 89.

617 J. A. Thompson, *The Bible and Archeology* (1982), pg. 15, cited from Kelemen, *Permission to Receive*, 90.

618 Noted historian Paul Johnson, *A History of the Jews* (1987), pg. 8.

619 Bones of whales have been found high above sea level in Michigan, Vermont, Montreal and many other places. One of many examples, see Carl Dunbar, former professor of geology at Yale University in his book *Historical Geology*.

620 Immanuel Velikovsky, *Earth in Upheaval* (1955), pg. 48.

621 Augusto Gassner, *Geology of the Himalayas* (1964), pg. 164.

covered in water; it is only in the timing that they differ.[622] Likewise found on high hills are the bones of rival animals, like deer and wolves, lying together without a trace of being gnawed or chewed. What else, other than fleeing from a catastrophic flood below, could bring such animals together *in such high places* without any signs of attack?[623]

THE MIRACULOUS NATURE OF THE FLOOD

The Torah describes an extremely unique event where rain poured down and the subterranean waters burst open. The Torah sources say that there were also major upheavals in the world taking place during the flood. In fact, Rabbi Naftali Zvi Yehuda Berlin *zt"l*, also known as the Netziv, a renowned biblical commentator, points out that many aspects of the Earth's geology as known today were a result of the flood.[624]

The Talmud makes reference to what may be asteroid impacts at the time of the flood.[625] Furthermore, the sages say that during this time the Earth got its 23.5 degree tilt, creating sudden climate changes and initiating seasons.[626] The sages also mention that the natural order as a whole disintegrated, causing even the astronomical bodies to function differently. The Talmud says that during this time there was a period where "the sun rose in the west and set in the east."[627] There may even be traces of these events captured in the annals of other cultures as well.[628]

---

622   One opines that their current form gradually formed over millions of years, and the other that it was catastrophic changes over a much shorter period of time.

623   Adapted from Miller, *Sing, You Righteous*, beginning at #122.

624   See *Ha'amek Hadavar*, Bereishis 7:19.

625   See *Brachos* 58a and *Rosh Hashana* 11b.

626   Malbim and Seforno, *Bereishis* 8:22; see also Netziv, *Bereishis* 7:20.

627   See *Sanhedrin* 108b.

628   Consider, for example, a source from Mexico that states: "The pillars of Heaven were broken. The Earth shook to its foundations. The sky sank lower towards the north. The sun, moon, and stars changed their motions. The Earth fell to pieces and the waters in its bosom uprushed with violence and overflowed...the system of the universe was totally disordered. Man had rebelled against the high gods. The sun went into eclipse and the planets altered their courses, and the grand harmony of nature was disturbed," see Hist. Sin. Lib. I., pg. 12. Also Martinus Martini, in his *History of China*, wrote of ancient Chinese

The Talmud explains that the water was not regular ocean water, but was boiling in many areas and contained sulfur or sulfuric acid.[629] Rabbi Yochanan mentions in the Talmud that even in his day there were several remnants of the fountains of the great deep that were still opened up and producing hot and cold water.[630] All in all, many places in Jewish tradition speak about the miraculous nature and total world transformation that took place as a result of the flood. Because of this, one cannot necessarily expect to observe the results of a natural flood.

EVEN POSSIBLE "NATURALLY"

While some may have a hard time wrapping their heads around a worldwide catastrophe, it is interesting to consider a scenario theorized by Bruce Masse, a respected environmental archaeologist at the Los Alamos National Laboratory. He believes that a global flood happened as the result of a comet strike approximately 4,500 years ago and killed eighty percent of mankind.[631] Masse presumes that a three-mile wide comet crashed into the ocean off the coast of Madagascar, resulting in global chaos. This would essentially be the most lethal disaster in history. According to Masse, the outcome of such a strike was six-hundred-foot-high tsunamis and massive hurricanes spawned when superheated water vapor and aerosol particulates shot into jet streams. There was also darkness caused by material expelled into the atmosphere. One cannot help but notice the startling parallels of boiling waters, major upheavals, civilization being destroyed, the blocking out of sunlight, and even the timing of when these events supposedly occurred. It would seem from here that traces of even some of the

---

records that mentioned a time before the deluge when "the planets altered their courses, and the great harmony of the universe and nature was disrupted...the sky sunk lower in the north."

629   *Brachos* 59b; *Rosh Hashana* 12a.

630   *Sanhedrin* 108a-b. Openings in other places around the world as well that he does not mention; see *Ben Yehoyada*. The *Margalios Hayam* mentions Josephus in *Wars of the Jews* VII: 6 that the remarkable spring in Beiram, which had twin fountains of hot and cold waters respectively, was renowned for its medicinal value.

631   Scott Carney, "Did a Comet Cause the Great Flood?" *Discover Magazine* (Nov. 2007).

miraculous elements of the global devastation are being uncovered through this research.

POST-FLOOD

Noah's three children—Shem, Ham, and Jafeth—divide up and populate the three surrounding continents respectively. Shem becomes the progenitor of all the Shem-ites, or Semites, in western Asia.[632] Ham, pronounced in Hebrew as Cham, goes to Egypt.[633] Interestingly, Egypt was originally called "Kem" or "Chem," and a remnant of that has remained embedded in words used today such as "**chem**istry" or "al**chem**y," which originates in ancient Egypt.[634] Jafeth became the ancestor of the European continent.[635] Jafeth descendants were blessed with beauty in nature,[636] and thus became the primary expression on Earth of the arts, philosophy, and science.

TOWER OF BABEL AND LANGUAGE ORIGIN

The Torah relates that G-d breathed into Adam's nostrils the "soul of life."[637] Targum Onkelos[638] translates this as a "speaking spirit." In other words, the part of a human being that gives him distinction as a spiritual being is his capacity for rational speech. The Torah philosophers and mystics also classify the human being as a *medaber*, a speaking creature.[639] Thousands of years after the sages spoke about speech

---

632   See, for example, "Shem, the third son of Noah, had five sons, who inhabited the land that began at Euphrates, and reached to the Indian Ocean"; see Josephus, *The Work of Josephus: Complete and Unabridged*, trans. William Whiston (1987), pg. 36.

633   The Bible itself refers to Egypt as the "land of Ham" in *Tehillim* [Psalms] 78:51; 105:23, 27; 106:22.

634   The word *chemistry* and *alchemy* are related. Majority opinion is that they are derived from the ancient Egyptian name of Egypt *khem*, *kem*, or *chem*. See "Alchemy" in J. A. Simpson and E. S. C. Weiner, *The Oxford English Dictionary*, vol. 1 (1989).

635   *Megilla* 9b mentions that Yavan, the Greek empire, was a descendant of Jafeth. See also Josephus, ibid., pg. 36.

636   *Bereishis* [Genesis] 9:27.

637   *Bereishis* [Genesis] 2:7.

638   Onkelos was a famous convert to Judaism in the second century. He authored an authoritative Aramaic translation and commentary on the Torah.

639   There are four kingdoms of life discussed: The inanimate, plant life (growing), animal life, and human.

being a key difference in the makeup of the human, modern science catches up and confirms the discussion as well.[640]

Besides for the aforementioned original theology and ancestry, there was also an original language. The Torah states that, "*All the earth had the same language and the same words...*"[641] and that the differences in languages were a consequence of the Tower of Babel.

Amongst researchers today, there are several theories and speculations about how languages came to be. Interestingly, some modern linguistic experts assert that it is very likely that all languages had an original mother tongue or proto-world language.[642] These experts group the estimated 6,000 world languages into "language families," which evolved from earlier protolanguages, eventually all developing from one protolanguage.[643] Dr. Joseph H. Greenberg of Stanford University has led the way in classifying most of the world's languages into just a handful of major groups. Merritt Ruhlen, a renowned American linguist who worked with Dr. Greenberg, has said that the strong resemblance between words describing a particular concept across language families proves that the world's languages come from a single source.[644]

---

640   "The ability to develop and articulate speech relies on capabilities, such as fine control of the larynx and mouth, that are absent in chimpanzees and other great apes." See W. Enard, "Molecular evolution of FOXP2, a gene involved in speech and language," *Nature*, vol. 418 (Aug. 14, 2002). See similar in Edmund Crelin, *The Human Vocal Tract* (1987), pgs. 83-88. Researchers in the Medical College of Georgia say that the brain is unique in humans that allows for true language: "We found evidence that the brain is organized differently in humans in this area of the brain, even though the outside looks the same." What Dr. Daniel Buxhoeveden was saying is that the brain is wired differently in the human being than in the chimpanzee; see News Brief from the Medical College of Georgia, Sept. 5, 2001.

641   *Bereishis* [Genesis] 11:1.

642   F. C. Southworth and C. J. Daswani, *Foundations of Linguistics* (1974); Philip E. Ross, "Hard Words," *Scientific American*, Vol. 264 (April 1991): pgs. 138-147; Peter MacNeilage and B. L. Davis, "On the Origin of Internal Structure of Word Forms," *Science* 288 (2000): pgs. 527–531.

643   For a sizeable amount of information, see the books and articles of Isaac Mozeson. In particular, his *Origin of the Speeches: Intelligent Design in Language* (2006). Mozeson also writes that the earliest human remains found with the hyoid bone (enabling speech) still intact was in a cave near Haifa, suggesting that this is strong evidence that the earliest language was a type of proto-Hebrew; see *The Word* (2002), pg. 4.

644   "Hard Words," ibid.; "On the Origin of Languages: Studies in Linguistic Taxonomy" (1994); "The Origin of Language: Tracing the Evolution of the Mother Tongue" (1994).

There was an interesting experiment done by Professor Linn Hobbs of the Department of Materials Science and Engineering at MIT. He has tried to measure out the possible height of the Tower of Babel. He manufactured bricks using clay, sand, and straw folded together, and gauged how much weight the bricks could withstand, to see how the numbers add up from an engineering perspective. Astonishingly, when they were baked in wood-fired furnaces, they could withstand 20,000 lb/sq in., which equates to a possible height for the tower of 10,500 ft., nearly two miles high.[645] This is actually near the height recorded for the tower in one of the extra-biblical works in antiquity.[646]

Additionally, much like the account of the flood, the recollection of the events of the Tower of Babel can be found in the annals of dozens of ancient societies from around the world.[647]

SODOM AND GOMORRAH

Sodom and Gomorrah were part of a metropolis consisting of five cities on the eastern bank of the Dead Sea, biblically referred to as the "Cities of the Plain."[648] The Torah describes how G-d destroyed these cities with fire and brimstone due to their overall moral corruption.[649] As late as the first century CE, the historian Josephus wrote that "traces of the five cities can still be seen."[650]

Over the years there has been speculation as to the exact location of these sites. In 1965 and 1967, archeologist Paul Lapp conducted

---

To see a further scholarly look at how the languages grouped, developed, and spread, see Nathan Aviezer, *Fossils and Faith* (2001), pgs. 165-175.

645   Instron TechNotes Publication, Issue 38, see www.instron.com/wa/library/StreamFile. aspx?doc=2107.

646   See *Book of Jubilees* 10:20–21, which says that the height was 5,433 cubits, around 8,150 ft.

647   It is significant as well that many ancient civilizations in different parts of the world also have remains of constructed ziggurats and step pyramids built in similar style and for religious purposes, perhaps echoing a common source. Even the oldest Egyptian pyramids near the city of Memphis were step pyramids. See Biberfeld, *Universal Jewish History*, pgs. 97–100, for extensive detail.

648   *Bereishis* [Genesis] 13:12.

649   *Bereishis* [Genesis] 19:24.

650   *Wars of the Jews* 4:8:4.

major excavations in Bab edh-Dhra in the Dead Sea Valley. These were later followed up by Walter E. Rast of Valparaiso University and Thomas Schaub of Pennsylvania State University in the 1970s.[651] During the excavations, thousands of tombs and bone repositories were unearthed, containing an estimated half-million people. Such a large amount of people in a single burial ground is clear evidence of a once-heavily populated region. The other cities, as well, were found to contain the remains of a once-large population. Bab edh-Dhra and Numeira are the only known inhabited towns in the region of the Dead Sea between 3300 and 900 BCE. It is very likely that these sites are associated with the Cities of the Plain.[652]

Based on the dating of pottery in Bab edh-Dhra, it would seem that this city existed for around a thousand years. Numeira, by contrast, existed for a very short period of time, less than one hundred years.[653] Notably, the Talmud relates that Sodom only existed for fifty-two years.[654] The experts estimate that the destruction of these two cities was around 2100 BCE.[655] This time period can correlate with the biblical portrayal.[656]

Significant, as well, is a parallel regarding the fate of Sodom and Gomorrah. The entire area of Bab edh-Dhra and Numeira are covered in ash, in some places up to nearly two feet.[657] The first supposition was that the cities had been destroyed by volcanic eruptions. When geologist Frederick G. Clapp visited the region he found no trace of

---

651 For the published reports of these excavations, see Rast and Schaub, "Survey of the Southeastern Plain of the Dead Sea," *Annual of the Department of Antiquities of Jordan* 1973, 19:5–54, pgs. 175–85.

652 Rast, "Bab edh-Dhra" in *The Anchor Bible Dictionary*, vol. 1 (1992), pgs. 559–61.

653 Rast, "Settlement at Numeira" in *The Southeastern Dead Sea Plain Expedition: An Interim Report of the 1977 Season* (1981), pg. 42; Rast and Schaub, "Preliminary Report of the 1979 Expedition to the Dead Sea Plain, Jordan," *Bulletin of the American Schools of Oriental Research* 240 (1980): pg. 43.

654 *Shabbos* 11a.

655 Rast, "Bronze Age Cities along the Dead Sea," *Archeology* (Jan/Feb 1987).

656 See Wood, "The Discovery of the Sin Cities of Sodom and Gomorrah," *Bible and Space* 12.3 (1999): pgs. 67–80. Further information can be obtained here concerning other details of the finds.

657 D. W. McCreery in "Preliminary Report of the 1979..." ibid., pg. 52.

volcanic ash or lava from as recent as 4,000 years ago.[658] Experts now suggest that subterranean pressure spewed a tremendous amount of combustible matter into the air that became ignited by lightning or some other factor and the flaming debris fell back to the Earth, producing remarkably similar imagery to the account mentioned in the Bible.[659]

When the archaeological and geographical evidence is reviewed in detail, it is fascinating how many clues point to the fact that the cities of Sodom and Gomorrah have now been found.[660]

PREFACE TO BIBLICAL ARCHAEOLOGY

Before moving onto the Patriarchal Age, it is important to preface with an overarching concept. Until the 1970s, few questioned the accuracy of the historical information of the Bible. The existence of the patriarchs, Moses, and the splitting of the Reed Sea were more or less accepted as historical events. At most, the questions of some scholars were to try to find "natural ways" in which some of the miraculous events occurred, but few doubted that they actually took place.

In the 1970s and 1980s, a new wind of Bible criticism began to blow from some European universities and much of the Bible's historical validity was thrown into question. There were not any new discoveries that aroused new questions that were never before heard; instead, it seems to have been more of a trend that happened to be in vogue at the moment.[661]

It is no secret that archaeology is a study that relies heavily on the interpretation of the researcher. In the recent past, there have become

---

658   Clapp, "Geology and Bitumens of the Dead Sea Area," *Bulletin of Petroleum Geologists* 20 (1936), pg. 906; see also Neev and Emery, *The Destruction of Sodom, Gomorrah, and Jericho: Geological, Climatological, and Archaeological Background* (1995), pg. 147.

659   Neev and Emery, ibid., pgs. 13–14.

660   For an over-all summary, see Wood, ibid.

661   "Our present-day minimalists are not a sudden, new phenomenon without precedent. It all began a long time ago, and the present efflorescence is merely a development of some 150/200 years that has in a way come to a head, but simply more scathing of others and more extreme in its views than were its precursors"; see Kenneth Kitchen, *On the Reliability of the Old Testament* (2003), pg. 449.

two camps in biblical archaeology: the minimalist and the maximalist, as they are often called. These terms refer to a whole spectrum of Bible-archaeology interpretation, with those in the minimalist camp insisting from the get-go that the Bible is utterly false from a historical point of view—and this perspective is what shapes the narrative of their findings, and the maximalist view—tending more toward agreement with biblical historical accuracy.

The Torah, and the entire Hebrew Bible, is a uniquely special book, at the very least, in the sense that it is the best-selling book of all time and a masterpiece that has intrigued humanity on every corner of the globe. It is a book of spiritual guidance, moral and ethical wisdom and inspiration—not a history book. In Jewish literature, the Scriptures are not viewed as a national history account, as the Talmud writes clearly that "chronology plays no significance in the Torah."[662] Torah is, instead, viewed as the blueprint of Creation, and the compass that guides one through life. This does not mean that the Torah does not contain bits of history—it certainly does—however these historical snippets are mentioned specifically to be spiritual paradigms that people of all future generations can live with and learn from, and not to be a detailed log of our national development. If the Bible omits certain events, this does not imply a lack of knowledge upon the biblical compilers, as only things needed as guiding lessons for all times were included.[663]

Many scholars today dismiss these original premises and treat the Hebrew Scriptures as a collection of randomly assembled pieces. They then set out to negate the Bible and deny its beauty and relevance. They then over-analyze the text based on these new pretenses that were seemingly culled from nowhere. The words of Israeli writer Yizhar Smilansky, that "when one engages overmuch in removing the innards, no complete animal remains,"[664] seem apropos.

---

662   *Pesachim* 6b.

663   Other historians from that era would have likely stressed other events that the biblical canon omitted.

664   Known by his pen-name S. Yizhar. Tal Bashan, "The Generation of the Desert," *Maariv Weekend Supplement*, Shvat 7, 5763, pg. 52.

This work seeks not to critique the worthy study of archaeology or negate its valuable role in seeking to reconstruct the past; instead, the stress here is to understand the uses and limitations of archaeology, which must be acknowledged. In this area of study there is much influence and shaping of results based on times, trends, and the cultural background of the scholars wording interpretations of evidence. It is also not an affront to the intellectual integrity or professional abilities of the scholars in their field, just perhaps a lack of objectivity that is recently being brought into question from biblical minimalists.[665]

As long as the facts are presented in full, scholars of both secular camps can continue to have legitimate discussion about how to interpret their findings. The following should be seen as food for thought, at the very least—some interesting findings that find parallel in the Bible, affirming much of its historical information.

THE PATRIARCHS

Renowned archaeologist William Albright writes about the Patriarchal era:

> Until recently it was the fashion among biblical historians to treat the Patriarchal sagas of Genesis as though they were artificial creations of an Israelite scribe of the Divided Monarchy or tales told by imaginative storytellers around Israelite campfires...archaeological discoveries since 1925 have changed all this. Aside from a few die-hards among older scholars, there is scarcely a single biblical historian who has not been impressed by the rapid accumulation of data supporting the substantial historicity of patriarchal tradition..."[666]

As Albright wrote, there has been significant archaeological evidence

---

665   Dr. Yizhak Meitlis makes a phenomenal case for the biblical-historical view in his 2012 work *Excavating the Bible*, where many facts on the topic were obtained.

666   "The Biblical Period," *The Jews*, Vol. 1 (1963); "The Biblical Period from Abraham to Ezra" (1960).

verifying details of the patriarchs and the times in which they lived. Many details mentioned in the book of Genesis are in sync with life in the Middle Bronze Age, and are even reflected in archaeological findings. Critics, nonetheless, continue to assume that the Bible was written much later than the events that it relates.

BIBLICAL SETTLEMENTS

All of the settlements mentioned in Genesis in connection with the travels of the Patriarchs (known today in Israel as "The Way of the Patriarchs")[667] like Shechem, Jerusalem, and Hebron, existed during the Middle Bronze Age.[668] Excavations in many of the Holy Land's cities that are mentioned in the Patriarchal timeframe have shown evidence of being occupied then.[669] Notably, the book of Genesis does not mention the Patriarchs traveling through the northern region of Israel. Research shows that the northern area was not settled yet in their times.[670] Those who claim that the Torah was written much later than it claims to be usually put its compilation somewhere in the Iron Age. They also claim that the author(s) of the Torah only had a vague grasp of the era in the past upon which they were writing. However, if the Torah was written sometime during the Iron Age, one needs to explain why the author(s) left out mention of cities like Mizpah or Ramah that were also on the main highway and central sites with religious significance during the Iron Age? How did the author(s), with only a vague knowledge of the past, manage to make the biblical description fit exactly the settlements of the Middle Bronze Age when it claims to be written?

---

667   It is also called the Hill Road or Ridge Route because it follows the watershed ridge line of the Samarian and Judean Mountains.

668   The town of Be'er Sheva is an exception, and its exact location as mentioned in the Bible is yet to be found. There is discussion whether it is at Tel Sheba (where nothing prior to the Iron Age has been found), or perhaps Bir a-Saba, a few miles away. Dr. Israel Rosenson suggests that it may not even be a town that archaeology could locate, because it was not a well-established area—described in Genesis as a cluster of wells; see Israel Rosenson, "The Story of the Past-Literature and History in the Bible—Contradiction of Complement?" (Heb.) Al Atar VII (1999-2000): pgs. 111–149.

669   Avi-Yonah, *Encyclopedia of Archeological Excavations in the Holy Land* (1975–78).

670   John Bright, *A History of Israel* (2000), pg. 82. In later periods of history, the focus is in different parts of the land; see also A. Parrot, *Abraham and His Times* (1971), pg. 66.

CAMELS

Another well-known issue brought up by the biblical critics is that the camel is described in the Torah early on as a domesticated creature.[671] However, scholars always thought that they were not truly domesticated until a much later period, which proved in their eyes that the Torah's authorship was from a later time. It is wondrous that this is still even used as an attack on the Bible, as it seems to have been disproven back in the 1970s.[672] Notwithstanding, recent research by Michael MacDonald of the Oriental Faculty at the University of Oxford suggests that camel domestication in Arabia began sometime in the third millennium BCE, fitting in line fine with Patriarchal timing.[673] Furthermore, Dr. Ofer Bar-Yosef, professor of prehistoric archaeology at Harvard University, suggests that the domestication of camels can be traced in surrounding regions back even further to the fourth millennium BCE, well before the Patriarchal Era.[674] Although it would seem that the use of camels was fairly uncommon at the time, their mention of use is limited in Genesis as well, and only is mentioned in regions of Israel where they would be likely to be utilized.[675]

CULTURAL CONSISTENCY

Additionally, Kenneth Kitchen, professor emeritus of Egyptology at the University of Liverpool, compiled an outline of over twenty-five

---

671   See for example *Bereishis* [Genesis] 12:16; 24:10.

672   See Richard Bulliet, *The Camel and the Wheel* (1975), pg. 64, describes a document piece dated from the seventeenth century BCE in Syria that mentions camels as a domesticated animal.

673   M. MacDonald, "North Arabia in the First Millennium BCE," *Pp. of Civilizations of the Near East*, Vol. 2 (1995), pg. 1357. See also Christopher Scarre, *Smithsonian Timelines of the Ancient World* (1993), pg. 176: "Both the dromedary and the Bactrian camel had been domesticated since before 2000 BC." *The Hebrew Encyclopedia* (vol. 8, pg. 918) also relates that archaeologists claimed that camels were not present in Egypt until the fourteenth century BCE. Recently, camel bones, seals, and images or people riding camels have been discovered there; see Yoel Schwartz, *Emes M'eretz Titzmach*, pg. 32.

674   Evidence has been found in Iran; see Ofer Bar-Yosef, "The Beginnings of Nomadic Societies in the Levant" (Heb.) in *Studies in the Archaeology of Nomads in the Negev and in Sinai* (Heb.), pgs. 7–25.

675   See footnotes and elaboration in Meitlis, *Excavating the Bible* (2012), pg. 46.

other known details about life in the Middle East/Mesopotamia, circa 2000 BCE, that line up nicely with the biblical account in the Patriarchs' time.[676]

In the Torah, Abraham complains to G-d that since he has no children his inheritance will be given to his servant Eliezer. G-d then responds that Abraham will have his own child.[677] It has been verified that it was common in Abraham's time and region for the childless person to adopt a stranger, or even a slave, as a son.[678] This is interesting because it was not prevalent in later times, and confirms a precise description of cultural life during the time that the Bible claims to be written. A later author would not have known the cultural norms of a millennium prior.

In a similar vein, when Sarah and Rachel were unable to have children, they gave a concubine to their husbands and the children produced were to be considered as their own.[679] This has also been identified as common in those days.[680] In fact, the chronology of Patriarchal events of the Bible matches up so well with archeological discovery that the renowned English Egyptologist Arthur Weigall said that "we can feel that we are dealing with facts carefully handed down."[681]

Additionally, even the historicity of the names used in Patriarchal times has been confirmed. The name "Canaan" is used in the Ebla tablets, showing the name to be much older than scholars had assumed.[682] Egyptian proscription lists that record enemies of Pharaoh or troublesome foreign neighbors contain the name "Abraham" and "Zebulun."[683] The Talmud identifies Abraham's mother as Amathalia the daughter of Karnebo.[684] There is no mention of this name in the

---

676   Kenneth Kitchen, *On the Reliability of the Old Testament* (2003), pgs. 352–54.

677   *Bereishis* [Genesis] 15:2–4.

678   Sarna, *Understanding Genesis* (1966), pgs. 122–23

679   *Bereishis* [Genesis] 16:2–3; *Bereishis* [Genesis] 30:3.

680   Bright, ibid., pg. 79. There are many more examples brought down in this work.

681   Arthur Weigall, *A History of the Pharaohs*, vol. II, pg. 109, brought down in Kelemen, ibid., pg. 92

682   See Biberfeld, *Universal Jewish History*, vol III, pg. 29, n9.

683   In addition, the Ebla tablets name the names: Adam, Ishmael, Esau, Saul, David, Israel, and Michael; see Biberfeld, ibid., vol IV, pg. 16.

684   *Bava Basra* 91a.

Bible; it was instead preserved orally for fifteen hundred years. Archaeologists have discovered Babylonian records in Ebla that mention the name Karnebo as a royal family name.[685] The name "Jacob" and some of his sons are found on other tablets.[686] It is significant that those names fell out of use after the Patriarchal age.[687]

These are just a few examples of the Torah's impeccable precision and testimony to its record being from the time it claims. There would truly be no way for the theoretical writers, a thousand years after the events supposedly took place, to know and so accurately record what the living conditions were one millennium back.

THE CAVE OF MACHPELAH

Furthermore, Jewish tradition teaches that Adam, Eve, the patriarchs and three of the matriarchs are buried in the Cave of Machpelah.[688] The book of Genesis describes in detail Abraham purchasing this property from Ephron, the Hittite. The acquirement of the cave described in the Bible is better understood in view of Hittite law of the time. According to Hittite law, if a buyer only acquires part of a land property, the tax responsibilities remain on the seller. It is only when the land is sold in its entirety that tax obligations are transferred to the buyer. This is likely why Ephron, the Hittite, insisted on selling Abraham the entire field, even though Abraham was really only interested in the cave at its end. Moreover, it is interesting that trees that were growing on the land were always registered at the time of sale, and the Torah, likewise, when describing the transaction, notes in the purchase that included in the sale were *"all the trees that were in the field"* (Genesis 23:17), thus in perfect alignment with Hittite law of the day.[689]

Moreover, by the end of the First Temple period, the Jewish nation

---

685   See Yosef Reinman, *One People, Two Worlds* (2003), pg. 119.

686   This is not necessarily a reference to the actual biblical figures. It is significant that those names were used in the time of the Patriarchs and then subsequently fell out of use.

687   See John Bright, (1964), pg. 70.

688   Abraham acquires it (*Bereishis* [Genesis] 23).

689   Manfred Lehmann, "Abraham's Purchase of Machpelah and Hittite Law," *Bulletin of the American Schools of Oriental Research* 129 (1953): pgs. 15–18.

was literate. Generations before the First Temple era, and how much more so many generations before, writing was a much scarcer art, known to a small elite. Notably, no mention of writing is found in the book of Genesis. It is not until the book of Exodus that the verb "to write" is first found.[690] As related above, all of the details of Abraham's purchase of the Cave of Machpelah from Ephron are recorded, yet there is no mention of the signing of any contract. All that the Bible mentions is a public agreement that they make, but no writing.[691] In the isolated town of Hebron where the cave was purchased, writing was not something that was familiar at that time. An author concocting this story thousands of years later would not be capable of accurately describing the transactions common to that era and in that remote city.[692]

Additionally, in 1985, Dr. Zev Yevin, former deputy director of the Israel Antiquities Authority, noted that the chambers in the Cave of Machpelah are similar to other burial chambers common at the time of Abraham 4,000 years ago. In the smaller chamber, they found clay shards dating back to around 900 BCE. In the upper cave, they found Latin script with the names Jacob and Abraham. The cave seems to have been in use at the time of the First Temple, and this sight has continuously been considered the actual burial place of the Patriarchs.[693]

JOSEPH

Scholars with Egyptological training have for quite some time been amazed by the corroboration of Egyptian elements in the story of Joseph. Egyptologist Alan Richard Schulman says that the writer of the Joseph narrative in the Torah "had an exceedingly intimate knowledge of Egyptian life, literature, and culture, particularly in

---

690   *Shmos* [Exodus] 17:14.

691   *Bereishis* [Genesis] 23:18.

692   Moshe Weinfeld, former professor emeritus of Bible at the Hebrew University of Jerusalem, wrote: "In Jeremiah 32 there is a story of a purchase carried out by means of a written scroll, while in Genesis 23, the text does not mention any document at all, and we can deduce from this the antiquity of the circumstances reflected in the tradition." Moshe Weinfeld, *The Encyclopedia of the World of the Bible: the Book of Genesis* (1982), pg. 147.

693   "Cave of Machpelah and the Monument Upon It," *Ha-Uma* (The Nation), No. 127 (Spring 1997).

respect to the Egyptian court," and as a "historical novel containing a core of historical memory."[694] The following are a sampling of some of these more interesting parallels.

THE PRICE OF SLAVES

Joseph is sold by his brothers for twenty pieces of silver and is the first of the would-be Israelite nation to descend to Egypt. It is intriguing that twenty pieces was historically the going rate for a slave in the time period that the Torah claims Joseph was living.[695] Just a few hundred years prior, the going rate was ten pieces of silver, and a few hundred years later the price was up to thirty pieces.[696] By the beginning of the first millennium BCE, the price had shot up to 50-60, and later during the Persian rule the price was 90-120. The price given in the Torah fits exactly with the going rate for a slave in the era in which Joseph is described as living in. Had an author recorded these events at a later time in history, slaves were much more expensive and there would have been no way of knowing the cost of a slave a thousand years prior.[697] There are many other examples of events in Joseph's life that could only be known if written during his lifetime.

---

694   Schulman in "On the Egyptian Name of Joseph: A New Approach," *SAK* (1975): pg. 236, based on James Hoffmeier, *Israel in Egypt* (1996), pg. 83. This correlation is not a new discovery. Charles Kent, former Woolsey Professor of Biblical Literature at Yale University, had this to say about the Joseph narrative: "The historical character of the Joseph stories is strongly attested by their remarkable archaeological exactness...Egypt lived apart almost as a hermit nation. Her customs, her language and her system of writing were shared by no other peoples of antiquity, and yet at every point the [biblical] narrator reveals a thorough familiarity with Egyptian life." Charles Kent, *The Historical Bible: The Heroes and Crisis of Early Hebrew History* (1904), pg. 148.

695   In other words, this was the price in the 18th and 17th centuries BCE.

696   This was the price in the 14th and 13th centuries BCE.

697   Kenneth Kitchen, *On the Reliability of the Old Testament* (2003), pgs. 344–45. Also see Kitchen, "The Patriarchal Age: Myth or History," *Biblical Archaeology Review* (March/April 1995). Average price listed in the Code of Hammurabi (Hammurabi section by T. J. Meek, in *Ancient Near Eastern Texts Relating to the Old Testament* (1969), pg. 170–76, and many other ancient documents.

CULTURAL AND LANGUAGE CONSISTENCIES

When in Egypt, Joseph becomes the "overseer" in Potifar's house, which has been validated as a common term for those who served nobility in the days that Joseph lived.[698] Joseph is sent to prison after false accusations by Potiphar's wife.[699] Prisons were not common in the ancient world, but were found in Egypt.[700] Following this, Joseph is given the highest leadership position, along with a symbolic ring and gold chain from Pharaoh, for his successful interpretation of Pharaoh's dreams. The procedure of bestowing these items has been attested to.[701] Joseph is meant to take steps to assist Egypt in getting through their pending famine. The Egyptian records speak of a Semite rising to power in the royal court.[702] Joseph describes his status as royal viceroy saying, "G-d has made me an advisor (lit. "father") to Pharaoh."[703] According to Egyptologist A. S. Yahuda, this title agrees with ancient Egyptian traditions, as the viceroy was called *Itf* or "father."[704] Furthermore, the Bahr Yusef is a canal that connects the Nile with Fayyum in Egypt. Not only does it literally mean "Joseph's canal," but according to ancient Arab tradition it is a reference to the biblical Joseph, viceroy of Pharaoh.[705] These are just a few brief examples out of many; however, it is clear that the story of Joseph is consistent with the Egyptian culture of the time he is described to have lived.

In summary of the first book of the Torah, historian Paul Johnson

---

698 Called "overseer" in *Bereishis* [Genesis] 39:4. That was a common term; J. Hoffmeier, *Israel in Egypt* (1997), pg. 84; William Hayes, *A Papyrus of the Late Middle Kingdom in the Brooklyn Museum* (1972), pg. 103.

699 Historian Paul Johnson in *A History of the Jews* attests to Joseph's historicity in part from this incident. He writes that ideas from this account were adopted into an Egyptian narrative called *A Tale of Two Brothers*, which is found on the Papyrus D'Orbiney.

700 Hayes, *A Papyrus*, pg. 37.

701 Thompson, ibid., pg. 48; Kent, ibid., pg. 149.

702 Johnson, *A History of the Jews*, pg. 24.

703 *Bereishis* [Genesis] 45:8.

704 Yahuda, *Language of the Pentateuch in Its Relation to Egyptian* (2003), pg. 23; see also Nahum Sarna, *Understanding Genesis* (1970), pg. 220.

705 Keller, *The Bible as History* (1995, Second Revised Edition), pg. 102; American engineer Francis Cope Whitehouse is credited with rediscovering the connection between Bahr Yusef and Joseph. See also Samuel Kurinsky, *The Eighth Day*, 87–90.

writes, "All this Genesis material dealing with the problems of immigration, of water wells and contracts and birthrights, is fascinating because it places the patriarchs so firmly in their historical setting, and testifies to the Bible's great antiquity and authenticity."[706]

SLAVERY AND EXODUS

Those who would deny the historicity of the enslavement and exodus also have an awkward time justifying why a nation would concoct such a dishonorable beginning for itself. It is counterintuitive in attracting potential members and could not be more opposite to what was practiced in antiquity.[707] Furthermore, there is no viable reason why Egypt, the ancient superpower, suddenly enigmatically "disappeared" from mention for several centuries.[708]

The book of Exodus begins with a new, unnamed Pharaoh[709] arising who did not know Joseph, enslaving the Jewish people and having them build the cities of Pithom and Raamses. Both of these cities have been identified in modern times.[710]

---

706 Johnson, *A History of the Jews*, pg. 15.

707 Levinstam, *Encyclopedia Mikraith* 3 (1958): 754; Hertz, *Pentateuch*, pg. 396 (in particular, quotation from Thomas Eric Peet, former professor of Egyptology at the University of Liverpool); James Jack, *The Date of the Exodus* (1925), pg. 10; V. V. Struve, *Izrail v Egipte* [Israel in Egypt] (1920), pg. 27. Soviet historian, Ilya Shifman, says that were the slavery a myth, created to give authority to "an early Hebrew cult," it would not only have been counterintuitive, but would have backfired in the ancient world; see Shifman, *The Old Testament and Its World* (Russian)(1987), pg. 121–22.

708 Avigdor Miller, *Behold A People* (1968).

709 Although the "new" Pharaoh is not mentioned by name, it was somewhat common up until 1000 BCE that the Pharaoh would just be addressed by that title without a name attached to it. This is as it appears in the Hebrew Bible as well, just "Pharaoh" from Genesis to the days of Rehoboam, and after Shishak (975 BCE) specifying a name (i.e., Pharaoh Neco); see "Pharaoh" in *International Standard Bible Encyclopedia*, vol. 3, pg. 821. Furthermore see Kenneth Kitchen, "Egyptians and Hebrews, from Raamses to Jericho," in *The Origin of Early Israel—Current Debate, Beer-Sheva* (1998), pgs. 105-106; Trude Weiss-Rosmarin, *New Light on the Bible* (1941), pg. 32.

710 In 1883, Swiss archaeologist Edouardo Naville, while doing excavations, found inscriptions with the name "Pitum" in Tel el-Maskhuta, making him believe that this was the biblical city (The Store-City of Pithom and the Route of the Exodus). Later, scholars William Albright and Kenneth Kitchen identified Tel el-Maskhuta as biblical "Succoth," and neighboring Tel er-Rebata as Pithom (see for example Kitchen, *Ramesside Inscriptions, Notes and Comments* Vol. II: Ramesses II, Royal Inscriptions [1999], pg. 270). Biblical Raamses is identified with

Sir Alan Gardiner was a renowned twentieth-century Egyptologist. Although he was a skeptic when it came to many aspects of the historicity of the Hebrew Scriptures, when it came to the Israelite's presence in ancient Egypt, he was forced to concede that "no historian could possibly doubt; a legend of such tenacity representing the early fortune of a peoples under so unfavorable an aspect could not have arisen save as a reflection...of real occurrences."[711] German scholar Martin Noth writes that the forced labor "corresponds with an actual historical situation."[712] Furthermore, professor Kenneth Kitchen has written comprehensively on evidence of Egyptian enslavement, including descriptions of fine details such as brick quotas and taskmasters.[713] Additionally, it is interesting that of the extensive record of slave names listed on the reverse of Papyrus Brooklyn 35.1446, belonging to a large Egyptian household, a large number have Semitic names like Menahem, a Shipra (Shifrah), Sakar (Issachar), Asher, and Aqob (Jacob).[714]

As far as the historicity of Moses, historian John Bright states with certainty:

> Over all these events towers the figure of Moses. Though we know nothing of his career, save what the Bible tells us...there can be no doubt that he was, as the Bible por-

---

the city of Tanis (San el-Hagar) in the northeastern Nile delta of Egypt. French Egyptologist Pierre Montet strongly asserted that this was the location of Raamses (*Revue Biblique* 39 [1930]), as do other contemporary researchers. Austrian Egyptologist Manfred Bietak, current chairman of the Vienna Institute of Archaeological Science at the University of Vienna, has modified Montet's findings and shifted the ancient site of Raamses about fifteen miles south. This city that he found dates to the period of the sojourn in Egypt, and even contains many Asiatic remains at the area of the slave residences.

711 "The Geography of the Exodus," in *Recueil d'etudes egyptologiques dediees a la memoire Jean-Francois Champollion*, pg. 204–205, cited from Hoffmeier, ibid., pg. 112.

712 Noth, *Exodus*, pg. 20. The enslavement is considered to have a ring of truth even by more skeptical scholars; see J. Maxwell Miller and John Hayes, *A History of Ancient Israel and Judah* (1986), pg. 67.

713 Kitchen, *The Bible in Its World: The Bible & Archaeology Today* (1977), pgs. 75–78; and also "From the Brickfields of Egypt," *Tyndale Bulletin* (1976).

714 Georges Posener, *Les Asiatiques en Égypte sous les XIIe et XIIIe dynasties* (Syria 1957) 34:145–63; Albright, "Northwest-Semitic Names in a List of Egyptian Slaves from the Eighteenth Century BCE" *Journal of the American Oriental Society* 74 (1954): pgs. 222–33.

trays him, the great founder of Israel's faith. Attempts to reduce him are extremely unconvincing. The events of exodus and Sinai require a great personality behind them...To deny that role to Moses would force us to posit another person of the same name.[715]

Likewise, noted historian William Albright takes the historicity of Moses as a given. He asserts, "Moses, probably born in the late fourteenth century BCE and died about the middle of the thirteenth, was founder of ancient Israel."[716]

The entire Exodus account shows very intimate knowledge of Egyptian culture of the time. Professor of Old Testament and archaeologist, Dr. John D. Currid, remarks that the Exodus account "is remarkably brimming with elements of Egyptian religious and cultural background. Only an author who was well-versed in Egyptian tradition could have composed such a poignant piece."[717] Likewise Scott Noegel, associate professor of Near-Eastern Languages and Civilization at the University of Washington, writes that "the scholarly world has known for some time that the book of Exodus demonstrates first-hand knowledge of Egyptian customs and beliefs."[718] The Exodus "story line" could not have been a later author's creative whims.

After Moses encounters G-d at the "burning bush," he returns to Egypt with signs that he was sent from G-d, including transforming his staff into a snake. This feat was then duplicated by Pharaoh's magicians.[719] The use of magic, including accounts similar to snake transformation, are well-documented in the Westcar Papyrus. There is evidence that snake charming was practiced by Egyptian magicians. There are depictions of men holding stiff serpents, and references to

---

715   Bright, (2000), pg. 127. For other scholars who support the historicity of Moses, see Pierre Montet, *Egypt and the Bible* (1968), pgs. 16-34; Dewey Beegle, *Moses the Servant of Y-ahweh* (1972); Edward F. Campbell Jr., *Moses and the Foundation of Israel* (1975), pgs. 141–54; Nahum Sarna, *Exploring Exodus* (1986), ch. 2, among many others.

716   Albright, "Moses in Historical and Theological Perspective," pg. 120.

717   Currid, "The Egyptian Setting of the Serpent," pg. 224.

718   Scott Noegel, "Moses and Magic: Notes on the Book of Exodus," published in *Journal of the Ancient Near Eastern Society* 24 (1996): pg. 45.

719   *Shmos* [Exodus] 7:8–12.

a king using a serpent-staff. Egyptologist Pierre Montet refers to several Egyptian scarabs showing snake charmers holding stiff serpents, and amulets with cobras being held by the neck.[720] Remnants of these snake-to-rod tricks, of paralyzing and later reawakening a serpent, are still found in modern Egypt.[721]

Pharaoh remains stubborn in releasing the Jewish people and the plagues ensue. Eventually the Jewish slaves are freed and leave with the wealth of Egypt. In ancient Egypt, as with many civilizations, it was unheard of to record defeat and devastation as a part of your history. The lack of extensive record of the Exodus events in Egyptian annals is, therefore, of no surprise. In the early 1800s, there was an interesting papyrus discovered containing an ancient poem called *The Admonitions of Ipuwer*. The Ipuwer Papyrus was written by an Egyptian sage and documents a series of catastrophes followed by social upheaval that he witnesses being afflicted on the nation. This manuscript dates to 1300 BCE, in close proximity to when the Exodus is claimed. The cataclysms described are eerily similar to those described in the Exodus, and there is no recorded history of any other such problem in the history of Egypt.[722]

The following are merely a sampling of the parallels:

BLOOD:

> "...there was blood throughout all the land of Egypt."
>
> (Exodus 7:21)

> "Plague is throughout the land. Blood is everywhere."
>
> (Papyrus 2:5-6)

---

720 Currid, *Ancient Egypt and the Old Testament* (1997), pg. 95.

721 David Freedman, *The Anchor Bible Dictionary* (1992), vol. 2, pg. 698; Walter Gibson, *Secrets of Magic: Ancient and Modern* (1967), pg. 13; D. P. Mannix, "Magic Unmasked," *Holiday* (Nov. 1960): pg. 32.

722 Introduction to Alan Gardiner, *Admonitions of an Egyptian Sage* (1909), pgs. 8-18. Gardiner believed that the events were taking place in front of Ipuwer's eyes, evidenced by his stated plea to take action, and his placing of blame for the kingdom's troubles on Pharaoh.

"...all the waters in the river were turned to blood..."

(Exodus 7:20)

"The river is blood...Men shrink from tasting..."

(Papyrus 2:10)

FROGS:

The Ipuwer Papyrus mentions crocodiles coming out of the Nile in a path of destruction.

There are also sources in Jewish tradition that crocodiles came out during the second plague.[723]

PESTILENCE:

"All animals, their hearts weep, cattle moan..."

(Papyrus 5:5)

HAILFIRE:

"...and the hail struck every herb and tree of the field."

(Exodus 9:25)

"Gates, columns and walls are consumed by fire."

(Papyrus 2:10)

"Trees are destroyed."

(Papyrus 4:14)

"That has perished which yesterday was seen."

(Papyrus 5:12)

"Neither fruit nor herbs are found..."

(Papyrus 6:1)

---

723   See how the Seforno translates the word *tzefardaya*, typically translated as "frogs" but here as "crocodiles."

LOCUSTS:

"... tomorrow I will bring the locusts into your country...
And they shall eat the rest of that which has escaped,
which remains to you from the hail, and shall eat every
tree which grows for you out of the field..."

(Exodus 10:4-5)

"...No fruit nor herbs are found. Hunger"

(Papyrus 6:1)

"Grain has perished on every side."

(Papyrus 6:3)

DARKNESS:

"... and there was a thick darkness in all of Egypt [for]
three days. They did not see one another, nor rise from
his place, for three days."

(Exodus 10:22-23)

"Destruction...the land is in darkness."

(Papyrus 9:8-11)

Dr. Hans Goedicke, professor of Near Eastern studies at Johns Hopkins University, has spoken about an ancient religious shrine found at El-Arish. The inscription there reads, "There was no stepping out into the open for a period of nine days...one face could not see its equal." The papyrus, "Prophecies of Neferti," describe the same happening.[724]

SLAYING OF FIRSTBORN:

"He who places his brother in the ground is everywhere."

(Papyrus 2:13)

---

724   Details and sources found in Kelemen, pg. 105. The "naos" was translated in 1890 by F. L. Griffith, see "The Antiquities of Tell el Yahudiyah and Miscellaneous Work in Lower Egypt During the Years 1887–88."

"It is groaning that is throughout the land, mingled with lamentations."

(Papyrus 3:14)

According to the Jewish tradition, the Egyptian firstborns got word of their fate and begged their fathers and Pharaoh to let the Jews go free. When their pleas were refused they revolted in uproar, erupting into a tumultuous civil war.[725] Alan Gardiner, who translated the papyrus, reveals that the "evils of civil war are everywhere felt." Some examples are:

"A man looks upon his son as his enemy."

(Papyrus 1:6)

"Many dead are buried in the river. The stream is a sepulcher and the place of embalmment has become a stream."

(Papyrus 2:6)

"Children of Princes are dashed against walls..."

(Papyrus 4:3)

Following this plague the Jewish people leave with the spoils of Egypt.[726] There is even allusion to this in the Ipuwer Papyrus:

"Poor men have become the owners of good things. He who could not make his own sandals is now the possessor of riches."

(Papyrus 2:4)

"Gold, blue stone, silver malachite, carnelian, bronze... are fastened to necks of female slaves."

(Papyrus 3:3)

"Behold the poor of the land have become rich, and [the possessor] of property has become one who has nothing."

(Papyrus 8:2)

---

725   Tosofos, *Shabbos* 87b.
726   *Shmos* 12:35.

There is discussion surrounding how the message of this papyrus is meant to be interpreted.[727]

At any rate, most scholars or historians, even those typically skeptical of biblical accuracy, usually agree that an exodus took place.[728] Solomon Dinkevich of the Courant Institute of Mathematical Sciences at New York University shows in practical and realistic figures how Israelite population grew from seventy members of Jacob's family to several million who left Egypt only several generations later.[729]

SPLITTING OF THE SEA

Following their departure from Egypt, the Jews arrived at the Reed Sea. The splitting of the Sea of Reeds can be traced in Egyptian monuments and Ugaritic texts.[730] It has been said about the Song of the Sea, sung as the Jews crossed through on dry land, as recorded in the book of Exodus, that it "certainly dates from the same period as the events themselves."[731] The *naos* (shrine) of el-Arish, now in the Museum of Ismailia, also describes how the king and his men fight "the evil ones at the whirlpool." The shrine continues with the name of the place where these whirlwind events took place: *Pi-Kharoti*. This is fascinating, as Exodus relates: "But the Egyptians pursued after them, all the horses and chariots of Pharaoh...and overtook them

---

727 Being that the modern "enlightened" person is not "supposed to believe in Bible stories," most historians say that the papyrus is speaking figuratively, for example: "Destruction of crops and livestock" really means an economic depression; "river being blood" means a breakdown of law and order; the "darkness" means lack of enlightened leadership. Although this is not at all what it says, it is more comfortable than the alternative.

728 William Jr. Steibling, *Out of the Desert* (1989), pg. 197.

729 Solomon Dinkevich, "A Calculation of the Israelite Population at Mount Sinai," *B'Or Ha-Torah* vol. 15 (2005), pgs. 105-113. Also see Nathan Aviezer, *Modern Science and Ancient Faith* (2013), pgs. 151–155.

730 Berl Haskelevich, "The Exodus and Egyptian Historiography," *B'Or HaTorah* vol. 15 (2005), pg. 85. Those who study Ugaritic poetry with Hebrew, like Professor Frank Moore Cross of the Harvard Divinity School and Professor David Noel Freedman, explain that the Song of the Sea, sung as the Jews crossed the sea on dry land, is one of the oldest in the Hebrew canon (see Freedman and Cross, "Studies in Ancient Y-ahwistic Poetry," *SBL Dissertation Series* 21 (1975): pgs. 31–33).

731 Georg Fohrer, *History of the Israelite Religion* (1972), pg. 72.

encamping by the sea, beside Pi-hakhiroth [in the Hebrew]."[732] At this place, this ancient relic recalls that the Pharaoh was thrown into a whirlwind high in the air, to be seen no more. Notably, the Pharaoh is called Pharaoh T'hom, which in Hebrew would mean "Pharaoh of the depths."

Furthermore, the Torah records this event as a miracle, as can certainly be seen in the elaborations depicted in the Oral Tradition. Notwithstanding, even from a purely rational look, some aspects of the sea-splitting event are deemed plausible in that region by prominent oceanographers.[733]

SINAI AND WANDERING THE DESERT

A few weeks later, the Israelites arrive at Mount Sinai. The location of the biblical Mt. Sinai is disputed amongst scholars, although generally associated with Jebel-Musa in the Sinai Peninsula.[734]

The Torah then tells over that the Jews sojourned in the desert for forty years. One of the issues that contemporary archaeologists have with the exodus account is the lack of evidence for the prolonged wandering. One would expect to find clothing, vessels, or bones from those who had passed on, yet to date they have come up short.

---

732 *Shmos* [Exodus] 14:9.

733 This is the theory of meteorologist Nathan Paldor of the Hebrew University in Jerusalem and the University of Rhode Island, and oceanographer Doron Nof of Florida State University. Their theory has been supported by another oceanographer, Gabriel Csanady of Old Dominion University in Norfolk, Virginia, who called the scenario "very plausible." Obviously, Torah does not need to be justified by naturalistic explanations. Although the very nature of everything timing perfectly is in itself a miracle of sorts, Jewish tradition elaborates on the far-reaching effects of the miracle of splitting the sea. In any event, it is interesting that modern researchers could deem significant aspects of the event as very plausible. See Richard Kerr, "Physics Parts the Red Sea," *Science* (April 24, 1992). Also Doron Nof and Nathan Paldor, "Are there Oceanographic Explanations for the Israelists' Crossing the Red Sea?" *Bulletin of the American Meteorological Society* 73/3 (March 1992): pgs. 305–14. Also Thomas Maugh, "Research Supports Bible's Account of Red Sea Parting," *Los Angeles Times* March 14, 1992, A1 and A25.

734 For more proposed locations of Mount Sinai by scholars over the years, see James Hoffmeier, *Ancient Israel in Sinai* (2005), pg. 124, which is a tremendous accomplishment in scholarship in its own right and will provide a wealth of information related to the sojourn.

It is very important to consider a few things. The Torah relates that when the Jews were living in the wilderness they were accompanied by the "clouds of glory" and had Divine protection. The Torah tells us that some of the benefits of these "clouds" were that for the forty-year period, the clothes and vessels of the Hebrews did not wear out.[735] Furthermore, the Midrash explains how the Jewish people would even pass away in yearly increments on the ninth of Av in self-dug graves, not gradually throughout the year.[736] The manner in which the Torah tradition describes the desert lifestyle is supernatural. That being said, what is there left to find? Archaeologists will argue that they do not believe in the miracles and want to find evidence for a *natural* sojourn. Surely they will not find evidence of a natural sojourn, as there never was one—*nobody believes in one.*

If one is testing the biblical story, he must test it on its own terms. One must accept all of it. It will do no good to take one element of the biblical story, and then graft onto it other non-biblical hypotheses and then test the conglomerate, because that is a conglomerate that no one believes in.

Furthermore, the Sinai desert is a big place and sands shift greatly over three thousand years. Even if one was looking for remains, where would one dig, and how deep? How many holes does one need to put down to have a reasonable probability of finding a few burial places dug on the ninth of Av? Therefore, the fact that they have not found the kind of evidence they are looking for is no proof against the historicity of the exodus.[737] In the words of David Hackett Fischer, professor of history at Brandeis University, "evidence must always be in the affirmative. Negative evidence is a contradiction of terms—it is no evidence at all."[738]

---

735   *Devarim* [Deuteronomy] 8:4.

736   *Eicha Rabbah, Petichta* 33: "Rabbi Levi taught: On the eve of the Ninth of Av, Moses would announce throughout the camp: 'Go dig!' The Jewish people would go and dig their graves and sleep inside them. When morning came, Moses announced: 'Let those who live separate themselves from the dead.' The live ones would rise, separate themselves from the dead, and count—and each year 15,000 would die."

737   Ideas about life in the desert are quoted from and/or based upon Dovid Gottlieb, *Living Up to the Truth* (1994), pg. 30.

738   *Historians' Fallacies: Toward a Logic of Historical Thought* (1970), pg. 47.

Still, there may be some interesting discoveries related to the Jews' sojourn in the Sinai desert. Archaeologists have found an inscription, dated to the time of Exodus, with the name Hobab on it. Hobab or *Chovav*, was another name for Jethro, the father-in-law of Moses.[739]

BALAAM

During the sojourn, Balak, King of Moab, fearing an Israelite attack, sent the wicked prophet Balaam to curse them.[740] The Talmud relates that Balaam had previously been an advisor to Pharaoh and initiated the killing of firstborn Hebrew boys and the subsequent enslavement of the Jews.[741] Interestingly enough, the early Egyptian historian Manetho also writes that it was Pharaoh's advisor who initiated the enslavement.[742] In 1967, at Deir Alla, Jordan, a team led by Professor Henk Franken of the University of Leiden found an inscription written on plaster fragments containing a previously unknown prophecy by Balaam dated to around the ninth-century BCE.[743] One of the fragments astonishingly had the full name in bold letters: "The prophet, Balaam son of Beor." It is interesting that the inscription is in a dialect of Aramaic and Balaam was originally from Aram.

---

739 William Shea, "New Light on the Exodus and on Construction of the Tabernacle: Gerster's Protosinaitic Inscription No.1," *Andrews University Seminary Studies* 25 (1987): pgs. 73–96. Dr. Shea has since published other articles on the subject.

740 *Bamidbar* [Numbers] 22. Most of the archaeological information about Balaam was gleaned from an article in the name of Rabbi Leibel Reznick (aish.com/ci/sam/48965991.html).

741 *Sanhedrin* 106a.

742 Josephus, *Against Avion*, Book I, sec. 26. Although Manetho himself is not from the same era as Balaam, it is interesting that there is a corroborating outside source for this Talmudic teaching.

743 Recently scholars have lowered the date closer to 600 BCE; see Jo Ann Hacket, *The Balaam Text from Deir' Alla* (1984), pg. 19.

JOSHUA, CONQUEST, SETTLEMENT, AND MONARCHY

JOSHUA SON OF NUN

Following the forty year sojourn, the Jewish people entered the Holy Land, which they conquered and eventually established a monarchy. Joshua, the son of Nun, led the Jewish people in laying claim to the Holy Land.

The Jerusalem Talmud and the Midrash relate that before Joshua led the way into Canaan, he allowed the peoples to either vacate, make peace and accept morality, or fight.[744] These sources continue, and say that the Girgashi vacated and were given a land in Africa.

Anthony Frendo, professor of Arabic and Near Eastern Studies at the University of Malta, writes that the Phoenicians who settled in North Africa were driven out of Canaan by Joshua, citing the writings of Procopius of Caesarea, a Greek historian:[745]

> They [the Canaanites] also built a fortress in Numidia, where now is the city called Tigisis. In that place are two columns made of white stone near by the great spring, having Phoenician letters cut in them which say in the Phoenician tongue: **'We are they who fled from before the face of Joshua, the robber, the son of Nun.'**"[746]

Moses of Khoren, an earlier Armenian historian, also referred to the two Phoenician columns.[747]

Later Greek historians[748] referred to this tradition as well, saying,

---

744   *Yerushalmi, Shvi'is* 6:1. Also *Vayikrah Rabbah* 17:6; *Devarim Rabbah* 5:14.

745   Frendo, "Two Long-Lost Phoenician Inscriptions and the Emergence of Ancient Israel," *Palestine Exploration Quarterly* 134 (2002): pgs. 37–43.

746   *History of the Wars* 4:10:14-24, circa sixth century CE, emphasis mine.

747   This story is also found in excerpts from the book written by a Christian historian named Yochanan of Antiochia, and Sueadas the Byzantine. Procopius and Yochanan of Antiochia are also independent sources. See book of Dr. Yochanan Levi of Hebrew University, *Olamot Nifgashim* (Worlds Meet), published by Mossad Bialik (1969), pg. 60.

748   See *Chronicon Paschale*, an anonymous work from the seventh century CE that attempts to chronicle the history of the world, cited by Frendo, ibid., pg. 40.

"The inhabitants of these islands were Canaanites fleeing from the face of Joshua the son of Nun."[749] Frendo claims that the original Greek text of this quotation is much earlier, going back to 234 BCE. According to Frendo, "The cumulative total of the biblical, archaeological and extra-biblical evidence presents a strong case for the historicity of the biblical account of the Conquest of Canaan as recorded in the book of Joshua."[750]

CONQUERING JERICHO

Jericho has access to the heartland of Canaan. Any military conquest from the east would have to conquer it.[751] Likewise, in Jewish tradition Jericho is called the "bolt" of the Land of Israel, that if it were conquered the entire land would be captured, therefore this was the first target of the Israelites.[752] The Jews circled the city seven times, sounded the *shofar* and the walls came crumbling down.[753] They then set the city aflame.

One of the points that actually led many scholars to claim that there was no such thing as an Israelite conquest of Canaan under Joshua is that we do not find any evidence for it—no debris, no bones, no broken walls. However, consider the following:

> In 1066, William the Conqueror conquered England. There are very few doubts about it. Yet there is no debris, no strewn bones, no broken walls to show us that that is indeed what he did. However, no one doubts it. In about 539 BCE, the Babylonian Empire, which spanned a huge area, the biggest of its day, ceased to exist. The empire was conquered by another, that of the Persians, but we do not find any rubble or debris amongst the ruins of Babylon to show it. In fact, if the ruins are all we had to

---

749   The Balearic Islands north of Algeria and east of Spain.
750   Frendo, ibid.
751   James Monson, "Climbing into Canaan," *Bible Times* 1 (1988), pgs. 8–21.
752   *Bamidbar Rabbah* 15:15.
753   *Yehoshua* [Joshua] 6:20.

go by, we'd be forgiven for thinking that Babylon never was conquered because it continued to flourish as a city with hardly any change. Yet, it was conquered. It was conquered by Cyrus, king of Persia.[754]

In the 1950s, Kathleen Kenyon excavated Jericho and said that the Israelites did not conquer it, based predominantly on the absence of a certain style of pottery from Cyprus that was imported into the area from 1550 to 1400 BCE. Therefore she concluded that Jericho must have been destroyed earlier than 1550 BCE. She calculated that the exodus from Egypt would have been later than that, and therefore the destruction of Jericho could not be from the Jews.[755] More recently, though, biblical archaeologist Bryant Wood claims that some of Kathleen Kenyon's conclusions were incorrect. Wood, an ancient-pottery expert, argues that Kenyon's excavations were made in a poorer part of the city, where the expensive imported pottery would have been absent in any case.

As renowned an archaeologist as Kenyon was, she was also reportedly politically opposed to Israel, and there may be question as to whether this disposition had an influence on some of her conclusions.[756] Notwithstanding, except for the disputed dating, Kenyon's discoveries at Jericho were largely consistent with the Bible. She found that the city's walls had fallen in a way suggestive of sudden collapse. Additionally, Kenyon found bushels of grain on the site. If the city had fallen after

---

754 George Athas, "Minimalism": The Copenhagen School of Thought in Biblical Studies, Edited Transcript of Lecture, 3rd Ed, (University of Sydney 1999), mentioned in Gottlieb's *Living Up to the Truth*.

755 These conclusions are very weak. Although she was respected in her time, her results can be questioned in at least four different ways. (a) Conclusions based on what is not found are weak. (b) Jericho was not on any of the major trade routes, as such, would one even expect to find pottery there? (c) She searched in what she described as the poor section of the city, likely to not have been there in any case. (d) She ignores the dating of local pottery that had been found in earlier excavations that do come from dates later than 1550 BCE (See *Biblical Archaeology Review* (March/April 1990): pgs. 44–56, where much of the information on Jericho excavations was extracted from).

756 Her sentiments are discussed in several places; one example is in Herschel Shanks, "Kathleen Kenyon's Anti-Zionist Politics—Does It Affect Her Work?" *Biblical Archaeology Review* 1 (1975), No. 3.

a long siege, the grain would have been used up. A thick layer of soot at the site, which according to carbon-14 dating was laid down about 1400 BCE, supports the biblical idea that the city was burned. Wood said, "It looks to me as though the biblical stories are correct." Other experts find little fault with Wood's archaeology.[757]

SACRIFICIAL ALTAR

Additionally, at Mt. Ebal a large rectangular structure made of uncut stone and with a ramp leading to the top was found containing ashes and bones of animals used in Jewish sacrificial service. The excavator Adam Zertal, professor of archaeology at the University of Haifa, interprets the site as the altar likely put up by Joshua in the Bible.[758] Whether it is the actual altar constructed by Joshua himself or not, it is certainly a fascinating piece that can be correctly identified as an Israelite altar dating from the period of the Judges.[759]

---

757 However they are more skeptical about his linking of the evidence with biblical events. Jericho conquering is discussed in Lemonick and Mihok, "Science: Score One for the Bible," *Time Magazine*, Mar. 5, 1990. It should be noted that five years after this article was published, a more updated carbon dating of charred cereal grains showed that Jericho City IV was destroyed "during the late 17th or the 16th century BCE," which is more in line with Kathleen Kenyon's findings. However, Bryant Wood defended his original dates, saying that his dating is based on pottery (likewise on Egyptian chronology). Jericho is just one example of the discrepancy between historical and carbon 14 dates for the second millennium BCE. Carbon 14 dates are often between one hundred and one hundred and fifty years earlier than the historical dates. There is a heated debate going on among scholars concerning this, especially with regard to the date of the eruption of Thera. An overview of the discussion can be seen in Manfred Bietak and Felix Höflmayer, "Introduction: High and Low Chronology," pgs. 13–23 in *The Synchronization of Civilisations in the Eastern Mediterranean in the Second Millenium* B.C. III, eds. Manfred Bietak and Ernst Czerny (Vienna: Österreichischen Akademie der Wissenschanften, 2007). Because of the inconsistencies and uncertainties of carbon 14 dating, many archaeologists prefer historical dates over carbon 14 dates.

758 *Yehoshua* [Joshua] 8:30. See Zertal, *A Nation is Born: The Altar at Mount Ebal and the beginning of Israel* (2000). See also Zertal, "Has Joshua's Altar Been Found on Mt. Ebal?" *BAR* (1986): pgs. 26–43.

759 Zertal's claims about this being the exact altar of Joshua are not widely accepted, yet the fact that it is an altar from the era of the Judges is clearer; see Meitlis, *Excavating the Bible* (2012), pg. 187.

GIBEON

As shown earlier, lack of evidence at a given time can be deceiving. Gibeon is described in the Book of Joshua as a "great city" at the time the Jews entered the land. After three years of excavation in the late 1950s, no pottery shards resembling ones from that era were found, which led archaeologists at the time to conclude that there was no evidence for this "great city" in the time of the conquest.

In 1960, two tombs were found filled with Late Bronze Age pottery, establishing evidence that Gibeon did indeed exist just before the conquest. Had they not continued digging or not found these tombs, the official archaeological conclusion would have been that there is no corroborating evidence.[760]

THE SUN STOOD STILL

Perhaps the most known accomplishment of Joshua was his making the sun and moon stand still for many extra hours.[761] Prolonged daylight in Israel means prolonged night in other parts of the world. This event is mentioned in the lore of peoples around the world, including the American Indians, the Chinese, and Greeks.[762] In the Mexican *Annals of Cuauhtitlan*, a history of the empire in Mexico, it states that "during a time in the remote past, the night did not end for a long time."[763] Likewise, Bernardino de Sahagún, deemed by many to be the first anthropologist, who came to America one generation after Columbus and gathered traditions of the natives,

---

760   This is comparable with the city of Ai that neighbors Gibeon, which many contemporary archaeologists dismiss as fabrication based on the exact same "lack of evidence." Perhaps something is just being missed? See James Pritchard, *Gibeon, Where the Sun Stood Still* (1967), pgs. 23, 136, 137. There is a link between Ai and Gibeon mentioned explicitly in Joshua 9:3, cited from Barry Freundel, *Contemporary Orthodox Judaism's Response to Modernity* (2004), pg. 26, note 52.

761   *Yehoshua* [Joshua] 10:12. The Talmud (*Avoda Zara* 25a) debates exactly how long the luminaries were delayed. See also Targum, *Chabakkuk* 3:11.

762   Matthew Williams Stirling, an American ethnologist and archaeologist, records in the 1945 Report of the Smithsonian Institute this idea in different cultures, cited from Miller, *Behold a People*, #171.

763   Sourced by Velikovsky, *Worlds in Collision* (2009), pg. 63.

writes that "during one cosmic catastrophe the sun rose only a little over the horizon and remained there without moving; the moon also stood still."[764]

SAMSON

After entering the land, the Jews were guided by the Judges. One famous biblical character from that time was Samson, who had super-human strength, a power that rested in his long hair. In the Bible, he kills a lion with his bare hands. Recently, a seal was discovered on the Israelite and Philistine border depicting a man with long hair fighting a feline figure. The seal was excavated in a layer of earth that dates to the eleventh century BCE, a time in which the Israelites were ruled by judges, including the biblical Samson.[765]

THE PEOPLE OF ISRAEL: SOME EXTERNAL SOURCES

THE MERNAPTAH STELE

"Isreal is laid waste, his seed is not."

One interesting find that is, to date, the earliest non-biblical refer-ence to the people of Israel is the Mernaptah Stele. A stele, or stela, is an upright stone or slab with an inscribed or sculptured surface, used as a monument or as a commemorative tablet. The Mernaptah Stele is a large granite slab detailing the victories of Pharaoh Mernaptah in

---

764 *Historia General de las Cosas de Neuva Espana*, new ed. 1938 (5 vols.) and 1946 (3 vols.). French translation by D. Jourdanet and R Simeon (1880), pg. 481, brought down in Ve-likovsky, ibid. There is no way to know for sure if these were the "actual" corresponding occurrences with the Joshua account, but interesting to consider that such accounts exist.

765 Charlie Wells, "Israeli Archaeologists Uncover Seal Lending Credence to Biblical Samson's Existence," *New York Daily News*, Jul. 31, 2012.

the early 1200s BCE. Known biblical locations like Canaan and Ashkelon are named among the ransacked sites. However, none compare to the fascinating inscription featured below:

In this hieroglyph there are "determinatives" that are used. These are symbols that show what genre the depiction is, be it geographical, ethnic, or otherwise. In this case the determinative "throwing stick" accompanied with the man and woman and under-strokes is a sign of a "foreign people," and not a town or city.[766] This is very significant, as it is a reference placing Israel, the people, in Palestine in the thirteenth century BCE. Furthermore, their power must have been significant enough to be mentioned on this Egyptian memoir.

Egyptian sources from the fourteenth and thirteenth centuries BCE mention a group by the name of "Asher" located in the Galilee, which is also incidentally where the book of Joshua fixes the location of this Israelite tribe.[767]

TEL DAN STELE

Several centuries after entering into the Holy Land, the Israelites finally solidified their monarchy. In 1993, a stele was discovered at Tel Dan in northern Israel by a team of scholars led by former head of the Institute of Archaeology at Hebrew Union College in Jerusalem, Avraham Biran. Its Aramaic inscriptions describe the defeat over local peoples including references to "Israel" and more significantly "The House of David." It was dated to the ninth century BCE, around a century after David's death. The archaeological consensus is that this is an authentic reference to the biblical King David—the first extra-biblical verification of his existence and dynasty.[768]

---

766 Carol A. Redmount, "Bitter Lives: Israel in and out of Egypt" in *The Oxford History of the Biblical World* (1999), pg. 97.

767 Shmuel Yevin, "Asher" in *Entsiklopedia Miqra'it* (Heb.) vol. 1 (1977–78), pg. 783, cited from Meitlis, ibid., pg. 73.

768 William Dever, *What Did the Biblical Authors Know, and When Did They Know It?* (2004), pgs. 128-9.

MESHA STELE

There is also the Mesha Stele, which was written in the ninth century BCE by Mesha, the king of Moab. Preserved upon it are some chilling external corroborations to the Torah. Mesha writes in line 10: "And men of God have lived in the land of Atarot from time immemorial." Compare this with the Book of Numbers, "And men of [the tribe of] Gad built Dibon and Atarot and Aro'er."[769] It also refers to the kingdom of Israel, saying, "Omri King of Israel," and perhaps the earliest extra-biblical reference to the Tetragrammaton, the Ineffable Name of G-d. Some would say that it contains a reference to "House of David," which, if conclusive, would make it the earliest external source of this term.[770]

DAVID AND SOLOMON

The backdrop painted by the Bible, describing the times of David and Solomon, seem to be in sync with much of the findings being uncovered today.[771]

David's son, Solomon, is said to have built fortifications—the "Gates of Solomon"—at Hazor, Megiddo, and Gezer.[772] They have now likely been found.[773]

---

769   *Bamidbar* [Numbers] 32:34.

770   Andre Lemaire, "'House of David' Restored in Moabite Inscription," *Biblical Archaeology Review* 20:03 (May/June 1994): pgs. 30–37.

771   Some of the following points are paraphrased from Meitlis, *Excavating the Bible* (2012), ch. 8. Over there, he gives a summary of findings and conclusions that are discussed and phenomenally referenced earlier in the book; see there for details about the forthcoming paragraphs.

772   *Melachim* I [I Kings] 9:15.

773   Paul and Dever, *Biblical Archaeology* (1973), pg. 97. Later on, excavations in the Negev were found to be similar to the "Gates of Solomon," although they were built after the days of Solomon. This led to gradual belief that the gates at Hazor, Megiddo, and Gezer were not linked to Solomon. In the late 1990s, professor Israel Finkelstein brought forth other questions in the link between royal construction and David and Solomon. Several counter-arguments have been put forth to Finkelstein; see Amihai Mazar, "Iron Age Chronology: A Reply to I. Finkelstein," *Levant* XXIX (1997): pgs. 157–167. For an interesting yet brief summary of the discussion, as well as a defense of the original dates, see Meitlis, ibid., pgs. 128–135.

Additionally, a combination of biblical sources and archaeological findings have shown the period of the Israelite monarchy to be a time of economic prosperity, sophisticated settlement patterns, and significant population growth in comparison to what it was beforehand. The written evidence also points to prevalent literacy in the days of David and Solomon.

Furthermore, skeptics believe that if David and Solomon even existed at all, they were nothing more than chieftains. According to them, they were certainly not kings, and there was certainly not a kingdom. Yosef Garfinkel, professor of prehistoric archaeology and of archaeology of the biblical period at the Hebrew University of Jerusalem, has, among many other accomplishments, served as co-director of the dig at an archaeological site called Khirbet Qeiyafa. In ancient times, it was a heavily fortified town on the Philistine border in Judah. They have found massive fortifications, pottery finds that correspond to the tenth century BCE, and carbon-14 dating on olive pits dated to the tenth century as well. Concerning his findings in just this place, he says, "The argument that Judah was an agrarian society until the end of tenth century BCE and that David and Solomon could not have ruled over a centralized, institutionalized kingdom before then has now been blown to smithereens by our excavations at Khirbet Qeiyafa."[774]

LATER KINGS AND PROPHETS

Omri's son, Ahab, was a wicked king who reigned from approximately 870-850 BCE. His name and contributions to the Battle of Qarqar are recorded toward the end of the Kurkh Monolith, an Assyrian document currently found in the British Museum. Jezebel, Ahab's wife, was a Phoenician princess who helped lure him into worship of the Baal. It was with Jezebel's "prophets" that the prophet Elijah faced off

---

774   Yosef Garfinkel, "The Birth and Death of Biblical Minimalism," *Biblical Archaeology Review* (May/June 2011), pg. 50. The discoveries demonstrate that a large bureaucracy was needed to construct the town. Garfinkel describes various examples why Khirbet Qeiyafa could not have been built, fortified, or administrated by a chieftain. It required a king.

at the encounter at Mt. Carmel. In the 1960s, a royal seal was found with her name upon it.[775] Marjo Korpel, professor of Old Testament at Utrecht University, later confirmed that this was indeed the seal of the infamous queen.[776] Seals, monuments, or other artifacts have likewise been found confirming nearly every other king of Israel and Judah chronicled in the Bible.[777]

In the Book of Kings II, King Hezekiah built a tunnel under the City of David in Jerusalem to prevent the Assyrians from having access to the water supply.[778] The Siloam tunnel has been confirmed and dated, both by the written inscription found on its wall and organic matter found in the original plastering, as the biblical tunnel.[779]

When the Babylonians conquered Judah in the sixth-century BCE and destroyed Jerusalem, Nebuchadnezzar the king of Babylon, appointed Gedaliah ben Achikam, a member of a prominent Jerusalem family, governor of Judah. He was soon murdered by an assassin sent by Baalis, king of the Ammonites.[780] As a result of his assassination, many Jews were slain and sent into final exile. This horrific event is commemorated with a yearly fast immediately following Rosh Hashana. A bulla giving mention to Achikam and several seals of King Baalis have been discovered.[781] Furthermore, a bulla found in Lachish (Tell ed-Duweir) inscribed "Gedaliah, who is over the house," is generally accepted as a reference to Gedaliah ben Achikam.[782]

Baruch ben Neriah was the secretary of the prophet Jeremiah. When Jeremiah was imprisoned, Baruch wrote out dictations of Jeremiah's

---

775 Nahman Avigad, "The Seal of Jezebel," *Israel Exploration Journal* 14 (1964), pgs. 274–6.
776 "I believe it is very likely that we have here the seal of the famous Queen Jezebel; see Marjo Korpel, "Fit for a Queen: Jezebel's Royal Seal," *BAR* 34.2 (2008), pg. 37.
777 See Miller, *Sing, You Righteous*, #127; *Rejoice O Youth!* beginning at #116.
778 *Melachim* II [II Kings] 20:20.
779 Amos Frumkin and Aryeh Shimron, "Tunnel Engineering in the Iron Age: Geoarchaeology of the Siloam Tunnel," *Journal of Archaeological Science*, vol. 33, no. 2 (February 2006): pgs. 227–237; see also the London-based *Nature* journal (Sept. 2003).
780 *Yirmiyahu* 40:13–41:2.
781 Avigad and Sass, "Corpus of West-Semitic Stamp Seals," *Biblical Archaeology Review*, (March/April 1999): pg. 181.
782 Avigad, "Baruch the Scribe and Jerahmeel the King's Son," *The Biblical Archaeologist*, vol. 42, no. 2 (1979): pgs. 114–118.

prophecies and read them to the people in the Temple, and Jehoakim, king of Judah. In the 1970s, a bulla containing the stamp and name of Baruch ben Neriah was chanced upon and then published and authenticated by Israeli archaeologist Nahman Avigad, and now sits in the Israel Museum.

PURIM

For some time, the name "Achashverosh" in the Book of Esther was criticized because it could not be found to have a corresponding name in the Greek writings. Greek historians[783] described several Persian kings from the biblical period: Cyrus, Cambyses, Darius, Xerxes, and Artaxerxes. The true identity of Achashverosh from among these choices was left to speculation.

In the 1800s, many ancient cuneiform inscriptions were decoded in the Persian palaces. The Greek "Xerxes" was merely a foreign corruption referring to King "Khshayarsha," which when Hebraised becomes "Achashverosh."[784] For this reason, Xerxes is typically identified by contemporary Jewish scholars as the biblical Achashverosh.[785] Among the countries that are listed under his rule are from "Hidush" to "Kushiya," likely a variant of the Hodu and Kush (from India to Ethiopia) mentioned at the beginning of the Megillah,[786] the scroll containing the Book of Esther that Jews read during Purim. Furthermore, the word "Purim" itself was found on Assyrian inscriptions to mean "lots."[787]

---

783 For example, Herodotus, fifth century BCE, and others.

784 First, Mitchell, "Identifying Achashverosh and Esther in Secular Sources," (2010). The first decipherer of the name in its Old Persian form tells how he found confirmation in the biblical name; G. F. Grotefend in A. H. L. Heeren, *Historical Researches…* (Eng. Trans. 1846), II, pg. 335. For an English summary of other plausible connections to Achashverosh, see Naphtali Winter, *Purim Revealed: The Inside Story of Megillas Esther* (2007), pgs. 35–48.

785 *Doros HaRishonim: Tekufas ha-Mikra* (1939), pg. 262; Miller, *Torah Nation* (1971), pg. 40; see also *Jewish History in Conflict*, pgs. 178–79.

786 Roland G. Kent, *Old Persian: Grammar, Texts, Lexicon*, pg. 151.

787 The Akkadian form is *puru*, which could be linked to the contemporary Persian. Also, from excavations of Dieulafoy at Susa, there was recovered a small quadrangular prism, each face engraved with a number, which must have served as a die. M. Dieulafoy, "Le livre d'Esther et le palais d'Assuerus," in *Revue des Etudes Juives* (1888), pgs. CCLXV–CCXCI.

Some were critical about the accuracy of the description offered by the Megillah about the conditions in Persia at the time. Marcel Dieulafoy, an official archeologist of the French government, made extensive excavations at the royal Persian palace in the ruins of Susa (Shushan) in the 1880s. He told over that the writer of the Book of Esther had tremendous accuracy in the description of the palace, and that since the ruins had been buried for 2,400 years, the writer of the book must have been there at the time.[788] It is for this reason that scholars refer to the Book of Esther as "a historical novel with the accent on the first word."[789]

CONCLUSION

These are only a few of the more prominent biblical accounts and personalities.

There are literally hundreds more remnants that have been excavated in the past hundred years that testify to other later or more "minor" biblical figures. It is surely without foundation when critics dismiss biblical accuracy when seen in light of the above pages. One who considers the facts objectively must assume the truthfulness of the biblical record.

---

788   Miller, *Rejoice O Youth!* #116. See also article by Morris Jastrow Jr., "Persian Art from Susa; 'Finds' by the Dieulafoys Taken to Paris. Palace an Artaxerxes Built and Prizes from Xerxes's Palace—Book of Esther Confirmed," *New York Times* December 9, 1888.
789   *The Anchor Bible* (1971), written from a scholarly perspective, quote cited in Freundel, pg. 19.

JEWISH IDENTITY

The Torah and its commandments are primarily instructed to the Jewish people. They are meant to be a manual for life. Who is traditionally considered a Jew, and thereby enjoined to uphold the Torah precepts? What are the unique roles of each gender in shaping the world? Why are the laws of kosher food and observance of the Sabbath so central to Jewish life?

Let's begin to explore.

MATRILINEAL DESCENT

The Code of Jewish Law states clearly that a child is considered a born Jew only if his mother is a Jew, regardless of the father's faith.[790] There is no mention of any dissenting opinion there or in any other classical *halachic* text. It is an established tenet given to the Jewish people at Mt. Sinai.

It is important to note that whether or not before Sinai there was a different precedent has no practical relevance to today. The Torah declares in reference to Sinai that "this day you become a people unto the L-rd your G-d."[791] Before the Sinai event, there was no community of Israel or binding Jewish legal system. The whole concept of the Jewish people's holiness and nationhood began at Sinai, as did the criteria for membership in this community.[792]

---

790   *Even HaEzer* 8:5. This is just talking about someone who is born a Jew; however, if someone converts in accordance with Jewish Law, then they are equally Jewish.

791   *Devarim* [Deuteronomy] 27:9.

792   In truth, there is a dispute as to when exactly matrilineal descent became the law: was it since Abraham or not until the giving of the Torah? One such instance where this debate shows itself is in the book of Leviticus. The Torah relates the story of the blasphemer, who is identified as the son of an Egyptian man and an Israelite woman. The Torah says, "The son of a Jewish woman—who was the son of an Egyptian man, in the midst of the community of Israel, and this son of the Jewish woman quarreled in the camp (24:10–15)." The words "in the midst of the community of Israel" imply that he was a Jew. Additionally, a few verses later, he is condemned to be put to death by stoning—which is a form of punishment only befitting a Jew. Non-Jews, who were subject to the death penalty for transgressing one of the Seven Noachide Laws are executed by decapitation; see Mishneh Torah, *Melachim* 9:14. Biblical evidence to this comes from the execution of Shechem (*Bereishis* [Genesis] 34:26), and Balaam (*Yehoshua* [Joshua] 13:22).

The *Toras Kohanim* comments on the words "in the midst of the community of Israel," saying that this teaches that the blasphemer converted before this event.

T   This is puzzling, as the Talmud (*Yevamos* 45a, among other places) states that a child born

Furthermore, some people tend to think that in biblical times, Judaism endorsed patrilineal descent by citing, for example, the children of Joseph or King Solomon, as children who were considered Jewish because of their father. However, the oral tradition and commentaries attest that these assumptions are incorrect. In all of these cases, the women, in fact, were Jewish or became Jewish through conversion.[793]

MATRILINEAL DESCENT DERIVED FROM TORAH

There is much evidence that can be brought to demonstrate matrilineal descent following the giving of the Torah. The following are merely two examples:

> **The Jewish Servant:** *"And if his master should give him a wife who will bear him sons or daughters, the woman and her children shall belong to her master, and [the servant] shall go forth by himself."*[794]

Here, a Jewish man is sold into temporary indentured servitude and given a gentile slave to father children. The verse explains that after his period of service ends, he goes free and his children remain. It is

---

from a Jewish woman and gentile man is a full-fledged Jew. The commentaries ask why the *Toras Kohanim* says that the blasphemer converted? Rabbi Chizkiyahu ben Rabbi Manoach, known as the Chizkuni, concludes that matrilineal descent only went into effect after the giving of the Torah, and beforehand went by the father. The *Mishneh Lemelech* writes that this touches on a broader discussion amongst the Torah commentaries: What was the status of the Jewish people before the giving of the Torah? Did they have the legal status as Jews, or as gentiles? A gentile inherits his father's status (*Yevamos* 78b). According to this perspective, the blasphemer would have been a convert, because he was born in Egypt before the giving of the Torah. The Ramban disagrees, saying that matrilineal descent was the rule since Abraham. The blasphemer was born Jewish.

793   In reference to the examples mentioned here, see *Nachalas Yaakov, Mesechta Sofrim* (end of ch. 21), which writes that Joseph's wife, Asnas, was Jewish. She was Dinah's daughter, conceived from Shechem. Jacob had given her an amulet with the Ineffable Name upon it. When Joseph saw the amulet he realized she was a Jew, and married her. In addition, the Talmud (*Yevamos* 76a) writes clearly that all of King Solomon's wives converted. All other biblical personalities used by secular academics to demonstrate "patrilineal descent" are likewise accounted for in Jewish tradition as inaccurate.

794   *Shmos* [Exodus] 21:4.

clear that the children inherit their mother's non-Jewish status, for if the children were considered Jewish, they would be exempt from permanent ownership by another Jew.[795]

Ezra:

> *"And Shechaniah the son of Yechiel, one of the sons of Elam, answered and said to Ezra, "We have broken faith with our L-rd and married foreign women of the peoples of the land, yet now there is hope for Israel concerning this thing. There-fore, let us make a covenant with our L-rd to send away all the wives* and all that were born from them, *according to the counsel of Hashem, and of those that tremble at the com-mandment of our G-d;* and let it be done according to the Torah.""[796]

The Jews returning to Israel vowed to put aside their non-Jewish wives and the children born to those wives. They could not have put aside those children if those children were Jews.

It can clearly be seen that matrilineal descent is biblical in origin. A person's Judaism or Jewishness being passed through the mother is an indisputable fact, with centuries upon centuries of history to attest for it.[797]

---

795   See *Yalkut Me'am Loez* on the verse.

796   *Ezra* 10:2–3.

797   In truth, even if it were not biblical, and instead "merely" a two-thousand-year-old insti-tution of the early sages, it would still be reasonable that it not be modified. "Similar to the American legal concept of *stare decisis*, legal systems recognize that settled law leads to expectations on the part of the community, develops a history and life of its own, and spawns derivative effects throughout its entire structure. For this reason, uprooting a law cannot be done lightly, and if splitting the community is the result, it is generally not worth it. Unfortunately only the deleterious outcome has emerged from the patrilineal debate." Barry Freundel, *Contemporary Orthodox Judaism's Response to Modernity* (2004), pg. 223.

Often times, modern people see themselves as more civilized or sophisticated than the people of long ago. This can, at times, lead some to think it necessary to modify the commands of the Torah or edicts of the sages. An interesting anecdote occurred when the "Who is a Jew" question first arose in Israel at the end of the 1950s. Ben Gurion sent letters to fifty people he considered Jewish scholars asking for their perspectives. Dr. Yosef Schechter, a medical doctor, received the letter by mistake. He still ended up writing back his opinion on the matter. He was very firm to not veer from tradition, writing,

It is worth probing in depth the source of this law both from a legalistic perspective and a spiritual one. The Talmud formally derives the law of matrilineal descent from the following verses:

You shall not intermarry with them; you shall not give your daughter to his son, and you shall not take his daughter for your son, for he will cause your child to turn away from Me and they will worship the gods of others.[798]

The Talmud clarifies that since the verse states "for *he* [a non-Jewish father] will cause your child to turn away," this implies that a child born to a Jewish mother is Jewish. "*Your* child," however, if a Jewish man marries a non-Jewish woman, the child is *not* Jewish—ergo there is no concern that "*she*" [the child's mother] will turn the child away from Judaism.[799]

Later, the law of matrilineal descent was likewise codified by the Rambam[800] and the Code of Jewish Law, as mentioned above.

"The argument that the position of the ancient authorities no longer fits the spirit of our time will undoubtedly be voiced. There is no need for deep analysis to convince ourselves that our time is one of the darkest, and almost certainly the darkest in history—a period whose crimes have brought mankind to the verge of destruction, similar to the generation of the flood and the people of Sodom. Can anybody seriously argue that we should bring the law of Moses, which bears the seal of G-d, into harmony with the spirit of our time?" (See *Zeihuyot Yehudiyot*, Sde Boker 2001, pg. 296.)

Furthermore, according to popular journalist Sue Fishkoff, the only ones who seem to be embracing the idea of patrilineal descent is American Reform-Judaism. She goes on to mention that even the Reform congregations in other countries have generally not accepted the notion. Some started to accept patrilineal descent and then reverted back. The edict was only "codified" in the United States in 1983, although it had more or less been the standard practice for a few decades prior. Even within the United States, not all congregations seem to abide by it. She mentions, for example, the dynamic of trying to incorporate patrilineal descent in France. She quotes a Mr. Jean-Francois Levy, a former president of a Reform organization, who says that even those in France who may be interested in things that Reform-Judaism has to offer them would likely not join if Reform in France embraced patrilineality. "They would say, 'Look, they don't even know the most basic Jewish traditions,'" Levy said. See Sue Fishkoff, "Why Is Patrilineal Descent Not Catching On in Reform Worldwide?" *The Jewish Week* (Feb. 13, 2011).

798   *Devarim* [Deuteronomy] 7:3–4.

799   *Kiddushin* 68b; *Yevamos* 23a.

800   Rambam, *Issurei Biya* [15:4]: "This is the general rule: The status of offspring from a gentile man or from a gentile woman is the same as his mother's; we disregard the father."

A DEEPER LOOK

It is interesting to ponder *why* Judaism goes solely according to the mother. What is it about the mother that makes her impart her Jewishness on her offspring?

Even in nature, amongst many animals the motherly bond with the child is firmer than the father's. The Jewish mother has the superior influence on the child's religious development.[801] This is because the mother gives over her essence to her offspring.[802] This is why the matriarchs in the Bible named their children, as the name expresses a person's essence. Furthermore, the womb has been compared to a *mikveh*, which has the capacity to convert a person to Judaism. "The mother determines the spiritual genetics of a child because of the impact that the womb has on the unborn child. The fact that the mother carries the baby within her reveals her capacity to carry on the Jewish lineage."[803]

In Kabbalistic terminology, male and female are both expressions of G-d's image, like it says, "In the image of G-d He created him, male and female He created them."[804] The difference between the Hebrew words for male and female is that man (*ish*) is spelled with a *yud*, and woman (*isha*) with a *hei*. The two letters together are the first two letters of the Tetragrammaton. *Yud* symbolizes wisdom, whereas *hei* alludes to depth and understanding. Wisdom is acquired information (*past*) and understanding is the *future* application of that wisdom.[805]

---

801 Lord Immanuel Jacobowitz, former Chief Rabbi of England, *The Timely and the Timeless* (1977), pgs. 198–217.

802 See, for instance, Rabbeinu Bachya, *Bereishis* 29:25. "Rachel's children inherited her silence. When Yaakov sent her gifts, Lavan took them and gave them to Leah, yet Rachel remained silent. Therefore, all her children were masters of silence. Binyamin knew that Yosef was sold, but kept silent. Esther did not reveal the identity of her people..." Chana Bracha Siegelbaum, *Women at the Crossroads: A Woman's Perspective on the Weekly Torah Portion* (2010), pg. 165.

803 In the name of the *Imrei Shefer*, Siegelbaum ibid.

804 *Bereishis* [Genesis] 1:27. Rabbeinu Bachya, *Zohar* 3:117a.

805 Wisdom related to beginnings and the past, as it says, "The beginning is wisdom" (*Mishlei* 4:7). It is also written, "I am the first and I am the last" (*Yeshayahu* 44:6). The sages teach that "first" refers to wisdom, and "last" to understanding. (See Ra'avad and Ramban on *Sefer Yetzira* 1:5.) For more elaboration in English on the subject, see Kaplan, *Immortality, Resurrection and the Age of the Universe* (1993), pgs. 57–59.

The symbolism of male and female can be seen in the following chart:

Male	*Yud*	Wisdom	Past
Female	*Hei*	Understanding	Future

It should therefore be of no surprise that women play primary responsibility in the creation and influence on the *future* generation.

Furthermore, the last two letters of the Tetragrammaton, *vav* and *hei*, represent male and female as well. The *vav's* shape represents a bestowal or flow of spiritual energy, and the *hei's* shape breadth and expansion. In Kabbalistic terms, the male aspect is the idea of bestowal or "giving," whereas the female is the idea of "receiving," as is even embodied in their distinct physical organs.

The Kabbalists describe the way G-d interacts with the world by means of different qualities or *sefiros*. The emotive elements symbolized by the letter *vav* are considered masculine, for they are expressions of G-dliness, the way in which G-d projects Himself to Creation. Divine expression is synonymous with the idea of "giving."[806]

The female soul, however, originates in G-d's attribute of *malchus*, royalty, and is represented by the letter *hei*. It is likened to the womb. It represents the power to "receive" and to eventually give back something more complete. Biologically, the man gives millions of sperm cells, one of which is selected by the woman. Her single fertilized egg brings forth one complete baby. The man's role is diversified whereas the woman's role is unified. It is for this reason, in part, that the Kabbalists describe *malchus* as rooted in G-d's unified *essence*, rather than one of many Divine "*expressions*." The *essence* of a Jew, his Jewish soul, is thus inherited from the mother.[807]

The chart below summarizes the above ideas:

---

806   *Tanya, Iggeres HaKodesh* 15 (122a); *Likkutei Torah*, Masei 90c.

807   See also: "One of the revealed reasons: The entire embryo is formed from an infinitesimal drop into a developed body, (the makeup of the body also affects the person's character traits, to a significant extent) by the mother alone (and during the period of pregnancy— it eats what its mother eats, etc.) so much so that we see openly that the spirituality of the mother (and whether she is joyful or in fear, and the like) influences, and also forms the character of the embryo..." *Likkutei Sichos*, vol. 14, pg. 205.

Male	Vav	Emotive Attributes	"Giver"	Expression
Female	Hei	Kingship	"Receiver"	Essence

CONCLUSION

The above ideas are brought together by the Lubavitcher Rebbe zt"l:
The blurring of the essential difference between man and woman is
even robbing women of their basic rights as mothers! Jewish law affirms that a child belongs to the people of which his or her mother is a
member, so that a child is Jewish only if the mother is Jewish. One of
the reasons for this is that the embryo is formed and nurtured in the
mother's womb. Flying in the face of this indisputable fact of nature,
there are those who are currently proposing that the father should be
the determining factor in establishing the child's identity. This is not
only unreasonable, but in effect—as in child custody suits—robs the
mother of the child whom she carried in her womb for nine months,
for whom she went through the pain of childbirth, and whom she willingly brought into the world. Women throughout the world, Jewish
and non-Jewish, should protest strongly against this unjust distor-
tion of the natural order.

It is time to restore balance to a world where light is called darkness
and darkness light. Above all, it is time to restore to women the dignity of their sacred role as molders of young Jewish lives—when and
where they are most needed.[808]

---

808   Quoted from "A Partner in the Dynamic of Creation," *Sichos in English*.

WOMEN IN JUDAISM

O ver three millennia ago, when the Torah was given, the world was not a very kind place for women. It was unfortunately all too common in many ancient civilizations that women could legally be forced into prostitution or treated like slaves or property.[809] Certain remnants of these practices even existed until fairly recently in history.[810] Even today, although it

---

809   In ancient Greece, infanticide of newborn girls was common practice. Infanticide of boys also took place but it was much more common in girls. Aristotle viewed females as "deviations" from nature, "necessary to keep the race going." See Aristotle, *Generation of Animals* (1943), pg. 406. Many women were forced into marriages against their will, and often locked in a women's pavilion called the gynaeceum. In historical Christianity as well, some of the most influential church leaders and reformers spoke rather unkindly about women. Paul tells women to be completely obedient to their husband, as they do toward G-d (I Timothy 2:11–15). Augustine viewed women as representatives of sin and seduction (Augustine, *On the Sermon on the Mount*, 1:15, 1:41). Thomas Aquinas questioned why women were even created, and concludes that they are "for procreation" (*Summa Theologiae* I). Martin Luther, the Protestant reformer, had an equally deleterious impression of women: "Men have broad and large chests, and small narrow hips, and more understanding than women, who have but small and narrow breasts, and broad hips, to the end they should remain at home, sit still, keep house, and bear and bring up children." (See Table Talk, "Of Marriage and Celibacy," quoted from *Oxford Dictionary of Medical Quotations*, pg. 62). Additionally, one need only review the "witch hunts" that took place between the fourteenth and seventeenth century and were endorsed by the church. (There are further examples that can be obtained from Michael Kaufman, *The Woman in Jewish Law and Tradition* (1995) and many other places.)

810   For instance, killing baby girls when sons were wanted or killing wives upon their failure to produce boys, as Henry VIII did. Truth be told, infanticide of girls was almost a universal practice. Surprisingly, the practice is present in some places even today. In fact, the common consensus is that the worldwide numerical deficiency in women is due to gender specific abortions, infanticide, and neglect. See Marc Michael, Lawrence King, Liang Guo, Martin McKee, Erica Richardson and David Stuckler, "The Mystery of Missing Female Children in the Caucasus: An Analysis of Sex Ratios by Birth Order," *International Perspectives on Sexual*

is not as prevalent, treating women as sub-human is something that can be found in various cultures.

Many people are under the misconception that since Judaism dates back to ancient times it must also contain some of these barbaric views, or at least some vestige of them. This is not at all true. George Foot Moore, former professor of theology and history of religion at Harvard University, said that "the legal status of woman under Jewish law compares, to its advantage, with that of contemporary civilizations, and represents a development of the biblical legislation consistently favorable to woman."[811] Judaism was very far ahead of its time, proclaiming that men and women were equal, and in some areas in fact acknowledged the superiority of female qualities.

The Hebrew Bible is replete with the priceless contributions of women throughout history. When Sarah and Abraham disagreed over Ishmael, G-d tells Abraham "whatever Sarah tells you, heed *her* voice." From here it is taught that Sarah had greater prophetic abilities than Abraham.[812] In line with that, the sages emphasize that there were as many prophetesses as prophets in the Jewish nation.[813] Rebecca

---

and Reproductive Health 39 (2) (2013), pgs. 97–102.

811   Moore, *Judaism in the First Centuries of the Christian Era*, vol. 2 (1971), pg. 126. Even feminist author Rosemary R. Ruether implies that Judaism did more than most other ancient religions or cultures to lift woman up in equality in civil rights and spiritual recognition. She cites the acceptance of the idea of women prophetesses as significant. She also says that "ancient Israelite women contributed more substantially and more significantly to the welfare of family and society than the modern Western woman in the same role." She also makes reference to the fact that women had considerable power, authority, and freedom of decision in this important realm that she managed. Ruether also makes mention that Old Testament references to women attributes to her intelligence, prudence, wisdom, and practical sense in numerous characterizations. She continues that "despite the family locus of most of the woman's activity, the knowledge and abilities of women were not confined to the family circle or limited to expression in strictly female activities... She was recognized as equal (or superior) in the possession and employment of certain kinds of knowledge and in religious sensibility and sensitivity. She was in general charged with the same religious and moral obligations as men, and she was held responsible for her acts. Man in the Old Testament recognizes woman as one essentially like him, as a partner in pleasure and labor, one whom he needs... In a sense she completes him—but as one with a life and character of her own. She is his opposite and equal." See Ruether, *Religion and Sexism: Images of Woman in the Jewish and Christian Traditions* (1974), pgs. 68–71.

812   *Bereishis* [Genesis] 21:12 and Rashi there. See also *Megilla* 14a.

813   The Talmud (*Megilla* 14a) says that there are forty-eight prophets and seven prophetesses

is seen as a role model of loving-kindness when she gives Eliezer and his camels water to drink. Later on, when the undeserving Esau was about to receive the blessing from his father Isaac, it is *her* insight that sees that Jacob is the more appropriate recipient.[814] The sages say that the righteous women were responsible for the redemption from Egypt.[815] In the era of the Prophets, Deborah was a Judge,[816] and she and Barak led the nation in battle. The essence of prayer is learned from Chana.[817] The delivery from Haman in the Purim story,[818] and victory over the Syrian-Greeks in the Chanukah story, are likewise attributed to women.[819] Not surprisingly, it's written that the final redemption with the messianic king will be in the merit of the righteous women.[820]

Jewish law also protects the rights of women in the family and society. One-sixth of the entire Talmud and a quarter of the Code of Jewish Law are devoted to women and the law. The marriage document, the *kesuba*, which has existed for 2,100 years, burdens the husband with ten areas of financial and marital responsibilities and the purpose of its creation was to prevent abandonment or "quickie" divorce of one's wife. The Talmud says about a man's wife that he needs to "love her as much as he loves himself and honor her more than he honors himself."[821]

---

mentioned by name in the Bible. However, in all, the Midrash (*Shir HaShirim Rabbah* 4:11) says there were sixty myriad prophets and sixty myriad prophetesses.

814 *Bereishis* [Genesis] 27.

815 *Sotah* 11b; *Shmos Rabbah* 1:12. The *Yafeh Toar* (on the Midrash) says that this refers to speeding up the redemption from the preordained 400 years to the 210 years that it turned out to be practically.

816 She was also a prophetess, unique in that time, and had a specific role needed for that particular generation.

817 *Brachos* 30b and on.

818 *Pesachim* 108b, Rashbam.

819 *Shabbos* 23a, Rashi.

820 "He recalled His loving-kindness and His faithful pledge to the House of Israel" (*Tehillim* 98:3). It does not say the "Children of Israel" but rather the "House of Israel," which is a biblical allusion to the women of Israel (See *Yalkut Shimoni, Rus* 606).

821 *Yevamos* 62b; *Sanhedrin* 76b. See also *Mishneh Torah, Ishus* 16:12.

MAN AND WOMAN: A SINGLE ENTITY

In the biblical account of Creation, there is an evolutionary progression of sorts: The first entities that were created were the inanimate, then plant life, then animal life. The Creation process culminates on the sixth day with the most refined and spiritually sensitive being, the human—Adam, and then from Adam—Eve. Adam and Eve were initially created as one androgynous entity made in the Divine Image, like it says, "In the image of G-d He created *him*, male and female He created *them*."[822] The sages explain that the shift in language hints at the idea that they were one being at the start.

A deeper look at how the Torah describes the formation of Eve is insightful. Popular English translation of the Hebrew world *tzela* states that G-d created Eve from the rib of Adam. While there is room for this translation in Jewish tradition,[823] it seems even more appropriate to translate it as "side," namely the side of Adam,[824] meaning that Adam and Eve are of the same inner substance, the same essence, and are inherently equal.

The Torah then immediately describes G-d's first command, "Be fruitful and multiply, fill the Earth and subdue it."[825] "Be fruitful and multiply" means to nurture children and uphold family life. "Subduing the Earth" means to build it up, to master, transform, and refine it. Consequently, from this command, mankind had the responsibility to both nurture future generations and build up the world.

---

822   *Bereishis* [Genesis] 1:27 with the commentary of Rashi.

823   See for example *Bereishis Rabbah* 17:6; *Targum Yonason, Targum Onkelos*, and *Yalkut Me'am Loez* on *Bereishis* 2:21–22.

824   See *Bereishis Rabbah* 17:6; Rashi and Ibn Ezra to *Bereishis* 2:21; Rambam, *Moreh Nevuchim* 2:30. There are two accounts of the creation of mankind, in Genesis chapter 1 and 2 respectively. In the first account it seems that Adam had male and female halves. In the second chapter this being was separated into two genders.

825   *Bereishis* [Genesis] 1:28.

MALE AND FEMALE: EXTERNAL AND INTERNAL SOUL ENERGIES

To do both of these jobs effectively seems contradictory. Building up the world is a public matter, which generally entails giving over of one's external abilities. On the other hand, cultivating and nurturing the next generation properly, to be fruitful and multiply, is something personal—a private matter—that essentially involves giving of one's inner, deeper self. By separating the human entity into male and female, G-d allowed each one to focus on one aspect of the human mission.

Some characteristics and drives were given to males and others to females; this gives each gender the ability to influence a different sphere. Males tend to be conquerors and females tend to be nurturers.[826] The male expresses most openly the public, external, or outward aspect of the soul and has traditionally used that energy working in an outside occupation. The female represents the inner or private aspect of the soul. Notably, modern psychology also attests to the fact that women tend to place more value in deep relationships, which are axiomatically private.[827] It is for this reason that traditionally the female has cultivated the private family life. This does not mean that genders are trapped in their tendencies; rather it encourages each gender to realize where their innate abilities lie.[828]

---

826   A woman's physical ability to provide nourishment to her children is a physical manifestation of her spiritual abilities to nurture in an emotional and spiritual way as well.

827   Consider the popular *Men are from Mars, Women are from Venus*, which elucidates on this. These qualities find parallel in modern psychology as well: "We know, for instance, from observations...that males are more aggressive than females, that young males engage in more rough-and-tumble play than females and that females are more nurturing." See Doreen Kimura, "Sex Differences in the Brain," *Scientific American* (May 13, 2002).

828   The contemporary view that joining the workforce is somehow more prestigious than caring for the family is misplaced. King David writes in *Tehillim* [Psalms] 45:14: "The complete glory of the princess is within." The royal princess is seen as the epitome of dignity, nobility, and glory. She shuns ostentation and seeks privacy (see Rashi). The sages compare every Jewish woman to the daughter of the king and the nucleus of the Jewish home to her royal domain. At the same time, the Rambam (*Ishus* 13:11) writes that every woman should go out to do mitzvos in the world and kindnesses for friends, and should not be imprisoned in the home as if it were a dungeon. Thus, the image of a woman as

Rabbi Shimshon Raphoel Hirsch *zt"l* explains that the human being was initially created as a single entity containing both male and female, and only later was split, to teach several important general lessons.[829] First, to emphasize that male and female each have unique abilities that complement one another in the task of uplifting the world. The sages teach about one outstanding and unique quality of women—their superior understanding. In the formation of Eve, the Torah uses the word "built," namely that she was built from Adam, as implied above. What is fascinating is that the root word *boneh*, "built," is related to the word *bina* or "understanding." The sages learned from this that women were endowed with greater natural intuition than men.[830] Men, on the other hand, have to learn and acquire understanding from their surroundings in the world around them.[831]

Rabbi Hirsch also teaches that G-d shows the equality of these two roles by creating Adam and Eve as one being, for if they were created as two separate entities, one could entertain the idea that one is better than the other. Since both were initially created at the same time as one, their complimentary characteristics and essential equality are affirmed.

THE ETHEREAL MALE AND FEMALE

From a mystical standpoint, G-d essentially created this dual balance of complimentary male and female "energies" in all aspects of Creation. Creation expresses itself and is upheld through "giving energy" and "receiving energy." The sun emits its own light, whereas the moon shines by receiving and reflecting sunlight. A planted seed con-

---

someone who is barefoot, pregnant, and in the kitchen, is not at all a Jewish concept.

829   See his commentary to *Bereishis* 2:22.

830   See *Niddah* 45b. Eve's body was already fully formed and only needed to be separated from Adam, therefore "He built" is interpreted as related to "understanding"; see Maharsha, based on *Brachos* 61a. This also implies that women mature earlier, see Tosafos HaRosh. The common term "women's intuition" does not give proper justice to the sensitivity in "understanding" of this spiritual principle, but is perhaps a glimmer into the fact.

831   Generally speaking, *chochmah*, or wisdom/conception, is attributed to males; *bina*, understanding, to females; and *da'as*, knowledge, to the two of them as a couple; see Ramban, *Iggeres Hakodesh*, ch. 2.

tains potential energy, and the earth, in receiving that energy, acts as a conduit for the seed to grow. What in the East might be called the *yin* and *yang*, the giver-and-receiver model is literally all over Creation.[832]

In Kabbalistic jargon, the "giving energy" is synonymous with male energy, and receiving is synonymous with female energy. That is not to say that a female cannot be a giver, or a male a receiver; instead, it signifies the primary energy force that each gender embodies.[833] The respective reproductive organs of a male and female are a biological manifestation of the spiritual paradigm of male as giver and women as receiver.

MALE-FEMALE PARADIGM IN CREATION

Light is often used as a metaphor for G-d expressing Himself, or, in other words, distributing His "Divine energy." G-d is neither male nor female, but, in a sense, His bounty emanates or manifests as two types of energy. One is the bestowing energy and the other is the receiving energy. This bestowing light or energy parallels the male aspect that G-d infused into Creation, while the receiver of the bestowal parallels female energy. Parenthetically, this is why G-d is almost always addressed as "He" in the prayer book, because the creations are asking that G-d *bestow* His bounty upon them. When Jewish tradition wishes to describe Divine energy as it is dwelling within Creation—namely as a part of what is typically the receiving end—it often uses the term "*Shechina*," which is feminine. It must be emphasized once more that G-d is neither male nor female; these are just borrowed terms to refer to whether Divine energy is being expressed though giving or receiving, as bestowed energy or embedded in Creation.[834]

G-d acts as the male in the relationship and Creation, while

---

832 This *yin* and *yang* is simply a borrowed term to demonstrate balance and does not attempt to compare the Torah concept to the way it is approached in the East.

833 Consider in the Talmud (*Taanis* 7a) where Rabbi Chanina said, "From my students I learned the most." The students, who are normally the receivers, were also givers; and Rabbi Chanina, who was primarily a teacher, actually received and learned from them.

834 Using the neutral word "it" instead of a gender word is impersonal and therefore not a good option.

humanity, or at times specifically the Jewish nation, are symbolic of the female or recipient of His bounty.[835] It is for this reason as well that G-d split up the physical male and female—two unique energies—in order to instill, in a tangible way, the concept of mutual need and dependency on one another. A human being should never feel completely independent, but must always take to heart his reliance on the beneficence of G-d. The presence of the concept of incompleteness in the physical world between male and female fosters the idea in the human being that his seeking of G-d is true as well.

MALE AND FEMALE: COMPLEMENTARY ENERGIES

In the same way that complementary energies exist all over Creation, they exist in the human male and female. Men and women are spiritually different; neither one better nor worse. Is red better than blue? Green better than purple? The question does not even make sense.

In contemporary Western society, nobody has a problem admitting that men and women are physically different. They are built differently and contain diverse anatomical parts. Neither one is superior, they are just built differently. Their anatomical parts are, in fact, meant to complement each other.

Likewise, it has become common knowledge that men and women are different emotionally. The father of sociobiology, Edward O. Wilson of Harvard University, said that human females tend to be higher than males in empathy, verbal skills, social skills, and security-seeking, among other things.[836] The same could be said psychologically and intellectually; not that one is by nature smarter than the other, but that they conceptualize things differently.[837] Not only are males and females

---

835   This metaphor of G-d and His people expressed as the love of male and female is the theme underlying *Song of Songs*. Likewise, there are many other verses that reflect this idea as well, see for example *Yeshayahu* 62:5; *Yirmiyahu* 2:2, 33:11; *Malachi* 2:11.

836   E. O. Wilson, *Sociobiology* (1992).

837   "The idea that male and female brains are organized differently has been around for a long time. After all, since men and women are dissimilar in size, appearance and sexual role, why shouldn't their brain organization differ too? Research has documented in the past twenty-five years that there are intellectual differences in the way the two sexes solve problems: On average, women do better in certain verbal skills and men in spatial and

different, but their brains actually parallel each other. As one researcher from the University of Pennsylvania recently remarked, "It's quite striking how complementary the brains of women and men really are."[838]

Physically, emotionally, psychologically, and intellectually, men and women are different, neither better than the other, and nobody has contentions with any of these. It is a fact of life. Is it really that surprising, then, that they are considered spiritually different as well?

Judaism teaches that men and women have two diverse spiritual paths that are meant to complement the other. The physical, emotional, intellectual, and spiritual differences in males and females are different levels of a united, multileveled, personal connection with each other—two halves of one whole. In creating this social order, each gender is granted the opportunity for complete fulfillment in their individual roles. Based on this concept, it becomes much easier to assess some of the differences between men and women in Jewish life and practice. The Torah shows each gender how to connect to G-d on His terms, and stresses that both men and women are afforded equal reward and connection with G-d, despite their differing means of attaining it.

Nechoma Greisman, a renowned author, scholar, and mentor to hundreds of women, laments the fact that people in Western society have lost sight of their purpose:

---

mathematical skills...Certain thinking skills are more lateralized—more dependent on one hemisphere—in the male brain than in the female," see Doreen Kimura, "Male Brain, Female Brain: The Hidden Difference," *Psychology Today* (Nov. 1985). For another interesting article, see also R. M. E. Sabbatini, "Are There Differences between the Brains of Males and Females?" *Brain & Mind Magazine* (October/December 2000).

838 Ruben Gur, cited in Ian Sample, "Male and female brains wired differently, scans reveal," *The Guardian*, December 2, 2013. Earlier in the article, Ragini Verma, a researcher at the University of Pennsylvania, said the greatest surprise was how much the findings supported old stereotypes, with men's brains apparently wired more for perception and coordinated actions, and women's for social skills and memory, making them better equipped for multitasking. "If you look at functional studies, the left of the brain is more for logical thinking; the right of the brain is for more intuitive thinking. So if there's a task that involves doing both of those things, it would seem that women are hardwired to do those better," Verma said. "Women are better at intuitive thinking. Women are better at remembering things. When you talk, women are more emotionally involved—they will listen more."

What a false and foolish world we live in! We call someone "successful" when we mean that the person has acquired some money! That's success? Is it a success when your children are estranged, when your marriage is on the rocks, when you're living on pills, and suffering from constant stress and anxiety in the rat race of today's corporate world, and you're too busy to take time out for family and friends, or for Hashem?

What then is success? It's hard to play a game if you don't know the rules. Success means knowing who you are and what you're supposed to be doing, and then doing it!

...It's just that in our society people are trying to play games that are not natural for them. The number of people in therapy and in need of psychological help is proof that there is only a certain amount a person can take of this without cracking.

The very first portion of the Torah tells explicitly about the creation of man and woman, and what their roles are. Within the definition of their roles lies tremendous flexibility. Who will balance the checkbook, who will take out the garbage, and who will make the major decisions is undefined. However, what is of major importance is that a man knows he is a man, and woman knows she's a woman. Both know that their purpose cannot be accomplished without the other.[839]

Dr. Tamar Frankiel, a feminist scholar who taught comparative religion at Stanford, Princeton, and the University of California at Berkeley, and author of the book *The Voice of Sarah: Feminine Spirituality in Traditional Judaism*, became so enamored with the teachings of feminine spirituality as carried out by the unique gender roles in traditional Judaism that she converted to Judaism and became an observant Jew. She identified it as an authentic way for women to spiritually develop in a naturally feminine

839   Nechoma Greisman, *The Nechoma Greisman Anthology* (2000), pgs. 64–66.

manner. She has described the separate spheres of male and female in traditional Judaism as something that facilitates a strong functioning family and society, and it is a key factor in empowering women.

In essence, the brain and the heart—intellect and emotions respectively—have very different roles and purposes, yet only when they both come together through their distinct powers does that make a person who he is. The male and female are corresponding energies, together making one essence, one complete person. Interestingly, this means that the contemporary phrase "soulmate" is actually accurate, because the man and woman are essentially the same soul in two bodies: one aspect of the soul that embodies the male energy and the other that is the female energy. A marriage is not merely a union of souls, it is a *reunion*.[840]

THE THREE SPECIAL COMMANDMENTS

It is fitting to mention that there are three fundamental commandments that the sages highlight as being special for Jewish women: *challah*, family purity, and lighting Sabbath candles.[841] These three commandments share the same theme and goal. In the words of Rebbetzin Malka Touger, "They help a woman to weave the physical and spiritual fabric of her home, to forge a link to posterity, and to transform her home into a lantern that will illuminate its environment."[842]

CHALLAH

Challah does not refer to the bread baked in honor of Sabbath, but rather to a more general term. When one would bake bread, there was a portion of the dough separated for the *Kohen*, the priest. This commandment is also representative of the more general commandment to eat kosher foods. The woman is entrusted to provide for her family foods that conform to the strict standards of *kashrus*. This is

---

840 *Bnei Yisaschar*, *Derech Pikudecha*, *Hakdama* 9:4. The inner connection between husband and wife stems from their initial creation as one being.

841 *Yerushalmi*, *Shabbos* 2:6; *Midrash Tanchuma*, Noach.

842 Malka Touger in *A Partner in the Dynamic of Creation, Actions Speak Louder: Three Pivotal Mitzvos*.

a very pivotal role, as food is literally the backbone of every Jewish celebration.

As the saying goes, "You are what you eat." Judaism speaks extensively about how the foods we eat not only influence our physical well-being but our spiritual well-being also. A woman, by taking care of her family and nourishing them, is not only involved in providing for and cultivating their physical sustenance, but more importantly, their spiritual sustenance.

FAMILY PURITY

Rebbetzin Nechoma Greisman explains that:

> *Taharas Hamishpacha*, or family purity, is a system which grants uniqueness to the private marital relationship of Jewish couples, and trains both partners to view each other as a whole human being, and express their love toward [one] another in more than one way. Each month contains a set time when the couple engage[s] in intimacy, followed by a period when there are no physical relationships at all. During this time, they must learn to demonstrate their concern for one another without any physical expression. This system provides a special element of renewal each month, when husband and wife eagerly anticipate their period of togetherness. Psychologists agree that one of the enemies which can poison even the best of marriages is simply monotony and boredom. Before the couple is reunited, so to speak, the wife immerses in a specially designated pool of water known as a *mikveh*.

The word *mikveh* means "pool" or "gathering" of water. The Torah makes very vague reference to what a *mikveh* is, or its use. Instead, all of its specifics are delineated in the Talmud.[843] The purpose of immersion in the *mikveh* has nothing to do with physical cleanliness. Incidentally, immersion in the *mikveh* is always preceded by a thorough

---

843   *Yerushalmi, Chagiga* 1:8, for example.

cleansing of the body. *Mikveh* is a renewal of the soul and the rebirth of spiritual purity. The human body is made of mainly water, and it is through water that life is able to exist and be sustained. It is for this reason that in most cultures around the world water is looked upon as a symbol of life and rebirth. The commandment of family purity, immersing in a *mikveh*, is considered suprarational, yet the theme that it touches upon is the spiritual recharge of the marital bond. The woman immerses in a pool of water that has a special design and holds a special quantity of natural water.

There is medical evidence that women who practice family purity and immerse monthly in the *mikveh* show fewer incidences of cancer of the reproductive organs and fewer infections of the reproductive system. In short, family purity seems to bring with it physical well-being, as well as emotional stability. In addition, children conceived within this framework are born with the greatest possible of spiritual benefits. This practice once again facilitates the physical and spiritual nurturing of the next generation as well.[844]

SABBATH CANDLES

As we saw above, every facet of Creation has a male and female element, a "giver" and "receiver." It follows that the same pattern exists in the days of the week. The weekdays represent the male, external flow of energy—as throughout each workday humanity is meant to toil and produce. Sabbath, on the other hand, is the culmination, the cessation of all work from the week. On this special day, which is strictly reserved for developing our spiritual nature, we refrain from anything resembling creative work. This model, carried out by the Jewish people, parallels the G-dly sequence of Creation that culminated in rest.

It is for this reason that the Sabbath is associated with the feminine, the *Shechina*, when there is a state of peace and G-dly presence in the world. The Sabbath is referred to as a bride and as a queen in Jewish literature.[845]

---

844   This section has been adapted from Greisman, *The Nechoma Greisman Anthology*, pgs. 74–78.
845   See *Shabbos* 119a; *Bava Kamma* 32b. The basis for the concept that Sabbath is bride and

At the end of the week, when entering into this new headspace, epitomized by the feminine, it is most appropriate for women to activate its commencement with the lighting of Sabbath candles. This is one of the special gifts given to women—the ability to add light to the world. At just a bit before sunset, a special portal opens that shifts energies from the bombardment of the weekday to the bliss of Sabbath—the inception of "feminine Divine energy."

There is a mystical teaching that the Hebrew word for "light," *ohr*, has the *gematria*, Hebrew numerology equivalent, of 207. The word Shabbos (Sabbath) has the value of 702, its mirror image. The symbolism of these words "light" and "Shabbos," and the parallel numbers that they represent, teach that by slowing down our usual fast-paced lives, we created a meditative space that encompasses all of our activities.[846]

Every Jewish woman is promised that "if you cherish the lights of Sabbath, I will show you the lights of Zion."[847] In other words, with this special mitzvah, one gains entrance into the World to Come. Sabbath is a called a taste of that experience. Lighting Sabbath candles every Friday night is a preview to, and helps usher in, the enlightenment of that future era.

TIME-BOUND COMMANDMENTS

A good place to start when looking at the distinct roles of males and females in Jewish practice is to examine women's exemption from time-bound commandments. Torah and its mitzvos were given to the world in order to facilitate the Divine plan of making a "dwelling place" for the Divine in the physical realm.[848] This goal is achieved when even coarse material existence becomes a conduit or means of expressing the Almighty.

Within the Jewish religion as a whole, there are many distinctions

---

queen seems to be based on a Midrash in *Bereishis Rabbah* 11:8. The *Zohar* says that the feminine aspect of Sabbath is most revealed on Friday night. One example of this can be found in the prayer welcoming the Sabbath, "*Lecha Dodi*," which says: "Come, my Beloved to meet the Bride; let us welcome the Sabbath."

846   Avraham Ariel Trugman, *The Mystical Nature of Light* (2008), pg. 124.
847   *Yalkut Shimoni*, Behaloscha, sec. 719.
848   *Midrash Tanchuma*, Naso 16.

as far as who is assigned to do each specific task. Some mitzvos are commanded exclusively to the Kohanim, some only to the Levites, and others are for the general populace. Kings have some mitzvos specialized for their position, as do prophets and judges. No one's part is less significant than the next. No person from one group may perform the mitzvos categorically reserved for another; instead, each one's assignment is something that they alone can carry out effectively. Each job aids that particular group in completing the overall Divine goal and reaching their fullest potential.

A similar phenomenon exists between men and women. Women are exempt from most positive mitzvos that are bound by a specific time.[849] This includes mitzvos like reading the *Shema* twice daily, hearing the shofar on Rosh Hashana, shaking the *lulav* on Sukkos, wearing a tallis or tefillin, and counting the Omer between Pesach and Shavuos. In almost all cases, this does not bar a woman from fulfilling these mitzvos, but it does relieve her of the obligation. Over time, women have actually taken on most of those mitzvos, and will be rewarded accordingly for doing so.[850]

One of the greatest misconceptions about traditional Judaism is the idea that women's obligation to fewer mitzvos is somehow connected with male superiority. In other words, men have more mitzvos in order to limit the women's role in the synagogue, allowing men to be the ruling sex. It is important to clarify why women are exempt from these mitzvos, both from a legalistic and a Kabbalistic perspective, since this view is completely erroneous.

LEGAL REASONS WHY WOMEN ARE EXEMPT

The Talmud derives,[851] through a process of biblical exegesis, that women are exempt from all positive time-bound mitzvos because they

---

849   Mishnah, *Kiddushin* 1:7.

850   Wearing a tallis and donning tefillin may be exceptions to this trend, see below.

851   *Kiddushin* 34a, using a *mah matzeinu* formula (deriving principle of *binyan av*).

are exempt from tefillin.[852] The Talmud states that just as women are exempt from donning tefillin, which is a time-bound positive mitzvah; so too, they are exempt from every positive commandment that time causes.

The biblical commentators throughout the ages have given various perspectives and insight as to why they are exempt. The following is a sampling of those reasons:

Family:

From a very superficial standpoint, one could say that a woman is excused simply because of her familial responsibilities.[853] Judaism, in contrast to other Western religions, puts primary importance of religious life on the home, as opposed to the house of worship. A woman is the core of a properly functioning home. In fact, the sages teach: "Greater is the reward of the woman than that of the man,"[854] because the woman empowers everyone in her household with the ability to reach their potential, and "the enabler of an act is greater than the performer."[855] This has nothing to do with a "second-class" status, but rather because her distinguished spiritual makeup forms the foundation of Jewish life.

There is, nonetheless, something lacking in this answer because even unmarried or childless women are exempt as well. What about after

---

852   As is learned from Mishnah, *Brachos* 3:3.

853   Avudraham, *Tefillos Shel Chol*, Sha'ar 3, *Birchos Hamitzvos*. Rabbi Saul Berman explains that Avudraham as follows: When the Torah exempted women from mitzvos, it was "to assure that no legal obligation interfere with...[their] role, which was centered almost exclusively in the home." Berman explains, "The wife-mother role is not mandated [by Judaism]...[but] it is clearly the preferred and therefore protected role." See Saul Berman, "The Status of Women in Halakhic Judaism," *Tradition*, 14:2 (1973): pgs. 5–28. For other sources that rule like the Avudraham, see Meiri, *Eruvin* 27a and *Brachos* 11a; Rabbi Shimon Duran, *Magen Avos* 2:6. See also *Kolbo*, *Hilchos Milah* 73; *Shitas Hakadmonim* to *Bava Kamma* (MY Blau: NY, 1976), pg. 334.

      This seems to also fit in line with Rabbi Shimshon Raphoel Hirsch comments to the verse in *Vayikra* 23:43. He writes that the time-bound mitzvos are procedures given to "afresh to our minds from time to time" all of the mitzvos. Traditionally, the man is the provider, and has all sorts of temptations in his daily business affairs. Women, who are more commonly dedicated to the inner well-being of the family, do not need such reminders.

854   *Brachos* 17b.

855   *Bava Basra* 9a.

the kids have grown and left the house? Familial nurturing, therefore, is not a complete answer. Other authorities point out, instead, that the exemption fits in line with the very nature of women.

Serenity:

The Maharal of Prague explains that the exemption compliments the nature of a woman's personality.[856] Man's gruff or aggressive nature is detrimental to his spiritual growth, and he needs extra religious duties to channel that energy.[857] It is common knowledge that the overwhelming majority of violence is committed by males.[858]

The old nursery rhyme that says little girls are made of "sugar and spice and everything nice," and little boys are made of "slugs and snails and puppy dog tails," may actually have a ring of truth to it.

The Maharal says that since a woman is closer to the peaceful state of the World to Come, she therefore requires less effort to attain it.

Naturally Attuned:

Some contemporary scholars point out that "a woman's menstrual cycle and her observance of the *niddah* laws invest her with an awareness of the sanctity of time."[859] She is naturally in sync with the domain of time and hence not obligated to observe many of the positive

---

856   Maharal, *Kol Kisvei Maharal, Chidushei Aggados* I; *Drush al HaTorah* 15.

857   Some studies suggest that there is even physiological evidence of male propensity to aggression. Husband and wife psychologists Ruben and Raquel Gur, researchers at the University of Pennsylvania School of Medicine, say they have evidence that shows men are more aggressive than women because the part of the brain that modulates aggression is smaller in men than it is in women. (See Lee Dye, "Women's Brains Better at Handling Anger," ABCNews.com, Sept. 25, 2013).

858   This fact is accepted; there are quite a few speculations as to why, but this is seen as a fact; see Jesse Prinz,"Why are Men So Violent," *Psychology Today* (Feb. 3, 2012). A quick glance at statistics from the United States implies that men commit significantly more acts of violence than women. One study found that 75.6 percent of all offenders were male and only 20.1 percent were female. (See U.S. Department of Justice, "Criminal Victimization in the United States, 2007 Statistical Tables," National Crime Victimization Survey, Aug. 31, 2010).

859   See Rabbi Emanuel Rackman in *One Man's Judaism*, pg. 300 and *Tradition* 1:1. See Avraham Weiss, *Women At Prayer* (1990), pg. 5.

commandments fixed by time. "Men learn the importance of time by fulfilling the time-bound mitzvos."[860]

Spiritual Completion:

Rabbi Aharon Soloveitchik zt"l examines the progressive order of created things mentioned in Genesis, and concludes that women are innately superior to men—hence created last:

> It appears from Genesis, that whatever is superior was created later…First light was created and with it other forms of energy. Then the inorganic world; then the organic world…vegetative life came first, and then animal life…The human being was created after all animals… male first and then the female gender. This proves the proposition that the woman has innate spiritual superiority as compared with man.[861]

Explaining himself more fully, he writes:

> There is an abundance of energy in the male gender which, if not tempered and controlled properly, might be released in a very destructive manner. Almighty G-d in His Infinite Wisdom, therefore imposed upon the male gender the obligatory mitzvos created by a time element and the obligation of constantly being engaged in Torah study so that man's psyche will always be preoccupied with spiritual and intellectual endeavors, thereby contracting man's disposition toward abusive energy…
>
> Man has to struggle in order to be good, compassionate, tolerant, and noble. A woman's personality was molded in such a way that she is naturally disposed toward compassion and consideration. Woman's character

---

860   See Rabbi Norman Lamm, *A Hedge of Roses*, pgs. 68-78.

861   "The Attitude of Judaism toward the Woman," in *Major Addresses Delivered at Mid-continent Conclave and National Leadership Conference* (Union of Orthodox Jewish Congregations: Nov. 27–Nov. 30, 1969), pg. 27.

was molded by G-d in accordance with the eschatological goals that Almighty G-d reserved for the world.[862]

Historically, Jewish women have shown stronger faith and more spiritual sensitivity than men. Women were not involved in the sin of the Golden Calf, nor were they involved in the incident with the spies, nor other complaints and skirmishes that arose when the Jewish people were traveling through the desert.[863] The male, unbridled energy needs to be tamed with extra commandments and responsibilities that serve as reminders not to waver from the straight and narrow. Women's exemption or non-involvement in certain areas of Jewish life is a far cry from a withholding of rights; rather it is a step up on the pedestal, a manifestation of the Divine faith in the greater strength of her moral self-discipline.

It is clear from this sampling of ancient and contemporary rabbinic literature that a woman is legally exempt from time-bound mitzvos because of the nature of her spiritual makeup and foundational role in Jewish family life.[864]

A DEEPER DIMENSION

The Kabbalists write that a woman has a natural connection to G-d, as expressed in the ability of her womb. A woman's elevated spiritual status is seen in her G-d-like ability to actually create new life. It is known that of the Torah's commandments, 248 are positive. The

---

862 Weiss, *Woman at Prayer*, pg. 2, note 6; pg. 5, note 9.

863 See *Bamidbar Rabbah* 21. In truth, a very small number participated in the sin of the Golden Calf. It was around three thousand, which is less than one half of one percent of the camp; see Ibn Ezra, *Shmos* 32:1, and "The Golden Calf" in Rabbi Eliyahu Dessler, *Strive for Truth*, ed. Aryeh Carmell, vol. III. The entire subject of these sins and how they were able to happen is beyond the scope of this work. It is a positive thing that the women did not participate, but not necessarily a "proof" of greater spirituality.

864 It should be noted that there are some that seem to have an opposing view to the aforementioned, see Ralbag, *Shmos* 13:21; and *Yismach Moshe* on *Shmos* 10:8-11. Possible suggestions as to how these sources can be seen as part of a bigger picture connected with earlier views are beyond the scope of this work. For further reading and a full treatment of the subject, see Rabbi Chaim Rappaport's article "Why Women Are Exempt from Positive Time-bound Commandments: Is There a True Torah View?" *Le'ela* 50 (2000): pgs. 53-64, where some sources from this work were gleaned from as well.

Kabbalists explain that this is the reason רחם (*rechem*), the Hebrew word for "womb," has the numerical equivalent of 248. Whereas men must do *all* 248 positive commands to connect with the Almighty, women are exonerated from some because their G-d-like power of creating life deems those mitzvos unnecessary.[865]

Furthermore, in Hebrew the word for "man" (*ish*), and "woman" (*isha*), are very similar. The only subtle difference is that *ish* contains the letter *yud*, while *isha* instead contains a *hei*. *Yud* and *hei* are the first two letters of G-d's Name.[866]

As we saw earlier, man corresponds to the *yud*, and woman to the *hei*. The Kabbalists teach that *yud* corresponds to "wisdom", and *hei* to "understanding." In other words, "wisdom" is the element of the male, and "understanding," the female.[867] The following chart will again help to view these representations more clearly:

Male:	*Yud*	Wisdom	Past
Female:	*Hei*	Understanding	Future

Based on the writings of Rabbi Aryeh Kaplan *zt"l*:[868] "Wisdom," the masculine element, consists of *accumulated* learning—therefore it represents the past. "Understanding," which a female embodies, is how information *will be* used—thus representing the future.

Positive and negative commandments also have a correlation to male and female. Positive commandments propel us into action, representing the past pressing into the future. Negative commandments hold us back, representing the future holding back the past. Positive mitzvos, therefore, are attuned with the masculine element; and negative mitzvos with the female element.[869]

Since the past influences the future, men must keep the negative

---

865   See *Tikkunei Zohar* 30 (74); *Pardes Rimonim* 23:13.
866   Rashi, *Sotah* 17a, s.v. "*Shechinah.*"
867   See *Zohar* 3:290a.
868   The following is quoted and paraphrased from Aryeh Kaplan, *Immortality, Resurrection, and the Age of the Universe* (1993), pgs. 57-62.
869   *Zohar* 1:48; *Eitz Chaim, Sha'ar Klipas Nogah* 5.

commandments just as women do. The future, however, cannot change the past, and therefore where time is involved, women are exempt from positive commandments. Where the commandment does not involve time, however, future blends with past, and women are also obligated.[870]

The roles and interplay of male and female are expounded further in the writings of the Arizal.[871] It explains there that men and women are really two halves of the same whole. The male's role is the "giver" (which even his physical makeup attests to) and the female the "receiver"; but at the same time, each is part of the same unified entity. This is, in fact, the deeper meaning of the sages' teaching that "[a man's] wife is like his own body."[872] Some mitzvos are performed by the male aspect of the [single] being, and others by the female. Once the male completes those that are obligatory to him, there is no need whatsoever for the female to do so as well.

The Lubavitcher Rebbe *zt"l* further elaborates on the writings of the Arizal, saying that this Kabbalistic concept—of one soul possessing two halves (male and female)—explains why **all** women are exempt from time-bound mitzvos, and not only those married and with children.[873] Single men and women are incomplete until marriage, yet they still retain a connection with their future "soulmate" that they will one day, hopefully, *reunite* with. Even though they are not united in a revealed way, i.e., through marriage, they still each complete the mitzvos for their unknown counterpart. Thus, even single women need not execute the time-bound mitzvos, as their unnamed other half is already completing them for her.

In conclusion, a woman's role is dignified and unique, significant

---

870 Time-dependent positive commandments are rooted in "hidden love," where the future element (*imah*) is completely concealed. Non-time-dependent commandments, on the other hand, are rooted in "revealed love," where the future is revealed to some extent. See *Eitz Chaim, Sha'ar Kitzur ABYA* 4. Until here is from Rabbi Kaplan, ibid.

871 Based on Rabbi Chaim Vital, *Ta'amei Hamitzvos-Bereishis*. Also see *Or HaTorah*, pgs. 349–350, 1199–1200.

872 *Menachos* 93b; *Brachos* 24a.

873 *Likkutei Sichos* vol. 31, pgs. 96-97. See also the *hemshech*, "Chiyav Adam 5638"; see Rappaport, ibid.

and respected. Her exemption of time-bound commandments is rooted solely in her inherent connection to G-d and to her spouse. It is through *refraining* from these mitzvos that these special bonds are realized and brought out.

WOMEN AND THE SYNAGOGUE

Perhaps the place where the different roles of men and women are most pronounced in traditional Judaism is in the synagogue. Traditionally, there has been a physical barrier, the *mechitza*, between men and women during prayer. This separation, coupled with women not being included in the number needed for a prayer quorum (minyan), and their exemption from certain rituals commonly associated with the synagogue, can give the impression of inequality to the uninitiated onlooker. Each of these issues must be addressed in its own right. One must always keep in mind the ideas stressed above about unique spiritual energies and roles that reinforce them.

THE MECHITZA: SEPARATION OF THE GENDERS

Mechitza refers to the physical separation between men and women during traditional Jewish prayer services. The first encounter with the concept of *mechitza* is on Noah's ark. The ark was made to be a place of holiness, a place of tranquility amidst a world of tumult—similar to the intended function of a synagogue sanctuary. On the ark, men and women were separated to preserve reverence and celibacy.[874] Later on in our collective Jewish history, when the Israelites crossed the sea, they all sang praises to G-d. The men and women worshipped separately though. Miriam, the sister of Moses, took a tamborine and led the women in dancing.[875]

Jewish law requires men to be separated from women while praying in synagogue. Historically, this practice was introduced in the Holy Temple in Jerusalem, the *Beis Hamikdosh*, the archetype of the modern synagogue. The Mishnah explains that a platform for women was con-

---

874   Rashi to *Bereishis* 7:7, wording borrowed from Ari Enkin, *Dalet Amot* (2008), pg. 11.
875   See Rashi, *Shmos* 15:21.

structed during the famous "water-drawing ceremony" on the holiday of Sukkos.[876] The Talmud elaborates that when men and women were in the same courtyard, there was levity between them. At that point it was necessary to make a complete divide by constructing a balcony to prevent further frivolity.[877] There is biblical direction to separate the genders, based on a verse describing the future messianic era.[878]

Since the destruction of the Holy Temple in Jerusalem in 70 CE, the synagogues and study halls around the world function as "miniature Temples" for the Jewish people.[879] In order to uphold this status, the synagogue must embody the original Temple in both philosophical doctrine and function.[880] Over the centuries, synagogues have built balconies or walls that separated the men's and women's sections. Some experts in Jewish law even suggest that having a *mechitza* is a biblical obligation.[881] In fact the esteemed contemporary sage, Rabbi Eliezer Waldenberg, writes that having a *mechitza*, or separation, was such an obvious and inherent part of the synagogue that the Code of Jewish Law does not even bother to discuss its details.[882]

---

876   *Sukkah* 51a.

877   "Initially women had been placed in the women's section of the *Beis Hamikdosh* and men outside. This had led to light-headedness. At a later stage men were placed inside with the women sitting outside, but again there were the same consequences. Finally, projections were inserted into the walls of the *ezras noshim* and each year a balcony assembled. The women sat in the raised section with the men below." Extracted from *Issues in Practical Halacha*, Issue #2 (22 Tammuz, 5755), produced by Kollel Menachem, Lubavitch (Melbourne, Australia).

878   There is a biblical source for the separation of men and women given by the Amoraic sage, Rav. He points to the following verses in *Zechariah* 12:12–14: "The land will mourn each of the families by itself: the family of the house of Dovid by itself, and their wives by themselves; the family of Nosson by itself and their wives by themselves...and all the families who remain, each of the families by itself and their wives by themselves." Rav, examining the verses, explains that even in a time of mourning, men and women will be seated separately. If separate seating is needed even when the Jewish people lament, how much more so must separate seating be required during joyous occasions—where the expectation of laxity is ever more increased; see Rashi in *Sukkah* there, s.v. "Kan." *Pri Hasadeh* 4:97; *Minchas Yitzchok* 2:20; *Oz Nedbiru* 12:48.

879   *Megilla* 29a.

880   It goes without saying, excluding functions such as the sacrificial order, which are forbidden outside of the Holy Temple.

881   *Iggros Moshe, Orach Chaim* 1:39. See also *Zichron Yehuda* 1:62.

882   *Tzitz Eliezer* 7:8.

Archaeological excavations in the Galilee have uncovered several synagogues dating from the second century CE and later that contain evidence of separate seating in the synagogue.[883] In slightly later periods, synagogues do not contain the same evidence of separate seating. The scholarly opinion surmises that in those places and at those times it was not customary for women to attend the synagogue. When the infrequent occasion where women would be attending would arise, provisions could be made to arrange appropriate seating.[884]

In 1845, the Reform Congregation of Berlin abolished the partition between men and women.[885] This new "custom" spread to other places in Europe. These nuances were met with tremendous opposition.[886]

---

883   These early synagogues were in the Basilica style, and had a balcony on three sides, which is the same as the Temple. These were synagogues in second century Galilee. Ernest W. Gurney Masterman describes the archaeological findings in the Capernaum synagogue and concludes from this that the gallery was likely for the women; see *Studies in Galilee* (1909), pgs. 112–114. Professor and pioneer in Talmudic archaeology, Samuel Krauss, said much more clearly: "We may consider these galleries the place for the women, who were thus separated from the men's section by a balustrade..."; *Synagogale Altertuemer* (1922), pgs. 355–357. The Talmud (*Yerushalmi, Sukkah* 5:1) clearly says that the Diplaston Synagogue in Egypt, which was destroyed in 166 CE, had a separate balcony for the women.

  Interestingly, even those break-off sects in ancient Israel, who had a different theology than the sages, also sat separately. Philo of Alexandria says that the Therapeutae, an ascetic group like the Essenes, had separate portions in their synagogues for men and women; see *The Contemplative Life*, Loeb Classical Library, IX, pgs. 131–133, 155. For many more sources and great insights, see Baruch Litvin, *The Sanctity of the Synagogue* (1987), pgs. 223–225.

884   Menachem Brayer, *The Jewish Woman in Rabbinic Literature: A Psychosocial Perspective* (1986), pg. 207. Also see Lisa Aiken, *To Be a Jewish Woman* (1992), pg. 74. In Litvin, ibid., there is discussion of other formats of making *mechitzas* throughout history, and in different lands. Many were done without balconies. There are a wealth of sources discussed in that work.

885   David Philipson, *The Reform Movement in Judaism* (1931), pg. 245.

886   In 1876, in response to these proceedings, Rabbi Shlomo Ganzfried, along with over seventy leading rabbis, joined together in a proclamation announcing that it was forbidden to pray in any synagogue that removed the separation between the two sections. Some of the key points discussed there: (a) It is forbidden to pray in a synagogue where there is not a full *mechitza*, i.e., where men can see women. (b) If the *mechitza* is not good, it is forbidden to pray there even if there are no women present. (c) It is better to pray alone than to pray in such a place, even on Rosh Hashana and Yom Kippur. (Full text is published in *Lev Ho'Ivri—Minhagei Beis Haknesses*). Other sages of the day soon filed suit as well, and their protests can be viewed in their responsa literature. For example, the *Maharam Shik* (*Orach Chaim* 77) writes: "G-d forbid to remain silent [to substandard *mechitzos*]!" Furthermore, in

Mixed seating was first innovated in America in the mid 1800s. Isaac Mayer Wise, a prominent reformer, borrowed a Baptist Church for his services in Albany, New York. There, "he found the 'family style' seating of the church so much to his liking that he decided to retain this feature in his temple."[887] In the ensuing years, even those who held fast to traditional Judaism began to modify the *mechitza's* height, style, or even its presence altogether. The leading Jewish legal authorities of the twentieth century were forced to confront the underlay of reasons for why the Talmud required the partition in the Holy Temple.[888]

The synagogue service is meant solely as a spiritual experience, not a social one, and the law of the *mechitza* is meant to enhance the concentration of all who are praying. In order to facilitate this concentration, possible sources of distraction are eliminated. It is potentially difficult for a male to concentrate on spirituality when a woman sits close by, because he is vulnerable to being distracted by her

---

the responsa of Rabbi Hillel Lichtenstein of Kolomea (Rosh Chodesh Adar 1873): "It has already been clearly stated that it is forbidden to make the partition in such a way that the men can view the women, and if the partition has already been so made, one should not enter there... Moreover, even if there is not a single woman in the synagogue, it is forbidden to pray there... it has become desecrated and is no longer a *mikdosh me'at*."

887   Thus, leaving behind the *mechitza* was only to become more like the church. See Norman Lamm, "Separate Pews in the Synagogue," *Tradition* 1:2 (1959).

888   There are two basic lines of reasoning when examining the purpose of a *mechitza* during prayer services. Perhaps the two most outspoken in their differing positions were Rabbi Moshe Feinstein *zt"l* and the Satmar Rav *zt"l*. According to Rabbi Moshe Feinstein, the *mechitza* prevents intermingling of the sexes; see *Iggros Moshe* 1:40 (see also *Teshuvos Seridei Aish* 2:20). According to the Satmar Rav, its purpose is that men and women not see each other; see *Divrei Yoel, Orach Chaim* 1:10 (also *Minchas Yitzchok* 2:20; *Oz Nedbiru* 12:48).

   The practical difference between these two opinions affects the minimum required height of a *mechitza*, and whether see-through materials like glass would be acceptable. According to Rabbi Moshe Feinstein, a shoulder-height *mechitza* [60–66 in] would be acceptable because it prevents "intermingling"; see *Iggros Moshe* 1:40, 42; 3:23; 4:31. According to the Satmar Rav, it would need to cover the heads of the women, where they could no longer be seen. Glass is improper because it allows the men and women to see each other, evading the whole purpose of separate sections (*Shevet Halevi* 1:29). According to Rabbi Moshe Feinstein it would be permitted, although this is the not the majority opinion; see *Iggros Moshe* 1:43. The Lubavitcher Rebbe rules that a *mechitza* needs to be of a height so as to prevent men from seeing women (approx. six feet), and rejected the idea of a *mechitza* whose upper section is made of glass; see *Sha'arei Halacha U'Minhag*, vol. 1, pgs. 198–199.

physical appearance. It is equally difficult for a married person to have the proper awe and reverence required for prayer—the individual's personal communion with G-d—when they have the security and comfort of their spouse sitting beside them.

The prayer service in Judaism, especially in America, has evolved into something much more theatrical than it ever traditionally was. The prayers are not meant to be a service in the sense of a collective performance, which goes through an established pattern of symbolic standings, sittings, and bowings. Instead, the prayer service in Judaism is a personal experience, a one-on-one time with the Almighty. Prayer is called the "service of the heart," and is meant to be one's private time to concentrate, converse, and connect with the Almighty without any distraction. Author Lisa Aiken puts it very eloquently, saying that "just as a married couple can relate most intimately to each other when they remove any distractions, we do the same when we want to focus our attention exclusively on our Maker."[889]

It should be noted that this only applies to the established service of the synagogue, which stands in place of the sacrifices and daily rituals of the Holy Temple. For this reason, the "miniature Temple" must conform, in construct and perspective, to the Temple as it was. At home, or anywhere outside of formal services, Jewish people are always welcome to pray their own prayers for their own specific needs. Families may, and are encouraged, to pray and sing together as a unit, and many do just that during the grace after meals at their Sabbath tables and throughout the week.

MINYAN: PUBLIC PRAYER

Traditional Judaism lays out what an individual is commanded to do based on the instructions of the Torah. Each command to a specific group of people is meant for one or both parts of a two-fold dichotomy: either to facilitate the expression of an essential energy that this person or group inherently possesses, or to rectify and correct something that this person or group is lacking.

---

889   Aiken, *To Be a Jewish Woman*, pg. 69.

Women are exempt from positive commandments that are designated for a particular time frame. Women are obligated to pray,[890] but communal prayer is among the acts that women are exempt from. They are certainly welcome to pray in the synagogue at any time they choose, yet being that they are not *obligated* to do so, they cannot count toward the unit of people required for this activity.

This is a general guiding principle in Jewish law—only one who is obligated in a command can be numbered in the unit necessary to complete it. The principle can be seen in certain scenarios with men as well. Between the death and burial of a close relative, a Jew is classified as an *onan*. An *onan* may attend synagogue services during that time should he desire, but he does not count toward the minyan since he is not currently obligated in it.[891] On the other hand, assuming women are obligated to read the *megillah* on Purim, and that a minyan is at least preferable, the Ran and the Meiri write that a woman may count toward this quorum.[892]

The only reason that Jewish men are meant to get together in a minyan to pray is to enhance enthusiasm, concentration, and unity. Jewish tradition teaches that men "need this," so to speak, in order to be effective in their spiritual growth. The personal prayer of the individual is carried a lot higher when standing together in brotherhood in a collective unit. According to traditional perspective, the entity of a minyan is greater than the sum total of the ten men involved.

Not so with women. As discussed earlier, a woman's unique status allows her to achieve the same spiritual heights in her prayers in the privacy of her own home. Praying alone is not a consolation prize, as even the *Kohen Gadol*, the high priest, on the holiest day of the year, Yom Kippur, prayed in solitude.

The verses from which the qualifying factors of a minyan are derived

---

890   *Shemoneh Esrei*; see *Shulchan Aruch, Orach Chaim* 106:1.

891   This individual is preoccupied with finalizing arrangements for the funeral and is exempted by Jewish law from communal prayer and other positive mitzvos.

892   See Ran to *Megillah*, end of ch. 2; Meiri, *Brachos* 47b. For the practical application of this idea, see Rama, *Orach Chaim* 690:18; also *Teshuvos Rav Pe'alim*, pt. II, *Orach Chaim* 62.

are connected with the sin of the spies recounted in the Torah.[893] Since women were not involved in this sin, they have nothing to rectify. Furthermore, it is interesting that a popular sociology work mentioned that when faced with challenges, men tend to retreat to solitude, while women seek out other people.[894] This need for rectification in community building may also contribute to why the obligation to pray in a group is commanded only to a man, because a woman has that drive to bond with others naturally.

It would seem that the real reason that not counting toward a minyan has started to bother some women is because modern synagogue services have become theater performances of sorts. However, the true center of Torah life does not take place in the synagogue but instead in the home. Traditionally, the synagogue, often just a little hole in the wall, was a place where men went to discharge their obligation to pray with a minyan, study, or listen to a Torah lecture from the rabbi. Women were not overall envious of that because the core of Jewish life was found in the home. To this day, the commandments that are essential to traditional Judaism, like keeping Sabbath and kosher, are all grounded in the home. With the secularization of Judaism, the synagogue became more like houses of worship in other faiths, by being considered the center of religious life. It is this that caused Rabbi Shimshon Raphoel Hirsch to so passionately write the following:

> If I had the power, I would provisionally close all synagogues for a hundred years. Do not tremble at the thought of it, Jewish heart. What would happen? Jews and Jewesses without synagogues, desiring to remain

---

893   In *Bamidbar* [Numbers] 14:27, Moses sent spies to scout the land of Canaan. Ten of them returned with a negative report, saying that it would be impossible to conquer the land. G-d, in His disappointment, turned to Moses and Aaron, asking them: "How long will this evil assembly provoke to complain against Me?" From here it is deduced that an "assembly" is ten men. A form of biblical exegesis using comparisons of words is called *gezera shava*. Comparing the verse (*Vayikra* [Leviticus] 22:32) G-d says, "I shall be sanctified amidst the children of Israel" and (*Bamidbar* [Numbers] 16:21): "Separate yourselves from amidst this assembly." The instruction is that an "assembly" must be present when G-d is being sanctified, like saying *kaddish*, *kedushah* and *barchu*, or the public reading of the Torah.

894   John Gray, *Men Are from Mars, Women Are from Venus* (1992), ch. 3.

such, would be forced to concentrate on a Jewish life and a Jewish home. The Jewish officials connected with the synagogue would have to look to the only opportunity now open to them to teach young and old how to live a Jewish life and how to build a Jewish home. All synagogues closed by Jewish hands would constitute the strongest protest against the abandonment of the Torah in home and life.[895]

Rabbi Hirsch's idea of closing synagogues would force Jews to once again see where the true priority and significance stands in Judaism. Living in a Western culture, it is easy to unintentionally absorb the ideology that the house of worship is the center of religion and G-dly connection, and thus feel indignant when the genders do not play the same roles in the synagogue. In reality, the home was and is the nucleus of faith and G-dliness, and women's task of nurturing faith to the family is no less holy, and is treasured as favorably by G-d.

BLESSING OF "*SHELO ASANI ISHA*"

The text of the prayers that men and women say is identical. There is, though, one minor difference. The Talmud records that a Jewish man must recite daily blessings for not being created a gentile, a slave, or woman.[896] As is clear from everything said thus far, Judaism holds women in the highest regard. Historically, the Jewish people are universally recognized for their highly developed social consciousness. That being said, this blessing seems peculiar. What, then, is the blessing on being created a male?

The question only becomes stronger by noting that speaking badly against anyone is considered a severe transgression. Therefore, the blessing instituted by the sages to be said every morning *cannot* be disparaging against women. What then does this mean?

---

895   Dayan Dr. I. Grunfeld, in his introduction to Rabbi Hirsch's *Horeb: A Philosophy of Jewish Laws and Observances.*
896   *Menachos* 43b.

Some people raise the concern that the three listed categories of people are considered equally inferior by the rabbis. Rashi, in his commentary to this segment, clarifies this. He explains that a shared characteristic between a gentile, slave, and woman is that none of them are obligated in the mitzvos in the same way that a man is.[897] Gentiles are bound only by the Seven Laws of Noah, not in the totality of the Torah's commands. Slaves are exempt from time-bound commandments because they have another "master" aside from G-d that they need to tend to. Women are exempt from time-bound commandments because of their innate serenity, natural spiritual completeness, and the other reasons elaborated upon earlier.

Western culture is very attached to the desire to become "number one." People often measure themselves according to their wealth, popularity, and beauty, among other things. Someone ranked higher on these scales is considered more important. One may thus erroneously think that the Torah also evaluates people based on this hierarchical value system, with the *Kohen Gadol*, the high priest, who works in the holiest chamber in the Temple, at the top of the scale, and the women just above the slave and gentile.

Torah does not evaluate people based on a hierarchical value system. The *Kohen* is given certain privileges and responsibilities, but from a Torah perspective these do not make him greater per se than anyone else. Only a *Kohen* can come forth and bless the people. Even the head of the *Sanhedrin*—the high court in Temple times, was not allowed. Does that make the *Kohen* superior to the other? Not from a Torah perspective. The Midrash states unequivocally and authoritatively, "I call Heaven and Earth to witness, be it Jew or non-Jew, man or woman, manservant or maidservant—only according to their actions will the spirit of holiness rest upon them."[898] Each player has his or her strengths and weaknesses, yet each is a significant player in uplifting the world, each one in his own defined way. The purpose of these

---

897   Rashi there, s.v. "*Kuli hai nami.*" Rashi's *siddur* also offers this explanation. Rashi's reasoning is also brought down in the *Tosefta* (*Brachos* 6:23. See also *Yerushalmi* 9:1) and later in the Rif, Rosh, and *Beis Yosef* (*Orach Chaim* 46).

898   *Yalkut Shimoni*, Shoftim 4:42.

external classifications is simply to ensure that society runs smoothly, and not to assign value on a hierarchy.

The sages' entire joy and zest was founded upon the fulfillment of G-d's commandments. This aspiration is meant to be embedded in the minds of every Jew. A Jewish man, therefore, is required to thank the Almighty for allowing him to serve Him in his unique way, with the responsibility to do even more mitzvos, and he thanks G-d for these added opportunities of connection. Every Torah commentary says that this blessing is a form of gratitude for this *particular* privilege, not a general thanks for not being created a woman.[899]

Thanking Hashem for not having the portion of another is not meant to imply inferior status of the other, and should not be taken as such.[900] By way of example, many would gladly thank G-d for not creating them a *Kohen*, who—in the times of the Temple—was regularly involved with slaughtering and gutting animals. The *Kohen* still retains his noble status, yet the person is thankful that he instead was designated to serve G-d in a different way.

Many women, in lieu of this blessing, are accustomed to say the blessing, "Who has made me according to His will."[901] The Midrash teaches that when G-d was preparing to create mankind, He consulted with his ministering angels. However, when He created the first woman, He did so strictly according to His own will. Only a woman can say, "Who has made me in accordance with His will [alone]."[902]

A man thanks G-d for the opportunity to do as many commandments

---

899   The sages framed the blessing in the negative, "Who has not made me a woman," as opposed to the positive, "Who has made me a man," for technical reasons. From a certain philosophical perspective, it would have been better to not have been created altogether. The sages reason this based on the arduous challenges and temptations that the soul faces while clothed in a body, in comparison to its purely spiritual involvements in the heavens before it comes down (*Eruvin* 13b). Now that the person has been created, he thanks G-d for allowing him to serve Him through all of the mitzvos.

900   Of note is the *Sefer Me'orei Or*, pt. 4, pg. 20, which suggests not saying the blessing aloud in the synagogue to avoid even the possibility that a woman might [mistakenly] feel shamed or "inferior" from it.

901   *Orach Chaim* 46:4.

902   *Yeshuos Yaakov, Orach Chaim* 46:5; see also Yehuda Levi, *Facing Current Challenges* (1998), pgs. 146–147.

as possible, while a woman, who inherently contains the connection to G-d achieved with the slightly fewer commandments assigned to her, thanks G-d for being made as a more finished product.[903]

A related idea can be gleaned from the creation of humanity. When G-d created Adam, He later changed him by removing a rib and making Eve. However, when Eve was created she was a finished product, so to speak, with no need for modifications. The blessing "who made me according to His will" means that Hashem made woman according to His ultimate desire, in contrast to the man who was not quite finished.

WEARING TALLIS AND TEFILLIN

As mentioned above, for all mitzvos that a woman decides to take upon herself—even though not obligated to—she merits reward for her deeds.[904] Furthermore, some authorities even say that mitzvos that women as a whole have traditionally accepted upon themselves, like *lulav*, shofar, and counting the *omer*, are now *obligatory* for them to perform.[905]

There are some exceptions to this rule. Women are highly discouraged from wearing a tallis[906] and laying tefillin.[907] Both of these mitzvos are advised against for their distinct reasons. The reasons are aspects unique to those particular mitzvah objects.

---

903   See *Siddur Olat Re'iyah* by Rabbi Avraham Yitzchak Kook.

904   This is the opinion of virtually everyone, except perhaps Rashi, *Rosh Hashana* 33a.

905   See *Magen Avraham, Orach Chaim* 489:1; *Chayei Adam* 141:7. Notable as well is that the Ashkenazi *poskim* write that she may even recite the blessing beforehand. Rama, *Orach Chaim* 589:6, based on Rabbeinu Tam, *Rosh Hashana*, ibid. Rabbeinu Tam learns out that phrase in the blessing, "Who has commanded us" refers to the collective whole of the Jewish people. The Rambam (*Tzitzis* 3:9) and the Sefardic *poskim*, say that this phrase refers to the individual (who in this is case is not commanded) and therefore prohibit a woman to say the blessing before doing these mitzvos.

906   The tallis is a four-cornered garment, worn during prayer, that the Torah instructs one to put fringes upon. These fringes are called the tzitzis. Many wear a small tallis with fringes even outside of prayer time.

907   These are a set of boxes and straps containing specific parchments describing the connection that a Jew has to G-d. One is worn strapped to the arm, near the heart, because that is the "seat" of the emotions; the other is worn strapped on one's head between the eyes, as this also is the "seat" of the emotions. Tefillin are discussed as to be a sort of spiritual antenna that paves a deeper connection between the wearer and G-d.

Wearing the fringes of a tallis is required only during the daylight hours. Therefore, they are a positive mitzvah bound by time, and a woman is exempt from wearing the fringes. Wearing these fringes differs from other time-bound commandments in that even for men it is an *indirect* obligation. The Torah does not command one to wear fringes; it instead says that *if* one is wearing a four-cornered garment, it must have fringes attached. There is no obligation to wear a four-cornered garment. If a man chooses not to wear a four-cornered garment, then he is not subject to the obligation of attaching fringes.

Pious men have accepted this deed upon themselves, making a point to wear a four-cornered garment throughout the day, so that they can even fulfill this indirect commandment. Women are permitted to wear four-cornered garments without affixing fringes.[908] For women, performing this mitzvah becomes very irrelevant; it is a time-bound mitzvah (which she is exempt from), and at the same time it is not obligatory for *anyone*.

Technically speaking, a woman may perform this mitzvah. One who wishes to perform a commandment that is *not obligatory* upon them must be sure that proper motives are sparking the interest. It is always important to remember that the Torah's commandments are instructions from our Father in Heaven for our benefit, and should not be used to prove political points, or advance social agendas or movements.[909] The Torah approach to growth in spiritual connection is better achieved through finding ways to enhance depth, concentration, and enthusiasm when performing the commandments that we already are instructed to do.[910] Because human nature is what it is, it is difficult to make judgments about personal piety on one's own. Instead, when taking upon new spiritual endeavors, one should consult a capable mentor or advisor who is an expert in traditional Jewish law.

---

908 Rambam, *Tzitzis* 3:10, 11.

909 Sometimes a person can perform a commandment not out of the sake of punctiliousness, or to better serve G-d, but out of a false "religious" pride. See Rama, *Orach Chaim* 17:2 to see how this can play out in the topic at hand.

910 Or if one is not proficient in all required tenets and obligations, better to work on fulfilling those than to carry out remote elective added "stringencies."

Regarding tefillin, they are a time-bound commandment as well. Women are discouraged from wearing tefillin for a slightly different reason than why they are discouraged from wearing a tallis.[911]

In a perfect world, tefillin are meant to be worn by men for the entire day. They contain a very high-grade of holiness and one must be in full control of his body while they are on. One's thoughts may not deviate from them while they are on, neither may one pass wind, doze off, or be involved with any frivolous behavior.[912] Only very saintly people are able to hold this level of purity over an entire day's span. Therefore, most men—who are obligated to wear tefillin—only do so during the morning prayers. Men wear them for a very minimal period of time because on the one hand they are obligated to wear them, but on the other hand are unable to retain, for an extended period of time, the proper sanctity that wearing tefillin requires. Along the same lines, Jewish boys, who generally begin performing mitzvos from a young age in order to be educated in the commandments, do not begin putting on tefillin until just prior to their Bar Mitzvah. Because of the great sanctity of tefillin, all "optional" wearing must be avoided. Hence, women—who are not obligated to wear them because they are time-bound—are deterred from doing so.[913]

Targum Yonoson takes another approach. On the verse, "A male shall not wear the garments of a woman, nor shall a woman wear the garment of a male,"[914] he writes: "Tzitzis and tefillin, which are male garments, should not be worn by a woman." Jewish mystic thought also connects tefillin to a male garment.[915]

---

911 Some of the information for this section was gleaned from Moshe Meiselman, *Jewish Woman in Jewish Law* (1978), pgs. 147–151, and notes.

912 See Rambam, *Tefillin* 4:14, 15, 25.

913 This is in line with the Raavad to *Toras Kohanim, Dibburah Dinedavah*, ch. 2. See also Tosofos, *Eruvin* 96a; *Chiddushei HaRamban*; Ritva, *Kiddushin* 31a. Additionally see *Responsa, Rulings and Customs of R. Meir ben Barukh of Rothenburg*, ed. Cahana, vol. 1:34, pg. 143. Furthermore, see *Tashbatz* sec. 270; *Kol Bo*, sec. 21, *Hilchos Tefillin* 13b; *Yam Shel Shlomo, Kiddushin* 1:64; *Beis Yosef, Orach Chaim* 38.

914 *Devarim* [Deuteronomy] 22:5.

915 "Men's garments" in reverse letter replacement (ש"ב ח"א) has the same *gematria* as "this is tefillin," because they are the secret of "the world of masculinity." *Shomer Emunim*, Ki Setzei.

Rabbi Aryeh Kaplan offers a spiritual perspective:

> Women resemble G-d in a way that no man could ever hope to: only a woman can create within her body, only a woman can bear a child. In this sense, a woman partakes of G-d's attributes more intimately than any man. The Kabbalists teach us that the hand tefillin represent the feminine element. The single hollow section in the tefillin box represents the womb, and the coils wrapped around the arm signify the umbilical cord. What a man partakes of with an object, a woman partakes of with her very body.[916]

With the words of Rabbi Kaplan in mind, I would like to suggest a further analogy: Hearing aids help keep those who have difficulty hearing connected with the world around them. If someone does not need a hearing aid, because they already hear well, wearing a hearing aid is both unnecessary and inappropriate. Tefillin function as a spiritual hearing aid that helps connect the wearer to the Divine. If one is already naturally connected and attuned, then wearing tefillin is superfluous.[917]

---

916   Aryeh Kaplan, Tefillin (1993), pgs. 56-57.

917   The Talmud mentions that Michal, the daughter of King Saul and wife of King David, donned tefillin and the sages did not protest (*Eruvin* 96a). Some say the sages did protest (*Yerushalmi, Berachos* 2:3; *Pesikta Rabati* 22). In any event, one cannot learn out from her actions. Jewish literature, in particular Jewish mysticism, highlights why her case was unique (see *Kaf HaChaim, Orach Chaim* 38:9, quoting the *Yafe Lilev*). Although the daughters of Rashi and a handful of other prominent and saintly women are rumored to have put on tefillin, there is no evidence for these claims. Rabbi Aryeh Frimer, a recognized expert on women's halachic issues, reports finding no source for this myth. Professor David Golinkin wrote, "There is a widespread story that Rashi's daughters wore tefillin, but I have been unable to find any written proof of this assertion" ("May Women Wear Tefillin?" *Conservative Judaism* (Fall 1997): pgs. 3–18). There is likewise no source for the first wife of the Ohr HaChaim donning tefillin, as is rumored; see Ari Zivotofsky, "What's the Truth About...Rashi's Daughters?" *Jewish Action* (Summer 2011). Although there is a small minority of early authorities who permit a woman to put on tefillin, the Rama seals the law, categorically forbidding it, for the first reason discussed above (see *Orach Chaim* 38:3. See also *Vilna Gaon* 38:3). Enactments such as these are codified to ensure proper performance of the Torah's commands, and cannot be disregarded.

ENHANCING DIGNITY

PHYSICAL CONTACT BETWEEN GENDERS

Judaism recognizes the power of human sexuality. While other faiths depict intimate relations as something to be shunned or a sin of the flesh, Judaism teaches that in the proper context it can be the holiest of acts. At the same time, when it occurs in inappropriate circumstances, it can also be the most repugnant.

Recognizing that the intimate relationship is the most intensely personal of the human experience, Judaism stresses that such relations should only be engaged in within the context of marriage. Within the long-term covenant of marriage, and universal framework for raising a family, relations are welcomed and holy.

Although often taken for granted in the modern world, any human touch is a sign of feeling and connection. As a relationship progresses, physical acts of affection proceed along a progression as well. In the Jewish view, the reality that physical contact will not remain casual for long is dealt with accordingly. Therefore, social situations between unmarried men and women are governed by strict rules. The door is never opened to allow an affectionate touch to become even more. Judaism provides the framework so that one need not test his or her own self-discipline.

The prohibition of *negiah*, literally "touch," is derived from two verses, elaborated upon in the Talmud, and codified by Jewish Law.[918] It should be made clear that the reason for men and women not touching each other in traditional Judaism has nothing to do with women being impure or unclean. Every forbidden relationship begins with a simple, non-intimate touch, so in truth even minor expressions of fondness are already a harbinger of negative consequence or inappropriate thoughts.

---

918 *Vayikra* 18:6 and verse 19, and elaborated in *Shabbos* 13a, although it is debated whether the prohibition is biblical in origin or Rabbinic with biblical allusion (see Rambam, *Issurei Biah* 21:1; *Sefer Hamitzvos Hagadol* 126). In contrast, see the Ramban (*Hasagos, Sefer Hamitzvos*, negative mitzvah 353) where it is ruled an *asmachta*. This is merely an academic dispute, as every Jewish sage agrees that it is forbidden for a man to touch a woman affectionately (*Shulchan Aruch, Even Haezer* 21:1, including hugging, kissing, jesting, etc.).

Certainly, most handshakes between men and women do not lead to intimacy and are not even thought about at the time, yet intimacy always begins with touching. It is also true that even a handshake can superficially convey feelings of intimacy. From a biological standpoint, when people touch, the body produces oxytocin that creates a serene feeling, physically and chemically bonding the parties and making them feel closer and wanting more.[919] Without the physical aspect, one can more easily control oneself.[920]

In essence, the reason that men and women refrain from contact is actually out of respect to each other and to themselves. When even casual physical contact is reserved just for a spouse or other close family members, the depths of those relationships are also enhanced.

MODESTY IN DRESS AND IN SPIRIT

It seems again most enlightening to learn the basics of this topic from the eloquent Nechoma Greisman:[921]

It is because the body itself is so holy that it must remain private and elusive. The holier something is, the more private it must be. Even the *Kohen Gadol*, the high priest, was allowed to enter the Holy of Holies only once a year.

Chassidic philosophy explains that a woman's body reveals the essence of G-d more than a man's body, since she is able to bring forth new life into the world, emulating G-d's power of creation, something from nothing.

In Torah, modesty and inwardness are central values. The opposite is true in the secular world. Modest attire is an expression of spiritual modesty. It is not due to shame. A woman who argues that she is "liberated," i.e., free to display her body and her intimate relationships

---

919   Sandra Ann Taylor, *Secrets of Attraction* (2001), cited in *Reader's Digest* (Nov. 2002).

920   It should be noted that there are many instances in which men and women can touch each other. One example would be applied to a person who is facing a life-threatening danger. Doctors and other health professionals may, likewise, touch members of the opposite gender when in the medical context. Even hairdressers or physical therapists may be permitted in the context of their work as well.

921   Greisman, *The Nechoma Greisman Anthology*, pg. 72.

openly, essentially states that she is nothing more than her body. "Look at me. This is who I am." She shows less sensitivity to herself than a modest woman. Modesty is not only the way you dress, it is also the way you speak, it is the way you relate to others on a personal level, it is also the way you express your emotions. Modesty is related to our own self-image. Who and what am I? My body is not the essential me, but an integral part of holiness, Jewish holiness.

CONCLUSION

In essence, Torah regards women as the "crown of Creation." She is holy, powerful, and is the center of Jewish life. While there are many misconceptions concerning the way in which traditional Judaism views women, hopefully the topics covered here have laid a foundation for further open-minded exploration of the topic of women in traditional Judaism.

KOSHER: DIET PLAN OF THE SOUL

F
ood is central to life. The need to eat is perhaps the most primal, basic, and recurring of human needs. Aside from the times during the day in which food is actually being consumed, time is dedicated to cooking it, exercising to keep its effects in check, and using the restroom to relieve the waste. Much of why people work hard all day is in order to make money to put food on the table. A large percentage of the life of the average person is occupied with food.

There is arguably nothing more misunderstood in the Jewish faith than the laws and meaning of *kashrus*, the dietary laws of the Torah. While almost everyone has heard of the idea of keeping kosher, few know its intricacies and significance. Kosher is not about lox, potato pancakes, and matzah-ball soup. Instead, Chinese, Italian, Mexican, and foods of every other ethnicity can potentially be kosher. Kosher is also not food that was simply "blessed by the rabbi."

Kosher is the diet plan for the soul, in that they are the foods prescribed by G-d in the Torah for consumption by the Jewish people.

WHAT IS KOSHER?

The word *kosher*, in biblical terms, means "fit" or "appropriate."[922] The sages elaborate that kosher means that something is usable, especially in reference to foods. It is worth briefly stating exactly which potential foods are kosher. A fully detailed explanation of the intricacies of

---

922   One example from *Esther* 8:5, "The matter was pleasing (*kasher*) before the king."

the Jewish dietary laws is beyond the scope of what is being dealt with here. The following is simply an overview of what foods are kosher:

- All fruits and vegetables are kosher.
- Animal kingdom:
    a. Any land animal that has both split hooves and chews its cud is considered kosher; if the animal only has one or none of those features, it cannot be eaten.[923]
    b. Birds are not given signs, but there are just twenty-four mentioned that are not kosher, and the rest are considered kosher.[924]
    c. Fish must have both fins and scales to be kosher.[925]

All land animals and birds must be killed through *shechita*, traditional ritual slaughter.[926] If the animal dies by any other means, it is not kosher.[927] Furthermore, it should be mentioned that the sciatic nerve,[928] blood, and forbidden fats[929] are also prohibited and must be extracted after slaughter.

Additionally, milk and meat may not be eaten together.[930] The byproducts of any kosher animal, like eggs or milk, are also kosher, and that from a non-kosher animal is not kosher.[931] Interestingly, insects are prohibited as well.[932]

---

923   *Vayikra* [Leviticus] 11:2–3.
924   *Vayikra* [Leviticus] 11:13. In practice, only birds that have an existing tradition of being kosher are eaten.
925   *Vayikra* [Leviticus] 11:9.
926   *Devarim* [Deuteronomy] 12:21.
927   *Vayikra* [Leviticus] 22:8.
928   *Bereishis* [Genesis] 32:33.
929   *Vayikra* [Leviticus] 3:17.
930   Or cooked together, or benefited from, as will be discussed below. Each prohibition is learned out from the three times it is mentioned in the Torah (*Shmos* [Exodus] 23:19, 34:26; *Devarim* [Deuteronomy] 14:21).
931   This does not include honey, as a bee is only a carrier of the honey, not the facilitator of the honey (see *Bechoros* 7b).
932   *Vayikra* [Leviticus] 11:20–21. There are some types of grasshoppers that are permissible, but like birds, there must be a tradition as to which are permitted.

NOT BASED ON PHYSICAL HEALTH

There is a common misunderstanding that the Jewish dietary laws are associated with ancient Israelite health concerns. Therefore, since contemporary health standards have solved these ancient health issues, the laws of *kashrus* are no longer necessary. From the beginning, this idea is simply not true. The kosher laws are not premised on bodily health at all.

Health would not explain why an animal must be ritually slaughtered, why fish with fins and scales would be specified, or why milk from a non-kosher animal would be unfit for consumption. Furthermore, there is no proof that kosher animals avoid health concerns. Sheep and freshwater fish could transmit tapeworm, and there is also risk of mad cow disease. Conversely, many non-kosher animals are not harmful to health at all. Arabs have enjoyed camel products for centuries, and the U.S. Department of Agriculture has praised rabbit meat as one of the most nutritious meats known to man.[933] Neither camel nor rabbit is kosher.[934]

Additionally, many Jews assume that the ancient Israelites avoided pig because they were concerned about deadly trichinosis or other ill effects of pork.[935] How do these people account for the Torah having the foresight to avoid pig for these reasons several thousand years before doctors discovered the connection between them?[936] This claim ironically seems to imply that the Torah is either Divine or written with wisdom far beyond its time. If it is the former, and the laws of kosher are divinely ordained, then how can human beings decide to change Divine instruction? If the latter, and it was merely a brilliant author with prophetic foresight, surely this insightful sage would

---

933   Based on *Kli Yakar* on *Vayikra* 11:1, and Abarbanel, who say that since non-Jews do not keep kosher and are healthy, it is clear that the reason for these laws is not for the body, but rather for the soul.

934   Ideas from this paragraph gleaned from an article by Professor P. B. Hutt, *The Jewish Dietary Laws and Their Foundations* (1994).

935   This is a parasitic disease caused by eating raw or undercooked pork or wild game infected with the larvae of a species of roundworm commonly called the trichina worm.

936   This strong question is asked in Dennis Prager, *Nine Questions People Ask about Judaism* (1986), pg. 58.

have also realized that much of the danger in pig consumption can also be avoided if the meat is cooked more thoroughly. So it can be safely concluded that the laws of *kashrus* are not rooted in the physical health of the Jew.

This is not to say, however, that there are no peripheral benefits to physical health when keeping a kosher diet.[937] Historically, Jews have been protected from several devastating epidemics that were adversely affecting their neighbors. One needs look no further than the Black Plague that stormed through Europe in the Middle Ages. The plight that the Jews suffered was significantly less than their gentile neighbors. This may be because they did not eat diseased animals. The requirement to salt meat may also have been a factor in preserving the meat and destroying bacteria.[938] Additionally, ritual hand-washing before meals, instituted by King Solomon, may have also helped contain the spread of disease in the Jewish community.[939]

Even throughout the twentieth century, many prominent doctors have recommended kosher diets as being healthier than other diets. Waldemar Haffkine, a renowned Russian bacteriologist, who laid the foundations of modern medicine by his development of certain vaccines, wrote: "Since the advance of research in microbiology, it has become well-known that all the procedures which in the Jewish laws of *kashrus* constitute a remarkable provision for preserving health."[940] Sir James Cantlie, a well-known Scottish physician, and author of thirteen medical volumes, once stated, "When I order a meat diet, it must be kosher meat."[941] Famous cardiologist and heart doctor to President Eisenhower, Paul Dudley White, said that kosher food is "easiest on the heart."[942] The contemporary and popular Dr. Myles Bader, internation-

---

937 An interesting compilation of health benefits can be found in Nissim Behar's *The Jewish Table*.

938 See Jack Cooper, *Who Knew?! Unusual Stories in Jewish History* (2010), pgs. 31–32.

939 Pre-meal hand washing, along with the other times in the day that a Jew is commanded to wash hands; see *Eruvin* 21b. See also Fred Rosner, "Hand washing and Infection Control," *Mt. Sinai Journal of Medicine* 74 (2007), pgs. 33–35.

940 Haffkine, "A Plea for Orthodoxy," *The Menorah Journal* (1916), pg. 6.

941 Harold Smith, *A Treasure Hunt in Judaism* (1950), pg. 149.

942 See Reuben Epstein, *The Torah Testifies* (1997), pgs. 112–113.

ally recognized leader in preventive care and wellness, says, "If you want healthy, clean-tasting chicken, buy kosher."[943,944]

Some of the sages over time have mentioned that non-kosher food is detrimental to the body and health. These statements, however, were not given as primary *reasons* for the commandment, rather as secondary matter-of-fact benefits that the Jewish dietary laws provide. In other words, all Torah authorities explain that non-kosher foods are harmful to the soul, and that is the primary reason for their prohibition. Some, however, say that the body is *also* adversely affected.[945] This means that nowadays, where many physical health concerns could be eliminated through modern breeding techniques and refrigeration, non-kosher food is still forbidden because of its spiritual effects.

REASON FOR KEEPING KOSHER

The basis of observance of all the commandments of the Torah is that they are given by G-d for the benefit of mankind. For every mitzvah, there is a benefit and a reason. In some instances, the reason and the benefit seem readily discernible, while others are beyond mortal understanding.

---

943   Jewishrecipies.org/food-for-the-soul.html.

944   This does not imply that the idea of a kosher diet is universally accepted as the healthiest. Modern medicine also has trends, and is constantly reevaluating what is healthy and what is not. Sometimes there is also a focus on a certain aspect of the food, or a certain aspect of its effects on the person who eats it. Consider eggs or coffee for example. It seems like every other week there is a different perspective as to whether they are good for or damaging to one's health. Some people might view this as flip-flopping; however, they can be good for some things and bad for some things without necessarily being inconsistent. Few foods are good for everything. Likewise, it is difficult to classify all varieties of kosher food as healthy or not in a single overarching view.

945   Ramban, *Vayikra* 11:9, where he mentions bottom-feeder fish as detrimental to health. Contrast with his commentary on *Devarim* 14:3, among other places, where the Ramban focuses on the spiritual maladies of non-kosher animals. Other examples of physical harm mentioned, see *Sefer HaChinuch*, mitzvah 73 and Rashbam, *Vayikra* 11:3. See also *Iggros Kodesh*, vol. 9, pg. 278, where it is also mentioned that kosher food is beneficial for the body. However, see the *Akedas Yitzchok*, (Shemini, *sha'ar* 60), Abarbanel, and Kli Yakar (*Vayikra* 11) among others, who disagree and say that *kashrus* has no impact on the body, only on the soul.

THREE CATEGORIES OF TORAH COMMANDMENTS

In Judaism, there are three types of commandments: *mishpatim*, *eidus*, and *chukim*. The *mishpatim* are completely logical edicts that facilitate a stable society. These basic rules include warnings against theft, murder, or engaging in promiscuity. Because of the blatant obviousness of these laws, humanity would be inclined toward many of them even if the Torah was not given.[946]

The second category, *eidus*, includes testimonies from events in the collective Jewish historical experience, for instance, eating *matzah* on Pesach. Although nobody would at random come up with these deeds, their commemorative value rings true enough with the rational mind to accept their observance.

The final ones, the *chukim*, are super-rational commands. These are the decrees that transcend human logic. The Jewish person is to adhere to their observance simply because of Divine instruction, without being privy at all to their reason or benefit.[947]

More generally, the commandments of the Torah can be broken up into two categories: logical and supra-logical—i.e., those that transcend logic. In Jewish tradition, the kosher laws are classified as super-rational.[948] Were they merely a health guide, they would not be categorized as such. Moreover, if keeping kosher was purely for physical health benefits, G-d would certainly have included them in his instructions for humanity at large, and not just the Jewish nation, as G-d cares about the well-being of all of His creatures.[949]

Some find observance of super-rational commandments more challenging, as their moral or symbolic meanings are not outwardly evident. However, when dealing with the Torah, which is Divine instructions, the real surprise should be that the human mind is able to comprehend *anything*, not amazement when it cannot. After all, one

---

946 We could have learned modesty from the cat, honest labor from the ant, marital fidelity from the dove, and good manners from the rooster (*Eruvin* 100b).

947 *Yoma* 67a: "I order you to observe My *chukim*, and you have no license to question them."

948 See Rashi, *Vayikra* 19:19, *Bamidbar* 19:2; Mishneh Torah, *Temurah* 8:8.

949 "His mercies are upon all of His works," *Tehillim* 145:9.

is dealing with the will and wisdom of G-d. G-d becomes extremely limited if His wisdom does not exceed human understanding. Worshipping a G-d that one *cannot* completely understand seems better than a god whom he can fully understand.

G-d gives different types of commandments to human beings in order that they connect with Him in a variety of ways, sometimes in a rational way and sometime in a way that transcends logic. Although the reasons for the commandments have been explored all over Jewish literature,[950] in their essence, all commandments of the Torah are meant to be followed earnestly because they are Divine instructions.[951]

PERSONAL BENEFITS

SELF-CONTROL

The sages explain that there are several beneficial outcomes that happen to a person by virtue of keeping kosher. Once again it must be emphasized that these are not the reasons for keeping kosher, but positive and practical effects it has on the human being. On the most basic level, keeping kosher enhances self-control. The Midrash relates:[952]

---

950 They are referred to as *ta'amei hamitzvos*. *Ta'amei* means both "reason" and "taste." The reasons attached to the mitzvos are similar to eating food. Food is essentially eaten in order to survive, yet enjoyment is gained from the variety of tastes and textures. These are the pleasant side-effects of eating. Similarly, G-d made the mitzvos with varied "tastes." In some, one can palpably experience the pleasant side-effects that accompany it. Just like a person does not eat food merely for taste, so too one does not do a mitzvah simply because of the reason; they can just provide added zest in their fulfillment. (Rabbi Dessler's response to the question of *ta'amei hamitzvos* posed by Rabbi Moshe Shapiro; see Becher and Newman, *After the Return* (1994), "Appendix—The Reason for the Mitzvos," pgs. 175-182).

951 As the well-known Chassidic adage goes, "If we were commanded to chop wood, we would do so with the same enthusiasm" as mitzvos that are perfectly understandable (*Likkutei Torah, Bamidbar* 40a). Also, "Whatever command or prohibition of G-d it may be that prompts one to ask why one should do this and not do that, there is but one answer: Because it is the will of G-d" (Rabbi Shimshon Raphoel Hirsch, foreword to *Horeb*). Nonetheless, even those in the category of the super-rational commandments, there are certain aspects, benefits, and positive outcomes that the rational mind can understand about them; see Rambam, *Temurah* 4:14.

952 *Midrash Tanchuma*, Shemini 8; *Midrash Sochar Tov* 10:12.

What does G-d care if a man kills an animal in the proper Jewish way and eats it, or whether he strangles the animal and eats it? Will one benefit Him, or the other injure Him? Or what does G-d care whether a man eats kosher or non-kosher animals? ...So you learn that the commandments were given only to refine G-d's creatures, as it says, "G-d's word is refined. It is a protection to those who trust in Him.[953]

One of the key purposes and Divine mission of the human being in this world is to achieve self-refinement. It is a worthy goal that is unfortunately not often pursued.

The sages teach that a person should never say, "I am not interested in eating pork, or engaging in lusts," rather he should say, "From my own standpoint it is entirely possible and desirable, yet I cannot because G-d has prohibited it."[954] Self-control is the distinctive feature marking man as superior to animal. The human being is able to call upon his nobler instincts and overcome his natural base drives. By not being allowed to eat just anything that he fancies, he will be disciplined to exercise the same self-control that he is called upon to display in the dietary field in other fields as well.[955]

POSITIVE TRAIT INHERITANCE

Jean Anthelme Brillat-Savarin, the nineteenth century author of the then best-known work of gastronomy, said, "Tell me what you eat, and I'll tell you what you are."[956] In the more widespread 1960s vernacular, the slogan was, "You are what you eat."

Modern science reveals that foods not only influence cells in the body, but also the personality. Every cell, likewise, possesses a spiritual

---

953   *Shmuel* II [II Samuel] 22:31.

954   *Sifra, Vayikra* 20:26.

955   See Nechama Leibowitz, *Studies in the Weekly Sidra*, First Series, Shemini, based on the *Akedas Yitzchok*.

956   M. F. K Fisher, *M. F. K. Fisher's Translation of Brillat-Savarin's The Physiology of Taste* (1971), pg. 3.

nature that gets passed on. Different foods create different character and temperaments within the human being that ingests them.

The sages explain that all of the non-kosher animals that the Torah forbids possess negative character traits. Ruminants, on the other hand, tend to be tranquil creatures. All kosher animals and birds are herbivorous and non-predatory.[957] With all of the foods that a Jew ingests, he is ingesting the characteristics of the animal as well.[958] By not eating from the meat of aggressive predators, one is protected from the transmission of cruel traits into his personality.[959] The only meat eaten is that of the passive grass-eaters who are themselves nearest to plant life—vegetarians.[960] Ergo, the kosher food chain is one of simple foods that do not influence the eater in a negative manner.

The consumption and absorption of the kosher species fosters sanctity and closeness to G-d, whereas other animals can instead dull and cloud this bond.[961]

COMPASSION

Some sages mention that one educational outcome implanted in the separation of milk, the life-sustaining liquid, and meat, which comes through taking an animal's life, is the idea that even those things permitted to the Jew must be treated with respect.[962]

Furthermore, the sages relate that one purpose of Jewish ritual slaughter is to perfect man by instilling within him proper character traits. The Ramban writes that although man was eventually granted permission to use animals for food, he must show respect for a

---

957   Mishnah, *Chullin* 3:6 mentions birds. See Ramban, Rabbeinu Bachya, *Vayikra* 11:13; Abarbanel, *Vayikra* 11 for other animals. *Toras Menachem* 5752, vol. 2, pgs. 131-132, mentions fish.

958   *Tanya*, ch. 7, 8.

959   Rabbi Shimshon Raphoel Hirsch, Shemini.

960   Feeding cows with sheep meat is the main cause of mad-cow disease; see Chaim Wilschanski, *For the Shabbos Table* (1999), pg. 140.

961   For further elaboration, see Horeb (ch. 68) by Rabbi Hirsch and commentary to *Vayikra* of Rabbi Dovid Tzvi Hoffmann, vol 1, pg. 310.

962   See Rashbam, Ibn Ezra, Abarbanel to *Shmos* 23:19. See also Rabbi Shimshon Raphoel Hirsch and *Noam Elimelech* loc. cit.

creature's life-soul.[963] Because of this, the Jewish people completely drain the blood before consumption, since that is where the life-soul of the animal is found. The *shechita* process benefits the animal and the slaughterer: a) It is the best way to reduce the pain that the animal feels, and b) it inculcates into the Jewish nation to be merciful—for when one is cruel to animals, that cruelty expresses itself elsewhere as well.[964]

Compassion for animal life is expressed in a variety of ways in Judaism. When one sees someone who has purchased new clothing, one wishes them: "May you wear it out and renew it." There are those that refrain from these words when seeing someone who acquired new leather clothing because another animal must be killed in order to make that new garment, and the Psalms say, "His mercy is upon all His creations."[965]

There have been times, even in recent history, when kosher slaughter was deemed inhumane. This is ironic, given that *shechita* is meant to cause as little pain for the animal as possible. *Shechita* requires one swift movement across the throat with a very sharp knife in which the animal dies instantaneously. As was mentioned earlier, within kosher animals, the carotid and vertebral arteries actually merge, so the *shechita* cuts off all blood flow to the brain, allowing the animal to die immediately and painlessly.[966]

Dr. Temple Grandin is an American doctor of animal science and professor at Colorado State University. She is arguably the most respected and well-known name in animal welfare. She commented about kosher slaughter as follows:

---

963   Ramban, *Bereishis* [Genesis] 1:29; see also *Sefer HaChinuch* 451. It is important to remember that the early sages were not necessarily giving a reason why the Torah mandates *shechita*. They were merely demonstrating that the laws of *shechita* reflect a Divine truth.

964   See Ramban, *Devarim* 22:6. See 14:21 in connection to milk and meat together.

965   *Shulchan Aruch, Orach Chaim* 223:6; *Rama*.

966   S. D. Rosen, "Physiological Insights into Shechita," *The Veterinary Record* (June 2004) 154: pgs. 759–765; C. J. G. Wensing, *Essentials of Bovine Anatomy* (1971). For a full treatment on the subject, as well as in-depth information of just how painless kosher slaughter is because of the above and other factors, see Rabbi Dr. Yisrael Meir Levinger, *Jewish Ritual Slaughtering and the Suffering of Animals* (Heb) (2004).

Recently, I participated in a ritual kosher slaughter—in this ritual, the way it was meant to be done, I must say. This was at a plant where the management really understood the importance and significance of what they were doing, and communicated this to their employees—and to the animals as well, I believe. As each steer entered the kosher restraining box, I manipulated the controls to gently position the animal. After some practice, I learned that the animals would stand quietly and not resist being restrained if I eased the chin-lift up under the animal's chin. Jerking the controls or causing the apparatus to make sudden movements made the cattle jump... Some cattle were held so loosely by the head-holder and the rear pusher gate that they could easily have pulled away from the rabbi's knife. *I was relieved and surprised to discover that the animals don't even feel the super-sharp blade as it touches their skin. They made no attempt to pull away. I felt peaceful and calm.*[967]

Studies have shown that kosher animals have shown no signs of fear in the slaughterhouse. Calves roamed freely without attempting to run away and a knife dipped in blood was licked by oblivious cattle.[968] As an extra precaution against any type of suffering, in case there may be one sensitive animal that could theoretically be aware of what is going on, animals are not killed in front of others.

KABBALISTIC EATING

The Jewish dietary laws come from the Torah, which clearly specifies their purpose: "You shall not draw abomination upon yourselves

---

967 Quote appears in Joe M. Regenstein, "Expert Opinion on Considerations When Evaluating All Types of Slaughter: Mechanical, Electrical, Gas and Religious Slaughter," (Cornell University: May 23, 2011). Professor Joe Regenstein of Cornell University dedicates himself to protecting the liberty to perform religious slaughter worldwide. More recent thoughts from Dr. Grandin are written in *Daf Hakashrus*, OU monthly newsletter for the OU, (July–August 2010).

968 See Yisrael Levinger's *Shechita and Animal Suffering*.

through beast or bird or anything with which the ground is alive, which I have set apart for you to treat as unclean. You shall be holy to Me, for I the L-rd am Holy, and I have set you apart from other peoples to be Mine."[969]

G-d is the source of holiness. The soul is G-dly, and therefore holy. The body, or physical aspect of any created thing, is the vessel for the soul. Ideally, the body is meant merely as a conduit for the spiritual—the means of expressing the selflessness and purity of the soul. Sometimes, however, the cravings of the material world can be alluring to the body, and the body begins to feel its own self-existence. At that point the body acts instead as an obstruction to the soul. Instead of being a vehicle for holiness, it becomes a barrier with its own self-interests. The more an entity is focused on its own existence, the more it perceives itself as a separate entity, and the farther away from holiness it falls. Only through self-abnegation can a person or entity become holy, or a vessel of expressing the soul.

Just as a craftsman cannot do his work without proper tools, so the soul cannot fulfill its task without a cooperating body. As it makes a great deal of difference for any precision work whether a craftsman possesses fine tools or not, so it is of great importance for the human soul whether the body consists of fine or of coarse material. The light shines brighter through a good lamp, and the same trees yield different fruit according to the soil in which they are planted.[970] Non-kosher foods coarsen the body, and thereby cloud the holiness of the soul.

The Jewish people are created to be a pure and holy nation and must, therefore, keep away from impurity more than the other nations. Just as the bulk of the nation may eat all manner of food without ill effects, but if the prince eats coarse food, he will become ill. So too, the Children of Israel are like the prince in that they are holy and noble, and contact with even the smallest impurity may cause them great harm.[971]

---

969   See *Vayikra* [Leviticus] ch. 11 and 20.

970   Rekanti, *Ta'amei HaMitzvos.*

971   Spoken in regards to priestly purity (*Divrei Sha'arei Chaim*, brought in *Ma'ayana Shel Torah*, Emor).

UPLIFTING THE PHYSICAL WORLD

The *Zohar* asserts that "the time of eating is a time of battle."[972] The purpose of the soul in coming to this world is in order to struggle, triumph, and achieve greater refinement and purity through conquering its temptations. Every moment in life is an opportunity to choose the Torah and G-dly path, or instead succumb to bodily passions. The *Zohar* underscores that eating is no exception from this Divine mission. Both *what* the Jew eats, and *how* he eats it, are ever-present battles in which the soul seeks to prevail over the body.

The battle of <u>what</u> to eat:

The Jewish dietary laws are for spiritual health. It is forbidden to eat impure animals because they bring impurity to the soul and can dull spiritual sensitivity.[973] Food has both a physical and spiritual component. The body gains its energy and benefits from

---

972 *Zohar*, 3:272a; see similar in 3:188b.

973 Jewish mysticism, in particular, speaks harshly about the spiritual damage caused by consuming forbidden foods. The following points are brought from different works in Jewish literature to show how serious the matter is treated.

When one eats something that the Torah deems impure, the mystics say that it desensitizes a person from connecting with G-d (See *Yoma* 39a; Rabbeinu Bachya, *Vayikra* 11:43; Shelah, *Sha'ar HaOsios, Kuf- Kedushas HaOchalin*).

Elsewhere it is taught that the heart is defiled from prohibited foods. (See Ramban, *Devarim* 22:30. See Rabbi Tzaddok HaKohen, *Kuntrus Eis HaOchel*. See also Rabbi Yosef Prager, *Pesach Hasha'ar*.)

The spiritually sensitive person should regard non-kosher food as poisoned, as it brings negative energy to the soul (See Shelah, ibid. See also Rabbeinu Bachya, *Shmos* 23:19; *Mesillas Yesharim*, ch. 11; *Shimush Chachamim*, p. 290. In addition, see *Peleh Yoetz*, "*achila u'shesiya*." See also the *Meshech Chochma, Devarim* 6:11. Also Rabbi Tzvi Hirsch of Nadvorna, *Alfa Beisa* "*achila*." See also *Bnei Yissachar, Maggid Ta'aluma* on *Brachos* 32a).

This contamination causes the Jew to lose his sensitivity in apprehending or appreciating anything spiritual, potentially leading down the road of turning away from G-d completely. (See related *Degel Machaneh Ephraim*, Eikev, quoting the Rambam.)

The Chofetz Chaim compares the waning spiritual sensitivity of a Jew eating non-kosher to a perfume store owner who began working in a tannery. Since he ordinarily was used to fine-scented working conditions, at first he struggled in the tannery, regularly getting nauseous and dizzy. As time passed he got used to the foul odor and after a while did not even realize it anymore. The Chofetz Chaim says that the soul is likewise accustomed only to experiencing the spiritual delights. Once the person starts enjoying and getting used to non-kosher foods numbing their G-dly experience, they begin to forget their previous state.

the physical component, while the soul benefits from the spiritual component.[974]

The eighteenth century Talmudist, Rabbi Shmuel Loew, known as the *Machtzis HaShekel*, elaborates. He asks why does the soul remain in the body by virtue of the fact that the person eats food, and why does the soul depart from the body when the body is denied food? How could our spiritual souls connect to our physical bodies? What nourishment does the soul gain from physical food? He answers that food has a spiritual component too.[975]

Thoughts on the Spiritual Component of Eating:

The Psalmist writes, "The heavens belong to Hashem and the Earth was given to man." Rabbi Yitzchak Meir Alter *zt"l*, the first Gerrer Rebbe, known as the *Chiddushei HaRim*, elaborates that the Earth was given to man in order for him to *turn it into* Heaven. Torah, the "blueprint of Creation," reveals what in the world is able to be uplifted, and specifies exactly how to uplift those things. When it comes to food, one only has the ability to uplift that which is kosher and upon which the proper blessing and intent have been performed.

The Torah says, "Not by bread alone does man live, but by the word of Hashem."[976] Everything in Creation is brought into existence by Divine utterance, including food. This Divine spark within food provides nourishment for the soul. When a Jew takes a kosher food and recites the blessing over it, he uplifts that spiritual essence and provides the "nutrition" that the soul needs. This is what it means that "man does not live on bread alone"; rather, the energy that keeps him alive is the G-dly spark hidden within that feeds the soul.[977]

> *Rabbi Shmuel of Lubavitch, the Rebbe Maharash zt"l, had two of his aides accompany him on a trip to Paris. The Maharash requested a room near the casino in the Alexander*

---

974 Cited by the *Magen Avraham*; see Yissachar Dov Rubin, *Sefer Talelei Oros* (2005), vol. 1, pg. 53.

975 See Rubin, ibid.

976 *Devarim* [Deuteronomy] 8:3.

977 See *Sefer HaLikkutim*, Eikev, also brought down in *Ma'ayna Shel Torah*.

Hotel, despite its great expense. Several hours after arriving, he approached a young Jew gambling, and told him, "Young man, yayin nesech (non-kosher wine) is prohibited, and clogs the mind and heart. Be a Jew." With that he returned to his room. Hours later the young man knocked on the Maharash's door and the two had a deep conversation for several hours. The following day, the Rebbe Maharash returned to Lubavitch. Upon his return he told the Chassidim, "For the last generations, the world has not seen such a pure soul. However, the soul had been steeped in the depths of klipah, negative energy…" The young man ended up becoming observant, and from him came many generations of Torah-observant descendants.[978]

The battle of <u>how</u> to eat:

Jewish tradition, and in particular the mystics, stress the further importance of having proper intent when eating kosher food. Every permissible act can be either uplifted to selflessness and holiness, or lowered to selfishness. According to the mystics, only through both eating the proper food, and having the proper intent, does the meal get uplifted to holiness, transforming it from a selfish act of pleasure eating into a vehicle to accomplish the G-dly mission.

When eating the kosher meal purely to satisfy one's natural cravings, the food remains mundane. When, on the other hand, the food is eaten with the intent of using the energy derived from this kosher meal to do more good in the world, the meal becomes a means to bring more light to the world. The meal becomes a spiritual experience, rather than an end in and of itself. Having this selfless intent on a regular basis is a constant struggle between body and soul.

The Talmud says that when the Holy Temple existed, the altar atoned for a person, and that now his table atones for him.[979] In order for his table to truly atone for him, however, he must have an ongoing

---

978   *Sefer HaSichos* 5705, pg. 28.

979   *Chagigah* 27a. This is one of the reasons for having salt on the table, and used with bread, for salt accompanied sacrifices (see *Vayikra* [Leviticus] 2:13).

keen awareness that he is eating for the sake of Heaven. Eating a meal, according to Judaism, is no easy task. The *Zohar* describes it as an outright war between the physical and the spiritual within. It has been said that it is easier to study an entire tractate of Talmud than to eat a single meal. The goal is not only to eat the foods prescribed by the Torah, but to eat them with the intent of harnessing that pure energy for the mission that the Torah lays out for this world.

It is no coincidence that the first command directed to mankind involved eating. The Torah speaks of the "Tree of Life" and the "Tree of Knowledge." The Tree of Life represents communion with G-d, whereas the Tree of Knowledge represents the experience of self-awareness. G-d tells Adam that he may eat of all of the trees of the garden except for the Tree of Knowledge.[980] From a Kabbalistic perspective, all of the trees in the garden had the potential to be Trees of Life, a G-dly experience, or Trees of Knowledge, a consciousness of self.[981] The Chassidic masters relate that this was the inner meaning of the challenge of Adam, and the challenge that every individual faces as well. Judaism does not set its goal on an ascetic lifestyle, but instead seeks that humanity infuse their mundane activities with holiness, direction, and purpose.

MYSTICAL SYMBOLISM IN KOSHER FOOD

Everything in the physical world has a corresponding spiritual energy that it parallels, symbolizes, or embodies. When looking at food with fleshly eyes, all that can be perceived is the superficial, tangible, and material entity. When gazing through the lens of the Torah, one can at least envision the inner, ethereal, and spiritual energy that the food embodies. In this light, one gains a glimpse into the symbolism represented by each category of kosher food law.

Kosher land animals must have both signs: split hooves and chews its cud. These *two* signs, of hooves split in *two* and *multiple* digestions, allude to multiplicity, as opposed to singularity. This is because kosher

---

980   *Bereishis* [Genesis] 2:9 and further.
981   Rabbi Tzadok HaKohen, *Pri Tzaddik, Bereishis* 8.

food has a *dual* nature and purpose, a physical benefit and a corresponding spiritual benefit. Forbidden foods, which lack one of the two, can only satisfy the physical cravings.[982]

Fish must also have this multiplicity: *two* signs—fins and scales. Torah is compared to water. The fins that navigate the fish remind a person to navigate through the wisdom of the Torah. The scales are the coat or protection given to all of those that carry out the mitzvos.[983]

The distinct energies unique to meat and milk respectively go against the Divine order of Creation when put together. Meat, which comes through the killing of an animal, and is red in color, embodies the Divine attribute of "harshness." Milk, which is gained only through a living animal, expressive of motherly benevolence, and white in color, which is connected with purity, embodies the Divine attribute of "mercy." These two physical manifestations of completely opposite spiritual energies can never mix.[984]

This is just a sampling of the enormous insight that can be gleaned from these miniature representations of the spiritual realms.

CONTEMPORARY PERSPECTIVE

PKU: A MEDICAL MODEL OF KASHRUS?

The Jewish soul is sensitive to the harmful spiritual effects of forbidden animals. The sages have written that the dietary laws, which are designated specifically for Jews, are likened to a doctor who gives out two different prescriptions for two patients who report the exact same symptoms. The doctor can diagnose what is best for them by examining their makeup, and what is most beneficial for their bodies. To the patients, upon superficial examination it may appear entirely similar, yet the doctor can see a more accurate picture. In this case, the doctor is Hashem who prescribes which diet is tolerable for each soul.[985]

---

982   *Ir Giborim*, cited by *Ohr Hatorah, Vayikra* 1:45.
983   *Ma'amurei Admur Hazaken, Inyanim*, pg. 130.
984   *Shulchan Hatahor* 321.
985   See similar in Rabbeinu Bachya, Shemini.

In Chassidic thought, everything in the spiritual world has a counterpart in the physical. This permits thought for the existence of spiritual molecules based on the knowledge of chemical structures. In other words, the molecules studied in chemistry could be thought of as the reflection of the intangible spiritual molecules the Creator used as a blueprint. Based on this, Dr. Velvl Greene provides an answer to those who reject *kashrus* because they lack empirical proof.

There is a medical condition called phenolketoneuria or PKU. It is a hereditary metabolic disorder affecting about one out of 15,000 children born in the Northern Hemisphere and leads to an irreversible and severe retardation.

The newborn child appears healthy and normal. He cannot really be distinguished during a routine physical examination from his 14,999 unaffected peers. Over the course of several years he develops a characteristic appearance and brain damage.

After a while, physiologists determined that the brain damage was a result of the accumulation in the body of phenylalanine. Normal people have the ability to metabolize phenylalanine and to convert it to other, non-harmful nutrients. But one child in 15,000 lacks the necessary enzyme and the phenylalanine accumulates until it harms the developing brain.

Around fifty years ago, American bacteriologist Robert Guthrie devised a blood test that permits the early diagnosis of PKU within a few days after birth. This test is now compulsory in most Western countries. Every baby born in a hospital is tested for PKU. If the results suggest that the condition is present, the mother is provided with nutritional advice and counseling. If the diet is modified early enough, if the phenylalanine-containing protein is replaced with a synthetic substitute and fed for the first four or five years, the retardation can usually be avoided. The solution is not simple. It is also inconvenient, unappetizing and expensive. But, it is effective.

Now consider the following scenario: a public health nurse visits a young mother who has just come home from the hospital with her precious newborn baby. The nurse conveys the frightening news that according to the lab tests the baby has PKU. She also provides the mother with a list of prescribed foods and instructions for preparing a suitable preventive diet.

Neither the nurse nor the mother is a chemist. The mother knows nothing about molecules or physiology or metabolism. She knows what she sees: a healthy, normal baby, like any other baby in the world, who enjoys eating and is apparently thriving on the diet being provided. The nurse knows a little more. She has studied a little chemistry and understands the best physiology of metabolism. Or at least she believes the teachers who taught her. The nurse doesn't really know the basis of the diagnostic tests, nor could she prescribe a diet out of her own experience. All she is doing is her job of transmitting the information she was taught. She believes she is acting in the best interests of the child and the community. But she is mostly acting out of duty and acceptance of higher authorities—such as doctors, chemists and nutritionists—who have studied more and know more and have better sources of knowledge.

The mother refuses to accept the diagnosis or the diet. She does not believe in the mysteries of chemistry or accept the authority of the doctors. Her baby looks normal and happy. Besides, the recommended diet is too expensive and inconvenient and unappetizing. What is all this nonsense about molecules anyway?

What could one tell the mother who demands, "Show me the danger now! Show me the difference between my baby and all the others!"?[986]

CONCLUSION

In essence, although the Jewish dietary laws are categorized as a command that transcends logic, the human mind can still get a glimpse of at least some of the benefits and meaning inherent in these laws. Through even brief investigation into the writings of the sages, it becomes evident that physical well-being is not at all the driving force. Instead, the Jewish dietary laws seek to prevent evil traits from

---

986   Example extracted and partially quoted from V. Greene, "Speculations on Kashrut," *B'Or HaTorah*, vol. 6 (1987), pgs. 159–164. Printed with permission.

becoming part of the Jew, and as the mystics stress, keeping away from spiritually detrimental energy.

For the one who is new to kosher observance, there is no need to jump into everything at once. Judaism is about progress, not perfection—climbing step by step, on the proverbial ladder of spiritual growth. Every step one does toward enhanced *kashrus* observance enhances his connection with Jewish tradition and with G-d.

THE SABBATH DAY
THE DESPERATELY NEEDED DAY

S habbos, the Sabbath day, is considered a pillar of the Jewish faith.[987] It has been described as an "island in time," a chance to recharge spiritual vigor. Throughout the week, our attention is focused on business affairs, toiling to make a living and provide for the family. Once a week, there is an opportunity to refocus on who we are and what is really important in life.

At first glance it seems like the Sabbath is merely a good idea—an opportunity to rest up and recharge physically and spiritually. While these aspects are certainly a part of the package, the Sabbath plays one of the most central roles in the Jewish faith, and is in fact even one of the Ten Commandments. Why the centrality of this day? Why is a mere "day off" an obligation at all, and given prominence and stature in no less a place than the Ten Commandments? Why not simply take a rest day when one gets tired or overburdened?

---

987   See *Yerushalmi*, *Nedarim* 3:14 where it is compared to fulfilling all of the commandments of the Torah. Through Sabbath observance, the Jew testifies that G-d created the world in six days, which is a core principle of Judaism. See also *Zohar*, Beshalach 47:1, 2. Another related idea is that in the ancient pagan cultures, the people assigned names of gods to the days of the week: Sunday for the sun, Monday for the moon, and so forth. In Judaism, the other days of the week do not have unique names, just the first day [until Sabbath], the second day [until Sabbath], etc. The focus of everything revolves around the Sabbath; see Ramban, *Shmos* 20:23.

THE SABBATH IS RATIONALLY PLEASING

The concept of "work" is a fascinating paradox. On the one hand it represents freedom, in that the ability to work gives people feelings of dignity and accomplishment. It is a way of expressing one's self and revealing innate talents, and waking up with a purpose can give a person definition and galvanize him to accomplish many great achievements. It is for this reason that people who do not necessarily need money continue keeping a job, and why many refuse to retire. On the other hand, it is also easy for one to become a slave to his job, making work the center of his life or his main identity. For the sake of physical, emotional, psychological, and spiritual health, balance in this area is essential.

Taking a break to regroup and refocus is of utmost importance in maintaining this balance. In modern society it is becoming seemingly more and more difficult to actually do this. He left work, but work did not leave him. Because of cell phones, email, and Internet, it is almost impossible to disconnect. Even when trying to take a break, life and work trail behind. It has become possible to leave a vacation not feeling refreshed. He never really rebooted; he just changed locations.

Professor Henri Baruk was a French psychiatrist and director at L'Ecole Pratique des Hautes Etudes, Sorbonne, University of Paris, and a member of the National Academy of Medicine in Paris. He once remarked that the Jewish Sabbath is truly beneficial, even on a practical level. He said, "The modern people are slaves of work, and of pleasure—people incapable of stopping for one single day to think. They believe themselves obligated, on the day of rest, to exhaust themselves with their automobiles and are the slaves of annual vacations, often returning from them ill. Such vacations may represent for many a goal of the whole year, but medically and psychologically, they are less beneficial than the weekly repose of the Sabbath."[988] Speaking from a purely secular vantage point, German historian of medicine Karl Sudhoff once said, "Had Judaism given nothing more to mankind than the establishment of a

---

988   Cited from Baruch Litvin and edited by Sidney Hoenig, *Jewish Identity: Modern Responsa and Opinions* (1965).

weekly day of rest, we should still be forced to proclaim her one of the greatest benefactors of humanity."[989]

This is also a recurring theme in a book by former Senator Joe Lieberman. A Sabbath observant Jew, Senator Lieberman wrote, "... In our harried and meaning-starved culture [the Sabbath] cries out to be rediscovered and enjoyed." He eloquently adds that the purpose of the day is not, as one may think, "to recharge our batteries so we can work harder," but instead "to recharge our souls so we can live better."[990]

ONE OF THE TEN COMMANDMENTS

The Ten Commandments are the fundamental principles of Jewish living. On the two stone tablets of the Ten Commandments, the mandates that had similar themes were grouped together. The first five commandments refer to the relationship between man and G-d, and the second five to the relationship between man and man.[991] Observing and remembering the Sabbath day is the fourth of the Ten Commandments, immediately following the prohibitions of idol worship and blasphemy. Because of its placement, we learn that Sabbath observance plays a pivotal role in our relationship with G-d. How so?

The Ten Commandments are actually mentioned twice in the Torah; once in the book of Exodus, and then reviewed in the book of Deuteronomy. In both of these times the Torah offers an added dimension to their observance. In the Exodus rendition the Torah calls the Sabbath holy because G-d *created the world in six days and rested on the seventh.*[992] In the repetition of the Ten Commandments in Deuteronomy, the Sabbath is to be observed to recall the fact that G-d *took the Jewish people out of slavery in Egypt.*[993]

Both of these reasons are true. The Sabbath attests to belief in G-d

---

989   See Ari Ben-Menahem, *Historical Encyclopedia of Natural and Mathematical Sciences*, Vol. 1 (2009), pg. 852.

990   Joseph Lieberman, *The Gift of Rest* (2001), pg. 221.

991   The commandments on each tablet actually correspond to those of the other. There is a correlation between each command from the G-d-man stone, and the one of similar position on the man to man stone, see *Shir HaShirim Rabbah* 4:5.

992   *Shmos* [Exodus] 20:11.

993   *Devarim* [Deuteronomy] 5:15.

and the pattern He set when creating the world, and also recalls that He redeemed the Jewish people from slavery in Egypt, where they were forced to work without taking rests. There is a lesson being etched into the psyche of the Jewish people by writing both reasons for Sabbath observance; the second principle is a continuation of the first. Not only did G-d create the world in six days, but He is also very much involved in our lives.[994] He took us out of Egypt and continues to oversee and interact with His Creation. Therefore, weekly Sabbath observance refreshes our faith, instilling within us that G-d is an active part in our lives.[995]

SABBATH OBSERVANCE IS LIVING JUDAISM

The Sabbath has such centrality in Judaism because its observance in deed is the embodiment of what our faith is based upon. Both the idea of G-d creating the world, and His involvement in human affairs, are cornerstones of the Jewish faith. One who denies either of these axioms is out of sync with the Jewish concept of G-d. Sabbath observance brings these theological concepts into action. It is not enough that faith remains a philosophical idea—something that we pay lip service to. The principles of Judaism must be lived.

When a Jew keeps the Sabbath, G-d remains an ingrained part in his life. His faith remains strong, because the Sabbath is something that he not only believes in but also lives, and with this secure faith he can better endure life's most grueling challenges. This spiritual fortitude to combat adversity has helped the Jewish people both on an individual and national scale. It has been said that "more than the Jew keeps the Sabbath, the Sabbath keeps the Jew." The Sabbath has preserved the richness of Jewish identity and spiritual growth. No matter what country the Jews found themselves in, or what kind of social pressures they were under, they always had their "island in time" to reinforce their beliefs in a tangible way. The need for contemporary Jewish people to experience an authentic Sabbath is of paramount

---

994   See *Kuzari* 1:1,2.
995   Rambam, *Moreh Nevuchim* 2:31.

importance. Harnessing and further strengthening Jewish spiritual passion in the coming generations will also largely depend upon how centrally Sabbath observance is portrayed.

THE NATURE OF SABBATH REST

On the Sabbath one rests from doing—and even thinking about—any forbidden labors. Even with a stack of important papers or bills sprawled across the desk and an Inbox full of messages that must be addressed, one should just allow himself to feel that all the work is done.[996]

THE DAY OF THE SOUL

The Sabbath is not only a time of rest from the physical world, but a day to actively engage in higher matters. It is a day to enjoy time with family and friends without all of the worldly distractions. It is a time to reflect on relationships with others, with G-d, and reestablish commitment to a purpose-driven life. For this reason, Rabbi Dov Ber, the Maggid of Mezritch zt"l, used to say that the word "Shabbos" is related to the Hebrew world *shov*, to return, as it is an opportunity to remove from one's mind all worldly concerns and return and reclaim the self. In any area where a person may have veered from the path during the previous week, the Sabbath is the time for realignment. The *Zohar*, the seminal work of Jewish mysticism, refers to Sabbath as *yoma d'nishmasa*, the day of the soul.[997] Rabbi Dovber Schneuri, the Mitteler Rebbe of Lubavitch zt"l, explained that a professor testified that there is a great change even in the pulse of a Jew on the Sabbath, due to the great pleasure that the soul is experiencing.[998] The face of a Jew is different on the Sabbath than during the week.[999] On this day every week, the Jewish people are given the opportunity to tear

---

996 See *Gur Aryeh* on *Bamidbar* 15:32.
997 *Zohar* 2:205a; *Bnei Yissachar*, Shabbosos 5:1.
998 See *Toras Chaim*, *Shmos* א:תרלב
999 See *Bereishis Rabbah* 11:2; *Tiferes Yisrael*, ch. 40. There is a story that echoes this theme in *Alei Shur*, vol. 2, pg. 382. Reb Eliyahu Lopian told how the Alter of Kelm always looked pale during the week, but had reddened cheeks on Sabbath.

down any spiritual blockages that hinder their connection with the Divine.[1000]

There is a different energy present in the air on the Sabbath than there is during the week. It is for this reason that the Jewish mystics describe the Sabbath as being on a higher plane of existence.[1001] The Sabbath is different in many ways, as we will see.

DEFINING "WORK"

Different people have different personal definitions of what the terms "rest" and "work" mean to them. The Torah, on the other hand, has very specific definitions as to what the nature of Sabbath rest from work is meant to be. Many newcomers to Jewish observance are initially confused when learning about the details of the Sabbath work restrictions. Things that are seemingly effortless actions, like writing a note or turning on a lamp, are deemed Sabbath prohibitions. These minor tasks hardly seem like work. The meaning of work, as it relates to the Sabbath, must be clarified.

Sabbath observance commemorates G-d creating the world in six days and resting on the seventh. Obviously G-d does not need a break from all of His exertion, so what then is the nature of this "rest" that He took? The answer is that G-d rested from creating. The previous six days He exerted His creative abilities and mastery over the world by speaking different entities into being. This is described at the beginning of the Torah, when each day G-d says, "Let there be such and such." On the seventh day He ceased from doing so, i.e., He ceased from creating. In effect, by ceasing to create anymore, G-d created the concept of rest.[1002]

1000 This fact is alluded to in that the word Shabbos is related to the word *shavas*, "to cease or tear down." See *Ma'amarei Hashabbosos* 41:1.

1001 Chassidic thought explains that the G-dly energy that sustains the world on the Sabbath is loftier than the weekday. This is because it comes from Divine thought as opposed to Divine speech, as the Torah describes G-d refraining from creating [through speech] on the Sabbath. Because of this more refined energy, it is easier to perceive the Divine in the world on the Sabbath; see *Sefer HaSichos* 5751, vol. 2, pg. 551. Elsewhere, the holiness of the Sabbath is compared to standing in the inner chamber of the king, whereas the weekday is standing outside of this area; see *Likkutei Sichos*, vol. 33, pg. 143.

1002 See *Bereishis Rabbah* 10:10.

Our Sabbath parallels G-d's resignation from the creative process. The "work" referred to is creative work, or certain labors that demonstrate stewardship over the world. Sabbath rest, then, is relinquishing any involvement in those types of tasks. Classifying something as work is not assessed by the amount of sweat that drips from the brow; it is whether this action, even in the minutest way, is a creative change or shows human mastery over nature. Refraining from these acts, in even the most minor manifestations, opens one up to be a conduit to experience the energy of harmony and tranquility that G-d made available during this day.

THE THIRTY-NINE GENERAL LABORS

The Torah writes that when the Jewish people were making their way through the wilderness they were instructed by G-d to build the Tabernacle. The Tabernacle was a precursor to the Holy Temple that would later be built in the Land of Israel. It functioned as a place of communion with the Divine. Although it was a physical structure with physical boundaries, it emanated the presence of G-d. Within its walls, G-dliness was most palpable and expressed most strongly.

The Torah elaborates in great detail as to how the infrastructure and utensils of the Tabernacle should be crafted. Despite the great holiness and necessity of the Tabernacle's construction, just prior to building, G-d reiterated to the Jewish people the importance of the Sabbath day. They were told that on the Sabbath they must abstain from even the slightest effort toward its construction.

The Talmud enumerates thirty-nine general categories of labors that went into the construction of the Tabernacle.[1003] These are the archetypal labors that must be refrained from on the Sabbath. All manifestations of these thirty-nine general labors make up the parameters for what is acceptable and unacceptable for the Sabbath today. Along with these general labors are rabbinic "fences" to prevent indirectly causing these labors, moving objects that are linked to them, and not invoking the assistance of a non-Jew to perform them. These safeguards were

---

1003 The analysis is found mostly in tractate *Shabbos*.

enacted to preserve the sanctity of the day. Each of the thirty-nine categories has sub-categories of labors that produce the same results and are, therefore, forbidden as well. The thirty-nine labors that are enumerated in the Mishnah are as follows:[1004]

1. Sowing
2. Plowing
3. Reaping
4. Binding sheaves
5. Threshing
6. Winnowing
7. Selecting
8. Grinding
9. Sifting
10. Kneading
11. Baking
12. Shearing
13. Cleaning
14. Combing
15. Dyeing
16. Spinning
17. Stretching the threads
18. The making of two meshes
19. Weaving two threads
20. Separating two threads
21. Tying a knot
22. Untying a knot
23. Sewing
24. Tearing
25. Capturing animals
26. Slaughtering
27. Skinning
28. Salting
29. Tanning hide

1004 *Shabbos* 7:2 (73a).

30. Scraping
31. Cutting
32. Writing
33. Erasing
34. Building
35. Demolishing
36. Extinguishing fire
37. Kindling fire
38. Giving something its finishing touch
39. Carrying in a public domain, or between private and public domains

Based on these archetypes it also becomes easy to assess if a new invention or technology is Sabbath-appropriate. One example of this is flicking on a light switch. True, these modern conveniences did not exist in the times of the Talmud, yet the underlying labors that they execute certainly were. Turning on an electric lamp falls into several categories from the abovementioned list. For example: kindling a fire—whether with actual sparks that come about or the fact that fire and electricity both create light and heat and thus share being prohibited. Although it takes no real exertion to switch on a light, one does create a complete circuit, which is an entirely new entity. This brief explanation hardly gives justice to the ruling, yet highlights how there are very clear modern-day applications to the Sabbath laws.

Furthermore, we must also view these seemingly minor tasks in the grand scheme of Sabbath purpose. The Sabbath is not primarily about physical rest. It is about entering a different state of mind and state of being that transcends the weekdays. During the week, we alter our surroundings; on the Sabbath we simply enjoy them. We temporarily exchange the creative conveniences that technology has given us and instead bask in the blessings that G-d has given us. Even the most minor of creative tasks, like turning on a light switch, disturb this unity and keep us tied to our physical amenities.

There is a link between our modern Sabbath observance and the labors performed in the Tabernacle. The Tabernacle, the place where the

Divine presence was most clearly revealed, is a microcosm for all of Creation.[1005] The world is our Tabernacle. When a Jew embarks on his tasks during the week, he is meant to elevate the world around him, making the physical world a conduit for the spiritual. During the week we construct our portion of the Tabernacle by impacting our circle of influence. Collectively, we transform the world.

When one builds or is creating in the world around, he loses focus on building or creating himself as an individual. When he puts the external creative opportunities on hold, he is granted the ability to look inward. In this sense, the thirty-nine labor restrictions of the Sabbath ironically enable him to have genuine liberation. True freedom of self is spiritual growth that fosters the achievement of one's potential. Eric Fromm, one of the most influential psychologists and scholars in Western philosophy, wrote:

> The Sabbath is a day of truce in the human battle with the world. Even tearing up a blade of grass is looked upon as a breach of this harmony, as is lighting a match... On the Sabbath one lives as if one has nothing, pursuing no aim except being, that is, expressing one's essential powers: praying, studying, eating, drinking, and singing. The Sabbath is a day of joy because on that day one is fully oneself.
>
> This is the reason the Talmud calls a Sabbath the anticipation of the messianic time, and the messianic time the unending Sabbath: the day on which property and money as well as mourning and sadness are taboo; a day on which time is defeated and pure being rules...One might ask if it is not time to re-establish the Sabbath as a universal day of harmony and peace, as the human day that anticipates the human future.[1006]

1005 See *Zohar* 2:162b.

1006 Eric Fromm, "To Have or To Be?" *Bloomsbury Academic* (2013), pgs. 43-44. Original published in 1976. The idea to incorporate this quote was gleaned from Nathan Cardozo, *Between Silence and Speech.*

THE SABBATH MEALS

The Sabbath meal experience is something lacking in a large segment of our society. The result of integrating it into one's life can have untold benefit. Even in purely physical terms, detached from any spiritual or religious implications, the Sabbath meals can be invaluable to having an enhanced personal and family life.

THE IMPACT OF FAMILY MEALS

Countless studies reveal the benefits of simply eating together and spending time with other members of the family or close friends. The National Center on Addiction and Substance Abuse at Columbia University has time and again shown a strong correlation between children eating dinner with family and overall well-being. The studies from varying years show that the more family meals that children attend per week, the less likely they are to smoke, drink, and use illegal drugs. They are also significantly more likely to be emotionally well-adjusted and to do well both academically and socially.

In 1997, a study by psychologists Blake Bowden and Jennifer Zeisz of De Paul University in Chicago also confirmed that meals, more than any other factor, served as a marker across ages and gender lines for perpetuating emotional health. It goes without saying that the positive results are exponentially enhanced when there is no television or other distractions present at the table.[1007]

Dr. Margaret Chesney, director of the Osher Center for Integrative Medicine at the UCSF School of Medicine, also says that those families that have religious practices or are highly spiritual likewise nurture these same positive results of well-being.[1008]

Family meals also can be an expression of the cultural or religious heritage of a family.[1009] By participating in these meals, everyone present strengthens their connection with their cultural or religious heritage. Interestingly, a study from Emory University found that

---

1007   Both of these studies can be found in Regan McMahon, *Revolution in the Bleachers* (2007).

1008   Joseph Califano, *How to Raise a Drug-Free Kid: The Straight Dope for Parents* (2009), pg. 18.

1009   See Miriam Weinstein, *The Surprising Power of Family Meals* (2005).

those who regularly participated in family meals that centered on religious or cultural celebrations had a closer relationship to family members, higher self-esteem, and a greater sense of control over their own lives.[1010]

Consider, then, the power of all of these factors combined: eating together, without a television, phones, or iPods, and in a religious or spiritual environment. The sum total of all of these positive effects on well-being are the most basic and practical gains that the Sabbath meal provides. With the addition of the spiritual element, the effect of the Sabbath meal is evermore lasting and impacting, satisfying not only the physical and emotional needs of the person, but also providing spiritual contentment.

THE MEALS INSTILL FAITH

The Jewish people are enjoined to "call the Sabbath a delight."[1011] This delight is brought about through the eating and camaraderie of the three Sabbath meals. Surrounded with family and song, the elegant table is set with one's finest utensils and a lavish display of food. Each part of the Sabbath meal possesses many layers of symbolic and esoteric meaning that naturally help to solidify the faith in those who take part in them.

The *Kiddush*, sanctification on wine, is recited as wine is a traditional symbol of a festive occasion.[1012] The hands are then washed and the *challah* is cut and eaten. The two *challah* rolls that are cut are reminders of the miracle of the manna that G-d sustained the Jewish nation with for forty years in the desert. It reminds us that there was always a double portion that fell on Friday, so it would not have to come on the Sabbath.[1013]

There is a ubiquitous custom to eat fish and later to eat meat. Fish

---

1010 M. P. Duke, R. Fivush, A. Lazarus, & J. Bohanek, "Of Ketchup and Kin: Dinnertime Conversations as a Major Source of Family Knowledge, Family Adjustment, and Family Resilience" (2003) (Working Paper #26).

1011 *Yeshayahu* [Isaiah] 58:13.

1012 *Sefer HaChinuch* 31. See also *Pesachim* 106a.

1013 *Shmos* [Exodus] 16:22; *Shabbos* 117b.

comes first because the Sabbath is a celebration of Creation. Since in the Torah's Creation account fish were created before the other animals, it comes first.[1014] There is a custom to have soup after the fish as the Talmud says that that a meal without soup is not really a meal.[1015] This is then followed by the meat. Meat is a food that typically brings physical satisfaction and enjoyment, and therefore, a perfect food for the Sabbath.[1016]

INNER MEANING OF THE SABBATH FOODS

Nothing is arbitrary or by happenstance in Jewish tradition. Right down to the very foods that are eaten on the Sabbath, everything in Judaism has meaning.

In the Kabbalistic tradition, *gematria,* or numerology, is used to gain insight into the essence of words and concepts and see how they relate to one another. Words or phrases that share numeric values often contain an essential similarity as well.

There are a variety of different numerology systems that are used. The Jewish mystics call one such system *mispar katan mispari,* which means the integral reduced value. In this system, the total value of a word is reduced to a single digit. If the sum of a word is more than nine, then the individual numbers in the total are added together again until reaching a single digit number. For example, the word חסד—*chesed* (kindness) has a normative numerological value of 72. The ח=8, ס=60, ד=4. The numbers of the sum of 72 are then added together 7 + 2 and brought to a single digit, 9.

The Vilna Gaon uses this method of *gematria* to reveal a fascinating insight about the items present on a traditional Sabbath table. He writes that everything connected with the traditional Sabbath table

---

1014 The Jewish mystics point out a more esoteric meaning in the order, explaining that the spiritual refinement of fish is easier, and this gives the power to refine the meat; see *Kaf Hachaim* 157:38. See also *Likkutei Torah* (Behaloscha 33b), which discusses how fish represent *alma deiskasya* [hidden (spiritual) world] and meat represents the *alma deisgaliya* [revealed world]. See also *Mamarei Admur Hazaken* 5563, vol. 2, pg. 790.

1015 See *Brachos* 44a.

1016 Although it is not a requirement per se, see *Shulchan Aruch HaRav* 242:1-2.

adds up to the number 7, symbolizing an intrinsic connection with the Sabbath, the seventh day. Thus:[1017]

Item (Eng)	Item (Heb)	Numeric Equation	Gematria	Sum Digit
Candle	נר	50+200	=250	2+5+0=7
Wine	יין	10+10+50	=70	7+0=7
Challah	חלה	8+30+5	=43	4+3=7
Fish	דג	4+3	=7	=7
Meat	בשר	200+300+2	=502	5+0+2=7

It becomes apparent that there is a lot more to the Sabbath meal than may meet the eye. Each of the pieces of the traditional Sabbath table is meant to be there, and the mystics give great esoteric meaning to each and every food traditionally upon it.[1018] The more one embraces the depth within each meal, the more one opens up to that special energy present on the Sabbath day and reaps its benefits.

CONCLUSION

Fully observing the Sabbath day is both necessary and beneficial, satisfying the broad spectrum of human needs. It is the time to rest physically, regroup emotionally, engage intellectually, and grow spiritually. It is the way in which the Jewish person maintains balance within himself, with his family and fellow man, with nature, and with G-d. Embracing and enhancing diligence in Sabbath observance will only lead to a better self, better family life, and better world.

1017 Chart is based on Michael Munk, *The Wisdom of the Hebrew Alphabet* (1983), pg. 111.

1018 All of the Sabbath foods are given tremendous mystical significance in Chassidic texts. Among all of the foods, kugel is mentioned in numerous places. The following is a sampling of its importance: The Chozeh of Lublin taught that just as one's merits and transgressions are weighed on the balance in our final judgment, so too they weigh all of the kugel that one ate in honor of the Sabbath (Hayim Grunfeld, *Sefer Pardes Hamelech* [Ruzhin-Sadigura] [Manchester: privately published, 1999], pg. 445). The Sabbath foods hint at the ten Supernal Attributes, the *sefirot*; see, for example, "Eating kugel symbolizes the *sefira* of Yesod." See *Mismeres Shalom*, Warsaw, 40b.

THE WORLD TO COME

What does Judaism believe about the soul? Is there any logical reason why one should believe in a soul? Is there any scientific evidence of a soul? What happens in the hereafter? What is the Jewish concept of the Messiah? Are we approaching the messianic era? How do we know? Can a contemporary person believe that there will be a physical resurrection, and that the dead will once again live?

Let's begin to explore.

REASONABLE APPROACH TO THE SOUL AND AFTERLIFE

In conjunction with belief in G-d, one of the foundations of Judaism is a belief in the immortality of the soul and an afterlife. This is a logical necessity for one who believes in Divine justice, as it resolves the apparent suffering of the righteous, or in common vernacular, why bad things happen to good people. The written Torah, being the outline of Jewish tradition and an instruction manual for *this* world, does not mention outright the details of immortality and the afterlife.[1019]

RATIONAL APPROACH TO THE SOUL

Definite knowledge of the soul and its immortality cannot be achieved in this world, as this would eliminate free choice and reward and punishment, which are fundamentals of Judaism and the purpose of Creation. However, there is good cause to believe that man is a dualistic combination of physical and spiritual, that man has a unique soul, and that it continues on after the demise of the physical body.

CONSCIOUSNESS

Before elaborating upon the idea of the soul, it is important to note that even the idea of full human consciousness is a scientific enigma. Human consciousness has been referred to as "one of the greatest of

---

1019 The Written Torah is not abstract or esoteric; it is pragmatic and intended for the many. It speaks to the average person who identifies with physical rewards, on a very basic level, with rewards that are verifiable; see Miller, *Rejoice O Youth*, pg. 215. See also *Kli Yakar* to *Vayikra* 26:12.

miracles."[1020] Its emergence and the growing complexity of the brain are irreconcilable with the naturalistic world perspective.[1021] Evolutionary theory holds that only those structures and processes that significantly aid in survival are developed in natural selection. What survival value or effects could consciousness have? What does consciousness have that neural signals and physical brain activity do not have?

Nobel Laureate neurophysiologist Sir John Eccles suggested that many of the scientific theories of human nature and development of consciousness denigrate the value of humanity. He calls the contemporary theory of evolution "defective" in this regard. He says, "It is of

---

1020 Karl Popper and John Eccles, *The Self and Its Brain* (1977), pg. 129.

1021 "If it is assumed that consciousness is a property of complex systems such as the human brain, and that such complex entities evolved much after the initial state of the universe, then consciousness was not present in the universe at its origin, or even near its origin. Therefore it follows that consciousness evolved from what was not conscious.

"However, even if consciousness is a physical property which could perhaps have emerged as the result of a random mutation in an evolved being, it would only become a property of an entire race if it gave its possessor a selective evolutionary advantage. To do so, however, it must be able to affect physical events. Therefore, if it is assumed that all humans are conscious, the very existence of consciousness in humans indicates that it must be able to affect the brain, to be a factor in the decision-making processes of the brain. This however is highly problematic, and is part of what is called in philosophy 'the mind-body problem.'

"If consciousness does interact with the physical universe in a way that provides conscious beings with an evolutionary advantage, somehow a conscious brain, using the same information, memory and so on that is available to a physically equivalent non-conscious brain, can arrive at a more survival-appropriate decision, and act on it. This, however, would mean that given the same physical conditions, information and so on, the physical output—action, behavior and so on—is different for a conscious and a non-conscious brain.

"However, if consciousness emerged into existence when brains reached a certain level of complexity, then consciousness must have evolved. But if consciousness is a qualitative phenomenon it cannot evolve unless it can interact with the physical universe. (It is also not clear why consciousness, which is non-physical, should be dependent on the complexity of the brain, which is physical; that is, how a physical—albeit higher-level—property such as complexity of interactions can motivate the emergence of a non-physical phenomenon.) Furthermore, the problem represented by the supposition that consciousness evolved is present as well in the supposition that conscious people originate in sperm and eggs which are non-conscious." Avi Rabinowitz, *The Retroactive Universe: Quantum Kabbalistic Cosmology & the Meaning and Purpose of Life—Mind, Free Will & the Garden of Eden* (1993).

the greatest importance to science that there be from time to time a critical examination of established theories, particularly when they tend to harden into dogmas. The amazing success of the theory of evolution has protected it from significant critical evaluation in recent times. However it fails in a most important respect. It cannot account for each one of us as unique self-conscious beings."[1022]

He further writes that "a complete theory of evolution must account for the emergence of consciousness. Since consciousness is the most complex phenomenon, and of an entirely different qualitative level than any other phenomenon, the theory that can account for it will presumably be far more sophisticated than the present-day origin theory. As consciousness involves elements of self-reference and holism, [and] is the source of subjectivity and crosses the mind-body divide, presumably the theory of it will do so as well. As such the complete origin theory will possibly take on features more reminiscent of some of the underlying themes of the Eden account."[1023]

WHERE IS THE "REAL" YOU?

When describing the soul, it must be made clear that it is distinct from the human mental capacity, as that it is only a single facet of the general human spirit. Neurobiology has revealed an ethereal mind that transcends the physical brain, supporting the idea of a soul.[1024] Acclaimed philosopher of science, Sir Karl Raimund Popper, put it this way, "I intend to suggest that the brain is owned by the self."[1025]

Consider your reflection in the mirror. The current image of yourself is different than your fifteen-year-old self or your five-year-old self, and also very different than what your eighty- or ninety-year-old self

---

1022   Quoting from Rabinowitz, ibid.

1023   See John C. Eccles and Daniel Robinson, *The Wonder of Being Human: Our Brain and Our Mind* (1984), pgs. 36–37. See also Richard L. Gregory, "Consciousness," *The Encyclopaedia of Ignorance* (1977), pgs. 273–281; paragraph quoted from Avi Rabinowitz, "Directed Evolution (A weak form of ID) & Possible Convergence of the Scientific and Spiritual Descriptions of the Universe," files.nyu.edu/air1/public/scirelig.htm.

1024   Wilder Penfield, *The Mystery of the Mind* (1975).

1025   *The Self and Its Brain* (1985). See also Gilbert Ryle's *The Concept of the Mind*, who calls the mind (not the brain) the "ghost in the machine."

will look like. Which one is the real you? Moreover, the vast majority of the cells in the body are constantly replenishing themselves, so over the course of several years you actually *are* a physically different person, in a manner of speaking.[1026] You also feel and think very differently at the moment than you did when you were fifteen or five, and will likewise feel and think differently when you are eighty or ninety. This means that a person is different emotionally and intellectually as well. The human being is perpetually changing—physically, emotionally, intellectually—which begs the question, "Where is the *real* you?" Is it your current self? How about your childhood self? Perhaps it is your elderly self? Where is the consistency or permanence that remains the same throughout life? Where is that essence or core?

There is no part or aspect of the physical human being, neither bone nor organ or limb, that can be pinpointed as the true self. There must then be an essential self, a unified animating force of all bodily capabilities, an ethereal source of thoughts, feelings, and willpower, a core of the human experience and being. The soul is the "spiritual self," the real "I" that inhabits the body and that operates through it.

The soul is the enigmatic human behind the human. The *Zohar* explains likewise: "Concerning the creation of the human it is written, 'You have clothed me with skin and flesh.' What, then, is the human— merely skin, flesh, bones, and sinews? No, the essence of the human is the soul; the skin, flesh, bones, and sinews are only a superficial covering, like garments, but they are not the human."[1027]

BEYOND PHYSICAL PLEASURES

Logically, only a non-corporeal entity should be able to comprehend infinite or refined spiritual concepts. No part of the physical human being can grasp the non-material concepts behind things like art, music, and philosophy.[1028]

1026   Quoting Dr. Jonas Frisen, a stem-cell biologist at the Karolinska Institute in Stockholm. See N. Wade, "Your Body Is Younger Than You Think," *New York Times*, Aug. 2, 2005.
1027   *Zohar* 2:75b–76a.
1028   Related in Rabbi Shem Tov Ben Yosef Falaquera, *Sefer Hanefesh*, ch. 15.

Consider music for example. Many people are profoundly moved after hearing a certain song. Where does this deep reaction come from? How are tears of joy or sorrow or feelings of inspiration generated from the combination of some chords?

The German poet Heinrich Heine described music as a strange thing, saying, "I would almost say it is a miracle. For it stands halfway between thought and phenomenon, between spirit and matter, a sort of nebulous mediator, like and unlike each of the things it mediates— spirit that requires manifestation in time and matter that can do without space...we do not know what music is."[1029]

Judaism explains that music is an expression of the soul.[1030] Listening to music can have an intense impact. Likewise playing music is described as revealing dormant aspects of the personality.[1031] Music is a tool that can lift one's spirits,[1032] generate and enhance joy,[1033] help one overcome temptations,[1034] and can even bolster intelligence.[1035] The therapeutic value of music is written about in scientific journals, and used in practice in modern society. Many therapists will listen to music with a patient and talk about the feelings or memories that it evokes, and other studies have shown a benefit from music therapy in the treatment for autism, dementia, learning disabilities, strokes and pain management during labor and birth.[1036] The refined appreciation experienced from music reaches a deeper place than the biological aspect of the person.

Furthermore, people feel good when overcoming a desire to do wrong. Additionally, the pleasure of doing kindness for another, or

---

1029 Macdonald Critchley, "Ecstatic and Synaesthetic Experiences during Musical Perception," (1977), in Macdonald Critchley and R. A. Henson, *Music and the Brain: Studies in the Neurology of Music* (1977), pg. 217.

1030 See for example *Heichal Haneginah* (Chabad), pg. 31. See also Rabbi Shaul Yedidyah of Modzhitz, *Imrei Shaul, Inyanei Zimrah* 43.

1031 There is a story of a sinful person playing music on a harp, and the Baal Shem Tov heard the tune. The Baal Shem Tov could recognize hidden in the music all of the wrongdoings that this person had done since the day he was born; see *Ohr Hameir*, Haazinu.

1032 See Rambam, *Shemonah Perakim* 5; see also Weintraub, *Iggros Da'as* 212. Regarding song moving one from sadness to happiness, see *Shomer Emunim, Ma'amar Tzahali V'roni* 2 and 9.

1033 See *Kedushas Levi*, Beshalach.

1034 See *Biur HaGra, Divrei Hayomim* 1:23:4.

1035 See the *Meiri, Tehillim* 47.

1036 See Tara Parker-Pope, "Using Music to Lift Depression's Veil," *New York Times*, Jan. 24, 2008.

the pleasure of intellectual discovery, transcends the fluctuating superficiality of the material world and is instead enjoyed solely by the spirit.[1037] These non-physical experiences and pleasures attest to the fact that there is a non-physical entity within that seeks them.

SEARCH FOR MEANING AND TRANSCENDENCE

Throughout his life, man is constantly in search of things that have nothing to do with his physical makeup. The thirst for enlightenment and meaning is hardly ever truly quenched, yet is ceaselessly pursued with tremendous enthusiasm and dedication of time and money. As the esteemed psychiatrist Viktor Frankl said, "In the healthy human being, there is a will to meaning, and it is this that sets him apart from the animals. One would never hear an animal ask himself, 'Does my life have meaning?' But this question is asked by homo-sapiens."[1038] How can the human being need transcendence, if transcendence has no actuality in the fabric of existence? What about a thirst for meaning—could the thirst be there with nothing to satisfy it? One cannot help but smile at the irony of the atheist who declares the human experience and the cosmos to be devoid of meaning and in the same breath that person declares their unending passion and commitment to investigating and understanding the human condition and the cosmos.

The heart of the average person desperately seeks that which is beyond the mundane. Animals do not have these cravings. When an animal's biological function or drive is fulfilled, it stops. Rabbi Abraham Twerski, who is also a clinical psychiatrist specializing in drug addiction, asks the following question: "Why is addiction unique to human beings?" He answers that addiction is born out of human discontent, and ultimately due to a lack of spirituality. The human being attempts to overcome discontent with things that have worked with other feelings, trying to fill a spiritual void with physical objects or pleasures.

1037 See grades of pleasure discussed in Rabbi Shalom DovBer of Lubavitch, *Kuntres U'mayon*, ch. 2.

1038 See Bill Short in *The Milton H. Erickson Foundation Newsletter*, vol. 3, Issue 16.

These give very temporary relief, but never satisfy the deeper spiritual craving. The individual is left as miserable as ever and tries to indulge in a futile attempt to feel better. The only true solution is to treat the spiritual void. Until the addiction is dealt with on this level, the person will never gain sobriety.[1039]

There is a dissatisfaction that drives a spiritual giant to accomplish greatness and uplift mankind that cannot merely be the product of natural selection. It serves no biological purpose. Where do these yearnings for something higher come from, if not from something "higher" that resides within?

The Midrash gives a parable related to this insatiable thirst.[1040] The book of Ecclesiastes writes, "All of the labor of a man is for his mouth, yet the soul will not be satisfied."[1041] What is the relationship between body and soul comparable to? To a commoner who marries a princess. Everything that this street urchin brings to her is like nothing, because compared to what she had in the palace, all is worthless. To him, it carries much importance, but she could not be any less interested. Likewise is the body and soul relationship. The body is very impressed by food, money, and fancy clothing, yet the soul is only concerned with things that really matter, i.e., the transcendent pursuits of a higher order that she, the soul, was involved in while in the spiritual palace on High.

Sadly, the average person will endeavor on an unending journey, striving to find lasting pleasure in the physical, yet try as he might, what he really seeks is not something that the body or mundane world can ever provide. The farther one removes oneself from faith, the more he lowers himself into despair. Carl Jung, the Swiss pillar of modern psychology, relates:

> During the past thirty years, people from all the civilized countries of the Earth have consulted me. I have treated many hundreds of patients. Among all my patients in the

---

1039 Twerski, *Seek Sobriety, Find Serenity* (1993), pg. 28.
1040 *Koheles Rabbah*, cited in *Mesillas Yesharim* 1:7.
1041 *Koheles* [Ecclesiastes] 6:7.

second half of life—to say, over thirty-five—there has not been one whose problem was not that of finding a religious outlook on life. It is safe to say that every one of them fell ill because he had lost that which the living religions of every age have given to their followers, and none of them has been really healed who did not regain his religious outlook.[1042]

A deep and pervasive aspect of the human condition is the longing for ethereal concepts like justice, freedom, and truth. Oftentimes, the quest for these ideals can even be accompanied by a certain willingness to give his life for their attainment. It seems ironic that nature could generate, preserve, and perpetuate a trait that is self-defeating and counterintuitive to organisms in their struggle for survival. Could nature really produce an organism containing probable predispositions toward its own destruction? Would nature produce a creature that cannot live a merely biological life, but must search higher for a reason for its existence? Could nature, which is devoid of intelligence, personality, vision, and spirituality, produce and preserve these very qualities in the organisms that it generates? These concepts certainly point to an elevated realm within a person that transcends nature, and at the same time, to a Creator who makes possible the emergence of these qualities that uplift the mortal out of the mundane.[1043]

THE SUBLIMINAL WHISPER

In the bestselling book, Tuesdays with Morrie, Morrie, who is a sociology professor nearing his end, says "Everyone knows they are going to die, but nobody believes it."[1044] There seems to be a part of the human system, coming from a subliminal whisper within, to confidently live life as though it will last forever. This itself attests to the soul's existence and immortality, for this state of mind and engrained outlook is an inseparable part of the human experience.[1045]

1042 Carl Jung, *Modern Man in Search of the Soul* (1933).
1043 See David Shapiro, "The Existence of G-d," in Robert Gordis, *Faith and Reason* (1973).
1044 Mitch Albom, *Tuesdays with Morrie* (1997), pg. 80.
1045 There is a similar idea expressed by Dr. Jacob Glenn in *The Bible and Modern Medicine* (pg.

JEWISH SOUL EXPRESSION

Perhaps the strongest proof of the Jewish soul and its inseparable connection with the Almighty can be found throughout Jewish history in the willingness of so many Jewish people to sacrifice their lives for G-d. Even threats of harsh torture have not stopped people from sacrificing their lives.[1046]

Self-sacrifice is fairly common, found among all cultures and creeds throughout human history. A wide variety of people, whether brave and praiseworthy military patriots or crazed and condemned religious zealots, have been willing to die for a cause. Intense convictions, be they personal passions or the product of brainwashing, can climax with the giving of the very self.

What is being discussed here is significantly more mind-boggling. In Jewish history, there are literally countless examples of the *unlearned*, *immoral*, and *non-believing* Jews giving their lives rather than renouncing their faith.

One such classic example is found in the city of Shpola, Ukraine, where there is a tombstone engraved with the words, "The grave of the holy martyr, Yossele the thief." Who was Yossele? In the eighteenth century there lived a degenerate thief who was caught burglarizing a church. His punishment for committing such sacrilege was to be burned at the stake. The judges of his case declared that if he would convert to their religion, he would only be charged with theft and hence receive a much lighter sentence. This thief, a denier of G-d and dissenter his entire life, replied that he would surely die rather than renounce who he was. Even as the fires consumed him, he refused to change his decision.[1047] Where does such devotion and willingness to embrace G-d on the highest level come from, if not from an essential, ever-connected but dormant soul?

In the more recent past, there is a story about a bleak Yom Kippur in

---

36). He writes that medical science has long noticed the irrefutable fact of the existence of an inexplicable phenomenon that could only be described as a spiritual resistance to ravaging diseases such as cancer, heart failure, and the like. The afflicted individual continues his purposeful life for extended periods of time, despite gloomy predictions for a speedy end.

1046 *Tanya, Likkutei Amarim*, ch. 18.

1047 From Shlomo Zevin, *A Treasury of Chassidic Tales: Festivals* (1981).

Auschwitz. One of the guards realized that the inmates were still making a point to fast, despite the fact that they were already completely emaciated. The guards singled out one Jew and said they had a present for him, a delicious ham sandwich. By chance, the Jew they singled out was a secular Jew who never fasted on Yom Kippur and also regularly enjoyed ham and other non-kosher foods. Here was his chance to finally have a meal, something nearly impossible to find. This secular Jew, who was the product of a secular family, refused to eat the ham. The brutal guards began to beat him viciously. When he continued refusing the sandwich, they beat him even harder and when they finished they left him for dead in the mud. A few Jews approached the dying man and asked him why he, as a totally assimilated Jew, refused to eat the ham sandwich? He replied to them, "I have always eaten ham—but never as a Jew. They wanted me, as a Jew, to eat ham. I could never do that."[1048]

THE BODY-SOUL COMBINATION IN JEWISH TRADITION

Jewish tradition teaches that mankind is composed of body and soul.[1049] In general terms, the soul is the animating force that separates a living person from one who is no longer living, as there is clearly a difference between the two.[1050] Jewish tradition reveals many layers that give meaning to what the soul is and how we should relate to it. Rabbi Moshe ben Maimon, known as the Rambam, is considered one of the greatest Jewish sages and philosophers of all time. He reminds the thinking person that the soul is not a combination of any physical elements. He explains that everything in the physical world decomposes, while the soul exists forever.[1051]

1048 See Daniel Eidenson, *Daas Torah* (2011), pg. 99.

1049 *Rama, Orach Chaim* 6:1, mentions the wonderous paradox of a physical body intertwined with a spiritual soul. In this section, the word "soul" is predominantly being used in generic terminology. Every human was created in the "image" of G-d; see *Avos* 3:14 and *Tosofos Yom Tov* there; also *Sefer HaMama'arim* 5702, pg. 105.

1050 The vultures in the jungles of Africa will circle a mortally wounded individual, but will not swoop down until the body becomes a lifeless carcass. Somehow the vulture can tell when the moment of death has occurred. See Abner Weiss, *Connecting to G-d* (2005), pg. 49.

1051 Rambam, *Yesodei HaTorah* 4:9.

BASIC BIOLOGICAL ANIMATING FORCE

One aspect of the soul, or human spirit, corresponds to the material self. It is the unnamable force on the biological level that enlivens and animates the body. On this natural or base plane there is little perceivable difference between the vitalizing force of human beings and animals. This aspect of soul is called the base soul, natural soul, or animal soul—as it is the base force that makes one alive.[1052] It is this energy that makes the heart beat, lungs open and close, and enables all of the other basic operations of a living person to function. This aspect of soul, being identified with nature, is self-serving, essentially centered on its pleasure and preservation.

THE G-DLY ASPECT

In addition, there is another soul described whose beginnings are distinct from everything else in the universe. All other creations are described in the Torah as being spoken into existence by G-d: "And G-d *said*, let there be—so and so." Adam is described as being formed from the dust of the ground, and that "G-d *blew* into his nostrils the breath of life."[1053] The *Zohar* elaborates that one who blows, blows from within. The Torah is metaphorically contrasting the air expenditure that occurs during speech and that which occurs during expulsion of a deep breath. In all other creations, G-d only invests His creative energies on an external or superficial level in creating and sustaining them; however, with the G-dly soul, He gave of His innermost and most essential life force. In Jewish philosophy the soul is referred to as an "actual piece of G-d."[1054] This aspect of the person yearns for "Higher" things, things that are outside of its own self interests.

1052 *Derech Hashem* 3:1:1; *Tanya, Likkutei Amarim,* ch.1.

1053 *Bereishis* [Genesis] 2:7.

1054 See *Iyov* [Job] 31:2, "Part of G-d above." See *Tanya, Likkutei Amarim* ch. 2, which adds the word *mamash* to show that this is meant in a most literal sense. See also Rabbi Chaim Vital, *Eitz Hada'as Tov,* Vaeschanan.

APPLYING THE SOUL: CHOOSING THE G-DLY PATH

Classifying the soul as "G-dly" helps give appreciation as to why it is so often hard to define. Human beings relate to physical terminology—things of this world. G-dly means outside of that realm. Jewish tradition teaches that one soul force within us is completely about self: self-serving and self-preservation. The other force within is directed outside of the self. These two forces are mutually exclusive. To have a connection with the "G-dly," the sense of self must be deflated.

The imagery of the G-dly soul as breath demonstrates the incongruence of the selfish path and the G-dly path. By way of analogy: the breath, like the soul, is usually unseen. If one breathes onto a mirror he can see his breath in the form of fog that forms on the mirror. The more one breathes, the less one sees of himself. In other words, when G-dliness is being pursued self-awareness fades, and vice versa. This, in short, is the story of our lives in this world— an ongoing struggle between choosing the self-serving path or the G-dly path.

In Judaism, choosing the G-dly path, embracing the G-dly aspect of soul, is the means of attaining spiritual health. Rabbi Chaim Vital *zt"l*, the primary student who passed down Lurianic Kabbalah, explains that just as a body requires certain foods to maintain its health, the soul likewise has a special system for maintaining its spiritual health.[1055] When one seeks guidance in health issues in life, one consults his doctor. The doctor knows his specific bodily makeup, its unique strengths and weaknesses, and can make a proper prescription based on this knowledge. The soul likewise has a prescription for its spiritual health. Judaism teaches that the Torah is the Jewish person's prescription for life. Jewish tradition explains that there are a total of 613 commandments in the Torah: 248 positive instructions, and 365 prohibitions to avoid. This corresponds with the 248 spiritual bones of the body and the 365 tendons or sin-

---

1055 *Sha'ar Kedushah* 1:1.

ews.[1056] Completion of the full spectrum of commandments enables a fully healthy soul.

In other words, the means in which the soul experiences the good for which G-d created the world are through fulfilling the commandments.[1057] The soul is rewarded or punished in the afterlife based on its adherence to the commandments while in the body. Every soul of Israel needs to be reincarnated many times in order to fulfill all 613 commandments of the Torah in thought, speech, and action.[1058] The nations of the world keep the soul healthy through their adherence to the Seven Laws of Noah, which uphold a moral code in the world. Through this they refine and uplift themselves and the world around them. All people of the world are charged to fulfill their purpose in this world by living up to their soul potential. This is essentially done by choosing the G-dly path and minimizing the influence of the base, self-concerned nature of the animal soul.

SCIENCE AND THE SOUL

The twentieth century, along with the nineteenth that preceded it, promoted a societal outlook dictated by science and rationalism. Academia had become increasingly closed-minded toward anything of the spirit. Souls, immortality, afterlife, and reincarnation were subjects initially placed in the realm of archaic taboos that had no place in the modern arena. These were topics reserved for religious fundamentalists and new-age occult practitioners. As the twenty-first century neared, however, some breaks in this shell of rejection began to emerge.[1059]

1056　See *Targum Yonasan* on *Bereishis* 1:27; *Zohar*, Vayishlach, pg. 170b. See also Chofetz Chaim, introduction to *Shemiras Halashon*. The number of bones in the human body changes over time. Infants start with less bone material and more cartilage. As the body grows cartilage solidifies into bone. The average eighteen-year-old male has 248 bones. As the person continue to grow, the number of bones lessens because when cartilage hardens, smaller bones fuse together to create larger bones. The 248 and 365 are spiritual anatomy.

1057　*Derech Hashem* 1:2:2; 1:4:5.

1058　Arizal, paraphrased in *Tanya*, *Iggeres HaKodesh*, 7:29.

1059　The following sub-sections discuss some aspects of the soul, as it is being discussed in secular circles. It attempts to make some comparisons between what they discuss and what Jewish literature mentions. It does not seek to imply that the context of the way

GHOSTS

Ghosts are departed souls who, for various reasons, continue to sojourn in the physical world rather than ascending to the higher spiritual realms. For over a century, the British Society for Psychical Research (SPR) has paid serious attention to ghost encounters. SPR was founded in 1882 in London by a group of eminent thinkers,[1060] and has had names like Sigmund Freud and Carl Jung as past members.[1061] They were known, for quite some time, to be meticulous in their evaluation of evidence.[1062]

The research society has explained that while most reports of ghosts turn out to be illusions, many seem to be verified. Their studies show that in cases where ghosts were reported as a result of sudden or tragic deaths, people completely unaware of the death corroborated "sensing some type of presence" in the home. Even animals reacted strongly to the same unoccupied chair in an allegedly haunted Kentucky home.[1063]

There seems to be validation in some writings of the Jewish mystics on the SPR conclusions. Sudden or tragic death is described in some texts as hurling the soul into a continued existence in this world. The "premature" death causes the bodiless soul to continue its occupancy

---

that these subjects are discussed is fully compatible with the Torah approach. This author heard in a *shiur* from Rabbi Zev Leff that the Steipler Gaon encouraged discussion about ghosts because it at least provokes thinking about there being more to existence than just the physical body. It is with this perspective in mind that the following is being presented.

1060 Ivor Grattan-Guinness, *Psychical Research: A Guide to Its History, Principles & Practices—in Celebration of 100 Years of the Society for Psychical Research* (1982).

1061 Renee Haynes, *The Society for Psychical Research 1882–1982: A History* (1982).

1062 William James, one of the prominent early members at the beginning of the twentieth century said: "Were I asked to point to a scientific journal where hard-headedness and never-sleeping suspicion of sources of error might be seen in their full bloom, I think I have to fall back on the Proceedings of the Society for Psychical Research." See Ian Stevenson, "Research into the Evidence of Man's Survival after Death," *Journal of Nervous and Mental Disease*, 185 (1977): pg. 152.

1063 Dr. John Gerald Taylor, *Science and the Supernatural* (1980), pg. 135. Although this work of a reputable scientist sets out to disprove all supernatural phenomena, the refutations are so weak that they end up reinforcing the ideas! (See Dr. John Beloff in *Journal of Parapsychology* 44 (September 1980): pgs. 270-271.) Further information on the topic of ghosts can be seen in Gershon Winkler, *Soul of the Matter: A Jewish-Kabbalistic Perspective on the Human Soul Before, During, and After Life* (1992).

in this world, yearning to complete its originally intended mission.[1064]

Additionally, in the Kabbalistic texts, there is reference to a semi-physical, transparent form of the soul called the *tzelem* or *guf dak*.[1065] It looks like the physical body in which it inhabits. Perhaps these are the apparitions or ghost figures that some encounter. Interestingly enough, this resembles how people describe themselves after having a near-death experience.

There are instances that the soul of someone who has passed on will appear again in the physical realm in what appears to be its body. There are dozens of eyewitness accounts, documented by reliable sources, coming forth from both secular scientific report and from contemporary Torah masters.

Swiss-American psychiatrist and pioneer in end-of-life care, Elizabeth Kübler-Ross, began as a skeptic early on in her career. As time went on and her experiences broadened, she became an avid believer in the continued existence of the soul after death and proclaimed on several occasions that "I know beyond a shadow of a doubt that there is no death the way we understood it. The body dies, but not the soul."[1066]

She tells a peculiar yet enthralling anecdote about one of her patients. A certain Mrs. Schwartz, who she had tended to before her death, appeared to her ten months after the funeral, looking as she did during her lifetime.

In her book, *On Life After Death*, she writes that she was considering other pursuits besides her care of the dying. One day as she approached an elevator, Dr. Ross noticed a woman standing in front of the elevator. The woman looked familiar. The woman approached her and asked her if she could accompany her to her office. Dr. Ross came to realize that it was Mrs. Schwartz and began to question her own awareness. She wondered if she had seen too many schizophrenic patients and was beginning to see things herself.

1064 See Gedalia ben Yosef ibn Yachiya, *Shalsheles HaKabbalah*.

1065 *Avodas HaKodesh* 2:26, pgs. 144–147; *Nishmas Chaim* 1:13.

1066 Holcomb B. Noble, "Elisabeth Kübler-Ross, 78, Dies; Psychiatrist Revolutionized Care of the Terminally Ill," *New York Times*, August 26, 2004.

When they reached the office door, Mrs. Schwartz said she had come to thank her for the help she had given her, and to ask her not to stop her work on death and dying.

Dr. Ross was completely dumbfounded and questioned her sanity. As a test, she asked the woman if she would write a note to Reverend Gaines. Mrs. Schwartz complied. She then got up from her chair, asked Dr. Ross to promise not to end her work, and then left. Dr. Ross later confirmed the wording and the handwriting as belonging to Mrs. Schwartz.

At the time, Dr. Ross was still very much a skeptic of such things; however, it goes without saying that after this encounter she no longer was. She continued her work with the dying and would come to believe in the world of the spirit. She became one of the foremost authorities on death and dying.

Another captivating account, offered from a Torah perspective, involved Rabbi Yosef Chaim Sonnenfeld *zt"l*, a great sage of a previous recent generation:[1067]

> *A certain respectable businesswoman took it upon herself to make sure that those who had passed on in her town always had someone to say Kaddish on their behalf. She would give sizable donations to the local yeshiva on condition that some of the students would be designated to say the Kaddish for poor souls who had nobody to say it for them. The woman partnered with her husband in their business, but after he passed away, the family fell on hard times, their financial situation deteriorating to the point where she did not have money for the dowries of her two daughters who would soon be married.*
>
> *She kept her sorrow quiet, yet was bothered that she would*

1067 This story is recorded in several places, abridged in Yechiel Spero, *Touched by a Story: Inspiring Stories Retold by a Master Teacher*, vol.1 (2003). See also book about Rabbi Yosef Chaim Sonnenfeld, *The Man on the Rampart* (Hebrew, 1977) part I, pg. 345 (translated in *Guardian of Jerusalem*, 1985). In the work *Sha'arei Emunah*, pg. 192, the author writes that Rabbi Avraham Bardacky of Jerusalem told him that he personally knew the grandson of the bank manager, who confirms this story.

not be able to maintain her previous contributions for Kad-
dish. She begged the yeshiva to continue this endeavor even
though she currently did not have the money to support
them. The school administration agreed. She was relieved
and confident that G-d would help her in some way to pay for
her daughters' wedding expenses.

While walking in the street soon after, she encountered
an older gentleman who greeted her and inquired about
her well-being. She described the challenging time that she
was going through, sobbing when enumerating the details.
The man asked her how much money she needed. When she
reluctantly specified an amount, he wrote her a check for
the amount that she needed. Because it was a substantial
amount, the man asked the woman to bring two witnesses to
attest that the money was given properly, and that the man
had actually signed his name and given the check. She com-
plied, and brought two young boys from the yeshiva. The old
man signed the check and gave it over to the woman.

The woman went to the bank the next morning to cash the
check. The clerk was baffled and showed the check to the man-
ager who fainted upon seeing it. They called the woman to a
small room for questioning, thinking the check to be a forg-
ery. The bank manager asked her who gave her this check. She
replied that it was a nice Jewish man with a white beard. She
said that there were even two boys from the yeshiva who wit-
nessed the entire exchange. The boys were brought and ques-
tioned by the bank manager if they would be able to identify
the man who gave the check. They nodded. The bank manager
showed them a picture, and asked if this was the man who
gave the money. They all agreed that this was that warm old
Jewish man. The bank manager said that this man was his
father—who had passed away ten years prior. The manager
processed the check and explained what was happening.

The father had appeared to him in a dream the night before,
saying that since the son had gone off the path of Judaism,

his (the father's) soul was tormented in the next world, as nobody was saying Kaddish on his behalf. Were it not for this woman arranging prayers, his soul would continue to not have a moment's rest. The son had laughed off the matter, until these three people walked in the bank attesting to the story.

Rabbi Yosef Chaim Sonnenfeld said that he was one of the yeshiva students, and that the other student was his friend, Rabbi Yehuda Greenwald. The bank manager did amend his ways, getting back in line with his Jewish observance.

NEAR-DEATH EXPERIENCES

In the mid 1970s, Dr. Raymond Moody introduced the concept of Near-Death Experience (from here on NDE) to the public in a way it had never been presented before.[1068] He painstakingly interviewed over 150 people who were declared medically dead and eventually re-suscitated. In all of these cases, the absence of detectable signs of life such as respiration and heartbeat were documented in their charts. He recorded their firsthand accounts of consciousness and awareness of their body undergoing operation, the hospital room, and the people inside. One such example from Dr. Moody's books reports a woman who during her NDE floated above her body and the hospital and saw a shoe on a multistory building, which was later confirmed in the exact location described. Since then, many teams of researchers all over the world have embarked on this new field of study, and as time progresses the evidence continues to build.

Initially, the secular establishment would naturally expect that during those times of medical death the person would only experience a blank void that would not be remembered upon their subsequent re-vival. Instead, the patients interviewed described themselves during their "death" and entrance to the "world beyond" as weightless, beyond the strictures of time, and encompassed by a feeling of unconditional

---

1068 See *Life After Life* (1975).

love in a way that is not describable in terms living beings can grasp. Some also communicated with relatives who had long passed, had an encounter with a bright light, and underwent a life review where they experienced the positive and negative effects and repercussions of all of the actions of their lifetime. Many told over that during that time they did not wish to return to the body, but were instead forced back in order to correct some earthly tasks not yet fully accomplished.

There was, not surprisingly, mixed reaction to Moody's findings. Many were very excited; however, others were hesitant and skeptical. Of particular note is work that Moody did with a Russian doctor who had a vivid recollection of his NDE, despite the fact that throughout his entire life the Soviets educated him to deny both G-d and a soul. Interestingly, several doctors who were initially cynical and vehemently disapproving of Moody became enthusiastic supporters of NDE research after conducting firsthand experimentation and interviews of their own.[1069]

There are those who would still rather dismiss the patient's entire experience as purely psychological or the beginnings of the natural neurological process of the brain shutting down. These researchers, however, are left at a stalemate, for instance, when grappling with how patients correctly related specifics about people or happenings in *other rooms* or *other places.*

Furthermore, these out-of-body experiences are particularly astonishing when described by children who have had an NDE, who in their innocence and simplicity are incapable of accurately fabricating a recollection of emergency room proceedings while their "dead" body lies on the operating table, or recall events taking place simultaneously in their homes that are later corroborated with impeccable accuracy. The evidence mounts further when the ones conducting the research of the children's experiences began as skeptics themselves.

There are many recorded stories about children having these experiences.

1069 See for example cardiologist Michael Sabom, *Recollections of Death: A Medical Investigation* (1982). He actually discussed in great detail the patient's exact experiences while in the hospital and not observably conscious, and compared it with their individual medical records.

One interesting case is about an eleven-year-old who had a cardiac arrest in the lobby of a children's hospital and was rushed to the intensive care unit to try to restart his heart. He was without heartbeat for at least twenty minutes, with fervent attempts at trying cardiac medications but to no avail. Finally, they tried to jolt his heart to start again with cardio paddles. Miraculously, the boy opened his eyes, and said, "That was weird. You just sucked me back into my body." A nurse later confirmed this peculiar line. The boy had emergency surgery, and survived the ordeal. Out of embarrassment, in thinking that he would be thought of as crazy, he did not share the details of his memories from the ordeal until he was questioned about it in high school. He described being "whooshed" out of his body, and was watching the procedure as it took place from a corner on the ceiling. He described in great detail what took place and the location of everything in the room. He accurately related specific phrases that the doctors and nurse in the room were saying and what they were doing. He confessed that he had never heard about NDEs and also did not watch very much television.[1070]

One particularly fascinating story is about a child named Mark who remembered an NDE that he had when he was only nine months old. At that time he had severe bronchiolitis. While he was in the emergency room he had a full cardiac arrest. For forty minutes the doctors frantically struggled to revive him. Thankfully they were able to, and he showed no signs of hindered growth or development. While at a holiday pageant at the age of three, he commented that the person in the play was "not what 'G-d' looked like," and went on to describe how he "encountered G-d" in the emergency room two years before. Mark had never been told of his operation or the details of that frantic night, yet he described the occurrences in the hospital as follows: "I saw the nurses and the doctors standing over me trying to wake me up. I flew out of the room and [went to the waiting room, where I] saw grandpa and grandma crying and holding each other. I think they

---

1070 Melvin Morse and Paul Perry, *Closer to the Light: Learning from the Near-Death Experiences of Children* (1991), pgs. 26-30.

thought I was going to die." He then described the process of crawling up a dark tunnel toward a light and having a detailed encounter with G-d.[1071] The descriptions that he gave of the hospital were confirmed as accurate by his startled father.

At the end of the day, the arguments of the doubters or detractors do not stand up under careful analysis.[1072] Although something only recently tackled by academia, Jewish tradition has been discussing this phenomenon at least since Talmudic times.[1073]

MANY LIVES

Reincarnation is another subject that the secular world often associates with Eastern religious traditions, storefront palm readers, or an article of faith accepted by the spiritually inclined; certainly not anything that can be documented or contain scientific value.

Dr. Brian Weiss is chairman emeritus of the Department of Psychiatry at the Mount Sinai Medical Center in Miami and Clinical Associate Professor of Psychiatry at the University of Miami School of Medicine. In 1980, a woman named "Catherine" stepped into his office with several severe issues and phobias that were not allowing her to function properly. After using conventional methods of psychotherapy, she agreed to allow him to hypnotize her. In this heightened sense

---

1071 Morse and Perry, ibid., pgs. 40-42.

1072 For example, those who say anoxia, lack of oxygen to the brain, is the reason for the NDE, have difficulty dealing with the clarity in which the patients describe everything. There does not appear to be any evidence that a brain before it completely shuts down is capable of producing such clear imagery. There is also no evidence that NDEs happen during times of anoxia. See Peter and Elizabeth Fenwick, *The Truth in the Light* (1995), pgs. 211–214. Furthermore, it is difficult to write the experiences off as hallucinations for several reasons. NDEs tend to have many similarities across a wide spectrum of people, which is uncommon for hallucinations. Also hallucinations are usually accompanied with anxiety or other negative feelings, whereas NDEs are by and large connected with feelings of peace and tranquility. Some theorized that NDEs were actually a memory of birth and travel through the birth canal. This theory became popular until it was shown that this is not a possibility. See Carl Becker, "Why Birth Models Cannot Explain Near-Death Phenomena," in Greyson and Flynn, *The Near Death Experience*, pgs. 140-162. There is also difficulty explaining how the people were able to know, see, and describe what was taking place in other locations during their NDE.

1073 See Ramban and Abarbanel to *Shmos* [Exodus] 20:15. See also the Maharsha to *Shabbos* 89a.

of awareness, she revealed some repressed memories of her childhood that Dr. Weiss believed would help relieve her fears, as is usually the case. They did not.

In their next session, she described in great detail a tragedy that had taken place in her village thousands of years prior. Dr. Weiss at the time was a highly educated intellectual who had been published in psychology journals and textbooks, and was very skeptical. He dismissed her story as imagination, yet was intrigued by her attention to detail. Then something unexpected happened; on her next visit Catherine said that many of her fears were gone or alleviated. Dr. Weiss remained unconvinced but proceeded with this method of treatment. She revealed other past lives to him and the experience of death itself, which incidentally parallels the accounts given by NDE patients. While reliving each life, she personified each past person that she was. Dr. Weiss was confused, as she had no evidence of being mentally deranged or any incentive for deception.

The final blow came when the woman revealed to Dr. Weiss several unknowable details about his father and son who had passed years before, including referring to his father by his never-used Hebrew name Avraham. This was the tipping point. This entire episode completely defied rational explanation. Dr. Weiss no longer felt that Catherine's descriptions were imaginary, as even the most lucid imagination would not be able to summon impossible facts or cure phobias. He published this case in his widely acclaimed, *Many Lives, Many Masters*.

Dr. Weiss is not the only one to start off with skepticism. Dr. Helen Wambach actually set out to research and to conclusively disprove reincarnation. She finished her mission with a complete change of heart. She did a ten-year survey of past-life recalls under hypnosis with over a thousand people. She asked her subjects very specific questions about the time periods in which they lived. She was astounded by the results. Aside for a handful of participants, eleven out of 1,088, she was able to verify the descriptions of clothing, footwear, and utensils that her subjects described with the actual historical record of when they claimed to have lived. She said that fantasy and genetic memory could simply not account for the results. Many other initially skeptical researchers have likewise come full circle in their views based on their investigations.

As is the case with NDE patients, the most telling research can be derived from children who remember past lives. Dr. Ian Stevenson was head of the Department of Psychiatric Medicine at the University of Virginia and spent forty years investigating over 3,000 cases of children who recalled past lives.[1074] Astoundingly, in over forty of these cases Stevenson encountered not only recollection of past lives, but also *physical* evidence of unusual birthmarks, scars, or birth defects of children that paralleled medical records for the individual Stevenson identified as the past-life personality.[1075]

Parenthetically, the concept of retaining physical characteristics that carry over lifetimes is not the norm, yet may have some rare parallels in Jewish tradition as well.[1076]

Stevenson was known to be a cautious, methodical, and conservative researcher. His choice to focus on children makes his research more scientifically sound, as it minimizes the possibility of corruption or forgery. Dr. Jim Tucker is the associate professor of psychiatry and neurobehavioral sciences at the University of Virginia School of Medicine and a protégé of Dr. Ian Stevenson. His 2005 book, *Life Before Life*, recounts over four decades worth of scientific research into the past-life accounts of children. Even the most steadfast skeptics, including the late Dr. Carl Sagan, could not help but concede that the research was carefully collected empirical data,[1077] and not mere embellishment or wishful thinking.

There are many documented accounts of children speaking about

---

1074 Tom Shroder, "Ian Stevenson; Sought to Document Memories of Past Lives in Children," *Washington Post*, Feb. 7, 2007.

1075 Ian Stevenson, *Where Biology and Reincarnation Intersect* (1997). See also Stevenson, "Birthmarks and Birth Defects Corresponding to Wounds on Deceased Persons," presented at the Eleventh Annual Meeting of the Society for Scientific Exploration, Princeton University, June 11–13, 1992.

1076 Rabbi Moshe Teitelbaum, known as the *Yismach Moshe*, said that the birthmarks on his arms that resembled stripes were caused because in a previous incarnation he was one of the sheep of the patriarch Jacob. See Jiri Langer, *Nine Gates to the Chassidic Mysteries* (1976). The journey from animal to human is also not the norm.

1077 Carl Sagan, *Demon Haunted World* (1996), pg. 300.

"when they were big" and giving precise depictions of another time in history, which can be verified, and are far too authentic and vivid to dismiss as mere exceptional imaginations.[1078]

Peter Fenwick is a fellow of the Royal College of Psychiatrists. He holds a research post as a senior lecturer at The Institute of Psychiatry in London. He has dedicated much study to documenting these cases. One story that he mentions is about a boy named Thomas Mather (pseudonym), who was born in British Columbia in 1982. He began to talk clearly when he was eighteen months old, and started having recurring nightmares when he was around two years. They were vivid and often about San Francisco. He began giving detailed reports about what appeared to be another life that he had lived. When seeing Princess Diana on television, he told his parents about another Diana that he knew when he "was big." He started to clearly depict actual places in San Francisco, which were verified to actually exist, and persistently spoke about when he was "big like daddy." Around the same time, he also spoke often of plane crashes, and how the people "at the airport were able to see me crash" when his plane crashed. He had a terrible fear of flying and of fires. The child also spoke about trees that he had "seen" in San Francisco, which were prevalent there, but not in British Columbia, and he complained to his teacher in preschool that the mail deposit boxes were the "wrong color" (as they are blue in the United States, but red in Canada). He also resented being treated like a little boy and did not understand why he could not do things that adults do, like going out alone. These are some of the key features that led to further investigation. Thomas's story is far from unique; in fact, these types of stories are being revealed much more often than one might imagine.[1079]

Children who experience "past lives" are a well-known field of para-

---

1078 For examples, see Ian Stevenson, *European Cases of the Reincarnation Type* (2008), pg. 105; Stevenson, *Children who Remember Previous Lives: A Question of Reincarnation* (2001), pg. 107; Stevenson, *Twenty Cases Suggestive of Reincarnation*, vol. 26 (1980), pg. 184. There are literally hundreds of examples of this in the vast amount of literature that is available on the subject.

1079 This story is mentioned in Fenwick, *Past Lives: An Investigation into Reincarnation Memories* (2001).

normal studies that is becoming more widely accepted. In fact, several universities even have departments devoted exclusively to its study. One of the most chilling stories of reincarnation in children began drawing attention several years ago. James Leininger is a child who lives in quiet Lafayette, Louisiana. His parents, Bruce and Andrea Leininger, are cultured and educated people. The following is a summary of some of the highlights of the Leininger story:

> In the year 2000, when James was just two years old, he began to have vivid nightmares. "Airplane crash! Plane on fire! Little man can't get out!" Andrea ran to his bedroom and saw James struggling. "He was lying there on his back, kicking and clawing on the covers." This dream would recur five times per week, with similar fear. James began to deliver incredibly accurate details later found out to be centered on a World War II pilot named James Huston, Jr. When Andrea asked who the little man in the plane was, James replied: "Me." When Bruce asked James who shot his plane down, James stated, "The Japanese." When he was asked how he knew that it was the Japanese who shot down his plane, James replied: "The big red sun."
>
> James had an obsession with World War II airplanes with propellers. In his car seat, James would put on imaginary headphones and facemask. He also continued to further demonstrate very detailed knowledge about airplanes. When Andrea gave James a toy plane with what looked like a bomb under it, James looked at it and said: "That's not a bomb, Mommy, that's a dwop tank." His mother did not even know what a drop tank was. When the nightmares persisted, they asked James more detailed questions about his dreams. The information he divulged was so clear that it became more and more difficult to dismiss. It is also difficult to say that he was being coached or the claim was a hoax, as the child was still in diapers and knew the flight characteristics of World War II–era fighter planes.

James was examined and tested by a renowned authority on children who have supposedly experienced "past lives," Carol Bowman. She vouched for his authenticity. Eventually, he revealed that he used to fly a Corsair and that his ship was named the Natoma. James knew that the Corsair would veer to the left on takeoff and that it had a tendency to blow tires out upon landing. He also knew that US fliers gave Japanese bombers girl names and Japanese fighters boy names. When his parents took him to the Lone Star Flight Museum, James was walking around a Corsair, engaged in a flight check, like a pilot normally does before boarding. Eventually James also told his father that his plane was shot down at the Battle of Iwo Jima.

His father Bruce was a hard sell. He was skeptical about these things and an evangelical Christian, claiming that re-incarnation was in conflict with his faith. After doing some research, he found confirmation for all of his son's claims. He also found that there was an annual reunion of surviving crew members of the ship that his son had named as his own and began to attend the reunions. He gathered up facts, all confirming the data fed by his son James, including that there was a pilot James Huston Jr. who was killed in the location and manner that his son described. However, being skeptical, and looking for flaws, he was pleased to find out that there were no Corsairs on Natoma Bay, which is the type of plane that his son claimed that he flew. However, Bruce later learned from another pilot, Bob Greenwald, that Huston had participated in a program in which Corsairs were tested for aircraft carrier landings.

They met up later with some of the crew that were part of the Natoma. James saw Bob Greenwald, who he recognized on sight and named correctly after "recognizing his voice." At the ceremony, little James was also reunited with his old friend, Jack Larson. The veterans could not get over the re-semblance of this little boy with their old friend.

Andrea later tracked down pilot James Huston's sister, Anne. Anne was eighty-four years old and they set up a phone conversation between Anne and James. The sister had never had any contact with the ship or the reunions. She sent a batch of photographs of her brother taken during the war, and in a couple of the photographs pilot James Huston was standing in front of a Corsair. In this conversation, James called her Annie, something that only James Huston did.

James mentioned their sister Ruth who was four years older than Anne, and that Anne was four years older than James, which was correct. He also said that their father was an alcoholic and broke things when drunk, and that he had to go to rehab. Anne confirmed all of this. When she sent James Leininger a drawing that her mother made of James Huston, the child asked where the other picture was. The other picture, which had been buried in the attic for about sixty years, was a drawing of Anne. Her mother had made two drawings when they were children. Anne was stunned. No one knew about that other picture, except for her dead brother.

This is the gist of the story. James Leininger's parents put together a book about this most intriguing story. It was compiled with the assistant of tough skeptic Ken Gross, so there is no fluff in the recap of the story. The story certainly demonstrates that there is good reason to believe that there is more to life and more to a person than meets the eye.[1080]

Perhaps even more intriguing is when children or adults start speaking, writing, or even fully conversing in a language they had never been exposed to, or even ones that are ancient and not currently known except to a few experts. The spectacle is common enough to have a name, "*xenoglossia*."[1081]

1080 For the full story, see Bruce and Andrea Leininger, with Ken Gross, *Soul Survivor: The Reincarnation of a World War II Fighter Pilot* (2009). These are consolidated quotations from that book.

1081 See Dr. Joel Whitton and Joe Fisher, *Life Between Life* (1988), pgs. 167–169. See also Ian Stevenson, *Children Who Remember Previous Lives: A Quest of Reincarnation* (2001);

These are just a sampling of compiled scientific research on the immortality of the soul, although there are many more fascinating documented occurrences that further the evidence as well.[1082] The reader is encouraged to explore these topics more comprehensively, using the cited footnotes as a guide, and see that "the evidence of human survival after death is strong enough to permit a belief in survival [of the soul] on the basis of the evidence."[1083,1084] The main idea for the reader in this section is to gain an enhanced appreciation of the fact that there is more to the human being than what meets the eye.

Unlearned Language: New Studies in Xenoglossy (1984); Twenty Cases Suggestive of Reincarnation (1966).

1082 For a further interesting compilation and more comprehensive look on these topics and others, see Yaakov Astor, Soul Searching: Seeking Scientific Ground for the Jewish Tradition of an Afterlife (2003).

1083 "The Evidence of Man's Survival after Death," Journal of Nervous and Mental Disease, pgs. 167–168.

1084 From a Torah perspective, it is possible that these cases are not actually remembering their past life, in the sense that they are a gilgul or reincarnation, but could be instead have the soul of another who has perhaps passed away cleaving to their own soul in a phenomenon known as an ibbur or dybbuk. See Nishmas Chaim, ma'amar 3, ch. 15.

REASONABLE APPROACH TO MOSHIACH AND REDEMPTION

The coming of *Moshiach* (the Messiah) and the era of redemption is a foundation of Judaism.[1085] Rabbi Israel Meir Kagan *zt"l*, the Chofetz Chaim, referred to this belief as the "principle of principles."[1086] It is a great mitzvah to await his arrival,[1087] and likewise this anticipation is one of the first things asked of a person upon entrance into the next world.[1088] It is a requirement to await his coming; however, if one *only* believes, but does not actively *await* the Messiah's arrival, he is not conducting himself properly.[1089]

In order to appreciate the significance of the coming of the Messiah, one must first appreciate the fact that the Jewish people are in exile, and have been for nearly two thousands years. Exile means that the

---

1085 Rambam, *Melachim* 11:2; commentary on Mishnah, *Sanhedrin* ch. 11. Number twelve of the Rambam's Thirteen Principles of Faith is that he is coming, and "if he tarries, wait for him" (*Chabakuk* 2:3). See also *Sefer Ikkarim* 4:42.

1086 *Chofetz Chaim al HaTorah*, Noach. Notably, *Iggros Moshe* (*Even Haezer*, vol. 1, 82:11, pg. 215) says that witnesses to a wedding who did not take this belief seriously are deemed heretics, and the wedding null and void.

1087 *Zephania* 3:8; Rambam, *Melachim* 11:1.

1088 *Shabbos* 31a. See also *Sha'arei Teshuva, Orach Chaim* 118:1.

1089 In some sources such a person is even classified as a heretic. See Shulzinger, *Mishmor Haleviyim* on *Brachos*, ch. 22. Rabbi Velvel of Brisk says that one must expect Moshiach at every minute, see *Ma'amarei Be'er Chaim Mordechai, ma'amar* 13. See also *Minchas Elazar*, vol. 5, ch. 36; *Alei Shur*, vol. 2, pg. 205.

Jewish people have been unable to dwell in the Land of Israel, in a society based on the precepts of the Torah, as once was, and instead are subject to the rule of foreign societies and ideologies. The concept of exile remains true even with the advent of the modern State of Israel. Exile, from a Torah perspective, is a state of mind and a state of being, not exclusively a geographical location; therefore, exile can occur even when the Jewish people are living in Israel.[1090] There have been several exiles in Jewish history, but the current exile, which has also been the longest, began with the destruction of the Temple in Jerusalem in the year 70 CE.

Many might be quick to think that the world community is so far from the messianic ideal, that it is very difficult to see such a vast change happen any time soon. However, situations can change very quickly, be they personal, communal, national, or global. One need only look at how Europe and the entire world were transformed in a negative way, literally overnight, over a short period in the early 1940s.

From a more positive vantage point, when one looks at the Torah, back to the first exile, one finds a very rapid change that took place as well. The first exile was the slavery in Egypt. This was the paradigm to which all future redemptions would be modeled after and parallel. In a matter of ten months, the slave nation, entrenched in excruciating labor with no sign of salvation, went from being oppressed to triumphant, was liberated, and decimated the greatest superpower of the time. One sees this transformation, on a small scale, with Joseph in prison. One day he finds himself in an Egyptian dungeon, and then through his ability to meaningfully interpret the dreams of Pharaoh, he becomes viceroy, ruler of all of Egypt—an overnight change for the better. Things may appear gloomy in the world at the moment, but salvation has been known to come suddenly and unexpectedly.

G-d is said to fashion the world "this one opposite the other."[1091] Good and evil exist simultaneously and proportionally. When neg-

---

1090 This was also the case during the Greek Exile, which ended with the miracles of Chanukah.
1091 *Koheles* [Ecclesiastes] 7:14.

ativity seems to prevail in the world, one should keep in mind that there is also an equal good transpiring in balance, albeit perhaps less openly apparent or reported. Therefore, the redemption could be at any moment.

WHO IS MOSHIACH?

Moshiach has many things that he will accomplish in the world. He will restore the monarchy of King David, rebuild the Holy Temple in its place,[1092] gather the dispersed Jewish people from around the world to the Holy Land,[1093] and establish a lasting world peace, ushering in an eternal reality devoid of evil.[1094] At some point, the dead will also be resurrected.[1095] The word *Moshiach* simply means "anointed one,"[1096] referring to his mission and status of king in the Davidic dynasty, all of whom were anointed with consecrated oil.[1097]

Contrary to the idea of the personal qualities of the Messiah present in other faiths, the Messiah in Judaism is a man of flesh and blood, born to two parents,[1098] and not any sort of quasi-deity. He will be a paternal descendant of King David,[1099] an exceptionally righteous person, and possess a deep care for every person.[1100] Like David his ancestor, he will be a rabbi, constantly immersed in Torah and its commandments, and strengthening its observance throughout the Jewish people.[1101] In truth, G-d prepares a candidate in every generation so that should the right time arise, this individual would assume the position in the grand role.[1102] He embodies or is the personification

---

1092 *Yechezkel* [Ezekiel] 37:26–28.

1093 See *Devarim* [Deuteronomy] 30:3–4; *Amos* 9; *Yirmiyahu* [Jeremiah] 23; *Yechezkel* [Ezekiel] 39.

1094 *Yechezkel* [Ezekiel] 37:23; *Zephania* 3:13; *Malachi* 3:19.

1095 *Yeshayahu* [Isaiah] 26:19; *Yechezkel* [Ezekiel] 37:12; *Daniel* 12:2.

1096 See *Shmos* [Exodus] 29:7; *Vayikra* [Leviticus] 4:3.

1097 See *Horayos* 11b for more details of this ritual.

1098 *Or HaChamah* on *Zohar* 2:7b.

1099 *Yeshayahu* 11:1; *Yirmiyahu* 23:5–6.

1100 *Pesikta Rabbasi* 37:1.

1101 Rambam, *Melachim* 11:4.

1102 See Bartenura on *Rus*; *Teshuvos Chasam Sofer* vol. 6, 98; R. Tzadok HaKohen, *Pri Tzaddik, Devarim* 13. See also *Sedei Chemed, Pe'as Hasadeh*, Alef, *Kellalim*, sec. 70.

of Moses in the generation.[1103] The Messiah's role is not in any way predicated on his miracles, or supernatural phenomena taking place in the world. Just as the Jewish nation did not accept Moses based on the miracles performed,[1104] so too will be with the Messiah. After Moshiach comes, there may be an extensive period where all of the laws of nature remain intact exactly as they are.

WHEN IS MOSHIACH COMING?

The Talmud relates that one time Rabbi Yehoshua ben Levi asked Moshiach, "When are you coming?" Moshiach answered him, "Today!" Rabbi Yehoshua ben Levi later disappointedly asked Elijah the Prophet why Moshiach had not come that day as promised. Elijah responded, that the Messiah meant "today" if the Jewish people would observe the commandments and thereby be ready for it.[1105]

The preordained date of the coming of Moshiach is a guarded secret.[1106] The only thing written about it is that it will happen "in its time."[1107] G-d will eventually send the Messiah whether the world is ready or not,[1108] yet the collected merit of the Jewish people can hasten his coming.[1109] Prayer for his imminent arrival is also essential in speeding up the process.[1110]

The Talmud and other sources speak harshly about those who try to calculate the exact time that the Messiah will come.[1111] The main concern about making precise calculations is because errors result in national disappointment, and theoretically, can also increase the

---

1103 See Rabbi Avraham Yehoshua Heschel of Apta, *Ohev Yisrael*, 110b; Rabbi Shlomo haKohen of Radomsk, *Tiferes Shlomo*, vol.1, Pinchas, pg. 304.
1104 Rambam, *Yesodei HaTorah* 8:1.
1105 *Sanhedrin* 98a.
1106 *Pesachim* 54b; *Midrash Tehillim* 9:2.
1107 *Yeshayahu* [Isaiah] 60:22.
1108 Ibid., 48:11.
1109 *Sanhedrin* 98a.
1110 Chasam Sofer (*Minhagei Chasam Sofer* 5:24) explains part of the blessing recited in the synagogue when blessing the new month says, "He will redeem us speedily." He explains that for the redemption itself, the prayers are unneeded as it is promised by G-d; instead they are meant to expedite his arrival.
1111 *Sanhedrin* 97b; *Derech Eretz* 11.

likelihood of false messiahs appointing themselves. Furthermore, the Rambam is clear that one must "await his coming every day," but if someone thinks that it will happen on such-and-such specific day, he will fail to await his coming earlier than *that* date.

Notwithstanding the fact, many of the greatest sages over the course of Jewish history did in fact attempt to predict the year or even the precise date of the Messiah's coming. The prohibition of calculating is perhaps not as prescriptive as it seems at first glance. One perspective is that it is only prohibited to make calculations based on astrology, but doing so by the means of Torah sources would be acceptable.[1112] Another approach says that the prohibition applied only to earlier generations, so as not to cause them anguish that the Messiah was so far off, but now that the world is on the brink of redemption, there is no prohibition.[1113]

Rabbi Meir Leibush *zt"l*, the Malbim, gives an enlightening analogy about predicting the end times: A father and son are traveling a long distance. At the beginning of the journey, the son asks if they will arrive soon, and the father does not answer, as their final destination is quite far off. As they near the town, the son asks the same question, and this time the father answers that it will only be a short while more. So too, as the time of the redemption draws nearer, it will become more readily identifiable.[1114] The sages of the past century have said on many occasions that the time is right for Moshiach to come now.

THE UNFOLDING REDEMPTION

The Chofetz Chaim used to say, "Even a blind man can see that we are the generation of Moshiach. All signs indicate that he is not far off."[1115] In fact, many contemporary sages have also stressed that the timing seems right for the Messiah to come now. Rabbi Moshe Sternbach writes that "exile is nearing an end... We have been told that by

---

1112 Abarbanel, *Maayeni HaYeshuah* 1:2.
1113 Ramban, *Sefer HaGeulah*, *ma'amar* 4.
1114 Based on the Malbim, Introduction to the book of *Daniel*. Similar analogy given by the Dubno Maggid.
1115 This is in fact the running theme in his work *Tzepisa LiYeshua*.

the year six thousand Moshiach must come." He also writes that "the conditions for his coming seem to be fulfilled."[1116] The Lubavitcher Rebbe zt"l announced and publicized countless times that Moshiach is imminent throughout all the years of his leadership.

SIX-THOUSAND-YEAR MAP OF HISTORY

The Jewish sages laid out a map in which world history would unravel, from the creation of Adam until the end of time. The world is described in the Torah as being created in six days. The sages draw parallel that these days also correspond to six millennia of history that humanity will experience following the creation of Adam. In other words, the events and trends of each millennium are foretold by the events of a corresponding day of Creation.[1117]

The Talmud says that the general layout of history is as follows: first two-thousand-year period will be years of *nothingness*, second two-thousand-year period will be years of *Torah*, and third two-thousand-year period will be *the days of the Messiah*.[1118]

- The years of *nothingness* (from year 1-2000) describe the world without Torah being taught.[1119] The year 2000 on the Jewish calendar was when a fifty-two-year-old Abraham began spreading the message of Torah and influencing others to go in its ways. This began the second "two thousand years": the era of *Torah*.

- The years of *Torah* (2000-4000) period saw the life of the patriarchs, the giving of the Torah at Sinai, the prophets, the settling of the Holy Land, and the destruction of both Holy Temples in Jerusalem. During this two thousand year period, Torah flourished like never before.[1120] The year 4000 on the Jewish calendar was the end of that era, marked by the passing of Rabbi Judah

---

1116 See *Rav Moshe Speaks—An Anthology of Talks by HaGaon Rav Moshe Sternbach.*
1117 See Ramban and Rabbeinu Bachya to *Bereishis* 2:3; *Iyun* 1 ch. 1; also *Beur HaGra* to *Tamid* 7:4.
1118 *Sanhedrin* 97a.
1119 Rashi to *Sanhedrin* 97a and *Avoda Zara* 9a.
1120 See Maharsha to the Baraisa on *Sanhedrin*, ibid.

the Prince, the end of the Tannaic era, growing tribulations of exile, and the decline of centers of Torah study.[1121]

- The years of the *Messiah* (4000-6000) is the opportune time that at any moment during this period Moshiach can arrive and bring salvation to the world.

Before the third two-thousand-year period, Moshiach could not have come, even if the world deserved it; during the last two-thousand-year period, Moshiach will definitely come, even if the world is undeserving.[1122] Even though it is a long exile, these days are prepared for Moshiach when the people deserve it. This period is likened to the winter months, which are called the rainy season; not because it rains every day, but because these days are more disposed toward rain than other days of the year.[1123]

SIGNS OF THE TIME OF REDEMPTION

The sages of the Talmud give various omens that will alert the Jewish people that Moshiach is very near.[1124] This downward spiral of events begins with large segments of the Jewish people scorning the traditional values of their religion: neither parents nor the elderly will be respected, the old will have to seek favors from the young and one's household will become his enemies. Insolence and impudence will increase, people will no longer have respect for authority and there will be none who can provide correction. Wisdom shall become putrid, truth abandoned, and religious study will be despised and used by nonbelievers to strengthen their false claims; the government will become godless, academies places of immorality, and the pious denigrated. This will be coupled with oppressing inflation, and many destitute begging with nobody to pity them.

Besides for the signs of despair, the sages and mystics also offer some positive signs that inform of the imminence of Moshiach. Included in

---

1121 Maharsha and Hagaos Yaavetz to *Sanhedrin*, ibid.
1122 Maharal, *Netzach Yisrael* ch. 27.
1123 See Abarbanel in *Yeshuos Meshicho*.
1124 Many examples given in *Sotah* 49b; *Sanhedrin* 97a; *Shir HaShirim Rabbah* 2:29.

these is a renewal of Torah study, the far-reaching dissemination of the mystical dimensions of the Torah,[1125] and the opening of the gates of wisdom from above and the wellsprings of wisdom below. The "wisdom from above" refers to the promulgation of Torah on a whole new level, and the "wellsprings of wisdom from below" are the marvelous discoveries in science and advancement in technology.[1126]

SCIENTIFIC DISCOVERY PARALLELS THE SAGES HISTORICAL LAYOUT

When looking back through history, it is quite interesting to see how the transformation of consciousness has been enhanced over time, as predicted clearly by the sages. After the death of Archimedes [circa 200 BCE], advancements in science took quite some time to start back up. There was very little scientific progress achieved until Copernicus and Galileo [1500s CE].[1127] This span of time incorporates a period of general intellectual darkness referred to appropriately as the Dark Ages. Not until the mid 1200s CE did history meet Roger Bacon, who is often credited as the first European advocate of the scientific method,[1128] but as mentioned, this method was not widely implemented until the days of Galileo in the 1500s. In the late 1600s and early 1700s, Sir Isaac Newton solidified the work of his predecessors and encapsulated the primary pillars of science into a few fundamental laws using mathematics. Newton's achievements were followed by great cultural change and progress. The mid-1700s saw the Industrial Revolution sweep across Europe and peak in the mid-1800s, when it spread to the United States as well. This time period saw unprecedented growth in inventions and technology.[1129]

1125   *Zohar* 1:118a. See *Zohar Chadash*, *Tikunim* 96c.

1126   See *Likkutei Sichos*, vol. 15, pg. 42.

1127   Some historians would estimate the gap even further, closer to eighteen hundred years, with the discovery of calculus and its more modern explanation by Newton and his contemporaries; see Benjamin Ginsberg, *The Adventure of Science* (1930), pg. 65.

1128   James Ackerman, "Leonardo's Eye," *Journal of the Warburg and Courtauld Institutes*, 41 (1978), pg. 119; see also Brian Clegg, *The First Scientist: A Life of Roger Bacon* (2003).

1129   The aforementioned dates and outline can be seen in Moshe Schatz, *Sparks of the Hidden Light* (1995).

With the onset of the twentieth century, something began to happen that is simply miraculous. New theories and approaches to looking at the universe were initiated that transformed the way in which mankind saw space and time, mind and matter. As the decades progressed after 1900 CE, there was an explosion of knowledge and technological advances. From the Garden of Eden until 1900, people rode around on horses like King David or Julius Caesar. Within the span of several decades, mankind went from inventing the automobile to the jet plane and later the space shuttle. Communications spread from telegraph to telephone to cellular phone, Skype, and beyond. Today one can literally speak to anyone else in the world, face-to-face, at any time he pleases, on his smart-phone. All of the world's data is in the palm of one's hands with the internet constantly at the fingertips. Medical research is progressing so fast that by the time a written book goes to print its information has already become obsolete. This century saw animals cloned, surgeries performed through lasers and robots, and operations carried out on a fetus while still in its mother's womb.

The trend continues nowadays at an even faster pace. It has been said that a week's worth of the *New York Times* has more information in it than what a person from the 1800s would encounter in his entire lifetime. Furthermore, it is estimated that this year alone there will be four exabytes[1130] of new and unique information generated, which is more than the sum total of all information generated in the past 5,000 years combined.[1131] The question is, why was scientific growth so slow during the Dark Ages, followed by a surprising revival in the 1500s, a dramatic increase with the Industrial Revolution, an exponentially skyrocketing growth in the past hundred years, and quantum leaps in the last few decades? There is, without a doubt, a flood taking place; one that begins with a trickle, expands, and leads to a completely unstoppable raging deluge.

1130 An exabyte is a unit of information equal to one quintillion bytes, or more clearly, one billion gigabytes.

1131 See Augusto Lopez-Claros, *The Innovation for Development Report 2010–2011* (2011), pg. 59.

THE ZOHAR PREDICTS

This exact development, in the stages whence it emerged, was detailed in the *Zohar* nearly two-thousand years ago:[1132]

> Rabbi Yossi said: Concerning the period prior to the Messianic Age, it is written, "I, G-d, will hasten it *in its time (b'itah)*."[1133] What is hinted at in the word *b'itah*? With vowels we can read it instead as *"b'et heh"* meaning "at the time of five." Our oral tradition teaches us that the world as we know it will last for 6,000 years—each millennium paralleling a day in the week of Creation described in the Torah. In the seventh millennium, corresponding with the seventh day or the Sabbath, the universe will go into a process of gestation and renewal. The fifth millennium is the darkest period of exile. For at least one thousand years, we must remain in exile.[1134] The fifth millennium represents the final *heh* of the Tetragrammaton. After the fifth millennium ends, and the sixth millennium begins,[1135] if we merit it, the Messianic Age will actually start. If not, sparks of the hidden messianic light will begin to appear, albeit in disguised ways, little by little...
>
> Then, 600 years into the sixth millennium,[1136] the gates of supernal wisdom *above* will open together with the wellsprings of wisdom below. This will begin the process whereby the world will prepare to enter the seventh millennium. This is symbolized by a man who begins preparing for Shabbos on the sixth day, Friday afternoon. In the same way, from the second half of the sixth millennium—noontime and onward—everything speeds up, just as everything speeds up on Friday afternoon in the Jewish

---

1132 *Zohar* 116b–117a, translation and some notes from Schatz, *Sparks of the Hidden Light*.
1133 *Yeshayahu* 60:22.
1134 This is the year 4000–5000 on the Jewish calendar, or 240 CE until 1240 CE.
1135 In the Jewish year 5000, or 1240 CE.
1136 Meaning the Jewish year 5600, or 1840 CE.

home and all preparations are made for the Great Shabbos. This is hinted at in the verse, "In the 600th year after Noah's life…all the wellsprings of the great deep burst forth and the flood gates of the heavens were opened."[1137]

The *Zohar* begins to reveal why scientific discovery and technology emerged in the way that they did. Nothing was produced during the Dark Ages because that was the main period of exile. Other points on the grand timeline contain potential messianic potential, but if humanity is not meritorious enough, only sparks of its light are revealed—veiled instead as scientific breakthroughs.

The *Zohar* says that "at the time of five," the messianic lights begin to shine. The fifth millennium ended in 1240 CE. In the timeline above, this is when Roger Bacon developed the scientific method. In that same generation, Thomas Aquinas recognized the necessity of merging science and religion into an integrated wisdom.[1138]

Of particular interest is the mention in the *Zohar* of the year 5600 (1840 CE), which is supposed to be around the time of a turning point—the real beginning of a spiritual and technological flood. When looking at the historical timeline, one will notice that in close proximity to this year is when the Industrial Revolution was really taking hold in America. Many scientific developments that would lay the foundation for future growth occurred very close to this time. Consider the work of John Dalton on gasses and chemistry, Michael Faraday on electric machines, Andre-Marie Ampere's investigations into the nature of electricity, and the insights into the connection between electricity and magnetism by Hans Christian Oersted; all of these came in this period beginning in 1820. Interestingly, Pulitzer Prize-winning commentator George Will, quoting DeMuth, in an article from *Newsweek* magazine, assures us that 1820 "marks the beginning of the modern age" where "science" has displaced other drivers of "social and economic development."[1139]

1137 *Bereishis* [Genesis] 7:11.
1138 See Schatz, *Sparks of the Hidden Light.*
1139 *Newsweek*, October 16, 2000. This excerpt from George Will, and also the scientific discov-

As the seventh millennium approaches, the world prepares itself and all scientific discovery and technology will speed up. The goal of Moshiach is to perceive the Infinity and Oneness of G-d within the *finite* and *diverseness* of the physical world. As scientific discovery advances, that unity unravels more and more.[1140]

Relativity, quantum mechanics, the uncertainty principle, and the anthropic principle are just a few of the contemporary revelations that show that the human mind must look beyond the physical reality. Seemingly unrelated concepts are now being joined into unified formulas. It is becoming more apparent that basic principles of Judaism and science are very much in sync:[1141]

- Modern physics presents a perspective that the universe depends on a higher consciousness that continuously creates and sustains all of the matter and energy of the universe.[1142] This parallels the idea in Jewish mysticism that G-d is constantly creating the world.[1143]

- "Quantum theory gives man the central role of being the pre-planned goal of the cosmos since its beginning, since for physical reality to emerge from a potential to actual state requires

---

eries surrounding the year 1820, were gleaned from Morris Engelson, *The Heavenly Time Machine* (2001), pg. 43.

1140 "According to the sages, knowledge (Torah knowledge or secular knowledge) comes from Heaven. This means that the sum total of all knowledge that flows into the world during any one period or generation is determined by Divine Providence in direct correlation to the merit of the generation and of those individuals who discover it. According to this principle, we can verify that in a period when knowledge is revealed in the non-Torah world, the same quality of knowledge is revealed in the Torah world. When the non-Torah world had a Newton and a Leibnitz, the Torah world had the Vilna Gaon and the Sha'agas Aryeh. In a generation of Einstein and Planck, the Torah world had a R. Chaim Soloveitchik and R. Abraham of Sochotchov... In short, the more science progressively reveals the secrets of our physical world, the more the secrets of the Kabbalah become indispensable in understanding the real meaning of the Torah. Divine Providence has determined that these two categories of knowledge develop and progress in parallel lines." Chaim Zimmerman, *Torah and Reason* (1979), pgs. 287, 291.

1141 Many of the following examples are based in Arnie Gotfryd, *Living in the Age of Moshiach* (2000), ch. 15. Any quotation marks are exact quotes from there.

1142 See Menas Kafatos and R. Nadeau, *The Conscious Universe: Part and Whole in Modern Physical Theory* (1990).

1143 See *Tanya, Sha'ar Hayichud V'Emunah*.

the participation of a conscious observer."[1144] This parallels the view in Jewish tradition that the entire universe was created for the purpose of man.[1145]

- "A large number of quantum physicists say that in order for physical reality to exist, the observer-participant must possess free will, since consciousness needs a physically unconstrained means to act on the quantum system."[1146] In this light, certain areas of science are confirming human free choice.

- Electromagnetism, one of the four basic forces in the universe, consists of waves. Intensity of frequency determines whether it will manifest as light, gamma rays, microwaves, or infrared waves. All matter consists of waves, on the microscopic or quantum level. This concept helps one understand the Jewish premise that G-d created the universe through "Divine speech." Furthermore, chemistry names over one hundred elements whose combinations form all matter in the universe, paralleling, as the mystics elaborate upon, that Divine letters (or building blocks) reconfigure themselves to form all things in the universe from Divine speech.

These scientific discoveries are the "lower waters" mentioned in the *Zohar*. The upper waters are the flood of Torah knowledge that has burst forth in the past few centuries and continues to proliferate. At key points in the grand timeline, the deepest insights of Torah could then penetrate the lower vessels. The purpose that the world was created for was in order to make the world into a dwelling place for the Almighty.[1147] This is achieved when even the coarsest of Creation reveals G-dliness.

As time progresses toward the messianic goal time of the year 6000,

1144 See John Wheeler, *Recent Thinking About the Nature of the Physical World* (1992): *It from Bit*. Ann. NY Academy of Science 655:349–363; J. VonNeumann, *Mathematical Foundations of Quantum Mechanics* (1955).

1145 *Derech Hashem* 1:2:5.

1146 This is described by Nobel laureate, Eugene Wigner. See also A. Rabinowitz and H. Branover, *Science in the Light of Torah* (1994), ch. 7, cited in Gotfryd, ibid.

1147 *Midrash Tanchuma*, Naso 16.

Torah insights too will be able to penetrate into lower levels, which in previous generations were not ready for them. As the messianic era approaches, even children will be able to understand the hidden wisdom. In the last generation they will be able to understand inner secrets of the Torah that were inaccessible to previous generations.[1148] It is for this very reason that the *Zohar* itself was not revealed until the thirteenth century, and not before.[1149]

SPIRITUAL UNDERPINNINGS

Rabbi Isaac Luria, the Arizal, founder of Lurianic Kabbalah, explains that spiritual refinement leads to the arrival of Moshiach. The mystics explain that beyond the physical reality, every physical thing in Creation is constructed of sparks of G-dliness embedded in husks of evil. The Divine spark is what keeps the matter in existence, its inner purpose in the universal scheme. The "evil husk" is that aspect of the object that conceals its inner G-dliness. Everything in Creation is precious and has purpose in the Divine plan. The commandments of the Torah are all about human interaction with those hidden sparks. In certain objects the G-dly spark is accessible, while in others, although present, it is not accessible. The word for "prohibited" in Hebrew is *assur,* which can also mean "bound" or "tied"—a reference to the G-dly spark inside. In other words, it is forbidden because the G-dly sparks inside are not able to be extracted and uplifted by human efforts. On the other hand, the word for "permissible" is *mutar,* which essentially means "unbound" or "untied"—meaning the spiritual energy contained within can be utilized and elevated through the means of a mitzvah. Doing a mitzvah with such an object causes the spark inside to resonate with the spirituality of the action and move upwards.

1148 See Rabbi Chaim Vital, Introduction to *Etz Chaim* (Jerusalem: Attieh ed., pg. 6). See also *Leshem Sh'vo V'Achlama, Sefer Biurim* 1, pg. 21: "What was forbidden to investigate and expound upon just yesterday becomes permissible today. This is felt by every true exegete. Numerous matters, whose awesome nature repelled one from even approaching in previous generations—behold, they are easily grasped today. This is because the gates of human understanding below have been opened up as a result of the steadily increasing flow of Divine revelations above."

1149 See *Chida, Shem HaGadolim,* Alef, 219, pg. 11.

When all of the sparks of the world will be uplifted, the messianic redemption will be underway.

When Moshiach comes, there will be no obstruction from the G-dly perspective of the world. Currently there is G-dliness that sustains existence, yet this element is concealed by the veiled perception of the human being. Currently, mankind views the physical universe as an entity in its own right, rather than as a mere expression of a Divine plan. This change in perception will be natural when Moshiach comes.

Perhaps a good analogy would be to imagine a cow looking at a work of art. He sees the colors and the images, but it is devoid of any value, depth, or meaning. If a professor of art examines the same painting, there is a world of difference. The colors depict something going on within the artist; the stroke style reveals even more; whether it is abstract or realistic points to another dimension of the artist. If someone is truly an expert, the painting becomes a window into the soul of the artist who painted it, to the point where every detail reveals some hidden purpose and meaning in the essence of the artist. The analogy is clear. The world need not change for it to look completely different. When the Messiah comes, the world will view everything in Creation as a masterpiece. Every detail will be seen as an expression of the artist who designed it. The signature of G-d will be evident on every bit of Creation. Increasing mitzvah observance hastens this realization.

REASONABLE APPROACH TO THE RESURRECTION OF THE DEAD

Based on what was discussed in previous sections, it is intellectually sound for the modern man to accept the premise that there is a soul, an afterlife, and even reincarnation. On the other hand, the average enlightened individual sees the idea of a bodily resurrection of the dead as a fantastic belief, set aside for horror films, and accepted only by religious fundamentalists. Moreover, many are often surprised to discover that resurrection is one of the main pillars on which the Jewish religion stands.

RESURRECTION: A JEWISH BELIEF

Resurrection of the dead at some point in the messianic future is very much a Jewish belief, to the point where the sages have said that one who denies the reality of the resurrection is as if he denied the entire Torah. Furthermore, the one who rejects this belief is the one who will not merit being a part of it, measure for measure.[1150]

The Talmud relates that the idea of resurrection is alluded to in the text of the Five Books of Moses.[1151] The books of the Prophets are full

---

1150 See *Sanhedrin* 90a-b.

1151 See *Sanhedrin* 90b, which brings from the verse (*Shmos* 6:4), "I established My covenant with [the Patriarchs] to give to them the land of Canaan." It does not say "give it to you," but instead "give it to them." Though it was given to their descendants, and not to them, there must be a time in the future when they themselves will get it. Additionally, it can

of outright predictions of a future resurrection. The book of Isaiah says in no uncertain terms, "Your dead will live, their corpses will rise. You who lie in the dust, awake and shout for joy..."[1152] In addition, Ezekiel assures, "Then you shall know that I am the L-rd, when I open your graves and lead you up out of your graves as My people,"[1153] and an angel tells the prophet Daniel, "Many of those who lie in the dust of the ground will awake..."[1154]

Jewish tradition maintains that all Jewish souls[1155] and those of righteous gentiles[1156] will be resurrected. It is a cornerstone of the faith; resurrection is a repeating theme in the daily Jewish prayer service,[1157] and is codified as one of the Rambam's Thirteen Principles of Faith.[1158] Resurrection is an essential component of the messianic redemption. The physical manifestation of the redemption, called the World to Come, includes a physical resurrection of the souls *along with their bodies.*[1159]

REASONABLE RESURRECTION

In truth, the future resurrection of the dead is not a difficult one to accept. It is already clear that G-d created the world *ex nehilo* once, "something-ness from absolute nothingness." Why, then, would it be difficult to comprehend and accept that G-d can create a second

---

be seen in a verse about bringing the heave offering to Aaron (*Bamidbar* 18:28). Since Aaron would not live forever, and did not enter into the Land of Israel, in order to receive *terumah*, he will one day be resurrected. See also *Sanhedrin* 91b, based on the verse, "I kill and bring back to life" (*Devarim* [Deuteronomy] 32:39).

1152 *Yeshayahu* [Isaiah] 26:19.
1153 *Yechezkel* [Ezekiel] 37:13, and in fact the entire chapter.
1154 *Daniel* 12:2.
1155 *Sanhedrin* 11:1.
1156 *Yefei Toar* on *Midrash Rabbah* 13:6. See also *Pirkei D'Rabbi Eliezer* 34, "[The Holy One, blessed be He, declares]: Every non-Jew who says, 'There is no other G-d,' I will restore to life in the World to Come."
1157 "*Modeh Ani*," which thanks G-d for the daily "resurrection," is a glimmer and reminder of the future resurrection (see *Anaf Yosef, Siddur Otzar HaTefillot*). Other examples are mentioned in "*Elokei Neshama*" and in the second blessing of the *Amida*, "The dead will G-d bring back to life in His loving kindness" (Yigdal).
1158 See commentary on Mishnah, *Sanhedrin*, Introduction to chapter 10.
1159 This is the majority opinion, see Ramban, end of *Sha'ar HaGemul*; Raavad, *Teshuva* 8:2; *Derech Hashem* 1:3:9; Tzemach Tzedek of Lubavitch, *Derech Mitzvosecha* 14b.

time, from something already existing that has merely disintegrated or dissolved?[1160]

Upon careful examination, one will find that there is a glimmer of resurrection built into the workings of the natural world. It has been said in the name of French philosopher Francois Voltaire that "it is no more surprising to be born twice than once; everything in nature is resurrection."

CATERPILLAR

A caterpillar spins itself a cocoon, remaining inside until it ostensibly dies, parts of it decay, and it becomes a thick liquid. Eventually this liquid glob becomes a beautiful butterfly with wings that bursts from the cocoon and flies through the air. The entire appearance, lifestyle, and eating habits of the butterfly are completely different than the caterpillar. Rabbi Israel Lipschitz zt"l, the Tiferes Yisrael, explains that one reason why G-d created a creature that had to undergo this process of "dying" and reemerging transformed was to echo what will take place on a grand scale in the future.[1161]

VEGETATION

An example of the nature of resurrection can also be seen in the cycle of growing vegetation and trees. A planted seed first rots under the ground, and only after quite some time does it sprout and grow into a healthy tree with beautiful fruits and flowers, many times greater than the original planted seed.[1162]

This was actually an analogy used by the Talmudic sages to convey the idea of resurrection to the pagans. The Egyptian Queen Cleopatra had trouble fathoming the concept of an enhanced life, back in the body, after it has decayed. Rabbi Meir responded with

---

1160 See *Emunos V'deos*, Seventh Treatise, *Resurrection of the Dead in the Present World*.
1161 See *Derush Or HaChaim*.
1162 In a similar vein, there is a custom of uprooting grass when leaving a Jewish cemetery. A verse connected with this act is from *Tehillim* 103:15, "Man's days are like grass, he blossoms like a flower." This indicates that just as grass seeds sprout after being buried in the Earth, so man will come forth alive from his grave (see *Beur Heitiv, Yoreh Deah* 376:4).

the example of a wheat seed, which decomposes before sprouting new life.[1163]

A related phenomenon is a forest in the winter. A superficial glance shows icy death covering the land, with bare trees, no visible animals and few, if any, signs of life. However, in just a few months, that same forest will be transformed, covered in lush foliage and filled with the life of spring birds and animals.

SCIENCE OF RESURRECTION

Perhaps it is difficult to grapple with how the structure of body and soul will be reunited after the body has decomposed for so long. In the modern era, this should not be challenging to grasp, for it is known that nothing can ever truly be destroyed; it merely exists in a different form. This is a useful idea for a rational understanding of the continued existence of the soul, afterlife, and resurrection.

NOTHING CAN BE CREATED OR DESTROYED

In the late 1700s, Antoine Lavoisier discovered that matter only changes form or shape, but always retains its mass. Later it was proven that a similar principle applies to energy: it can change form but always retains its force. Einstein further proved that mass and energy are in fact two sides of the same coin, thus furthering the same concept. In practice, this means that no part of Creation can be completely eliminated; it just simply changes its state of being. No matter how much something is pulverized, it is not gone forever.[1164]

It is worth noting, at least parenthetically, that Judaism made note of this concept centuries before academia caught up. King Solomon said, "I know that whatever G-d does, it shall be forever; nothing can be added to it, or anything taken away."[1165] The *Zohar* also relates, "Even a human word, yes, even the voice is not void, but has its place

---

1163 *Sanhedrin* 90b. Same comparison offered by R. Chiya bar Yosef in *Kesubos* 111b.

1164 Together, these principles have come to be known as the Law of Conservation of Mass and Energy, or as the first law of thermodynamics, which is a specific manifestation of the Law of Conservation and Energy.

1165 *Koheles* [Ecclesiastes] 3:14.

and destination in the universe."[1166] Rabbi Saadia Gaon elaborates on the topic: "Even if [an object] is burned with fire, it can never be annihilated, because it is impossible to destroy something to the point that it becomes nothing; this is something reserved for the Creator who Himself created it from nothing."[1167]

Taken in this context, resurrection of the dead refers to rebuilding the body from the matter and energy conserved in the universe.

Furthermore, the relatively recent discovery of the genetic code found in DNA makes the idea of resurrection intellectually acceptable and feasible to even the most ardent rationalist. The fact that every cell contains the information to reconstruct the entire body, and the scientific success in cloning a living creature from a single cell, shows that the idea of a bodily resurrection is not as far-fetched as once thought.

One of the main materials from which the body will be resurrected, mentioned in the classical sources, is the *luz* bone.[1168] It is a small bone of the spine[1169] that never decays and can never be destroyed. The rational mind could see the *luz* bone as a receptacle that preserves the DNA necessary for rebuilding the body in the future.

In 2008, researchers sought to bring back a variety of extinct animals, including the woolly mammoth. The bulk of the discussion surrounding the question of whether to carry this out or not was not based on whether or not it was possible, but on the ethical ramifications of doing so. Researchers were fairly convinced that they would be able to bring back these extinct creatures. Tom Gilbert, an expert in ancient DNA at Copenhagen University, optimistically predicted

---

1166 *Zohar*, Mishpatim 100b.

1167 *Emunos V'deos*, essay 7, ch. 1. Parenthetically, this should not be taken as Jewish tradition endorsing burning the body—cremation. The body is considered sanctified and "on loan" from Above. One must return it intact when the soul is finished with its mission.

1168 *Koheles Rabbah* 12:5.

1169 Some of the sages have linked it with specific bones as either the coccyx, the lowest bone of the spine (*Aruch, maareches luz; Avodas Hakodesh* 2:40; *Avkas Rochel* 2:4), while the Arizal maintains that it is the bone at the back of the skull where the tefillin are placed (*Likkutei Nach LehaArizal*, Shoftim). Its inability to decay or be destroyed is a spiritual principle.

that "if you can do a mammoth, you can do anything else that's dead, including your grandmother."[1170]

MODERN TECHNOLOGY AS A SPIRITUAL ENFORCER

Modern technology can be a tangible reminder of a neglected spiritual concept. Rabbi Israel Meir Kagan zt"l, the Chofetz Chaim, gave an example of this. He said that many people would falsely claim that G-d does not pay attention to what occurs in the world, since He is so far away. To counteract this, G-d gave humanity the inspiration to build the telescope, showing that even mankind has the ability to see the heavens, despite their great distance from the Earth. The doubting mind can conclude that surely G-d has the ability to see from above to below concerning all matters.[1171] When car GPS systems were first becoming popular, contemporary rabbis often used this as an analogy for G-d knowing where a person is at all times.

Likewise, the cloning process example cited above is not intended to minimize the future resurrection that will take place in a miraculous way. It merely notes that if human beings can more or less recreate an entire organism, how much infinitely more so is it possible from the Creator.

FORETASTES OF RESURRECTION

There are other examples of foretastes of the resurrection in the field of biological science. In recent years, scientists were able to regenerate cells of biologically dead nervous tissue in the ears of some vertebrates and mammals. Inner-ear biologist Yehoash Raphael of the University of Michigan has successfully identified a gene that, when injected into the cochlea of deafened animals, caused reorganization into living cells.[1172] He hopes to advance his research to

---

1170 Tom Mueller, "Recipe for Resurrection," *National Geographic Magazine* (May 2009).

1171 *Shem Olam* 1:24. He also used other inventions to bring out other lessons in Divine service.

1172 P. Viastarakos, T. Nikolopoulos, E. Tavoulari, G. Papacharalambous, "Sensory cell regeneration and stem cells: what we have already achieved in the management of deafness," *Otology & Neurotology*, 29(6) (2008): pgs. 758–768.

humans, and anticipates success. This is another allusion to resurrection taking place.

Additionally, consider this true story: A woman named Maureen Khadder had an aneurysm in her brain. The surgeons could not operate on the tense artery while the blood was circulating out of fear that it may burst. A special medical team performed an obscure procedure that drained the blood out of her body into a refrigeration unit. Her body temperature dropped 30 degrees, and her heart and brain waves stopped. She was medically dead at this point. They performed the operation, reheated the blood and circulated it back into her body. She, as well as nearly forty others, have come back unscathed from the procedure, once again showing a glimmer of resurrection.[1173]

Hints of resurrection are not limited to biology. Frank J. Tipler is a professor of mathematical physics at Tulane University. A noted scientist, he concludes that the resurrection of the dead is a necessary outcome destined to take place in the future. He deduces his findings through the laws of physics as they are presently understood. He soothes anyone who may have lost a loved one by saying, "Be comforted, you and they shall live again."[1174] While the details of his Omega Point Theory are not fully in sync with Torah, his general deductions about the eventual pinnacle of the universe are certainly eye-catching, reminiscent of Jewish tradition, and a novel conclusion to find in major academic journals, to say the least.

In essence, the concept of resurrection is being revealed more and more across the scientific spectrum. The theoretic belief is becoming more of a tangible reality as time passes. Technological advances made the concept of resurrection plausible, even to modern skeptics.

PURPOSE OF A PHYSICAL RESURRECTION

The question of how a bodily resurrection is possible has been defused, and the only remaining point of interest is *why* the soul would be returned to the body. Would it not be more appropriate

---

1173   "Welcome Back Mrs. Khadder," *60 Minutes*, April 2, 1995.

1174   Frank Tipler, *The Physics of Immortality: Modern Cosmology, G-d, and the Resurrection of the Dead* (1994), pg. 1.

to bask in the pleasure of G-dliness in the afterlife without the confines of the body? What purpose does a physical resurrection serve?

Judaism fundamentally disagrees with the common approach of religion as to what the role of the body is. In other circles, the body is seen as a seductive penitentiary, constantly seeking to lure the innocent and imprisoned soul to the enticements of the flesh. For that reason, the physical body and natural drives are to be stifled and quashed through fasting, asceticism, and celibacy.

Not so in Jewish tradition. The body and soul are a team set out to accomplish the goal of uplifting the physical world through Torah and mitzvos. The objective is not to escape the world by donning robes and endlessly meditating on the cosmos, but instead to bring Heaven down to Earth by sanctifying the physical world that one is a part of.

The soul cannot attain the heights of spiritual experience without clothing itself in a body and performing physical mitzvos, neither can the body be refined without the aid of the soul. The body is the only means to draw down spirituality into the physical realm. For example, the spiritual energy revealed in the physical world through the act of charity could not be accomplished without a physical hand, nor could a kind word be spoken without a physical mouth. In its intended state, the body serves as a conduit of expressing the spiritual, an interface between the soul and physical world. As Rabbi Moshe bar Shem-Tov de León poetically put it, "Just as the craftsman needs the instruments and the instruments need the craftsman to show that they can create, so does the soul need the body to show its accomplishments."[1175]

The ultimate goal of the spiritual self descending to the physical world is to uplift and transform it into a dwelling place for G-d in the lower realm.[1176] In other words, the goal of Creation will be attained when even the place that was created to conceal G-dliness will reveal G-dliness. Although now they are material entities with conception of self, they will then allow the infinite light of G-d to reveal itself through

---

1175 *Sefer HaMishkol*, part 1, *sod hanefesh*.
1176 See *Tanya*, ch. 36, based on *Midrash Tanchuma*, Nasso, sec. 16.

them. This can only be achieved through the body-soul combination. People generally recognize the holiness and sanctity of the soul, but in Judaism the body itself is holy and G-dly as well.[1177] With the body upholding its end of the deal and fulfilling its mission, why should it not also be rewarded in the hereafter for its accomplishments?

The Talmud relates a parable about the resurrection told by Rabbi Judah the Prince to Antoninus:[1178]

> A human king once had a beautiful garden, full of figs. He set two guards over it, one was crippled and one was blind. The crippled one said to the blind one, "I see beautiful fruit in this garden. Carry me on your shoulders and we will share it." So they did: the blind guard carried the crippled, until they ate all of the best fruits in the garden.
>
> The king returned and asked them, "Where are my choicest fruits?" The cripple said, "Do I have feet?" The blind one said, "Do I have eyes?" But the king was not fooled; he placed the cripple on the shoulders of the blind and judged them together.

In the same way, in the future G-d will judge the body and soul together, either rewarding or correcting them both, as one unit. In the messianic future, when the dead will live once again, the entire world will have reached its pinnacle, and the true purpose of G-d's Creation, to bestow His goodness on His handiwork, will be experienced forever.

1177 The Jewish mystics even explain that each limb of the body corresponds with some Divine reality; see *Toras Menachem* 5749, 1:37.

1178 *Sanhedrin* 91a–92b; *Vayikra Rabbah* 4:5.

AFTERWORD

The prominent psychologist Carl Jung identified the mentality of our age as only embracing that which has been sanctified by society. He writes, "Where the many are, there is security; what the many believe must of course be true; what the many want must be worth striving for, and necessary, and therefore good."[1179] It is my sincere hope that the brief presentations of the Jewish ideas within this book will whet the appetite toward introspection, reevaluation, and further exploration into the pillars of our faith.

The Rambam, Maimonides, quotes the Greek philosopher Alexander of Aphrodisias as saying that there are three causes that prevent mankind from embracing and pursuing truth: (1) arrogance and the love of freedom, (2) subtlety and difficulty of the subject at hand, and (3) ignorance, lacking the capacity to comprehend. The Rambam also adds a fourth cause: habit and training.[1180]

In essence, the major tenets of Jewish thought are intellectually pleasing. The reasonable person can, without hesitation, fully embrace Jewish tradition. Be they principles in the realm of faith or in practical observance, the Jewish outlook is a satisfying elixir for life. However, a person can think to himself, "Where do I go from here?" Judaism makes sense, and is very deep and meaningful, but the idea of becoming more active in the traditional Jewish lifestyle seems daunting. At times, the novice can feel overwhelmed because a Jewish lifestyle

---

1179 Carl Jung, *The Undiscovered Self* (1969), pgs. 70–71.
1180 See Rambam, *Moreh Nevuchim*, (Guide I, ch. 31, 108–9).

seems all-encompassing. A person may feel hypocritical unless taking on everything in full. He may also feel social pressures to remain in the status quo. For these reasons, he may never begin to do anything new at all.

In times past, one would gain their Jewish identity simply through birth. They were born in a *shtetl,* a small Jewish town, with the local kosher baker and fish market, with pious people in the study halls and roaming the streets on a daily basis, and the spirit of every upcoming holiday permeated the air. Life was rich. People were sincere. Embracing Judaism was automatic. Why would someone choose anything else?

In our own times, the ghetto walls have come down, and the average Jew finds himself in places bereft of Jewish practice or values, and tempted to blend in as much as possible with the surrounding society. In our days, when one acts "Jewishly," it is out of one's own free choice more so than it has ever been before, and there is seemingly no consequence when one rejects Jewish living. In this regard, the modern era ranks highest as one of the most challenging times in history for the survival of Judaism.

Yet at the same time, and for the same reason, this generation also achieves the highest standing when embracing tradition. In our days, every little thing that a Jew decides to do, in embracing his Judaism, has immeasurable value. The gratification, so to speak, that is caused on High is infinitely greater now than in previous generations. For someone in a previous generation, keeping kosher, for example, was a natural part of life; something that was done at home and in all family and friends' homes as well. When a Jew kept kosher then, there was no inner challenge connected to it. Nowadays, it is a different story. In our times, when a Jew, who for many years had not known any better and didn't keep kosher, decides that he wishes to live more in accordance with his Jewish faith and begins to keep kosher—the accomplishment is much greater *because* he has that inner challenge. When he walks by the fast-food restaurant and smells the cheeseburger that he had for so many years been accustomed to, and rejects it to further embrace Judaism, the accomplishment is extraordinary. Likewise, by any other aspect of Jewish life that is currently a challenge to him.

Our Jewish connection is about growth and learning, not about all or nothing.

Does G-d really care about our little actions? Do our thoughts, speech, and actions make any real difference to G-d?

G-d is Infinite. Infinite does not just mean infinitely big, it also means infinitely small. In that sense, G-d is just as much involved in all of the little details and decisions that we make throughout our lives. Even the smallest step up the ladder of self-refinement and Torah wisdom contains boundless value; all the more so when it is a challenge to do so. Imagine just how much Divine delight and personal success we can create in our own lives.

BIOGRAPHICAL SKETCHES

Baal Shem Tov: Rabbi Israel ben Eliezer (1698-1760), often called the Besht. His title means "Master of the Good Name." He was a Jewish mystic and taught appreciation for earnest Jews who lacked scholarship. He is the founder of the Chassidic movement.

Chazon Ish: (1878-1953) Rabbi Avrohom Yeshaya Karelitz, who is often referred to by the name of his magnum opus the *Chazon Ish*. He was a prominent rabbi in the Holy Land in the earlier half of the twentieth century.

Chofetz Chaim: Rabbi Israel Meir Kagan (1838-1933) was an influential Lithuanian Jewish rabbi of the Mussar movement, expert in Jewish law, and widely known as well for his ethical works.

Crescas, Rabbi Hasdai: (1340-1410) A prominent medieval Jewish philosopher and renowned teacher of Jewish law.

Dessler, Rabbi Eliyahu Eliezer: (1892-1953) Talmudic scholar and Jewish philosopher. He was known as the spiritual counselor of the Ponevezh Yeshiva in Israel.

Emden, Rabbi Yaakov: (1697-1776) Known also as the *Ya'avetz*. He was a prominent German rabbi and Talmudic scholar who combated against influence of the Sabbatean movement.

Hirsch, Rabbi Shimshon Raphoel: (1808-1888) A German rabbi, and defender of traditional Judaism. He is perhaps best known as the intellectual founder of the *Torah im Derech Eretz* school of thought.

Liadi, Rabbi Shneur Zalman of: (1745-1812) The founder and first Rebbe of Chabad Chassidism. He was the author of many works, and best known for the *Shulchan Aruch HaRav, Tanya* and his *Siddur Torah Or.* He is commonly called the Baal HaTanya, the Alter Rebbe, or an acronym the GRaZ, as well.

Lipschitz, Rabbi Israel: (1782–1860) Rabbi of the later period of Jewish Community of Danzig. He was the author of *Tiferes Yisrael,* widely used commentary on the Mishnah.

Lubavitcher Rebbe: Rabbi Menachem Mendel Schneerson (1902-1994). Known also as simply "The Rebbe," he was a prominent Chassidic rabbi and the seventh Rebbe of Lubavitch. Aside from tremendous scholarship in both the realm of Torah and secular knowledge, he perpetuated a worldwide network of institutions to spread traditional religious practices among the Jewish people.

Maharal: (1520-1609) Rabbi Yehuda Loew, his Hebrew acronym of *"Moreinu ha-Rav Loew,"* was an important Talmudic scholar, Jewish mystic, and philosopher. He served predominantly as the leading rabbi in Mikulov and Prague.

Rabbeinu Bachya: Rabbi Bachya ben Joseph ibn Paquda (eleventh century) was a Jewish philosopher and rabbi who lived at Zaragoza, Spain. His most famous work is the *Duties of the Heart.*

Ralbag: (1288–1344) Rabbi Levi ben Gershon, sometimes called by his latinized name Gersonides. He was a very prominent medieval Talmudic authority, philosopher, mathematician, and astronomer.

Rambam: Rabbi Moshe ben Maimon (1135-1204), also known as Maimonides. He was one of the most famous medieval Jewish philosophers and codifiers of Jewish law. He was also well-versed in the sciences of astronomy and served as a physician.

Ramban: Rabbi Moshe ben Nachman (1194-1270). He was a leading medieval Jewish scholar, philosopher, physician, kabbalist, and biblical commentator.

Ramchal: Rabbi Moshe Chaim Luzzatto (1707-1746). He was a great scholar and teacher of Jewish ethics and philosophy.

Rashi: Rabbi Shlomo Itzaki (1040-1105). Medieval French rabbi, perhaps the greatest commentator on the Written and Oral Law, and is studied universally in both areas.

Vilna Gaon: Rabbi Elijah ben Shlomo Zalman Kremer (1720-1797), was a tremendous Talmudic scholar, authority on Jewish law and mysticism, and regarded as the foremost leader of non-Chassidic Jewry of the past few centuries.

Vital, Rabbi Chaim: (1543-1620) Rabbi in Safed and the foremost disciple of Rabbi Isaac Luria, the Arizal.

Wasserman, Rabbi Elchonon: (1874-1941) A prominent rabbi, a noted Torah scholar, and dean of *yeshiva* in Europe before the Second World War. He was killed by the Nazis during the Second World War.

GLOSSARY OF TERMS

Amalek: A biblical character mentioned in the Torah. He was the son of Eliphaz, the grandson of Esau. His descendants were called Amalekites, or the nation of Amalek. They were notorious for their baseless hatred of the Jewish nation. Haman, the antagonist in the miracle of Purim, was a descendant of this people. Many groups that collectively hate the Jewish people are said to be at least "spiritual descendants" of Amalek.

Chassidism: A philosophy of traditional Judaism, which was initiated in the eighteenth century by the Baal Shem Tov. It stresses piety and strong commitment to Torah and mitzvos, but fused with joy and mysticism.

Halacha: The practical way in which to act, as determined by Jewish law.

Holy Temple: Also known as the *Beis Hamikdosh*. This was the central spot of Jewish worship, located on the Temple Mount in the Old City in Jerusalem. It was this location that G-d chose as the place where His Divine Presence would be found most palpably in the physical world. It was destroyed and rebuilt and destroyed again, and has remained destroyed for the past two thousand years.

Kabbalah: A general reference to the mystical teachings of Judaism. Kabbalah means "received," and was part of the oral code passed on in the collective body of Jewish knowledge. The *Zohar* of Rabbi Shimon bar Yochai and the writings of the Arizal are perhaps the most well-known texts of this genre.

Kosher: The Jewish dietary laws.

Mitzvah or Mitzvos: A commandment of the Torah. Mitzvos is the plural. There are 613 commandments outlined in the Torah—365 of them are positive instructions, and 248 are restrictions of what to avoid.

Midrash: One of several classical collections of the sages' homiletical teachings on the Torah.

Pesach: The springtime festival of liberation, also known as Passover, celebrating the Jewish redemption from slavery in Egypt.

Purim: Festival celebrated in the Hebrew month of Adar that commemorates the victory of the Jewish people against annihilation by the wicked Haman in the days of King Achashverosh of Persia.

Shabbos: The seventh day of the week, the Jewish Sabbath.

Shavuos: A holiday observed fifty days after Passover begins, celebrating the Jewish people receiving the Torah at Mount Sinai.

Sukkos: An autumn holiday commanded in the Torah that commemorates the booths in which the Israelites would live, and also the clouds of glory that provided their protection while wandering in the desert.

Talmud: Central text of the Oral Tradition. It expounds on the Hebrew Bible and upon the Mishnaic writings. It was compiled over a span of time and covers the full scope of Jewish law and lore.

Tosefta: A compilation of the Jewish oral law from the period of the Mishnah, around the beginning of the Third Century.

Tosofos: Medieval commentary on the Talmud, found opposite Rashi in contemporary printings.

Tefillin: Often translated as "phylacteries," they are one of the most important commandments in the Torah. They are a Jewish ritual prayer belt, worn daily during morning prayers by Jewish males. The Torah mentions it most explicitly in Deuteronomy 6:8: "You shall bind them as a sign upon your hand, and they should be for a reminder between your eyes."

Zohar: The foundational work in the literature of Jewish allegorical and mystical thought known as Kabbalah. The teachings of Kabbalah were revealed by G-d to biblical figures such as Abraham and Moses and were transmitted orally from the biblical era. The *Zohar* is a redaction of these mystical ideas, compiled by Rabbi Shimon bar Yochai, a great sage in the second century CE.

ABOUT THE AUTHOR

From an early age, Pinchas Taylor showed a particular interest in history and science. A top student, he decided to pursue the path to the rabbinate. After graduating from the Rabbinical College of America, he completed his formal rabbinic studies in Los Angeles, CA, and began teaching and counseling people in addiction recovery. After expanding Jewish educational and outreach activities in several communities around the globe, he and his wife Miriam returned to teach at the Rabbinical College of America.

In 2010, the Taylors moved to south Florida, where Rabbi Taylor serves as the Director of Adult Education and Outreach at the Chabad of Plantation. His regular Monday night lectures in Jewish Thought are very popular, and his writings and classes can be found all over the Web.

As an erudite and inspirational young scholar, Rabbi Taylor has become a sought-after educator and speaker. To contact him, please visit PinchasTaylor.com.

ABOUT MOSAICA PRESS

Mosaica Press is an independent publisher of Jewish books. Our authors include some of the most profound, interesting, and entertaining thinkers and writers in the Jewish community today. There is a great demand for high-quality Jewish works dealing with issues of the day — and Mosaica Press is helping fill that need. Our books are available around the world. Please visit us at www.mosaicapress.com or contact us at info@mosaicapress.com. We will be glad to hear from you.

MOSAICA PRESS